# STEFAN BUCZACKI'S
# GARDENING
# DICTIONARY

# STEFAN BUCZACKI'S
# GARDENING
# DICTIONARY

HAMLYN

Introduction  6

# GARDENING TECHNIQUES 9

**Publishing Director** Laura Bamford
**Creative Art Director** Keith Martin
**Executive Editor** Julian Brown
**Editor** Karen O'Grady
**Design Manager** Bryan Dunn
**Designer** Louise Griffiths
**Picture Researcher** Mel Watson
**Production Controllers**
Julie Hadingham and Clare Smedley
**Illustrator** Vanessa Luff
**Researcher** Liz Dobbs

First published in Great Britain in 1998
by Hamlyn an imprint of
Reed Consumer Books Limited,
Michelin House, 81 Fulham Road,
London SW3 6RB
and Auckland, Melbourne,
Singapore and Toronto

Copyright © 1998 Reed Consumer
Books Limited
Text © Stefan Buczacki 1998
ISBN 0 600 59377 0

A catalogue record for this book is
available from the British Library

Printed in Europe

# PLANTS AND GARDENS 119

# INTRODUCTION

Gardening is a vast subject. It is also, in large measure, an inexact science. And whilst there are generally recognised correct and incorrect ways of performing many of the essential tasks, there is also huge scope for personal experience and personal opinion. No one book can possibly contain everything that every gardener will ever need to know; not even those books entitled 'Encyclopaedia'. This book and its companion volume, 'Stefan Buczacki's Plant Dictionary', are quite deliberately called dictionaries rather than encyclopaedias therefore; but they are also personal dictionaries. Both volumes stand alone as works of reference, but fully complement each other. They are books that describe, discuss and explain gardening as I see it and do it. There is nothing here that is outside my own experience and my text is liberally laced with hints, advice and ideas that I have discovered or found especially useful.

The book is divided into three principal sections. The first encompasses the general wherewithal of gardening, its planning, the tools and equipment needed, the ways of gaining the best from your site; the essential information that will I believe enable all gardeners to perform the vast majority of their gardening tasks in a meaningful and efficient way. The second section describes the types of plant that you might wish to grow in terms of the individual parts of the garden and the way they should be created and managed: the vegetable plot, alpine garden, herbaceous border and so forth. The third section, the Glossary, extends the 'Dictionary' theme to explain those gardening terms and phrases that my experience has indicated are most frequently puzzling or ambiguous.

# Gardening Techniques

This section of the book will equip you to understand the scope, limitations and constraints of your own garden. A basic knowledge of soil, climate and other factors will make your gardening more meaningful and enjoyable. It will also make it less wasteful too, as you won't be tempted to try plants or techniques for which your site is inherently unsuited.

I explain some of the design features that you might wish to consider, give advice on gardening with children and the disabled and describe the essential tools and other equipment that will help you. Finally, I give accounts of the important operations and techniques of gardening, stressing throughout those that my experience has shown are really important and omitting those that I think arcane or merely curious.

# Climate and Weather

Gardeners, like farmers, are notorious for their preoccupation with weather although this is perfectly understandable because it is so unpredictable. A basic understanding of the climatic features that make up the weather can help us organise and plan garden activities to cope with the unexpected, but for all plants, the key climatic factors are the same: precipitation, sunshine and wind.

### Precipitation

I hardly need to stress the importance of water to plants. Approximately 90 per cent of the protoplasm of actively growing plant cells is water and most of the total plant is protoplasm. It's in aqueous solution that nutrients are taken up from the soil and it's also in water that they and the chemicals manufactured by the plant itself are moved from one region of leaf, shoot or root to another. Deprive a plant of water and it will die from a combination of starvation, structural instability and general biological malfunction. Most of the water is taken up from the soil and the amount of water present at any particular time depends on the soil's physical characteristics (see page 17), the prevailing temperature, the drying effect of the wind and, of course, the volume of precipitation that has fallen upon it.

Precipitation is a useful word for all the forms in which water falls to earth. Most, of course, falls as rain, although drizzle, dew, fog, hail, snow, sleet and hoar frost also contribute small amounts. There are obvious regional variations in annual rainfall but in general, the nearer you are to the sea and to high ground, the more rain you will have.

In Britain, this rain is due mainly to warm westerly or south-westerly winds passing over the Atlantic Ocean and causing water to evaporate. When this moist air reaches the high land of the west and central parts of the country, it rises, cools and expands. The moisture condenses, clouds form and rain falls. This is called relief rain.

Cyclonic rain is rather different and is produced in the low pressure systems that you see depicted on weather maps. Here, warm and moist air rises above cold and dense polar air moving in the opposite direction. As with relief rain, the rising moist air expands and cools, but

**below and below right**
The contrast between summer and winter in a temperate climate garden is huge; and is something that influences almost all our gardening activities.

10

**left** A summer storm threatens the garden but the beneficial effects of such short periods of very heavy rainfall in drenching dry soil are more than off-set by the physical and other, more insidious, damage they can cause.

with the significant difference that cyclonic rain can occur over low as well as high ground and that, as low pressure systems, unlike mountains, are constantly moving, outbreaks of cyclonic rain are much harder to predict.

Finally, there is the least predictable of all, convectional or thunder rain. Localised heating of the earth gives rise to powerful upcurrents of warm, moist air in which large raindrops form, buoyed up by the rising air. The very heavy, short-lived rainfall of thunderstorms can have considerable impact in gardens, however, because of its sheer physical force; flowers and vegetation generally are beaten down or broken and the soil may become compacted and capped.

Lack of rain, a drought, is of course, rather more important than an excess. It's because of the unpredictability of drought that you should plan for water shortages carefully. I'll come to this shortly but first a word about snow. The amount of moisture contributed in this way is never excessive as approximately 25cm (10in) of snow represent only 2.5cm (1in) of rain; and most, of course, falls in winter at times when plants have little use for moisture. Nonetheless, odd as it seems, a blanket of snow, although itself frozen, will protect plants and soil – a covering of about 7.5cm (3in) will usually prevent them from freezing. When falls of snow are very heavy, however, its sheer weight will break branches of shrubs and trees; particularly those evergreens that present a large surface area on which the snow can settle.

**Making the Most of Rainfall**

Rain never seems to fall when it is wanted and most gardeners have to supplement natural rain with hand watering or irrigation. Unfortunately, the time you most need water for the garden is the time when water companies are liable to restrict its use, so it makes sense to plan ahead. Water butts will conserve rain water during the summer months, but you should use this mainly outdoors as

**above** Snow should be left on cloches and cold frames for although it does cut out some light, it offers valuable additional insulation against frost.

greenhouse and indoor plants may suffer from the micro-organisms it will accumulate. Concentrate on watering where it will yield most benefit. Except in the most long severe drought, established lawns will survive so use the water elsewhere. Water plants when the parts that you most want are maturing: flowers at flowering time and vegetables and fruit as the edible parts develop. Recently planted trees, shrubs and perennials will need watering during dry spells for the first couple of years, but once their roots have developed they can be left for longer periods. Plants in containers, however, will always need regular watering. The improvement of the moisture retentiveness of soil is also extremely important and I cover this in the next chapter.

## Sunshine – Temperature

All life on earth depends on solar radiation; radiation from the sun. Less than half of the sun's radiation reaches the earth's surface, the remainder being lost, mainly by reflection back into space. For plants and gardens, there are two important components of the radiation: the shorter wavelength visible light, and the warming, longer wavelengths tending towards the infra-red. Although neither penetrates the soil, the surface warming effect of the sun's heat is conducted into the top few centimetres of soil and the re-radiation of this into the air is a very important factor in dictating the temperatures that plants experience. The temperatures that occur in any region depend mainly on the angle at which the sun's rays strike: at the Poles, where this angle is shallow, the warming effect is much less than at the Equator where the sun is higher in the sky. In most countries there can be considerable north-south differences in temperature.

All plants have their own maximum and minimum growth temperatures and, of course, they are higher for tropical than for polar species. Although all green plants grow in the same, basic, biochemical way, it's clear that mechanisms have evolved to permit particular species to survive satisfactorily in extreme conditions. Nonetheless, survival isn't the same as active growth and almost all plants grow little below 5°C (41°F) or above 25°C (77°F) and grow best between 10°C (50°F) and 25°C (77°F). This explains why plants in very cold or very hot climates (alpines and cacti, for instance), are usually slow growing.

Most of the long-wave radiation leaving the earth's surface during the night-time cooling period doesn't pass back into space, for it's largely retained through the absorbing properties of the atmosphere. With clear skies, however, at a time of year when the compensation of day-time warming by the sun is low, the heat loss from the earth can be sufficient to cause temperatures at ground level to drop below freezing and so form a frost. This type of frost is called a radiation frost and when it occurs in spring, it is crucial. The dates of the first and last frosts of the year are among the most important in any gardener's calendar.

Some gardens are more prone than others to spring frosts: a dry, free-draining soil, for instance, is a poorer conductor of heat than a wet one and there is less transfer of heat from reserves at depth in the ground. So dry soils are more likely to give rise to radiation frosts. A good cover of vegetation, such as grass, can also limit the amount of heat loss and shrubs growing in lawns are less liable to spring frost damage than those in bare soil. Overhanging trees can also limit the loss of heat upwards and serve to protect the plants beneath them.

Of course, frosts also occur throughout the winter, and not always when the sky is clear. Most winter frosts arise when cold air is transported over land but as plants are pretty well dormant at this time, these are of much less significance to gardeners than radiation frosts.

We need to distinguish between ground frosts and air frosts. A ground frost arises when the temperature at or just above ground level has fallen to 0°C (32°F), but this doesn't usually cause much harm to plants. An air frost, however, which occurs when the temperature is 0°C (32°F) or less at a height of 120cm (4ft) above the ground, can be much more serious. Even so, air frosts aren't generally damaging to plants during the winter when they are dormant, but spring air frosts, occurring after growth has begun, can be disastrous.

The mechanism of frost damage to plants is complicated and no-one fully understands it, nor indeed, what determines hardiness. It seems to be related, however, to the ease with which water can be drawn out from plant cells and frozen in the spaces between them; and to the rapidity with which subsequent thawing takes place. A slow thaw, allowing the cells to rehydrate gently, is much less damaging than a rapid one.

## Frost Protection

Tender plants are those that can only be grown outside in the period between the last and the first frosts. Once frosts do occur, these plants need protection, either in a greenhouse, a conservatory or under cloches. Heavy plants in large containers that can't be moved may be wrapped in insulating material such as bubble polythene film. Container-grown plants, even if they are normally hardy, may need protection from severe frosts as their roots will be more vulnerable to damage in a small container than in the open ground. Plants that are marginally hardy should be protected by mulching with organic matter around their crowns in autumn,

although, when practicable, it makes sense also to take cuttings and overwinter these under cover as back up if the parent plant fails.

Spun fleece is a relatively new product that gives quick and easy frost protection for gardens. It comes into its own for those unexpected late spring frosts when any bedding plants or vegetables already outside can be quickly covered up with a double layer overnight.

## Sunshine – Light

Light from the sun allows photosynthesis to take place and so enables plants to manufacture food and develop. It's not always true, however, that the more light a plant receives,

**above** The consequences of late frost can be dramatic in scorching the tender tips of young shoots although in most cases, the effects are relatively short-lived and the plant will recover in the subsequent weeks.

**opposite bottom** Much of the care taken in planting a new shrub correctly can be undone if it isn't given a mulch around the crown for frost protection.

the better it will grow. As with temperature and other factors, each type of plant has an optimum light requirement. Many camellias, rhododendrons or mahonias that are naturally shade species won't thrive, even in our latitudes, when planted in full sun. The fact that different plants have differing requirements for, or different tolerances of, light intensity is something that gardeners should appreciate when making mixed plantings. Very high light intensities can also be damaging, and many gardeners will have seen the symptoms of greenback on tomato fruit that are growing too close to greenhouse glass.

Another, rather different role for light lies in the phenomenon of daylength; the fact that the daily light period varies during the year. Special chemicals in plants are receptive to this variation and when certain thresholds are crossed, internal processes in the plant are triggered,

most importantly that of flower initiation. This is called photoperiodism and it's of most importance to commercial growers who adjust the length of the period of artificial illumination to induce flowering in plants like chrysanthemums or poinsettias at all times of the year. The retention of leaves by urban trees growing close to street lights is a common example of another photoperiodic effect.

## Making the Most of Sunshine

To make optimum use of sunshine, especially the warming infra-red component, we need to capitalise on something called the greenhouse effect. At its simplest, this occurs when relatively short wavelength radiation passes through a surface or layer, strikes a reflecting surface and is re-emitted as longer wavelength radiation that is unable to pass back out again. The greenhouse effect we have heard about in

the media relates to the trapping of warmth in this way at the earth's surface because of chemicals in the atmosphere that prevent it from being re-emitted. Do remember, however, that the greenhouse effect itself is vital; without it life on earth couldn't survive. The concern is strictly with an *enhanced* greenhouse effect leading to global warming.

This phenomenon is used in real greenhouses, and also in cloches, polythene tunnels and similar garden structures. Solar radiation passes through the glass or plastic, is re-emitted in the form of long wave-lengths which can't pass back through the glass and is, therefore, trapped. We tend to refer to any greenhouse that depends on the sun's warmth alone as an *unheated* greenhouse to differentiate it from one in which some form of artificial heat is supplied in winter.

Artificial heat may be supplied minimally, to maintain the temperature at just above freezing so that non-hardy plants may be kept over winter, or, more elaborately, to enable warm climate species to be grown actively all year round – see chapter 15 on the use of greenhouses in gardens (page 92).

## Wind

The final climatic factor to consider is wind; the movement of air over the earth's surface. Although wind at any one place may blow from any point of the compass, there are general, global wind patterns.

I've already mentioned the importance of wind in carrying rain but dry wind is equally significant in gardens. It's the medium for the dispersal of pollen, of many seeds (including weeds), insects, spores of pathogenic fungi, salt spray from the sea and, on occasion, of noxious artificial chemicals. The drying effect of wind on leaves results in the evaporation that in turn draws water up plants from the soil but in more extreme circumstances, the drying effect can be great enough to have damaging consequences if the water can't be replaced sufficiently quickly.

Wind is also a powerful physical force and can be seriously damaging in gardens; gales may smash greenhouses, uproot trees or, at least, break branches, whilst lesser strengths can rock shrubs to and fro or remove fruit from trees. I am convinced that almost every garden would benefit from some wind protection.

## Windbreaks

Exposed sites can be made more favourable for plant growth if a wind-break is erected to provide shelter. Some form of shelter will also help to protect structures such as greenhouses, cloches and arches which can be vulnerable to wind damage. Research into the best types of wind-break has shown that the most efficient is one that is 50 per cent permeable (half solid and half holes) rather than entirely solid, while a barrier 2m (6½ft) high has been demonstrated to protect a garden 20m (60ft) wide. Temporary wind-break netting is invaluable for giving a hedge or individual shrub a better chance to establish but for a more permanent barrier you should consider the relative merits of fences, walls and hedges which I discuss on pages 25 and 214 respectively.

**above** High light levels on tomatoes can produce greenback.

**below** A modest wind-break can produce dramatic effects on plant growth.

# Soils

Plants rely on the soil for water, nutrients and physical support, so the well-being of both plant and soil are closely linked. I've always believed that gardeners should understand something about the nature of the soil in order to manage it properly and also to encourage them to treat it with the respect that it merits. First, it must be realised that soil isn't a single static entity but a changing mixture of different components. To look at these soil constituents in more detail, it's useful to divide them into three groups: non-living, once-living but now dead, and living.

### Non-living Matter

The non-living component of soil consists of minerals. A mineral is defined rather technically as 'one of a group of naturally occurring solid inorganic substances with a characteristic crystalline form and a uniform chemical composition'. In everyday language, the group embraces such substances as quartz, vermiculite, calcite and dolomite that many gardeners will have heard of. Minerals originate in rocks (a rock as we see it lying in our gardens is no more than a collection of minerals) but over thousands of years they have been eroded by the action of the weather, earth movements, seas and rivers to end up as small particles. Together, these millions of small particles form the basis of soil.

Mineral particles may be derived from the local rock underlying your garden or from parent rock situated some distance away. Mineral matter can be swept many kilometres from its origin by rivers or glaciers and it's for this reason that the chemical characteristics of your soil may be significantly different from those of the rock that outcrops on a nearby

hillside. The degradation of the minerals from rock results in three main types of particle: sand, silt and clay; I discuss the influence of these on the physical structure of soils later (see page 17).

There are two other non-living components of soil that are vital to plant life, water and air. These are held within the soil, usually in the spaces between the small solid particles, and the way that the solid particles are aggregated together to form crumbs controls the relative amounts of air and water and in large measure this dictates the soil's characteristics (page 18).

### Once-living But Now Dead Matter

When a small mass of mineral particles first accumulates in a particular site, it begins to be colonised by relatively simple forms of plant life such as mosses and liverworts. When these plants die, their remains become added to the mass of mineral matter and this blend then forms the very beginnings of soil proper. The dead plant remains are called humus or organic matter.

In time, other plants grow, the relatively simple types soon giving way to more advanced, flowering plants, and they too in turn will add more humus to the soil. One of the commonest examples of this process, and one that many gardeners will have seen, takes place on the undisturbed tiles of old roofs. Mineral particles are blown to accumulate in the crevices, cushions of mosses soon grow and within a few years, if they are left undisturbed, small flowering plants will be seen to colonise.

In gardens, much of the organic matter is removed before it has a chance to form humus; crop plants are harvested, weeds are removed promptly and dead herbaceous material is taken away at regular intervals in the cause of tidiness. This is why we need to add extra organic matter or humus to the soil in the form of composts and manures to compensate for what we have removed.

## Living Matter

All of us are aware of the larger creatures that make their homes in the soil: mammals, like moles and voles; amphibians, like frogs and toads; and reptiles, like snakes and lizards. There are also, however, vast populations of much smaller living organisms: eelworms; earthworms; countless arthropods including insects; myriapods (centipedes and milli-pedes); mites and woodlice; and astronomical numbers of bacteria together with fungi, algae and representatives of other groups.

There are three main ways in which these living organisms can affect soil. First, fungi and bacteria, together, most importantly, with earthworms, digest the remains of plants and animals and break them down into chemically simpler nutrients that are then available for plants to take up through their roots. Some specialised bacteria also play a very valuable role in the recycling of the important element nitrogen by converting atmospheric nitrogen into inorganic salts which are also then made available to plants.

Second, there is the physical effect of the soil being disturbed and mixed as the animals themselves move around and make burrows which aerate the soil. The volumes of soil that are moved in this way are quite remarkable. As long ago as the nineteenth century, the subject fascinated Charles Darwin who calculated that over 100 tonnes of soil are moved per hectare every year solely through the action of earth-worms. This activity improves drainage and makes it easier for plant roots to penetrate the soil. And finally, before we leave the subject of living things in soil, it should be remembered that many soil organisms do use plants as a source of food, so as well as the fount of nutri-ents and water for plants, the soil can also be a source of pests and diseases.

Many of the constituents of soil are easy to see simply by digging and handling it. What are

harder to assess visually are the physical and chemical characteristics that affect plant growth, although I shall show you how, by understanding some simple science, and by observation and simple tests, much important information about your soil can be obtained.

## The Physical Characteristics of Soil; Soil Texture

As I explained earlier, in the course of soil for-mation, mineral particles are broken down into sand, silt and clay, the difference between them lying in the size of the particles. Sand comprises particles 0.06-2.0mm in diameter, silt comprises smaller particles of 0.002-0.06mm while clay particles are minute, less than 0.002mm in diam-eter. The proportion of these three types of particle in a soil is used by soil sci-entists to classify soils, each type having a characteristic texture. You can feel the differences yourself if you rub moist samples of soil between your finger tips and thumb: the large sand particles will feel gritty, the silt feels smooth, and

**above** Mosses are among the earliest plants to colonise bare rock and their small clumps accumulate the very first particles of true soil on which tiny flowering plants then begin to grow.

**below** The importance of earthworms in breaking down organic matter and mixing the soil can't be over-stated.

**above** The closely packed, fine particles of a clay soil act as a barrier to the penetration of air and water.

smaller particles of clay will be sticky. By shaking up a small sample of soil with water in a clear jar then leaving it to settle, you will see the proportions of sand, silt and clay in layers, the dense sand at the bottom, then the silt and then the clay.

Humus also contributes to soil texture; a soil with a high humus content will stain your fingers when touched and when shaken up with water the humus itself floats on top.

## Soil Structure

Mineral particles clump together to form larger aggregates called crumbs. Within a crumb, and between neighbouring crumbs, are spaces. These are known as pores and it is within the pores that air and water are to be found. And whilst the relative amounts of sand, silt, clay and other materials make up a soil's texture, the relative proportions of solid matter and pores are an expression of its structure. The ideal garden soil, one with a mixture of large and small pores, is therefore said to be well-structured.

Both the texture and structure of a soil will determine how well it holds water. Water will drain much more rapidly through a sandy soil where there are many more large pores than through a clay soil where the tiny particles are very close together. The addition of humus to a soil will improve its ability to hold moisture, humus acting like a sponge in soaking up and holding the water without causing water-logging.

## Chemical Characteristics of Soil

Soil chemistry is a very complex subject but there are a few important aspects for gardeners to consider. The most significant are the relative amounts and relative availability to plants of soil nutrients, and the soil's relative acidity or alkalinity, expressed as its pH.

Almost all the plant nutrients in a soil are derived from the mineral matter and are a feature of the type of rock from which that matter was derived. Some types of plant thrive better on some soils than others simply because of the different proportions of nutrients present. Plants growing wild rarely suffer from or display the characteristic symptoms of nutrient deficiencies. They tend to grow only in those places to which they are most suited and the nutrients taken up by them are returned to the soil when the plant dies and decomposes. The situation in gardens is rather different as plants are grown intensively together, often not on the most appropriate type of soil, and are then harvested and their remains removed (see page 80). Although we attempt to compensate by applying additional organic matter and fertiliser, shortages of individual nutrients may still occur (page 87).

The expression pH stands for 'potential of hydrogen'. It is a complex measurement related to the number of charged hydrogen atoms or ions present in solution and is expressed on a logarithmic scale. This means that a solution with a pH of 6 contains ten times as many hydrogen ions as one of pH 7 and one hundred times as many as one of pH 8. The practical significance of this is that a small difference on the pH scale can represent a big difference in acidity or alkalinity. The pH scale runs from 0 to 14 with pH 7 being neutral; values lower than 7 are acid and values higher are alkaline.

An alkaline soil means the presence of large amounts of calcium, often in the form of chalk or limestone. Under such alkaline conditions and the presence of large amounts of calcium, some nutrients are difficult for plants to absorb (they are said to be unavailable) as they combine with other chemicals in the soil. Many plants have no strong reaction either way to this situation but some have a particular ability to tolerate it (these are known as calcicoles) while some are quite unable to tolerate it (these are called calcifuges). The optimum soil pH in which most plants can take up nutrients satisfactorily is about 6.5 and this is the ideal to which vegetable gardeners especially aspire.

## Soil Tests

The nutrient level and pH of a soil can be tested and analysed, either by taking a sample and sending it to a soil laboratory or by purchasing a test kit from a garden centre and doing it yourself.

Nonetheless, whilst I consider pH tests are worth doing, nutritional soil tests can at best raise more questions than answers and at worst be seriously misleading. I say this because the limiting factor for plant growth in most gardens is likely to be the amount and availability of soil nitrogen. Yet simple test kits don't generally distinguish between total nitrogen in the soil and the proportion available for plants to use, while nitrogen levels can fluctuate considerably depending on weather and other conditions. Nitrogen is highly soluble and the level in soil can diminish very quickly following heavy rain; which is why gardeners often need to apply additional nitrogen fertiliser to their crops in significantly wet seasons. The nutrient status of an unknown soil is often rather effectively revealed by looking for plants that indicate specific nutrient deficiencies (see page 87).

To check your soil pH, use an inexpensive chemical kit that relies on the colour change of chemical dyes rather than a pH meter. The meters sold for garden use don't measure pH directly but an electrical parameter which is sometimes but not always directly proportional to it. Results from them can therefore be misleading. The kits are reliable but great care must be taken to obtain a representative sample of soil. You should collect between five and ten samples per 100 sq.m and these should be taken from soil before fertilisers and manures have been applied. Dig a small hole and take samples from the sides rather than the surface, remove any debris such as stones or fibrous organic matter, break up any lumps you find and mix the samples together with distilled or deionised water using clean equipment. You will then need to take sub-samples from your original sample in the small test-tubes provided. The kit will then require you to add a dye or use coloured indicator paper impregnated with dye. Follow the instructions offered with the kit and compare the colour produced by your test sample with the colours on the chart supplied to find the pH of your soil.

## A Soil Profile

To examine a soil profile in your garden, dig a flat-sided hole in an undisturbed (not recently cultivated) area. Examine the vertical sides of the hole and you should see fairly distinct horizontal layers. By studying the depth and composition of these layers, soil surveyors classify soils and deduce the processes that led to the soil's formation. For gardeners, it's sufficient to be able to identify the darker

**above** The characteristic yellowing between the leaf veins which shows a deficiency of iron symptomatic of alkaline conditions.

**below** Soil pH is the only really important soil measurement that need concern gardeners and is best obtained with a colourimetric test.

**above** Large clods left on the soil surface during autumn digging will be broken down gradually and efficiently by winter frost.

**below** Digging a straight sided hole in your garden will reveal the soil profile: an upper humus-rich layer of top soil lies over a much poorer layer of sub-soil which in turns grades in to the bed rock.

upper layer of top soil, the lower sub-soil and the underlying rock. Look also for the presence of a hard, crusty horizontal layer of deposited mineral salts about 20cm (8in) down within the soil. Such a layer is called a pan and it can impede drainage and root growth even on soils that otherwise are free-draining. The presence of a pan may explain why you have had problems with poor plant growth and water-logging; some deep digging will be needed to break it up (see page 55).

The top soil is the uppermost fertile layer containing the living and once-living but now dead constituents. An ideal top soil should be at least one spade deep but the depth can vary greatly from one site to another. Sub-soil, which lies beneath, is often lighter in colour and has a coarser texture than top soil. Avoid mixing the two together as the sub-soil lacks organic matter and micro-organisms. Normally, organic matter should be added to the top soil region but if the top soil is shallow, or the site has been neglected for a few years, double digging (see page 56) will be needed to take it deeper. Double digging will also gradually enable you to increase the depth of a shallow top soil.

## Soil Conditions

A clay soil is hard to cultivate, poorly drained and tends to be wet in winter then very slow to warm up in spring. In summer the surface can become hard and impenetrable. On the plus side, the minute particles present in clay do hold plant nutrients very effectively so fertility is high. A sandy soil, by contrast, is easy to work and quick to warm up in spring but plants can suffer as water drains through very rapidly, taking nutrients with it. Of course, there are plants that have become adapted to both but in order to grow the widest range of plants, the ideal soil is a medium loam, a readily workable blend of sand, silt and clay.

Most of us, at least initially, don't have that ideal loam but soils at either extreme can be improved by adding humus in the form of organic matter. The sponge-like properties of humus will help a sandy soil retain moisture while the natural glues that it contains will help bind mineral particles into crumbs. Paradoxically, humus will also improve clay soils as it helps crumb formation, so opening up the soil and making it less sticky and prone to water-logging.

Eventually, humus is broken down by micro-organisms so adding organic matter to the soil is a continuing activity. On a large scale it can be both tiring and expensive, so concentrate on one bed at a time. In a conventional vegetable plot, digging in organic matter should be an annual activity undertaken in the autumn when the bed is clear of plants and it can be rough dug. The advantage of autumn digging is that large clods of earth can be left over winter and will be broken down by winter rains and frosts. Then, in the spring, it will be easier for you to form a tilth, a fine surface of level soil suitable for seed germination. The digging will also help improve the soil structure as soil that has become compacted by heavy feet or equipment can be opened up. With a deep bed system, the incorporation of organic matter may be done through the operation of double digging every four or five years. In a herbaceous border or soft fruit garden, the whole bed can be dug over when plants are replaced, say every seven to ten years. Of course, organic matter will be added when individual plants are replaced or in the form of a loose mulch in spring that will gradually be absorbed into the soil during the summer.

After finding out the pH of your soil, you may wish to adjust it in order to grow a wider range of plants. Raising the pH of an acid soil is fairly straightforward and simply requires applications of garden lime (ground limestone). The best time to add lime is in the autumn and a rotary cultivator will help to incorporate it thoroughly. To determine the correct dose, follow the instructions on the packet (the amount to add will depend on the soil type and the pH) and remember to wear gloves when handling lime. Don't be tempted to add too much as over-liming can cause nutrient deficiency problems. Also don't apply lime within one month of applying animal manure to the soil, for the two can combine to liberate ammonia which is harmful. Check the pH again after about nine months and lime again if necessary but once the desired pH level has been reached no further liming should be needed for four to five years.

Soils that are very alkaline (pH 7.5 and above) are harder to alter. Proprietary sulphur chips can be added over a small area to reduce the pH but the results are not as effective as when using lime to raise pH. Applying fertilisers that contain ammonium sulphate as a nitrogen source will also help to lower the pH but it isn't good practice to add soluble nitrogen simply as a pH adjuster. The best approach is to grow plants that prefer alkaline conditions and to grow any favourite calcifuges in potting compost in containers. Any borderline plant that shows deficiency symptoms can be treated with a fertiliser containing sequestered iron (see page 86).

## Limitations of soil improvements

Most soil improvement will consist of adding organic matter (see page 59) or increasing the pH by adding lime. It isn't practical to import into the garden large quantities of non-living constituents like top soil, sand, silt or clay in an attempt to change the entire garden. The quantity needed to effect a difference would make such an exercise extremely hard work and very expensive. Small areas, however, can sometimes be improved in this way, especially when there is a particular benefit: using fresh top soil when replanting a rose garden to help avoid rose replant problem, creating a raised bed to enable root vegetables to be grown in a garden with heavy clay, or digging in grit around

shrubs that need a well-drained soil are instances of this. New housing developments often have the top soil removed during construction, and as plants will not grow satisfactorily in sub-soil anyone purchasing a new house should ensure that their builder is contracted to replace the top soil before they move in.

Chemicals are available that claim to help improve soil structure by aggregating the particles into crumbs. They are sometimes called soil conditioners and are of variable effectiveness. They include products derived from seaweed which are rich in alginates; whilst they may be helpful on a small scale, the cost of trying to 'improve' large volumes of soil in this way would be prohibitive. Moreover, adding soil improvers will not help improve drainage if a heavy clay soil lies over a poorly-draining sub-soil. Such severe water-logging can generally only be corrected with a drainage system which is best installed under professional guidance.

**above** When buying a new house, be sure that your contract includes a requirement for the builder to re-instate the top soil or your gardening activities will be blighted for years.

# Structural Fabric of the Garden

A garden is much more than a collection of plants. It contains important non-living elements too. Some, such as a drive, serve a clearly defined and functional purpose; most, however, like gates, paths and paved areas are not only functional but also set a style or create a feel to a garden. So when choosing the structural elements - strength, durability, ease of use and maintenance - there are also design and aesthetic elements to consider. Here I shall consider the functional aspects; the significance for garden design is dealt with in the next chapter.

**above** Bark chips make an excellent pathway for more informal parts of the garden

**below** Gravel is a versatile material for paths in the ornamental garden.

## Paths, Paved Areas and Driveways

The hard landscaping materials used for paths, paved areas and drives are functionally similar and although the range available increases year by year, I shall concentrate on those that I feel have the widest and most important application in the garden.

**Brick:** Bricks are aesthetically pleasing and functionally fairly adaptable as they can be obtained in a wide range of colours and finishes and, most significantly, can be laid in a variety of patterns (known by such names as stretcher bond, basket weave and herringbone). Being small, they are easy to handle and simple horizontal bricklaying is a relatively straightforward task although complicated effects are best done by a professional. By choosing a garden brick with similar colouring to the house you can link the two areas together visually. It is very important, however, to use bricks that are suitable for outdoor use. They must be frost tolerant and robust enough for the intended purpose. Normal building bricks aren't adequate; you should use old blue bricks, modern 'engineering' bricks or specially made paviours.

**Gravel:** I consider this to be one the best materials. Inexpensive and easy to lay, it can be used informally for curved paths and difficult corners or to create formal straight paths with an edging at either side. Large areas of gravel can be relieved by plants or by small patches of other materials such as paving slabs. There is a wide choice in particle size and shape; true gravel has rounded particles through having been rolled in a river but chippings, produced by artificially crushing rocks are equally valuable. A surprisingly wide range of colours is available also, including browns, greys and off-white. The sound made as cars and feet move across gravel is a satisfying one, and also has a security element as intruders will find it difficult to walk unheard along a gravel path. It's important, however, to take precautions to avoid weed growth and this is most readily achieved with a purpose-made permeable plastic sheet, laid beneath the gravel itself. A gravel depth of about 2cm (¾in) is normally sufficient as deeper layers can be difficult to walk on. Small-sized pea gravel will attach itself to muddy boots so a gravel path is less successful close to a vegetable garden; a rigid material is more appropriate there.

**Pre-cast Slabs:** Natural stone slabs are now virtually unobtainable new and prohibitively expensive second-hand. Those made of reconstituted or artificial stone are, however, very attractive and often cost little more than plain concrete. When laying a large area, try to break the monotony of the surface by laying slabs in patterns or by introducing other materials.

**Sets and Blocks:** Sets are brick-like blocks made of natural stone such as granite. They are expensive but can sometimes be obtained second-hand. Blocks are passably convincing artificial versions available in a range of colours and shapes. Both are ideal for arranging in geometric patterns and look particularly attractive in formal, town gardens.

**Bark Chips:** Various grades of bark are available for different purposes. Use specially designated splinter-free ornamental bark for laying under swings or climbing frames, and cheaper shredded bark, confined by wooden boards, to make rustic paths. A deep layer of 4–5cm (1½–2in) is adequate though it slowly degrades and must be topped up annually or biennially.

There are other materials that, although widely used, I feel have significant disadvantages and I mention them here so you may be aware of their drawbacks before embarking on costly projects.

Concrete is a useful foundation for a shed or greenhouse but on its own, used over large areas, is extremely dull. It can also become slippery and although the surface can be tex-

tured to overcome this, the results often look amateurish. It is inexpensive but hard work to mix and lay.

Grass can make an attractive foil between borders and has a limited function as a path, but used frequently, even with a plastic mesh underlay, it soon becomes worn and muddy. Slabs or stepping stones can be inserted but these will require extra maintenance as the grass edges will need trimming.

Wooden decking is currently a fashionable surface but though it may work well in dry climates, it warps and soon becomes slippery and covered with algae in wetter regions.

Pebbles and cobbles are difficult to walk over, although can create a pleasing pattern.

**above** Brick paving can be extremely attractive, especially in older or town gardens but be sure to use engineering bricks or substitutes that are resistant to frost damage.

**above** The siting of an area for sitting, dining and barbecues should be given careful consideration. Be sure that it is sunny and warm at the time of day when you are most likely to use it.

and the sharpness of any bends need to be considered carefully.

**Paved areas:** Patios, courtyards or sun terraces are for people as well as plants, so it is advisable to plan out what activities are likely to occur on them (like siting of barbecues, setting aside room for a table and chairs and placing of parasols) and choose appropriate materials. You will find that different materials are required for different areas of activity and may well enhance the appearance. Drainage is important too and the safety aspect of changes in level should be considered.

**Drives:** A higher specification is needed for a drive as the weights involved are considerable. Cost is likely to be uppermost in your mind if the driveway is large but try to choose a material that links visually with the house. Always use a recommended contractor and ascertain if local regulations or other legal requirements may affect your plans.

## Gates

A gate is so important in dictating the appearance of your garden that it could well be worth having one made specially to order. Wooden gates are the most popular and although hardwoods such as oak are more expensive than softwoods, they are longer-lasting and require less maintenance. Red Cedar is a durable softwood, and is certainly appropriate for garden buildings, but I find it too soft for gates. Wrought iron is impressive but expensive and heavy; coated aluminium or mild steel alternatives may be cheaper.

And so finally, to my *bête-noir*, tarmac; fine for roads and pavements, but not, please, in anyone's garden.

Once you have chosen your material, remember it will need to be adequately bedded. All hard materials should be laid on mortar or sand but do take into account any drainage requirements beforehand. And an edging material will be needed to contain loose material laid as a path.

**Paths:** The purpose of a path is to allow people to move about the garden easily and safely. When planning a path, however, do consider how often it will be used and for what purpose. Any path that is likely to have a wheelbarrow or lawnmower transported along it should be at least 60cm (24in) wide while its slope

**Front gates:** Depending on your property, the all-important front gate may be a small path entrance or something much wider at the opening to a drive. The type and height of the boundary either side of the gate should be considered in making your choice. If the boundary is tall, as it may be in a town garden or very large country one, then for privacy, or to block out unattractive surroundings, a solid wooden gate up to eye-level may be appropriate. Wrought iron gates are considered stylish and allow more light in to a small, dark town garden but offer little privacy. If you drive into your garden from a busy road, automatic opening gates could make your entry safer.

**Side gates:** These tend to be practical rather than elegant as most people simply require a high, strong and solid barrier. For convenience, a self-closing gate is useful if people are entering and leaving through the gate with great frequency, or if a dog needs to be confined.

All gates must have adequately strong posts or piers of wood, metal, brick or stone. For small gates these are best kept simple but larger gates can accommodate impressive piers with ornaments on top. Hanging a gate is not a task for the faint-hearted and hanging a large drive gate is best left to a professional.

For smaller openings, use the gate itself to calculate how far apart the post or pier should be, make allowance for hinges and latch and use a spirit level to ensure both piers or posts are parallel. Finish off brick piers with a capping stone to protect against weather and allow three days for mortar or concrete to set before hanging the gate.

## Boundaries

There are often legal requirements to define or maintain a boundary. They will protect and shelter your garden and give your family privacy but they can make your garden more shady, so don't automatically opt for the highest possible fence or wall as it could restrict the type of plants you can grow. In general, I favour hedges for boundaries (see page 219 for the merit of the different plants available) but where hedging is not practical or appropriate, fences and walls need to be considered. Traditional walls are solid and do not offer the 50 per cent permeability that is desirable in a windbreak. They will create eddies and debris may accumulate in your garden. Dry stone walls are a feature of the landscape in some areas, but for most people the choice will lie with brick or screen blocks, the decision usually dictated by cost.

Although inexpensive, softwood fence panels are not durable in strong winds. Where cost

**above** Choice of gate can play a large part in dictating the feel of a garden. Wrought iron is ideal for formal situations but not for country cottages.

**left** Brick walls make very attractive boundaries in formal situations; but remember that being impermeable to the wind, they will result in eddies and possibly the accumulation of debris on the leeward side.

makes them a necessity, do use panels pressure treated (not simply painted) with preservative and posts sunk at least 60cm (2ft) into the ground. Modern metal sleeves for posts minimise rotting and make replacement easier. Lengths of trellis along the tops of fences (and walls) will help to break up the monotony.

Interwoven hazel or, better, willow hurdles are attractive and wind permeable. I rate them very highly and use them extensively in my own garden. Picket fencing, made from vertical, pointed timber boards spaced slightly apart and nailed to two horizontal lengths, is inexpensive for a low fence. Traditionally, it is painted white and modern micro-porous paints make repainting a less frequent chore.

## Ornaments

A well-placed ornament can contribute much more to the style and feel of a garden than a single plant but there is a danger of overdoing it. The choice is really very personal so I offer two pieces of advice. Use high quality objects for their original purpose and you won't go far wrong: statues to look at and admire, fountainheads to spout water, sundials to tell the time, bird baths to bathe birds, bird tables to feed birds, bat boxes to shelter bats, pavilions to sit under, arbours to harbour; the choice is huge, but significantly excludes staddle stones which aren't for gardens but for keeping farm stores free from rats.

The pros and cons of stone, wood, lead and concrete are similar to those that I outline in my chapter on containers (page 112) but other considerations relate to security and safety. Chaining or cementing in place may be necessary and photographing of valuable ornaments would be prudent.

## Garden Buildings

A shed is important for storing tools and equipment and if it has windows it can be used to work in during wet weather. Site it so it is easily accessible but not an eyesore; although screens and plants can offer some disguise.

Most sheds are made of wood (red cedar is more expensive but much more durable than deal or similar softwood), but you should check if locks, glass, shelving, wood treatment, delivery and assembly are included in the price. Visit several sites to see assembled sheds to check height and space requirements but also to examine the workmanship and finish; doors especially vary greatly. A foundation of concrete is ideal although on a well-drained soil, paving slabs might suffice. Make sure the shed is secured with a suitable lock; your insurance policy may not cover you if the shed is left unlocked.

Summerhouses, of course, must be placed where they will capture the maximum sunlight and care will be needed to ensure that their presence doesn't conflict with the needs of sun-loving shrubs, vegetables, greenhouses or other warmth requiring garden components. Most summerhouses appear far too stark because there seems to be a general reluctance to plant climbers against them. My first action on purchasing a summerhouse is to clothe the structure with trellis and plant perfumed climbers like roses, jasmine or even honeysuckle to scramble over it. Be sure to have a small paved area in front of the summerhouse on which to stand chairs and table.

**below** Interwoven hurdle fencing is flexible and partly permeable to the wind and so most unlikely to be damaged in a gale. It's also extremely attractive.

Garden furniture should be part of a garden's structure, and not only when a seating area like an arbour is enclosed. As with everything else, buy the best you can afford. Wood is better than any plastic although Victorian or replica cast iron benches are magnificent. Position the seats where you have a good view of the garden and, if the garden is large enough, plan both for social seating where people can gather together, and more solitary areas where they can be alone with their thoughts.

## Supports for Climbing Plants

Although I've discussed the way that different types of plant should be supported in the appropriate accounts later, some of the supports used for climbers are large enough to be parts of the garden's structure. Archways, for instance, are invaluable for marking the change between one part of the garden and another as well as providing support for climbers. Pergolas are more ambitious structures, useful in large gardens to divide off an area as a walkway or shady retreat. In a small garden, a 2m (6½ft) tall obelisk can add height to a border. Arches and pergolas must be strong enough to support heavy climbers

such as roses and honeysuckle. Posts should be sunk into the ground to a depth of at least 60cm (2ft) although concreting will not be necessary.

Trellis is versatile and the wide range of microporous paint and wood stain colours now available can make it a very attractive feature in the garden. Use it as a screen in sheltered gardens or fixed to a wall on battens which allow air to circulate behind climbing plants, so reducing the likelihood of mildew.

Sections of trellis are readily available at garden centres but do remember that only the smaller sizes will fit in an average car. Large and irregular climbers can be attached to walls by lead-headed nails or, much better, by a system of wires attached to screw-ended vine eyes inserted in wall plugs.

**above** Sundials, statues and other garden ornaments need choosing with very great care as they can be major influences in giving a garden its overall feel.

**left** A pergola, provided it is made of materials appropriate to the garden, can play the roles of supporting climbers, dividing the garden and adding a vertical dimension.

# Design and Planning in the Modern Garden

Climate, location and geology all play their part in determining how well plants will succeed in a given situation, but when designing and planning how a garden will appear and function, the needs of the people using it are just as important. And these in turn depend on lifestyle and, very often, age.

**below** The all-important accommodation of children's needs in the modern garden needn't result in something either unsightly or dominating.

During our lives, there will be periods when we have time for gardening, but relatively little to spend on it; later, we may have more money available but are frustrated by lack of time to put changes into effect. Later still, it may not be time or money but physical strength that is lacking. So, when planning your garden, you shouldtry to ensure that it matches your current needs, and ideally, that it can be adapted as those needs change. In this way, you'll gain maximum enjoyment from it and minimise, although not of course remove, the frustrations. The planning and design of a garden is particularly important if you or members of your family have special needs because factors such as safety and access will take precedence over aesthetic considerations. I discuss this in detail in the chapters on gardening for the disabled and gardening with children; here I shall concentrate on some general principles.

It hardly needs to be said that the way we live now is very different from the way our gardening ancestors lived but the modern garden is nonetheless the embodiment of all that has gone before. Rather than see today's garden as an isolated entity, frozen in time, I think it's both instructive and interesting to realise how our present day gardens evolved.

## The Evolution of the Modern Garden

Until very recently, little more than a century ago, the specifically ornamental garden was the grand garden. Poor and ordinary folk were too busy with survival to have time or room for such things and the bulk of their gardening activity was centred on growing vegetables. Nonetheless, by allowing some of the more attractive weeds to survive, they became the unwitting catalysts for the development of a gardening style that has remained unchanged for hundred of years: the hotchpotch of flowers, vegetables, fruit and animals that has became known as the cottage garden. And ironically, this is many people's ideal garden today, a Utopia for urban estate and village home alike.

The earliest ornamental gardens of any significance in Europe were those of the Romans and their planting styles reflected the gardens of their Italian homes. The plants they used were a blend of the herbal and ornamental, usually planted in lines or squares but often in containers too. Roman gardens were highly advanced yet after the empire's decline in the fifth century AD, there are few records of any gardening activity until the practice surfaced again 500 years later in the kitchen and herbal gardens of the monasteries. The typical Medieval monastery garden had arbours, courtyards, raised beds and quadrangles: a place to harvest food but also for contemplation. Then, over the next 200 years, the ornamental garden became an adjunct to the stately home and the palace. Intricate geometric patterns of plants were produced by training and pruning; labour was almost limitless.

The garden remained formal until the early eighteenth century when Britain led the way: Lancelot 'Capability' Brown (1716-1783), and later Humphry Repton (1752-1818), led the abandonment of huge, formal, rigid geometric patterns, confined the flower garden close to the house and created instead sweeping landscapes. They were shapers of the countryside rather than gardeners and so inevitably their immediate influence on small home gardens was minimal. I like to believe, however, that it was their notion of a remodelled, more natural environment, combined improbably with the total informality of the cottage garden, that was to surface in the embryonic modern home garden of the nineteenth century.

As the western nations expanded their influence throughout the world in the late 19th century, vast numbers of new plants were collected and the introduced to gardens. Many wealthy landowners took up plant collecting and had impressive gardens with a large staff to match. Their new acquisitions were grown either in beds or in borders. William Cobbett in his *English Gardener* published in 1828 described the difference: a bed contained predominantly one type of flower, a border was a mixture. Cobbett would have been familiar with hardy annuals, biennials and bulbs such as tulips but it wasn't until around 1840 that a fall in the price of glass led to the much wider availability of greenhouses and cold frames. It was

**above** Early gardens were both formal and functional and it was to be many centuries before both of these attributes were changed significantly.

**left** The repeal of the tax on glass in the nineteenth century bequeathed to the people of Britain a legacy of greenhouse building and use that is as important as ever today.

this that encouraged an interest in half-hardy annuals, plants such as pelargoniums, tagetes, petunias, fuchsias, verbenas, salvias, ageratums and lobelias, so familiar to us today.

But gradually gardeners came to rebel against this formal bedding style. Inspired by what Brown and Repton had done for the landscape, they began to bring elements of informality and the cottage garden to the fore. One of their aims was to produce a mixed flower border that had colour for months rather than just a few weeks without the need for replanting. So the border that came to such pre-eminence was the herbaceous border. The Irishman William Robinson (1838-1935) synthesised many of the border's guiding principles in his book *The English Flower Garden* published in 1883. Gertrude Jekyll (1843-1932) took Robinson's ideas to heart and adapted them to creating herbaceous borders for the houses and gardens designed by her friend Edwin Lutyens.

**above** The Second World War stimulated vegetable growing in the most improbable of situations

**below** The ability to buy plants for planting almost all year round has revolutionised modern gardening.

The first half of the twentieth century saw times of war and economic depression and meant the returning of the home garden to its role of providing food. After the end of the Second World War, people wanted a change from the drab and merely useful and longed again for colourful flowers in their gardens; roses and bedding plants in bright colours were popular. A generation or two later, such gaudy colours were out of fashion and pastel became *de rigueur*. But more importantly, the whole approach to gardening came to be questioned. There grew up a generation that questioned the use of artificial (or indeed, and less advisedly, any) chemicals, both on farm and garden, that wanted 'pure and wholesome' food, and that wanted to do its bit in saving the planet; a movement that led to what I call 'free-range gardening'.

### The 'Typical' Modern Garden

The typical garden today is less than 200 sq m in area. As gardens have become smaller (or we want to use them for more activities so they simply seem smaller), the plants we grow must really earn their place. In a large country house garden for instance, setting aside a large area for a double herbaceous border through which to walk in summer was quite feasible. Out of season one would simply move to another area of the garden (or another house). In small modern gardens, by contrast, there might be room for one small border, visible all year round from the house. It makes far more sense today for the border to contain a mixture of plants, one that offers something in each season: bulbs in spring, herbaceous perennials and annuals in summer, berries, foliage and the bark of shrubs in autumn, evergreen colours and shapes in winter.

Many people today wish to spend less time on gardening chores, staking, weeding and digging and more on planning colour schemes and using their garden for leisure. The garden industry is very aware of this and now offers us a variety of labour-saving tools and labour saving plants: dwarf varieties that need no staking, weed suppressing ground-cover shrubs that need no pruning, and dwarf rye grass mixtures for lawns that are harder wearing and need less mowing. The deep bed system for growing vegetables has reduced the need to dig, and mulching beds and borders has lessened the

need for weeding and watering. Growing plants in containers close to the house fits in well with many people's way of life. Half-hardy plants no longer have to be raised but can be bought at almost any stage of growth. An increasing environmental awareness has led to an interest in organic gardening and native plant gardening. Even perennials have been rescued from the border and experiments are now underway to grow them in more natural groupings with the aim of reducing maintenance.

Gardeners are more than ever before influenced now by fashion and marketing. Part of this is, of course, due to greater communication through the broadcasting and publishing media but the growth of garden centres, superstores and garden shows has also played a part. Even non-gardeners are encouraged to think of their 'room outdoors' and there are plenty of people willing to help them fill it, if not with plants then with furniture, barbecues, swimming pools, summer houses and the other necessities of modern gardening life.

## Garden Styles

Trying to decide in advance on a garden style rather than buying things on impulse will help ensure that your house, the non-living parts of the garden and the plants all work together to create a pleasing environment. In a small garden, you may be restricted to a single style but larger gardens are often most successfully subdivided into smaller areas or garden rooms, each embodying a rather different approach. What follows are some of the possible approaches (not all mutually exclusive) that you might want to consider.

**The Formal Garden:** Here, the hard landscaping is usually based on a geometric shape, often symmetrical. At least some of the plants are used in regular patterns; clipped yew or box are popular choices but formally trained roses, lavender and other flowering shrubs play a part as well. Lawns, if used, are neat, regular and well-maintained but paving and gravel are often more appropriate, especially in smaller

**below** It's almost impossible to define an 'average' modern garden and one of the more unexpected trends has been a return to formality, but on a much reduced scale.

areas. Attractive containers and ornaments play an important part; the formal approach probably finds its greatest value in small town gardens.

**The Informal Garden:** In an informal garden there is an absence of obvious patterns and order. The planting seems more natural, with plants in irregular drifts rather than straight rows. Paths and lawns should flow and wander, structures of wood and natural stone are often used and the rigid shape of boundaries is concealed with plants.

**The Classical Garden:** The classical garden needs a highly disciplined approach with clipped green hedges, a symmetrical layout and classically inspired ornaments. It is uncluttered and relaxing but impractical for plant collectors or those with young children. The classical garden is rarely successful in a small space and is a style that most often fails today.

**The Cottage Garden:** Flowers, herbs and vegetables grow together in informal plantings. At least some of the flowering interest is produced by plants self-seeding but although the planting is very informal, careful management is required to keep it under control and to distinguish between the good and the bad among wild species; a cottage garden still needs weeding. Ornaments and structures are simple: hazel hurdles, picket fencing, terracotta pots and rustic arches.

**The Architectural Garden:** Here there is bold and very obvious planting with specimens chosen for their shape rather than flower colour. Grasses, bamboos and large foliage plants are often used in very conspicuous groupings with modern hard landscaping materials. This is a low-maintenance garden but one for people whose interests lie more in art than horticulture.

### Colour in the Garden

An individuals' idea of which colour combinations can give the greatest pleasure vary enormously. And as with other areas of life, fashionable colours come and go in gardening, although changes tend to be rather slower to put into effect. I have no wish to try and tell anyone which colours or colour combinations they should use in their gardens. I do want, however, to indicate a few, fairly general accepted principles of colour perception and appreciation; most people wouldn't argue for example that among individual colours, reds and oranges are perceived as being hot and aggressive while blues, greens and whites are cool and restful.

For colour combinations, a colour wheel can be used to demonstrate different effects. Here the spectral colours of white light: red, orange, yellow, green, blue, indigo and violet are drawn as segments of a wheel. Adjacent colours are then seen to harmonise; colours on the opposite side of the wheel make strong contrasts. These strong contrasts don't appeal to every one and are often referred to as 'colour clashes' but there are occasions when they can be effective. The combination of certain yellows with certain blues for instance is one that I find very pleasing in part of my own garden.

When 'painting' your garden, bear in mind that unlike real paints, more plant colours are

**below** The cottage garden is many people's ideal of horticultural perfection but it is in reality one of the hardest types of garden to manage; and it can look pretty bleak in winter.

available at certain times of the year than others. Early spring, for instance, is predominately a season of yellows and oranges, the height of summer brings the greatest variety while autumn brings browns, oranges and reds but rather fewer blues. It will always be easier to follow nature's inclinations rather than fight them; but by all means create a few surprises by seeking out unusually coloured plants in nursery catalogues.

Colour can be used in your garden in two main ways: group together plants of predominately one colour or blend them. At its extreme, the single colour approach is often seen in white gardens (not surprisingly as there is only one shade of white) or silver borders. In a mixed or herbaceous border, I can do no better than refer you to Gertrude Jekyll. In the early part of this century, she experimented for many years with long deep borders in her own garden at Munstead Wood in Surrey, England. She used intense, strong colours like oranges and reds in the centre and gradually introduced paler colour at the ends.

## Design Principles

Most gardens appear as they do more by accident than design. There are two main reasons for this. First, a gardener taking over an established garden is generally loath to change the existing layout; or at least to change it very quickly or extensively. This may be because of lack of time, inclination or simply appreciation of how significantly his or her gardening life could be improved by relatively small but well thought out design changes. And secondly, on a new site, the financial constraints after purchasing a house, or simply a belief that the task is just too daunting, prevents many new gardeners from planning their garden in its entirety. They are content to let things evolve piecemeal.

I hope that I can persuade you that planning your garden is really a matter of applied commonsense and I find it useful to think of the key elements of garden design in the form of three questions: how do you make the most of what your garden site offers; how do you make your garden function effectively for your needs; and how do you make your garden appear larger than it really is?

First, therefore, what does your garden site offer you as a garden planner? As I have already

indicated, the type of soil will dictate to a greater or lesser extent the plants that you can grow: to a greater extent if it is markedly acid or alkaline; to a lesser extent if it is merely very sandy or clayey. Nonetheless, I doubt if there are any garden *features* that any soil prevents you from having if you are prepared to compromise slightly on the choice of plants.

The topography of the site, the humps, hollows and slopes can influence the ease with which digging or lawn mowing can be performed, but should be considered positively too. A slope is always the best position for a rock garden; the top of a slope is the best place in an overall sloping garden for a fairly formal pool while the foot of a slope is best for an informal one where natural spilling over of water at the edges enables the margins to be softened with bog and waterside plants. The base of a hollow or even the foot

**above** A Colour Wheel is a useful device to demonstrate how some colours blend together much more harmoniously than others

**below** Always make use of the topography of your garden, in this case a slope.

Does your garden have special and unusual natural features? Among those that I consider valuable and important enough to justify reorganising other garden activities are a natural outcrop of rock that offers you the chance to have a real rock garden; and a stream or even a wet ditch around which you can plant a bog garden.

There are two aspects to making your garden function effectively for you. The first is to position features thoughtfully. A vegetable garden must have as much sun as possible yet, as it is not usually a particularly attractive feature, it should be carefully screened to separate it visually from the rest of the garden without the screen itself casting much shade. Positioning the vegetable plot on the sunny boundaries of the garden is the easiest way to do this.

Conversely, a herb garden is functional and attractive, both ends being served by having it as close as possible to the kitchen. When positioning purely ornamental beds and borders, be sure to place them where they can be appreciated at the time of year they will be at their best. This is most important in relation to a shrubbery grown for winter colour; there's little point in placing it at the furthest point from the house where no-one will venture in winter time.

The second way in which your garden can be made to function well is to ensure that it's designed for labour saving maintenance. At various places in the book, I've mentioned how the choice of plants and use of particular techniques can be very important but the basic design of the garden is significant too. The single most annoying and time consuming gardening task is in trying to mow twists and corners of a lawn that are too small for the mower and are therefore either left untidy or must be cut laboriously with shears. A gravel path adjoining a lawn is visually lovely, but you must be prepared for occasionally having to brush stones from the grass. A gravel path adjoining a vegetable plot, however, can be a nightmare as you walk from soil to gravel and pick up vast quantities of the path on your muddy footwear.

Creating a false illusion of space is not difficult in most gardens; and very rewarding too. Give the impression that there are a great many plants in your garden whilst at the same time filling relatively little of the area with them.

**above** The presence of a large tree will always be a major influence both in the design of your garden and, to some extent, in the types of plant; they must tolerate the shade and impoverished, dry soil that it creates locally.

**opposite bottom** Arches, short lengths of hedge or trellis and other devices can be used to subdivide a garden and make it very much more interesting.

of a slope is often a poor place for a fruit garden because dense, cold, frosty air accumulates there and will damage the blossom and such a site is also no place for slightly tender or early blossoming ornamentals. Conversely, the top of a slope is often a windy place and this too will make for an unproductive fruit garden because pollinating insects are blown away.

The only already existing plants that are worth considering seriously in a garden design are trees because they can't be moved or quickly replaced. Many very good gardens are largely designed around one or more mature trees as these generally dictate where much of the light and shadow lies and, because they draw heavily on the food and water reserves of the soil, also dictate where you can't place vegetable and fruit gardens or mixed borders. The presence of trees, especially deciduous ones, will also influence the positioning of the pools and the greenhouse; neither of which benefits from shade or falling leaves.

The simplest way to achieve this apparent conjuring trick is to keep the centre of the garden open – a lawn is the easiest way – and confine most of your plants to the periphery. This also has the advantage of obscuring the boundary fence or wall, making it impossible to see where your property ends.

This effect can be improved still further if there is open space beyond your garden (fields or parkland for instance) that can be glimpsed through gaps in these marginal plantings. And make good use of curves in lawns, beds, borders and paths to suggest that there is something beyond what can actually be seen. Placing a focal point so that it is glimpsed through an archway or a gap between two plantings also helps to take the eye a long way and enhance the feeling of distance.

Having decided, I hope, that your garden would benefit from a degree of design or re-design, how many of the changes must be worked out in detail beforehand? I have a suspicion that many would-be designers are put off by the detailed scale plans (often beautifully executed in water-colours) that they may

have seen in books and magazines. These might be fine for professionals and theorists but I have never seen such a plan translated into practice without considerable modification. I find it much more effective simply to equip yourself with several sheets of plain paper on which the outline of your garden is shown, place yourself at an advantage point (usually a bedroom window) and start to sketch in the various features that you want to retain or introduce. The most important single feature is a focal point but the precise positioning of this can only be decided from ground level when you look from the various possible viewpoints: windows, doorways, gates or paths. In a large garden, you will probably require more than one focal point to provide visual satisfaction from different spots.

**above** By keeping the centre of the garden open and confining the bulk of the planting to the periphery, you will create the feeling of the area being much larger than it really is.

# Specific Problem Sites

In the previous chapters, I have looked at the ways in which you can go some distance towards capitalising on the climate and soil in your area and how to set about designing a garden to meet your individual needs. But frequently, plans are thwarted or frustrated by some over-riding factor that superficially seems insurmountable; as people frequently tell me, 'it's never as simple as it appears in the books'. I can understand this frustration. No two gardens are identical simply because every location has its own special features. In many ways, this is what makes gardening the fascinating activity that it is; local or regional diversity in gardens, dictated by individual variations in site, are to be encouraged. Nonetheless, I've realised that there are certain areas that offer more problems than others and so in this chapter, I've set out some guidelines for dealing with them.

**above** Plants in coastal gardens must be tolerant not only of strong winds but also of the effects of salt spray.

**below** Hill gardens inland also experience the problems of exposure; but often to winds much colder than those at the coast.

In the plant lists that accompany each description, I've excluded fruit and vegetables. These will always prove difficult in marginal gardens of any type, although in the detailed accounts of fruit and vegetable gardens (see pages 120 and 134) I have indicated when particular types are likely to be successful in less than optimal conditions. And of course, the ornamental plant lists aren't exhaustive but I hope they will point you in the direction of genera that contain a considerable proportion of species relevant to each situation. For more information on individual types, I refer you to the detailed plant descriptions in the companion volume *Stefan Buczacki's Plant Dictionary*.

## Gardens by the Sea

The difficulties of gardening by the sea are those of wind, salt and salty water – if the garden is very close to the seashore, within reach of wave splash, plants can be almost inundated during the winter. Salt carried on the wind is the more general problem, however, and its effects can be apparent for several kilometres inland.

I don't think that anyone has determined why some plants are more tolerant of salt than others but it's evident from the richness of the seashore's natural plant life that a great many have adapted to it. Some like the sea buckthorn (*Hippophae*) or the sea aster (*Aster maritima*) can be grown in gardens in their natural unaltered state and make very attractive subjects. Others, like thrift (*Armeria maritima*) may be grown either in their native form or in one of a small number of selected variants. Yet others, like many roses, bear little resemblance to the wild species. And finally, there are the numerous plants like *Eucalyptus* that will never have experienced the coast in their natural homes yet still possess a valuable tolerance of salt.

Every seaside garden will be the better, however, for the provision of some shelter; even salt tolerant species will grow more luxuriantly if the force of the wind can be lessened. In the tree and shrub lists, I have indicated those species that make particularly good coastal wind breaks.

## Some Plants for Seaside Gardens
### Herbaceous plants and bulbs
*Achillea, Agapanthus, Allium, Alstroemeria, Anemone, Anthemis, Armeria, Aster, Bergenia, Campanula, Centaurea, Crambe, Crocosmia, Dianthus, Dierama, Echinops, Erigeron, Erodium, Eryngium, Euphorbia, Geranium, Gypsophila, Heuchera, Iris, Kniphofia, Limonium, Linaria, Melissa, Mimulus, Morina, Nerine, Oenothera, Origanum, Penstemon, Phygelius, Pulsatilla, Ruta, Salvia, Santolina, Scabiosa, Schizostylis, Scrophularia, Sedum, Sisyrinchium, Stachys, Veronica, Zantedeschia.*

### Trees and Shrubs
*Acer pseudoplatanus* (windbreak), *Arbutus, Castanea, Chamaerops, Choisya, Colutea, Cordyline, Corokia, Cotoneaster, Crataegus* (windbreak), *Cupressus,* x *Cupressocyparis, Cytisus, Elaeagnus, Ephedra, Erica, Escallonia, Eucalyptus, Euonymus, Fraxinus, Fuchsia, Garrya, Genista, Griselinia, Hebe, Helianthemum, Helichrysum, Hippophae, Hydrangea, Ilex, Juniperus, Laurus, Lavandula, Lavatera, Leycesteria, Lonicera, Myrica, Olearia, Parahebe, Phlomis, Phormium, Pinus* (windbreak), *Pittosporum, Podocarpus, Populus, Prunus, Pyracantha, Quercus, Rhamnus, Rosa, Rosmarinus, Salix, Sambucus, Santolina, Senecio, Sorbus, Spartium, Spiraea, Tamarix* (windbreak), *Ulex, Viburnum, Yucca.*

## Exposed Inland Gardens
Exposed gardens away from the coast do have some features in common with seaside locations. The wind is the constant factor but in hilly inland areas, it tends to be colder; and in really elevated locations, very much colder. Salt is not present to cause spotting or scorching but the searing effect of the wind on foliage can have much the same effect.

Weather forecasters now frequently refer to the chill factor – the reduced temperature effect that we feel when a cold wind blows very strongly; plants will experience this just as much as humans. In very windy places, you are likely to see, even on the toughest species, the characteristic effect called wind pruning, in which the buds on the windward side of plants shrivel and die, resulting in a plant apparently leaning away from the wind. And, exactly as at the coast, a windbreak or shelter will immeasurably improve the quality of your gardening. I know of many an upland garden that simply could not exist without a screen of durable trees. However, whereas cypresses, including the very fast-growing Leyland cypress, are generally unsuccessful as wind breaks on the coast because of their susceptibility to salt damage, they will often survive when used in the same way in hilly sites. Although not the loveliest of trees, this does mean that a wind break can be provided relatively quickly; there's no need to wait the many years required for more conventional native plants to reach maturity. Although no tree can be guaranteed to survive the gales that are frequent at high altitude, there's no doubt that many species do have particularly brittle wood and should therefore be avoided.

I should add that the plants I suggest here (at least, the smaller ones) will be valuable for another common problem garden that, whilst superficially very different, does in have much the same cause. These are what I call 'wind-tunnel' gardens; those sites where there is a very narrow gap, very often one adjacent to a town house with little space between the house and neighbouring property.

In the lists that follow, I haven't specifically included alpines, although they are the one large group of plants that will thrive in most exposed gardens (see my comments on page 196). Nonetheless, within familiar herbaceous genera such as *Geranium* or *Campanula*, it's not surprising that where alpine and lower growing species exist, they will generally be the most successful.

**above** Far too many gardeners perceive shade as a problem; it isn't and a shaded garden offers you the opportunity to grow some of the loveliest of ornamentals.

Most have also adapted to a relatively moist environment as shaded places are generally damp. It's for this reason that gardens that are both shaded and dry are those that present the biggest challenges for there are relatively few plants that have adapted to this combination.

One feature of shade tolerant plants (or at least, of those tolerant of deep shade) is that flowers tend to be sparse or insignificant. The shaded garden therefore is one that relies very largely on foliage; but it is none the worse for that. No foliage plants exemplify the shaded garden more than ferns; flowerless by definition but in a delightful array of foliage shapes and textures. All ferns will be suitable and I haven't therefore listed them individually by name.

## Some plants for Shaded Gardens
### Bulbs
*Anemone nemorosa, Arum, Colchicum, Convallaria, Cyclamen, Eranthis, Erythronium, Fritillaria, Galanthus, Hyacinthoides, Iris foetidissima* (dry shade), *Leucojum, Lilium, Trillium, Ranunculus, Scilla.*

### Herbaceous perennials
*Aconitum, Ajuga* (dry shade), *Alchemilla, Anemone x hybrida, Aquilegia, Astrantia, Bergenia* (dry shade), *Brunnera* (dry shade), *Campanula, Carex, Cimicifuga, Deschampsia* (dry shade), *Dicentra, Digitalis* (dry shade), *Epimedium* (dry shade), *Euphorbia robbiae* (dry shade), *Galeobdolon, Geranium* (dry shade), *Hakonechloa, Helleborus* (dry shade), *Hepatica, Holcus, Hosta, Lamium* (dry shade), *Luzula, Lysimachia, Mentha, Milium, Mimulus, Molinia* (dry shade), *Omphalodes, Pachysandra* (dry shade), *Polygonatum* (dry shade), *Pulmonaria* (dry shade), *Sanguinaria, Symphytum* (dry shade), *Thalictrum* (dry shade), *Tiarella* (dry shade), *Valeriana* (dry shade), *Vinca* (dry shade), *Viola labradorica* (dry shade).

### Shrubs
*Arctostaphylos* (dry shade), *Aucuba* (dry shade), *Berberis, Buxus, Camellia, Cornus canadensis, Cotoneaster, Daphne, Euonymus fortunei, Fothergilla, Garrya, Gaultheria, Hamamelis, Hydrangea, Hypericum calycinum, Ilex* (dry shade), *Kalmia, Leucothoe,*

**above** There's no easier place to create a garden water feature than at the foot of a slope to which water drains naturally.

**below** Planting around a pool can be immensely satisfying as you can select a range of plants, tolerant of increasingly drier conditions.

## Some Plants for Exposed, Inland Gardens
### Herbaceous plants and bulbs
[In very exposed sites, all herbaceous plants will require some shelter]

*Achillea, Anemone, Anthemis, Armeria, Aster, Campanula, Crocosmia, Dianthus, Erigeron, Erodium, Euphorbia, Geranium, Gypsophila, Heuchera, Iris, Origanum, Pulsatilla, Ruta, Salvia, Scabiosa, Schizostylis, Scrophularia, Sedum, Stachys, Veronica.*

### Trees and shrubs
*Acer pseudoplatanus, Cotoneaster, Crataegus* (windbreak), *Cupressus* (windbreak), x *Cupressocyparis* (windbreak), *Cytisus, Elaeagnus, Erica, Euonymus, Fraxinus, Genista, Ilex, Juniperus, Laurus, Lonicera, Pinus* (windbreak), *Populus, Prunus, Pyracantha, Quercus, Rhamnus, Rosa, Rosmarinus, Salix, Sambucus, Sorbus, Spiraea, Ulex, Viburnum.*

## Shaded gardens
Plants that thrive in or at least tolerate shade, are those that have evolved to cope with low light levels.

*Ligustrum, Mahonia* (dry shade)*, Ruscus, Pieris, Prunus laurocerasus, Rhododendron, Ribes, Rubus* (dry shade)*, Sambucus, Skimmia, Stranvaesia, Symphoricarpos.*

## Gardens on Very Wet Sites

A garden can have a permanently wet soil for a number of reasons. Generally the drainage is impeded, commonly although not invariably because there is a clay soil or sub-soil. A clay soil alone doesn't mean a wet garden, however, for there must be a continuing influx of water more or less throughout the year to create constantly wet conditions. A spring beneath the garden is one cause. Drainage from nearby land is another and, for this reason, permanently wet gardens are often situated near the foot of a slope. Plants that thrive in these conditions are those that aren't liable to having their root tissues asphyxiated and succumb to decaying organisms in consequence. Yet again, however, the exact way that this tolerance operates seems obscure. Choosing plants that grow naturally in the permanently wet areas of ditches, the margins of pools or in bogs will help ensure success.

## Some Plants for Very Wet Sites
### Herbaceous perennials and bulbs
*Acorus, Astilbe, Caltha, Cardamine, Carex, Filipendula, Gunnera, Hemerocallis, Iris* (some)*, Ligularia, Lysichiton, Lysimachia, Lythrum, Mimulus, Primula* (many)*, Rodgersia, Trollius, Zantedeschia.*

### Trees and shrubs
*Alnus, Amelanchier, Betula* (some)*, Cornus, Crataegus, Gaultheria, Mespilus, Myrica, Photinia, Populus, Pyrus, Salix, Sambucus, Sorbaria, Sorbus aucuparia, Spiraea, Symphoricarpos, Taxodium, Vaccinium, Viburnum.*

## Hot and Dry Gardens; Free-draining Soil

With the increase in global warming, a number of countries that previously experienced cool summers are now experiencing a high proportion of hot and dry summers, conditions in which gardeners with light soil have experienced most difficulties. And although no-one seems clear whether we are truly passing through a period of general climatic warming, there's no doubt that requests for plants toler-ant of hotter, drier environments now reach me much more frequently.

Elsewhere in the book, I've described the importance of improving the soil's moisture retentiveness and of collecting and storing rain water. Both are essential in the conditions under discussion but a great deal can also be done in the careful selection of plants. Those that originate in warm and dry climates will be most likely to survive. Plants from regions with a Mediterranean climate (which extends of course far beyond the Mediterranean itself) are often both durable enough to survive a hot dry summer and hardy enough to come through a cold winter. Also, a silver or grey appearance to the foliage often betrays a plant's adaptation to limit water loss; species that display this characteristic are also good dry garden subjects.

## Some Plants for Hot, Dry Gardens
### Herbaceous perennials and bulbs
*Acaena, Acanthus, Achillea, Agapanthus, Allium, Alyssum, Anaphalis margaritacea, Antennaria, Anthemis, Arabis, Armeria, Artemisia, Asphodeline, Asphodelus, Bupleurum falcatum, Calamintha, Centaurea, Centranthus, Cerastium, Chamaemelum nobile, Cheiranthus, Coreopsis, Cotula, Crambe, Crepis incana, Crinum, Crocosmia, Cynara, Dianthus, Diascia, Dierama, Echinops, Erodium, Eryngium, Erysimum, Euphorbia, Ferula, Festuca, Foeniculum, Gaura, Genista, Glaucium, Gypsophila, Hermodactylus, Holcus, Iberis, Ipheion, Iris unguicularis, Linaria, Linum, Lychnis, Nepeta, Oenothera, Onopordum, Origanum, Osteospermum, Pennisetum, Penstemon, Perovskia, Phlox douglasii, Phygelius, Potentilla, Raoulia, Romneya, Ruta, Salvia, Santolina, Saponaria, Sedum, Sempervivum, Silene maritima, Stachys, Stipa, Verbascum, Zauschneria.*

**below** A hot, dry garden invites you to mimic the plantings that occur in places with Mediterranean and similar climates; but always remember that they must also be tolerant of rather colder winters.

**Shrubs**

*Brachyglottis, Buddleja, Callistemon, Ceanothus, Cestrum, Cistus, Colutea, Convolvulus cneorum, Cytisus, Euryops, x Halimiocistus, Hebe, Helianthemum, Hypericum, Lavandula, Luma, Myrtus, Olearia, Ozothamnus, Phlomis, Potentilla, Spartium, Thymus.*

## Gardens With Clay Soil

In my account of soil types, I've described the advantages and disadvantages of clay soil. But it's true that no gardener with a very heavy clay will ever concede any advantages and I don't deny that gardening in these conditions can be extremely dispiriting.

My advice of improving a small area at a time with as much organic matter as is available still stands. But in truly extreme conditions those small areas will be bound to

remain fairly small and selecting plants that are at least reasonably tolerant of the conditions will be the only realistic option. The list that follows includes some of the most reliable; but bear in mind that some are not particularly hardy so the list must be read in conjunction with information on relative hardiness.

## Some Plants Tolerant of Heavy Clay
### Herbaceous perennials and bulbs

*Acanthus, Alchemilla, Anemone x hybrida, Aruncus, Bergenia, Caltha, Carex, Deschampsia, Epimedium, Euphorbia robbiae, Helleborus, Hemerocallis, Hosta, Lamium, Molinia, Panicum, Polygonatum, Primula* (many), *Prunella, Rheum, Rodgersia, Symphytum.*

### Trees and shrubs

*Acer, Aesculus, Amelanchier, Aucuba, Berberis, Betula, Carpinus, Chaenomeles, Chamaecyparis, Choisya, Colutea, Cornus, Corylus, Cotinus, Cotoneaster, Crataegus, Deutzia, Escallonia, Eucalyptus, Forsythia, Genista, Hamamelis, Hibiscus, Hypericum, Ilex, Juniperus, Laburnum, Lonicera, Mahonia, Magnolia, Malus, Philadelphus, Pinus, Populus, Potentilla, Prunus, Pyracantha, Quercus, Rhododendron, Ribes, Rosa, Salix, Senecio, Skimmia, Sorbus, Spiraea, Taxus, Thuja, Tilia, Viburnum, Weigela.*

## Gardens with Extremes of Acidity or Alkalinity

There is a major dichotomy between gardens that display extremes in soil pH. For in practice, whilst there are a great many plants that are tolerant of high acidity, rather few are seriously intolerant of it. Or, to put it another way, a plant that will grow well in an alkaline soil will very often grow well in an acidic soil; the reverse isn't nearly as true, especially with perennials. Very few herbaceous perennials and bulbs must have acidic conditions. I think that this difference arises because of the peculiar chemistry of an alkaline soil, as I've already described (see page 18). Some plants simply cannot take up iron from an alkaline soil; but there's no comparable chemical problem in acidic conditions.

The lists here therefore are necessarily rather limited but give suggestions of plants for soils at the extremes of the pH spectrum.

**below** Roses will always succeed in a clay soil and should be the first choice among ornamentals although many other types of plant will also thrive in these conditions.

## Some Plants for Gardens with Highly Acidic Soil

### Herbaceous plants and perennials requiring high acidity

*Carex pendula, Dicentra, Fritillaria* (some), *Osmunda, Pachysandra, Tricyrtis, Trillium.*

### Trees and shrubs requiring high acidity

*Acacia, Andromeda, Arctostaphylos, Calluna, Camellia, Cassiope, Clethra, Daboecia, Desfontainea, Embothrium, Empetrum, Erica, Eucryphia, Fothergilla, Gaultheria, Kalmia, Ledum, Leucothoe, Liquidambar, Magnolia, Myrica, Nyssa, Pernettya, Phyllodoce, Pieris, Rhododendron, Stewartia, Vaccinium.*

## Some Plants for Gardens with Highly Alkaline Soil

### Herbaceous perennials and bulbs tolerant of high alkalinity

*Acanthus, Achillea, Aconitum, Anchusa, Anemone* x *hybrida, Arum, Bergenia, Brunnera, Campanula* (some), *Centranthus, Corydalis, Dianthus, Doronicum, Eremurus, Eryngium* (some), *Geranium* (many), *Gypsophila, Helenium, Helleborus* (some), *Heuchera, Kniphofia, Linaria, Lychnis* (most), *Paeonia, Saponaria, Scabiosa, Sidalcea, Stachys* (most), *Verbascum.*

### Trees and shrubs tolerant of high alkalinity

*Acer, Aesculus, Aucuba, Berberis, Buddleja, Buxus, Caragana, Carpinus, Ceanothus, Cercis, Cistus, Colutea, Cotoneaster, Crataegus, Cytisus, Deutzia, Elaeagnus, Euonymus, Fagus, Forsythia, Fraxinus, Fuchsia, Genista, Hebe, Hibiscus, Hypericum, Juniperus, Laurus, Ligustrum, Lonicera, Mahonia, Malus, Olearia, Philadelphus, Phillyrea, Photinia, Pinus, Potentilla, Prunus* (some), *Rhus, Rosa, Rosmarinus, Sambucus, Sarcococca, Senecio, Spartium, Spiraea, Symphoricarpos, Syringa, Taxus, Thuja, Vinca, Weigela, Yucca.*

## Walls in Shade

I've linked these sites together, for although their problems are rather different in cause, the plants that will tolerate one will often-tolerate the other. The partially shaded wall presents a problem because it is subject to rather little sun in winter and plants that grow there must therefore be very hardy. The wall in

full shade is a difficult situation by contrast simply because it does receive sun; early morning sun in winter when plant tissues are frozen therefore thaw out and damage quickly. If you require wall shrubs for these situations, you will generally find that those on my list of plants for exposed gardens will be generally reliable.

### Climbers for Walls in Shade

*Akebia, Celastrus, Clematis* (some), *Hedera, Hydrangea, Muehlenbeckia, Parthenocissus, Schizophragma.*

**above** Gardening on an acidic soil needs careful thought; although there are many appropriate plants, a large proportion flower only in the spring.

**below** North-facing walls are often very sheltered. East-facing walls present a greater challenge as they can thaw very quickly after night-time frost.

# Gardening with Children

Almost anyone in the gardening business will tell you how sad they are that so few young people attend gardening society meetings, exhibit at shows or even buy gardening magazines. But let's distinguish between young people and children. I can understand that for teenagers and over, there are many other attractions and demands on their time. Only when young adults first own a garden do they begin to take gardening seriously. But children are another matter for most have access to some sort of family garden (even if it is only a window box) and encouragement given at this early stage of their lives will reap its rewards when they have their own gardens later.

**above** For children to succeed in their own small gardens, they must be given one of the most favoured and sunny positions.

**below** Nothing will stimulate a child's interest like quick growing annuals.

I always think that much of gardening with children is concerned with psychology. Be very careful with your 'don'ts' in the garden. Saying 'no' too frequently when children venture onto your own beds and borders will cause them to associate plants and gardening in general with something untouchable. It's far better to explain carefully why it is not a good idea to walk through the newly emerging potatoes or jump on the courgettes. Let them envisage gardening from the plants' point of view and see them as living things; although do please spare them the ridiculous notion that plants will be 'hurt' if they are damaged.

Encouragement is the appropriate word with children, for most have relatively little patience and expect results both quickly and dramatically. I am convinced that setting aside a small area specifically for the children to use is the ideal way in which to stimulate their interest. But please don't be tempted to give them a spot in which you are unable to grow anything yourself; you should do quite the reverse.

In the open garden, choose a place where the growing conditions are good, where the soil has already been well amended with organic matter and where there is good exposure to sunshine. An area of about 3.5-4sq.m (38-43sq.ft) will allow them plenty of scope although in a small garden, of course, this may need to be scaled down. Choose an area also that is close enough to a tap for the children not to have to carry cans of water long distances.

In a world increasingly aware of the damage that can so easily be caused to the natural environment at large, inform children about the importance of recycling. A compost bin of their own may be impractical but children must certainly be encouraged to contribute the debris from their own plot to the family bin. And, most importantly, explain to them how the thing works.

Dissuade them from using any pesticides on their plants; there will time later for them to be selective enough to make minimal use of the safer, less persistent substances on a few occasions. Whilst they are young enough to be impressionable, let their garden plot teach them the value of all animal and plant life (including the species that we call pests). But

let it also serve to show them that life is a struggle; the plants they choose to grow will not survive if weeds, too, are allowed to flourish.

What are the types of plants most appealing to children? Hardy annuals raised from seed sown directly outside are almost always the most satisfactory, offering so much in return for so little.

Vegetables are rewarding too for they offer something edible (although I am uncertain if having grown spinach themselves, easy as it is, necessarily renders them more likely to eat it). Among other vegetables, radishes are the easiest of all, closely followed by lettuce (the small varieties such as 'Little Gem'), carrots (especially the quick growing early, spherical rooted types), peas, runner beans (which produce more dramatic results more quickly than almost any other vegetable), and courgettes. But almost all vegetables are worth trying and available space need really be the only limiting factor.

Among flowers, the list is longer still. Sunflowers are almost essential because of their size but candytuft, calendulas, nasturtiums, pansies, poppies, schizanthus, and ten-week stocks are all rewarding. When choosing seeds, however, either from a mail order catalogue or from a garden centre display, do allow your children some choice; there may be items that appeal to them from the pictures on the packets and only by trying them will they discover if they are easy or frustratingly difficult.

It may also be worthwhile buying a few plants, partly to give them encouragement while their seeds germinate but also to demonstrate to children that some garden plants can only be propagated by cuttings; and allowing them to take cuttings themselves will of course prove tremendous fun later.

Teach your children the value of their garden tools – some manufacturers produce ranges of good quality small tools specially for children. Show them that they should wipe over the tools and put them away at the end of their gardening activities; although I am not naive enough to expect your children to be inherently any better than mine were at tidying away but in the garden at least, they can always follow a parental example. Teach them garden hygiene also; always to wash their hands after gardening.

So much for gardening *for* children. It is also important to consider gardening *with* children, especially those too young to understand even the basics of horticulture. The most important rule here must be a don't: don't have a garden pool (and fill in any existing pool) while children are very young – a small child can drown in a very few centimetres/inches of water.

Children of course also expect swings, sandpits, tree-houses, rope ladders and similar essentials. But there's no reason why the entire garden should take on the appearance of a municipal playground. If the garden is large enough, set aside an area for play things, preferably an area visible from the house (or, at least, from the kitchen). Alternatively, choose items that can be put away easily and simply and that are made from materials that blend with the environment. Children's garden equipment needn't be of luridly coloured plastic; relatively inexpensive wooden items are readily available. Nor need such features as sand-pits be planned as permanent garden features; they can be constructed in such a way to be capable of being changed later into rock gardens, or even into pools.

Let your children garden with you. Choose a day when you are feeling relaxed and are prepared to potter rather than when you are undertaking major activities that need your full

**above** Play areas need placing carefully. They must be visible from the house and yet discreet enough not adversely to affect the remainder of the garden.

**above** Whilst children should be encouraged to take part in parents' gardening activities, some tasks must be done without their distracting presence.

concentration or where you need to work quickly. Young nimble fingers are ideal for dead-heading bedding plants, harvesting fruit and planting up hanging baskets. Take the opportunity to explain that by taking off the faded old flowers new ones will be produced. When harvesting, give them a small basket and explain which fruits are ready and how you judge ripeness.

A few gardening activities are best done, however, without the distraction of young children. Above all, using electrical or powered equipment such as mowers, trimmers, hedge cutters and shredders is better done in adult company – you must be able to concentrate on the task in hand without distractions.

## Poisonous Plants

Recent legislation requires garden centres and plant producers to label plants for relative toxicity. There are those among us who feel that this has over-emphasised a relatively rare hazard; very few garden plants are dangerously poisonous so it's important to keep a sense of proportion. Nonetheless, children need to learn that they should never eat any plant (including toadstools of course) without parental guidance.

There are two main problem areas that people confuse: those plants which if eaten can cause poisoning, and those plants that can cause skin irritation. The difficulties in establishing guidelines will be immediately evident, however, as some people's skin is more sensitive than others; and skin irritation can range from a mild rash to painful, large, blisters needing hospitable treatment. The plants in the box below are those that should be officially designated on their labels as toxic to some degree.

---

### Poisonous Plants

**Category A**
Plants that are poisonous if eaten and also cause severe skin blistering. The sale of these should be restricted.

*Rhus radicans*
*Rhus succedanea*
*Rhus verniciflua*

**Category B**
Plants that require a warning on the plant label and also on the bed label at point of sale. Should be labelled as indicated:

| | |
|---|---|
| *Aconitum* | CAUTION toxic if eaten |
| *Arum* | CAUTION toxic if eaten |
| *Atropa* | CAUTION toxic if eaten |
| *Colchicum* | CAUTION toxic if eaten |
| *Convallaria majalis* | CAUTION toxic if eaten |
| *Daphne laureola* | CAUTION toxic if eaten/may cause skin allergy |
| *Daphne mezereum* | CAUTION toxic if eaten/ may cause skin allergy |
| *Daphne* (all others) | CAUTION toxic if eaten |
| *Brugmansia* | CAUTION toxic if eaten |
| *Dictamnus albus* | CAUTION toxic if eaten |
| *Dieffenbachia* | CAUTION toxic if eaten/skin and eye irritant |
| *Digitalis* | CAUTION toxic if eaten |
| *Gaultheria* (Section Pernettya only) | CAUTION toxic if eaten |
| *Gloriosa superba* | CAUTION toxic if eaten |
| *Hyoscyamus* | CAUTION toxic if eaten |

| | |
|---|---|
| *Laburnum* | CAUTION toxic if eaten |
| *Lantana* | CAUTION toxic if eaten |
| *Nerium oleander* | CAUTION toxic if eaten |
| *Phytolacca* | CAUTION toxic if eaten |
| *Primula obconica* | CAUTION may cause skin allergy |
| *Ricinus communis* | CAUTION toxic if eaten |
| *Ruta* | CAUTION severely toxic to skin in sunlight |
| *Solanum dulcamara* | CAUTION toxic if eaten |
| *Taxus* | CAUTION toxic if eaten |
| *Veratrum* | CAUTION toxic if eaten |

**Category C**
Plants that require a warning on the plant label as indicated

| | |
|---|---|
| *Aesculus* | Harmful if eaten |
| *Agrostemma githago* | Harmful if eaten |
| *Alstroemeria* | May cause skin allergy |
| *Aquilegia* | Harmful if eaten |
| *Brugmansia* | Harmful if eaten |
| *Caltha* | Harmful if eaten |
| *Catharanthus roseus* | Harmful if eaten |
| x *Cupressocyparis leylandii* | May cause skin allergy |
| *Delphinium* | Harmful if eaten |
| *Chrysanthemum* (except pot mums) | May cause skin allergy |
| *Echium* | Skin irritant |
| *Euonymus* | Harmful if eaten |
| *Euphorbia* (except poinsettia) | Harmful if eaten/skin and eye irritant |
| *Ficus carica* | Skin irritant in sunlight |
| *Fremontodendron* | Skin and eye irritant |
| *Gaultheria* (except Section Pernettya) | Harmful if eaten |
| *Hedera* | Harmful if eaten/may cause skin allergy |
| *Helleborus* | Harmful if eaten |
| *Hyacinthus* (except planted bowls) | Skin iritant |
| *Hypericum perforatum* | Harmful if eaten |
| *Ipomoea* | Harmful if eaten |
| *Iris* | Harmful if eaten |
| *Juniperus sabina* | Harmful if eaten |
| *Kalmia* | Harmful if eaten |
| *Ligustrum* | Harmful if eaten |
| *Lobelia tupa* | Harmful if eaten/skin and eye irritant |
| *Lupinus* | Harmful if eaten |
| *Narcissus* (except planted bowls) | Harmful if eaten/skin irritant |
| *Ornithogalum* | Harmful if eaten |
| *Polygonatum* | Harmful if eaten |
| *Prunus laurocerasus* | Harmful if eaten |
| *Rhamnus* | Harmful if eaten |
| *Schefflera* | May cause skin allergy |
| *Scilla* | Harmful if eaten |
| *Thuja* | Harmful if eaten |
| *Tulipa* (except planted bowls) | Skin irritant |
| *Wisteria* | Harmful if eaten |

Gaultherias are very attractive and appealing shrubs but their fruits are toxic if eaten.

Aquilegias are among the many plants that are safe if handled but harmful if eaten.

Laburnum is toxic, the seeds especially, although 'Vossii' produces fewer of them.

# Gardening for the Disabled

It would have been unthinkable, only a few years ago, for a chapter in a general gardening book to be devoted to this topic. Things have changed partly because many people who have gardened all of their lives now wish to continue doing so, with relative ease, as they grow older. And second, and perhaps even more importantly, because gardening itself is now seen as a highly beneficial and therapeutic activity for those, gardeners or not, who have or who develop a disability. In consequence, several organisations now exist to give advice and assistance and I'm grateful for their publications in guiding me in much of what follows.

**above** A slope for wheelchairs must be gentle and wide enough for good control.

**below** There is no need to compromise the entire design of a garden to accommodate wheelchairs; a little thought is all that's needed.

## Garden Design

The basic principles of garden design still apply: deciding your needs, recognising your local conditions and drawing up a plan (see page 35). If your mobility is restricted, the main consideration will be ease of access around the garden, so paths, steps and raised beds must be designed to make this as simple as possible.

**Paths:** More paths will be needed than in a conventional garden and the additional cost shouldn't be underestimated. Bear in mind that in a small plot, several wide paths will reduce the area available for growing plants. One option is to have narrower paths with turning spaces at intervals; if done with attractive materials and in a regular fashion as part of the overall design of a garden, this can be very striking. The relative merits of different materials are outlined on page 22, but slipping is a hazard so brick paviours and some types of slab are the best options. Loose gravel is difficult for wheelchair use but by using a 5mm (¼in) layer of mechanically compacted chippings on top, the surface will be easier to grip. A low edging to a path that will prevent wheelchairs slipping off the path is also useful to the visually impaired as is a tapping rail.

**Steps:** Wide, shallow steps are the easiest to use but a slip-resistant surface is again important. Keep steps clear of obstacles such as pots and try to avoid positioning them under overhanging trees that drop fruit and leaves. A firm handrail can be helpful but choose a style that fits in with the rest of the garden. Providing the slope is gradual, ramps can replace steps to

keep costs down, but in positioning steps, try to work with the shape of the garden. Ramps are best made of concrete and the gradient should be at least 1:15; the ideal is 1:20. This does of, course, increase the length and in a small area, could be considered unsightly. Try to provide some screening or use a focal point therefore to draw the eye away from the ramp.

**Raised Beds:** These are expensive to install, so try working with one in another garden first to satisfy yourself that they really are what you want. If you do decide to go ahead, you have the option of free-standing raised beds or those that are built against an existing wall or slope. Free-standing beds are more expensive and look unnatural but access to both sides is possible. Cutting into a slope and using a retaining wall to hold back the soil is cheaper and more attractive. Piling up soil against a garden wall and building a retaining wall in front is both quick and inexpensive and worthwhile if you have an existing wall in a suitable position.

A width of 60cm (2ft) – or 120cm (4ft) if there is to be access from both sides – is ideal for a raised bed but the most suitable height will depend on the height of the person using it and the types of tools they have. As a guide, assume that the shoulders are flat and the soil is below elbow level. The walls must be strong enough to hold the soil whilst being as thin as possible so the user can get close to the plants. Most raised beds are constructed from timber, concrete slabs or brick but weep holes may be needed for drainage and lining the inside with polythene can help to prevent damp from penetrating the materials.

## Growing in Containers

An alternative to raised beds is to grow plants in containers on a level surface but make sure that you have easy access to an outside tap or water butt. There are many types of container now available (see page 112) but half barrels are popular: they are large enough to grow a wide range of plants, inexpensive, fit into many gardening styles, can be left out overwinter and are firm and stable. Containers needn't be considered permanent fixtures, however, and can be moved on trolleys or fitted with castors. Hanging baskets and window boxes are also practical, especially if a long-handled sprayer or other device is used for ease of watering.

## Equipment

A great deal of research and study has been made in recent years into the design of tools that are appropriate for different types of disability. I have followed the experts' categories here and it's evident that by defining the problem, the solutions almost present themselves.

**Difficulty in Bending or Kneeling:** Long-handled tools can enable most gardening activities to be done while the back is straight. A jacket with plenty of wide pockets for holding small items avoids the necessity of having to bend down to reach into a bag. Kneeler stools and knee pads are other useful options.

**Weak Grip:** Arthritis can cause both pain and weakness in the hands and arms, making pruning and digging difficult. Careful choice of shrubs and correct spacing can reduce the need to prune while extensive use of mulches can reduce the need for digging. Pistol-grips are more comfortable to hold than conventional handles and you can either fit your own or buy tools already equipped with them; they often also have arm supports. Fixing foam padding to existing handles can make them more comfortable, while ratchet pruners need less strength than conventional models, although they do take longer to cut.

**above** An elevated water garden is a rather complex feature to build but will give immense satisfaction to wheelchair bound gardeners.

**above** Modern power tools with single-handed operation have revolutionised gardening for many disabled gardeners.

**Visual Impairment:** This covers a range of conditions and individual solutions will be needed to enable you to move around the garden safely and measure out materials you need. Apart from a safe layout, clues will be needed so a visually impaired person can orientate themselves: the sound of chimes or water (a pool is dangerous), a change in texture on a path, the provision of hand rails, the avoidance of trip hazards and the provision of defined edges to borders, paths and other features. Planting should include not only scented and aromatic plants but also those with contrasting textures.

### Tools and Equipment

There isn't one set of tools that will suit all disabled users but there is now a wide range available, which means that finding out by trial and error shouldn't present a problem. Often a slight adaptation to a conventional tool is just as useful as buying an expensive specialist aid. Make contact with a local centre or group where you can try out a range of tools before buying. Large garden centres generally stock a reasonable range but a wider selection will be obtainable by mail order.

Instead of buying separate tools, several companies now offer so-called multi-change systems. These allow you to buy handles separately from the heads; many handle lengths are available (some are telescopic) with a wide range of tool heads. These systems, however, are only as good as their fixing mechanisms so check both their effectiveness and that also you can operate it easily. Among the tasks for which special tools might be able to help are :

**Weeding:** Long-handled hoes and weed-pullers save having to bend down but remember that the use of mulches and other techniques may help reduce the amount of weeding required.

**Digging:** This is a strenuous activity for all gardeners and it is worth using techniques such as mulching that help to reduce the need for digging. Lightweight digging tools are available but you may also consider those with either shorter or longer than average handles and those fitted with an auxiliary handle or a pistol-grip. Spring-aided spades are used by many able-bodied gardeners and they are suitable for many disabled gardeners too.

**Chronic Fatigue:** Lightweight tools may help but learning to pace your activities so that you do 'little and often' is the best approach. Try to be well organised so you don't waste physical energy looking for tools or simply walking to and fro. If chronic fatigue is a long term concern, you should seriously consider redesigning the garden so that it creates less work.

**One Hand or Arm:** A number of one-handled tools are available while cordless (battery operated) versions of many tools are also helpful.

**Wheelchair:** Using the correct tools (long-handled or light-weight for instance) can be a big help when trying to garden from a wheelchair but the physical handling of materials is the hardest problem to solve. Tools should be stored somewhere accessible and be carefully organised on tool racks.

**Pruning:** The problems with most conventional pruning tools are their weight and the strength required to make a cut. Longer handles can reduce the need to bend down or reach up while a ratchet action requires less strength. Cut and grip cutting tools (those that hold the item once it has been cut) reduce the need to bend over and pick up clippings. Bear in mind that there are many versions of conventional garden shears, including the extremely useful one-handled models.

**Watering:** The installation of an automatic watering system is a relatively costly option but one that could be amply repaid in the time and effort that it saves in the daily chore of summer watering. Another way to reduce watering is to choose plants that are more drought tolerant and to mulch generously in early spring. Watering cans vary greatly in size and shape so try several to find the one that suits you best. Remember that carrying two small cans might be easier than one large one. A hose that rewinds itself on a reel might save effort and be safer than leaving it out, while seeping hoses, spray guns and sprinklers can also be useful.

**Moving Materials:** One-handed wheelbarrows and the ascender barrow that can be lowered to the ground in order to load goods at ground level are both excellent aids. Other options include adapting a trolley to hold tools or using ground sheets to drag materials rather than carrying them.

**Greenhouses and sheds:** For wheelchair access, make sure there is no door threshold, and the door width is adequate (double doors can be fitted to most garden buildings). For a greenhouse, automatic vent openers are valuable in summer and thermostatically controlled electric fan heaters in winter. Sheds should be well-organised with tools kept on racks.

**above** Gardeners who are blind or have impaired sight will gain enormous pleasure not simply from a scented garden but also one with tactile plants that are pleasing to handle.

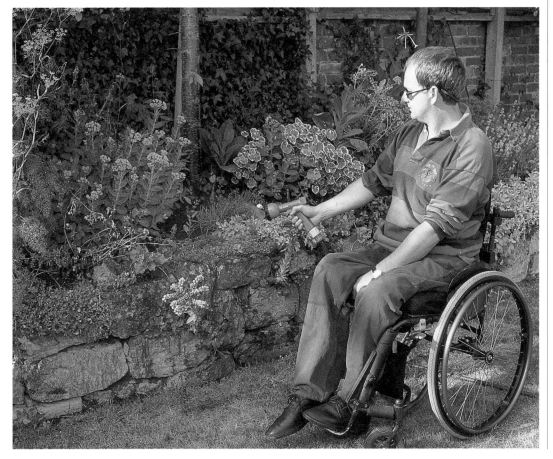

**left** Modern hose-end watering devices obviate any problems with moving heavy watering cans.

# Equipment and Tools

I don't think there is any area of gardening activity where more conservatism has been shown for so long by so many as in the design and use of tools. Hand tools like the spade and hoe are still recognisably the same as those used many centuries ago. Constructional materials have changed, especially in the past few decades, but the relatively unchanging nature of the designs should at least suggest that they are effective. Allowing for the basic principles, the individual style of tools is a personal matter and I would strongly advise you to sample and handle any tool before you buy it. The notion of giving a gardening friend or relative a new spade as a present is an appealing one; but do let them choose it themselves.

### Modern Trends

Although the basic design of many hand tools has not changed, the influence of the science of ergonomics has made us more aware of the need to match the tool to the user. As a result, longer and shorter handle lengths are available for those gardeners taller or shorter than average. Many manufacturers also now produce entire ranges of lighter and smaller tools, generally called 'ladies' ranges'.

The multi-change or detachable head system is valuable but nothing new. The same handle is used for a number of different tool heads which are easily interchanged. The system offers you a choice of handles so once having found one that suits you, all of your cultivating tools will be of the right length; and will be easier to store. If you are buying a set of

tools from scratch, such a system should be cheaper and also has benefits for disabled gardeners (see page 46). The only disadvantage that I have found is if you are undertaking a task that requires constant swapping of tools, from say rake to hoe.

It is an oft-repeated maxim that the more you pay, the better the product; by and large this is true of garden tools. But remember that you are not buying disposable merchandise but acquiring the means to enjoy your gardening for many years. Therefore, buy the best you can afford. For all hand tools, with the exception of forks, I'm convinced that stainless steel offers the ultimate in quality, although they are considerably more expensive than basic carbon steel models. They move more easily through the soil, they remain sharper for longer and require the minimum of maintenance (a mere wiping with a cloth after use).

The reason that I exclude forks from this general eulogy is that I find that tines on stainless steel tools bend far too easily – here carbon steel is to be preferred. If your finances are limited, however, your priorities for stainless steel should lie with those tools that most benefit from the smooth finish: the digging appliances like spades, trowels and the push hoe.

### Essential Tools

And so to my short list of essential cultivating tools for every gardener with open soil to till: a

**above** Choosing tools is a very personal matter. English gardeners are among the few in the world who don't prefer spades with long straight handles.

**right** Forks and other tools are now commonly available in full-sized and smaller, or female, versions.

spade and fork (initially, I suggest that you buy small border varieties rather than full-sized versions as these can be purchased later if you progress to large scale vegetable growing); a hand trowel and hand fork; a push hoe; and a spring tine rake (sometimes called a lawn rake). Lightweight, aluminium handles are to be preferred for cultivators while slightly pliable wood is best for spades and forks (where ash is the norm for long-handled versions and beech for the small, hand tools).

Cutting Tools: Among tools with cutting edges, secateurs are the most important and here the choice lies between scissor action or by-pass tools – with two blades working against each other – and anvil action models with one blade cutting against a solid surface. The former are more gentle with soft stems while the latter are valuable for cutting hard, woody tissue without being damaged. I am still unsure which I would choose if I could have only one but in less experienced hands, I think it would be the anvil pattern. Even more than with cultivators, quality pays in cutting edge tools but if cheap, poorly made secateurs are frustrating, then cheap shears are even more so.

Powered hedge trimmers (see below) mean, I'm sure, that the days of the short-handled garden shear are numbered but modern single-handed shears, based on the ancient sheep shear principle are nonetheless very useful for trimming into difficult corners or cutting back small bushy plants, such as heathers. It's extremely useful to be able to hold the shoots in one hand whilst cutting with the other. And for lawn edging, no power cutter in the world can give anything remotely like the finish of a long-handled lawn edge shear.

Lawn Tools: Apart from the long-handled lawn shear, the half-moon lawn edging knife is relatively inexpensive but gives a perfect straight edge at the start of the season so is well worth the investment. Lawn mowers themselves now come in an astonishing array of types but there remain two basic principles in lawn mower design: that based on a cylinder of rotating blades and that based on some form of slasher, which these days is more likely to be of nylon than metal. After years evaluating a large number of machines, my preferences are: large petrol-engined wheeled rotary mowers; petrol-

**left** Single-handed shears allow you to hold the plant in one hand whilst trimming it with the other.

**below** Among many ingenious modern devices is the lawnmower with interchangeable cassettes of mowing blades and scarifier tines.

engined cylinder and electric cylinder mowers (all with grass collectors); and small electric hover rotary machines. If I had one small lawn, I would use the electric cylinder. With fairly large lawns of good turf, you can find work for all of the remaining three, using the big rotary (which is really at home on rougher grass) early in the season when the surface is uneven, wet and littered with the debris of winter, the big cylinder machine during the summer to give a smooth finish and attractive stripes and the small hover mower to reach beneath overhanging shrubs and into difficult corners.

**Rakes:** Whilst I have suggested a lawn rake as your only garden rake, it will be of little use for one particularly laborious task: the periodic removal of moss from the lawn and it is here that electric or, better, petrol-engined lawn rakes are invaluable. At least one manufacturer offers a machine with interchangeable cas-

settes that can be switched from mower to rake. Their collection boxes, however, are all too small; much the best plan is to use the machine without the collector and rake the moss and 'thatch' into heaps afterwards.

## Powered Tools

For many years gardeners have managed solely with hand tools but the effectiveness and relatively low cost of modern powered appliances mean that they have a crucial part to play in relieving the more routine and tedious tasks. In all except the very small garden, therefore, I rank some power tools as very important. I have already discussed lawn mowers and lawn rakes but other powered appliances have now joined my list of gardening indispensables.

**Compost Shredder:** I have chosen this for two reasons, the first being that my garden, as everyone else's, benefits from as much com-

**below** The compost shredder has enabled many gardeners to make fuller use of the organic debris from their garden; although it does itself consume significant energy.

post as can be provided. The shredding enables me to compost a great deal more coarse material, and more quickly and efficiently than otherwise. The second is that in enabling me to compost so much more material, I am spared the problem of transporting it elsewhere as rubbish. But I would also add that if a large and powerful shredder is invaluable, a small, under-powered one can be a frustration in other than small gardens for it will jam with annoying regularity. So while the debris from a small garden can be coped with by an electric shredder of around 1000 watts, larger gardens really will only be served by large electric or, better still, petrol-engined machines. But there is one other feature of compost shredders that anyone who has any experience of them will know: they are very noisy. Do therefore be very careful in choosing the time for using any shredder to avoid disturbing the neighbours.

'Vacuum Cleaners': The second powered machine that I now find extremely useful is a device generally referred to as a 'garden vacuum cleaner'. The effectiveness of these appliances has improved beyond measure in recent years and whilst I'm still not convinced that they can double up as municipal road sweepers, as the manufacturers seem to believe, they have one essential role. There is nothing quite like them for collecting hedge trimmings; even from gravel surfaces.

**Cultivators:** Powered cultivators (often called rotavators, although this is a brand name) are only worth considering if you have a large vegetable garden; even then they have drawbacks. Their weight and the action of L-shaped tines can encourage a hard pan to form, especially on heavy clay soils, and they can very effectively chop up and disperse couch grass and other perennial weeds. Choose a petrol-engined machine of at least 25hp with variable handle positions and a good range of attachments; and check that you can handle the machine in operation as they are not easy to steer.

**Trimmers:** Grass trimmers (often called strimmers, also a brand name) are useful for trimming around awkward areas for which you should choose a model with an automatic nylon-feed. They can't, however, cope with

very long rough grass; for this you will need a brush-cutter with a rotating metal blade, a dangerous machine in inexperienced hands.

**Hedge Trimmers:** I've already referred to the widespread acceptance of powered hedge trimmers of which a large range of brands is now available. Assuming that you choose a modern appliance with all modern safety devices (two switches, short stopping time and so forth), the two practical considerations relate to length and quality. Cheaper (and longer bladed) models are more noisy and have more vibration. Rechargeable electric models are available but I find them heavy and with too short a running time.

**Safety:** Finally, having touched on safety, do be sure that you have a circuit breaker (popularly called a trip switch) with any electrical appliance and also use gloves and eye protection.

**above** Rotary cultivators aren't easy to use and their benefits need to be weighed against the likelihood of compacting the soil and dispersing weeds.

# Cultivation Techniques

I have already described the composition of soil and the way that the various components of it affect plant life (see page 16). I now want to consider the way in which it should be cultivated. The word cultivation describes all the physical operations on the soil: digging, forking, raking, trenching and hoeing. You may wonder why any cultivation is necessary; no-one cultivates the soil for wild plants and yet they still grow perfectly well. It's important to realise, however, that when we grow plants in a garden we may be using natural principles but many of the ways that we treat them and our expectations of them are distinctly unnatural.

We grow plants that are alien to the habitat, they may be removed before the end of their life span, they are grown in artificial spatial arrangements and we expect much more from them than nature can manage: bigger flowers, larger fruiting heads, more leaves and so forth. In the course of all this unnatural behaviour the soil is subject to a great deal of interference. We walk over it and compact it with machinery, we neglect the natural processes of organic matter recycling, and we use powerful hoses and sprinklers that may fall with much greater force than rain droplets. Our abuse of the soil is mainly, therefore, a matter of physical compaction. The additional weight causes the soil crumbs to be pressed together, resulting in loss of pore spaces for water and air. Loss of pore spaces adversely affects root development and soon this in turn leads to poor plant growth overall.

At its most severe, the lack of air can limit the growth of the aerobic bacteria and fungi that are needed to break down organic matter into humus. These organisms may be replaced with populations of anaerobic bacteria, which bring about a different chemical degradation of organic matter resulting in the formation of a dark unpleasant material and the liberation of gases such as hydrogen sulphide (with its characteristic smell of bad eggs), hydrogen and methane. Available nitrogen is lost more quickly when there is insufficient oxygen and there may also be an accumulation of chemicals that at best are useless as plant nutrients and, at worst, may be toxic to plant growth.

When water is unable to drain freely through the soil, it accumulates in puddles on the surface, so further restricting air from entering. When the soil crumbs disintegrate and block pore spaces, this causes an effect

**below** Each tool has several uses and the back of the fork is valuable in breaking down the largest of soil clods.

known as capping. It is a special problem on clay soil as the minute particles pack together very tightly making them particularly impenetrable. Most compaction occurs near the surface of the soil but a breakdown of physical structure can also occur at some depth, even when the soil above is unaffected. The result of this is called a pan or hard pan, a compacted layer at about 20cm (8in) below the surface.

The presence of a hard pan prevents water from moving downwards, although it may initially appear to drain away from the surface. Pan formation can arise naturally in regions of very high rainfall when soluble minerals are precipitated from solution or when small insoluble particles gradually accumulate. But pans can also form if the soil is not properly managed. For example, if the soil is dug repeatedly and frequently to the same shallow depth or if a mechanical cultivator is used regularly.

As the soil structure deteriorates in the way I've described, so the conditions become less favourable for earthworms and other soil life and the end result is that plant growth can decline. All these adverse physical effects on soil can be corrected but it is, of course, better to avoid or minimise them happening in the first place. The way to do this is to cultivate your soil using one or more of a variety of techniques that I describe below.

## Digging

Of all cultivation techniques, digging is the most important as it breaks through compacted soil and allows water and air to penetrate. As the soil is turned over, lumps or clods of soil are exposed to the weather (especially frost) which then breaks them down into smaller particles. Digging also provides the opportunity for organic matter to be added to the soil. To dig the soil thoroughly, the plot must be free of plants, so most digging takes place in early spring (before planting or sowing) or autumn (after the area is cleared). However, you should take into account the weather conditions; ideally, frozen soil should not be dug nor should soil that is heavily waterlogged.

The most familiar type of digging is called single digging – the cultivation is limited to one spade's depth. From time to time, however, the lower levels of the soil should be broken up too and this is referred to as double digging. It offers the best way of preventing pan develop-

ment and ensuring that deep rooted plants have the best growing conditions.

Before explaining the detailed differences between single and double digging, let me stress that proper digging, and double digging especially, is strenuous exercise and so it is an activity that should be undertaken at a steady pace, not in a rush. Divide up the area to be dug and aim to tackle a section each week, from, say, early autumn to just before Christmas. Ideally, you should warm up your muscles beforehand by gently bending and stretching. Wear suitable clothing and

**above** Neglect of deep digging can result in the development of an impervious pan several centimetres (inches) below the soil surface.

**above** Double digging entails working methodically from one end of a plot to the other.

It's worth reminding ourselves of the correct tools to use. A spade is used for moving soil from one place to another but a fork is better for breaking down the soil into smaller pieces. It's also easier to lift, spread and mix in soil improvers such as organic matter with a fork rather than a spade. Some soils are hard to penetrate with a spade and a fork may be easier to push in. Further breaking up of clods in spring is often easier with the back of a fork.

### Single Digging

With single digging, the cultivation or disturbance of the soil is limited to the depth of the spade and the penetration of organic matter below this level is solely by the activities of earthworms and other soil animals. Because soil can only be dug by spade when it is fallow (free from plants) and not frozen, you have a choice between autumn and early spring. Both times are important. In autumn, soil should be rough dug; that is, the spade inserted approximately to its own depth (usually called a spit) and the soil turned over but then scarcely broken down. During this autumn digging, manure or compost should be forked over the surface and roughly mixed with the soil. The water within the clods will be frozen during the winter and the soil will thus break down naturally into smaller pieces as a result of the expansion of the ice.

Even after this breakdown, however, the soil will still be in too coarse a condition for sowing seeds or planting plants when spring arrives. A second digging, either with a spade or fork, should be performed then, making liberal use of the back of the tool to break down the clods into finer pieces. If the soil is broken down in this way in the autumn, effort is being expended wastefully (the frost will do the task for nothing) but more importantly, the heavy winter rains beating onto the fine surface will bring about capping once again.

footwear; leather boots are preferable to rubber Wellington boots. Take regular breaks by doing other lighter tasks around the garden. And when digging, try to keep your back as straight as possible; a spade or fork with an appropriate handle length for your height will help. Avoid making awkward jerking movements; aim to build up a steady rhythm.

**right** A trench in which organic matter has been incorporated offers the most effective way of preparing the positions for rows of plants like runner beans that require a moisture-retentive soil.

### Double Digging

Double digging is digging to two spade's depth. It's also known as bastard trenching (using, I've always believed, 'bastard' in the sense of 'counterfeit' or 'spurious': it looks like proper trenching but isn't). Work your way in a line across the plot to form a trench, removing the soil by barrow to the end of the plot. Fork organic matter into the base of the trench and then dig another trench, parallel to the first, using the soil from the second to re-fill the first. Gradually work your way along the plot, making parallel trenches and filling the final trench with the soil that you barrowed away at the start. You should only double dig when the ground has not previously been dug for some time; and also when it won't be dug again for some time. The two most obvious occasions when there will be no digging for some while are when planting a new herbaceous or shrub border and when preparing a new deep bed for vegetables (see below).

## Use of Trenches for Crops

Trenching (real trenching, not bastard trenching) is a traditional technique used for providing certain types of crops, such as runner beans and sweet peas, with sustained moisture through their growing season. The principle is to incorporate organic matter up to a depth of 30-50cm (12-20in) in order to hold the moisture. Care must be taken, however, not to add

**above** For most gardeners, the best flavoured celery is trenched which is partly buried, rather than self-blanching which grows on the surface.

**left** The deep bed system requires initial deep digging but should then not require further deep digging for several years. But it must be narrow enough to reach from the sides without being walked on.

layers of manure continually to the base of the trench. This can led to a sump forming which provides ideal conditions for root-rotting organisms to which the pea and bean family is especially prone. Rather than put the organic matter in layers at the bottom of the trench, incorporate it uniformly, therefore, throughout the depth of the trench as you refill it.

Trenching is also used to produce traditional trenched celery. Celery is a plant that grows naturally in wet, boggy places and therefore grows well in a moist trench. Blanching or whitening of the stems is enhanced by back filling the trench with soil as the plants grow (see page 140).

## The Deep Bed System

Sometimes called a no dig system – although this can also refer to blanket mulching (see page 83) – this approach seeks to minimise compaction by feet and machinery so that routine annual digging is no longer necessary to improve the soil's physical structure. However, the facility for incorporating organic matter at some depth is also lost too. To replace this, there is a need to dig very thoroughly by double digging when the bed system is set up and every four to six years thereafter.

The beds should be constructed so that all parts can be reached from the pathways without the need to tread on the beds – a width of about 1.2m (4ft) is ideal – and if access is required for tasks such as planting or thinning, then planks can be placed over the beds supported on bricks or blocks.

## Hoeing

There are two main types of hoe: the draw hoe, used to earth up or cover vegetables with soil to protect them from frost or to exclude light, and the Dutch hoe which is used to sever annual weeds and also to loosen the soil surface. In dry weather, pulling and pushing a Dutch hoe over the soil surface exposes darker, more moist soil underneath.

Two contrasting beliefs have grown up around this type of hoeing. One is that moisture release is encouraged as damp soil is brought to the surface, the other is that moisture loss is minimised by keeping the surface friable. There is some truth in the first although in drought conditions the soil is best left not hoed as the dry layer does act as a mulch. Hoeing is a very valuable practice but always remember its function in weed control and take care not to disturb shallow- or brittle-rooted crops such as onions.

## Raking

Even after the soil has been forked over in spring, the soil surface is still too coarse for seed germination. The pieces of soil need to be further broken down and if the soil is very stony, then some should be removed if seeds are to be sown direct (some stones are valuable nonetheless as they retain warmth and act as a positive aid to early growth). A fork will help initially but a soil rake is needed to create a seed-bed. The aim is to produce a level area

**below** The gardener here must be careful; whilst hoeing between the lettuces, she mustn't disturb the fragile roots of the onions nearby.

where the soil is friable and the soil particles form small, uniform crumbs. Such a soil is said to have a good tilth although this is a strange word and you will seldom hear gardeners talk of a bad tilth; all tilth is good tilth. A friable soil enables the surface to warm up more evenly and provide more uniform conditions of moisture and light for the seeds. There is no merit in raking and creating a fine tilth in autumn as the heavy winter rain will cause capping on the surface and a hard crusty layer will form.

## Use of Powered Cultivators

I have already discussed powered cultivators as tools on page 53 and have pointed out their drawbacks, most notably encouraging the formation of an impervious pan within the soil. They also cause smearing of clay soils by breaking down the crumbs. If a powered cultivator must be used, because the area is too large to dig, it is important to cultivate more deeply than usual (this is called sub-soiling) every two or three years so any pan is broken up.

## Mulches and Organic Matter

Mulching is a technique that can be used instead of hoeing to control annual weeds; it also helps retain moisture within the soil. A mulch is simply a layer of material placed over the surface of the soil. Traditionally, it is some form of organic matter such as garden compost or manure but there are now other materials, often called sheet mulches, made from various forms of plastic or paper. The pros and cons of the various materials and how to apply them are dealt with in more detail on page 82 but it is worth mentioning that it is only the organic mulches that contribute to improving soil structure. The material works as a mulch while it is on the soil surface but in time earthworms and other animals drag it down into the soil where it is broken up.

The need for well-rotted as opposed to fresh organic matter to add to the soil is often emphasised and it is worth understanding why this distinction is important. If fresh organic matter, such as plant debris, is placed on or mixed into the soil it will begin to decompose as it comes into contact with the soil organisms. The organic matter provides the bacteria and fungi with nutrients. Fresh plant remains are rich in cellulose; the ratio of the two important elements of carbon and nitrogen in them is

about 33:1, whereas in partly-decomposed organic matter the ratio is 10:1. The explanation for this is that as fungal and bacterial activity increase on the plant remains, some of the carbon is used by them (some is lost as carbon dioxide) but there is a shortage of nitrogen. A convenient source of nitrogen is the soil itself and in time as the decomposition process proceeds, the carbon to nitrogen ratio falls to 10:1 and the nitrogen becomes mineralised so there is a time when soil nitrogen is depleted or unavailable to plants. This is why applying fresh manure or plant remains directly to the soil is not recommended; the material should be composted in a compost bin first (see page 81 for details).

**above** A rake should be used carefully and in alternate directions to create a fine tilth in a seed bed.

# Training and Pruning

Although many gardeners imagine that pruning is performed only on trees and shrubs, any removal of shoots, branches, flowers or other parts from a growing plant amounts to pruning, and many of the same underlying principles apply. In this part of the book, I have followed convention, however, and these accounts relate only to the pruning of woody plants. Methods of training and pruning herbaceous plants and vegetables will be found in the appropriate sections later in the book.

**above** Pruning and training this climbing rose will allow it to flower from top to bottom.

**below** A careful cut, just above and sloping away from a bud, is the key to pruning.

Continually pruning a young plant will dictate its overall shape as it matures. This operation is called training, and the process by which it is done is generally known as formative pruning. The choice of training method can have a considerable bearing on the plant's productivity, and cordon or fan-trained fruit trees grown against walls are good examples of this (page 67). The need to train a plant into a chosen shape is, therefore, the first of the reasons for pruning. The routine pruning performed on it thereafter is usually called maintenance pruning, and this is done mainly to increase the production of leafy shoots (part of the reason for pruning or clipping hedges), or of flowers and fruits (the usual reason with ornamental and fruit plants). A further reason is to encourage overall vigour by removing overcrowded shoots and branches and letting light and air penetrate. Finally, pruning can actually improve the health of a plant when it involves removing either diseased parts, or any redundant or moribund tissues (like dead flowers) that are likely to provide disease-causing organisms with a foothold.

Using pruning to shape a plant makes use of the fact that taking off the end of a shoot, with its associated buds, stimulates those buds

lower down to burst into life. This is why regular clipping of a hedge will thicken its overall growth. This important principle of pruning and training is based on disrupting a phenomenon called apical dominance, in which the growing buds at, and close to, the tip or apex of a shoot produce chemicals that inhibit the growth of those below them. Sometimes, simply bending the leading shoot from a vertical position towards the horizontal is enough to reduce apical dominance and stimulate flowering lower down.

## Tools for pruning

For most pruning tasks, a pair of secateurs (sometimes called pruners) will be adequate although for thicker, tougher stems, loppers and a pruning saw are necessary. Hedge-clipping is achieved either with hand shears or powered trimmers. The important features of all of these tools are considered on page 50.

## How to prune

In order to follow pruning instructions you need to identify the main stem (known as the leader), the laterals (the side-shoots that arise from the main stem) and the sub-laterals (side-shoots that arise in turn from the laterals). When pruning fruit and blossom trees you may also need to recognise a spur, which is a short, stubby shoot on which flowers and fruit develop.

Always make pruning cuts immediately above a bud, leaf, flower, branch division or other actively growing structure; never in the middle of a length of shoot. This ensures that natural healing of the cut surface takes place swiftly. Always position the cut approximately 6mm (¼in) above the bud or other growing part and sloping away from it. To control the direction of future growth, look at the way the buds face. By cutting above outward-facing buds you will encourage shoots to grow outwards, leaving a more open centre to the plant. By cutting above an upward-facing bud, you will encourage shoots to grow upwards, giving a narrower, more upright habit overall, but with a much greater likelihood of shoot congestion. Take special care when removing large branches from trees, especially from the main trunk. Never allow the saw cut to damage the swollen base or collar of the branch, for within this zone are the tissues that promote healing; and never apply wound-sealing compounds to the cut surfaces of pruning cuts.

## When to prune

Flowering and/or fruiting shrubs, trees and climbers fall into two groups: those that flower early in the year on wood produced during the previous season and those that flower after midsummer on wood produced during the current year. In order not to remove flower buds, pruning is performed after flowering. Those shrubs that flower on the older wood are pruned as soon as the flowers fade, and this usually involves little more than a general tidying up and removal of dead flowerheads. Plants that flower on the current season's wood may be pruned at any time between late autumn and early spring, but the advantage of leaving the work until spring is that the old growth provides some protection over winter.

The timing of pruning for foliage plants is less critical but their ability to withstand frosts and cold winds needs to be taken into account. Any plant of borderline hardiness (and also many evergreens) are best pruned in the spring, although long growths that could be blown about and damaged in the wind may be removed in autumn.

There may be other factors to consider with particular species. Vigorous plants, such as wisterias and many hedges may need pruning twice a year, while trees such as willows and walnuts have a strong sap flow in spring and early summer so pruning cuts made at this time can weep badly and weaken the plant. Plums and related plants are prone to silver-leaf disease and as the spores of the causal fungus are produced in autumn and winter, pruning must be done in spring or summer.

## How severely to prune

I mentioned earlier that the removal of apical buds stimulates others (usually called lateral or side-buds) to grow. Essentially therefore, the more of the main shoot that is removed, the greater will be the stimulation of the side shoots. And the greater the severity with which these, in turn, are cut back, the greater is the proliferation of shoots overall. The practical consequence is that severe (or, as it is usually called, hard) pruning should be used in order to encourage more growth from a plant that is growing feebly or is inherently weak. Conversely, a very strongly growing plant should, in general, be pruned lightly in order to contain its vigour.

## Basic Pruning Methods
### Annual renewal pruning

This is a very important pruning technique for plants that flower after midsummer. Either the whole plant is cut back to just above ground level in early spring, as with *Buddleja davidii*, autumn-fruiting raspberries and some dogwoods (*Cornus*); or, and much more generally, only a proportion (usually the oldest one-third) of the stems is removed each season. The remaining stems are left unpruned or are lightly pruned (to less than half their length)

**above** Hard pruning, as with this *Buddleja davidii*, can look brutal but will guarantee a more attractive and efficient plant later.

**below** Annual renewal pruning: the oldest third of the shoots have been cut from this shrub in spring.

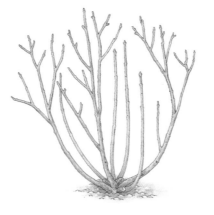
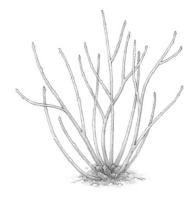

**above** Shrubs like lavender that produce a mass of individual small flowers can be 'dead-headed' with shears after flowering.

and so the plant is entirely renewed every three years.

### Light pruning or trimming after flowering

This is the most common pruning technique for those plants that flower before or shortly after midsummer. It is a more extensive version of dead-heading; the dead flowerheads are cut back well beyond the base of the flowers and some re-shaping of the plant is done at the same time. Hand shears may be used to trim lightly over bushy plants as the flowers fade; trim to below the base of the dead flowerheads but not more than a few centimetres into the older wood.

### Restorative pruning

Overgrown and neglected trees and shrubs can often be rejuvenated by pruning and removing dead and diseased parts, overgrown and crossing branches and weak shoots. This stimulates new young growth although it is best to spread the task over three years, doing one-third of the pruning each year. Much of the benefit results from improved penetration of light and air to the centre of the plant.

### Pruning for damage and disease control

If a part of a plant has simply been damaged (a branch broken by a gale, for instance), that damage won't itself spread and it might be thought that no treatment is needed. Complications arise, however, if the broken tissues are then invaded by a disease-causing fungus, but the likelihood of this arising can be minimised if the wound is 'cleaned up' promptly. Branch stubs should be cut off neatly, broken branches cut back to the basal collar and any damaged tissues cut back carefully to healthy wood or bark.

Understanding disease biology will also help to indicate the value of pruning as a control. For example, during the winter the rose black spot fungus survives in small lesions on the shoots. Hard pruning in the spring to remove these diseased shoots is of much greater value, therefore, than collecting diseased leaves. It's important, also, to recognise the difference between localised diseases and much more

**right** Damaged or diseased wood, like this cankered branch, should be cut back to just above the basal collar.

deep-seated or widespread problems. Most fungal cankers (like apple canker) are classic examples of localised problems: there isn't much infection beyond what can be seen, so if a branch bearing a canker is cut away neatly, there should be no further spread. Bacterial cankers (like those on plums and cherries) are often associated with extensive contamination of the tree, however, and so cutting out an individual lesion may have little overall effect.

## Training and pruning notes for the main groups of garden plants

### Shrubs
#### Training
No training is needed with free-standing shrubs, although standards will need staking like young trees (page 64), but shrubs can be trained against a wall to form a more-or-less two-dimensional structure, simply by cutting away any shoots that point directly towards or away from the wall and then tying the main branches to the wall. Spur-pruning will also be necessary on many flowering wall shrubs: the side-shoots arising from the main framework should be cut back to within about 10cm (4in) of their bases each year to produce short flowering shoots or spurs.

#### Pruning
**Flowering shrubs** Be guided especially by flowering time and always prune after flowering is complete. Remember that dead-heading will generally encourage repeat flowering, either immediately or later in the season: cut back the dead flowerhead to just above the first leaf with a plump bud in its apex. Many flowering shrubs also benefit from three-year renewal pruning.

**Foliage shrubs** Most foliage shrubs perform reasonably well without special attention, but many will benefit from three year renewal pruning. Timing is less critical than for flowering plants, but spring is the best pruning time overall.

### Trees
#### Training and support
Newly-planted trees are usually top heavy and likely to be rocked by the wind, so support in the form of a tree stake will help their roots to

establish more quickly. A typical tree stake is 5cm (2in) in diameter with 2m (6½ft) above ground and 75cm (2½ft) below; these stakes are still very popular, although more recent research has shown that shorter ones, with only 75cm (2½ft) above ground allow the tree to flex and so develop greater wind tolerance. Stakes are best positioned at planting time when there will be less damage to the roots. Place the stake on the side of the stem facing the prevailing wind so the tree is blown away from, not on to it, and secure it with an adjustable tree tie with a buffer between the bark and the stake.

#### Pruning
When tree branches overhang buildings or other types of obstacle and for the wholesale reduction in size of trees that have grown too large for their site I urge gardeners to use a tree surgeon, preferably affiliated

**above** Many types of shrubs, like these pyracanthas, may be grown either free-standing and pruned little, or carefully shaped against a wall.

**below** I still prefer to dead-head roses the traditional way: by cutting back to the first leaf with five leaflets.

**below** Some otherwise good garden trees and shrubs produce suckers, especially when grafted onto a different rootstock, and these should be pulled away regularly.

to a recognised professional body. Not only do tree surgeons have the necessary practical experience, but they will also have insurance protection in the event of any mishaps. The complete removal of unwanted trees is also generally a matter for a professional. Apart from the difficulty and danger of felling the tree itself, the stump must be dug up, ground down or winched out, the latter two requiring expensive equipment.

Suckers are produced by trees and shrubs where the chosen variety has been grafted on to a different rootstock. Suckers should always be removed, for they will invariably draw nutrient away from the grafted variety, but they should be pulled, not cut away, if the result isn't merely to be the stimulation of yet more suckers.

Remember that care in choosing varieties of trees and shrubs and simple routine attention (such as rubbing off buds or leaf clusters that arise on the bark of standard specimens) will very often obviate the necessity for any remedial pruning later.

All of the above relates to the pruning of the above ground parts of trees and shrubs but there will be a few occasions when root pruning is desirable. Usually the need only arises when a plant has been chosen inappropriately for a site and, for various reasons, it is undesirable completely to remove and replace it. Root pruning is most commonly used with apples, pears or a few types of ornamental trees but should never be done on plums or other *Prunus* species, willows or poplars as they will respond by excessive production of suckers. Root pruning is achieved by carefully digging a circular trench in autumn approximately 45cm (18in) deep and at a radius from the trunk determined by allowing about 12cm (5in) for every 1cm (½in) of trunk diameter. The fine roots should be left intact and the thickest roots severed. After the operation is complete and the trench refilled, the plant will almost certainly require the added support of a stake.

## Roses
### Training and pruning

Training is usually only required with climbing and rambling roses, which may be treated in the same way as other climbing plants (below). Large shrub roses will benefit from tripod or similar stout supports. Most types of rose, however, do require rather careful pruning and, for the best results, you should use one of eight techniques appropriate to the various rose groups (page 222). The task is best done in the spring and the only autumn pruning I do is to remove long whippy shoots to prevent the plants being rocked by winter winds. Rambler roses (page 225) are the only group to require summer pruning although, of course, dead-heading should be done throughout summer to prolong flowering.

## Climbers
### Training

Although a few common climbers like ivy and Boston ivy (*Parthenocissus tricuspidata*) are self-clinging and therefore require no additional support, most climbers need tying and training. Twining climbers, like wisteria, grasp supports by wrapping their entire stems around them and growing upwards. These are most successful, therefore, where the principal supports are vertical.

Climbers such as clematis and grape vines have tendrils which are much more effectively supported by horizontal wires. Trellises, if strong enough, having both vertical and horizontal elements, are useful for both twiners and tendril climbers.

Climbing roses are grapplers that rely on backward-facing spines, a rather crude system, and although to some extent they may be twisted around vertical supports (as with pillar roses) they also need to be tied securely to their supports to prevent them from becoming tangled.

Walls offer the best support for climbers and all except self-clinging types need horizontal wires fixed 20-25cm (8-10in) apart. Use 2mm (⅛in) diameter, plastic-coated wire that can be tensioned without snapping and attach it to looped vine eyes, screwed into wall plugs. For large climbers, stronger wires with straining bolts may be needed, although very heavy plants like established wisterias are best secured with individual vine eyes.

Trellis can be an attractive feature in its own right but its strength depends on the thickness of wood and method of construction, so be sure to choose a type appropriate to your plant. It may be made free-standing but if it is being attached to a wall, fix it first to 2.5cm (1in) battens so that air can circulate behind it. Trellis may also be used as a top to increase the height of fences or walls, as screening and as an in-filling in arches and other structures.

There are many free-standing supports like archways, pergolas, pillars and tripods that provide an opportunity for training climbers. But choose a climber with vigour appropriate to the size of support; many arches and obelisks are only strong enough for the less rampant types. Train the stems so they are almost horizontal to encourage flowering all along their length.

### Pruning

The same basic pruning principles relating flowering time to pruning apply to climbers as well as shrubs, and if climbers are thought of as long thin shrubs, their pruning will seem much more logical. Clematis, which many gardeners find confusing, illustrate this well. They can be divided into three main groups for pruning purposes, depending on when they flower:

**Group 1.** Clematis that flower early in the year on wood produced the previous season. Prune immediately after flowering by cutting back all weak and dead stems to just above a bud.

**Group 2.** Clematis that flower on wood from the previous season but in early summer, rather later than the Group 1 types. Prune in early spring by cutting out any dead or weak stems and cut back remaining shoots by about 30cm (12in), cutting to just above a pair of plump buds.

**Group 3.** Clematis that flower later in the summer on the current year's wood. Prune hard in early spring to remove the previous season's growth, cutting back to just above a pair of plump buds about 75cm (30in) above soil level.

### Fruit Trees
#### Training and pruning

To reach their full potential, fruit trees must be trained and pruned from a young age and I have subdivided the descriptions here according to fruit type, as each requires rather different treatment.

### Apples and pears

The easiest way to grow apples or pears is as a free-standing bush. No support is necessary other than a tree stake and only winter pruning is required. It is simplest to start with a one-year-old tree (called a maiden). During the first winter after planting, cut back the single shoot to a healthy bud at about 60-90cm (2-3ft) above soil level. This will result in several upright shoots being produced over the next year.

The second winter, cut out the middle shoot to give the tree an open centre. The four strongest shoots remaining should be cut back by about half their length. Remember, always cut to an outward-facing bud to maintain the open centre. Remove any other long shoots and also cut back laterals to about three buds.

In the third and subsequent winters, maintenance pruning takes over from formative pruning and the trees should be pruned in winter by cutting back the side-shoots on each branch to two or three buds above the base and shortening the leading shoots on each branch by up to one-half. The less you need to cut back established trees, the better.

**above** Root pruning can limit the vigour of trees. In this plan view, a trench has been dug around the tree at a distance equivalent to 12cm (5in) for every 1cm (½in) of trunk diameter. The thickest roots uncovered have been severed.

**below** The success of many climbing plants depends on having firmly attached wire supports. Use screw pattern vine eyes to secure the wires.

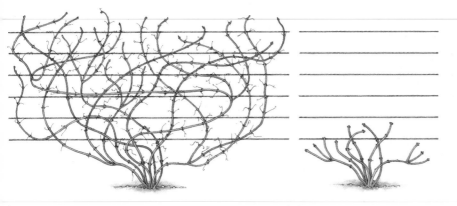

**above** The later flowering the clematis, the harder should it be pruned. This is a late flowering Group 3 variety before and after spring pruning.

**below** Cordon apples need pruning in late summer and again in winter. The labour is well-rewarded, however, by your ability to have many plants in a limited space.

Growing apples or pears as cordons can save space but requires summer as well as winter pruning. Set up a system of horizontal wires between firmly braced posts, spacing the wires 60cm (2ft) apart to a height of 2m (6½ft). Plant a maiden tree with a supporting cane at an angle of 45 degrees and tie both tree and cane to the support wires. Prune all side-shoots longer than 10cm (4in) to a point just above the third bud from their bases. Thereafter, every year in late summer, cut sideshoots longer than 20-25cm (8-10in), and growing directly from the main stem, at a point just above the third leaf above the basal cluster. At the same time, cut shoots arising from the side-shoots at a point just above the first leaf beyond the basal cluster. Prune established cordons in late summer by cutting back all the side-shoots longer than 20cm (8in) to a point three leaves above the base. Also cut back any small shoots arising from the side-shoots to one leaf above the basal cluster. Once the leading shoot has reached its allotted length, treat it in exactly the same way as the side-shoots.

Pears especially are very successful when grown as espaliers. An espalier consists of a central stem bearing tiers of paired horizontal branches, trained flat against a wall or support wires. After planting an unfeathered maiden in winter, cut it back to about 40cm (16in) above soil level, just above three plump buds. The topmost of these buds will grow to become the central stem, and the two below will develop as the two lowest branches.

In summer, tie the top shoot in to a vertical cane, and the two lower ones to canes placed at angles of 45 degrees. Then, in late autumn, carefully lower the two branches so they are horizontal, and tie them into support wires. If one is weak, cut it back by about a third to an upward-facing bud. Otherwise, do not prune. At the same time, in order to create the next tier, prune back the central stem to about 45cm (1½ftin) above the lower branches, again just above three strong buds. Cut back any other shoots to three buds. In the following summers, as before, tie in the side branches at first at an angle of 45 degrees, and then in late autumn lower them to the horizontal. Continue this system of summer and autumn pruning until the required number of tiers has been formed, at which point the central leader should be cut back in summer to check further growth. The arms of the espalier are then maintained in a similar way to a cordon in order to encourage fruiting.

**Plums, cherries, peaches and apricots**

A maiden plum tree is best planted in late autumn, but should not be pruned until budbreak in early spring. Then cut back the leader to just above four or five plump buds at the required height, allowing for a stem of about 90cm (3ft) for a bush and 1.4m (4¾ft) for a half-standard. Any laterals should be cut back to about 7.5cm (3in). They will eventually be removed but for the time being help to strengthen the main stem.

The following summer, pinch back any new growth on the laterals, leaving no more than four or five leaves. By early spring of the second year, several strong new shoots will have developed. Choose four that are well-spaced and wide-angled to form permanent branches. Cut each back by one-half to two-thirds to an outward-facing bud. Remove all laterals.

In the spring of the third year choose up to eight strong outward-growing secondary branches to form a balanced framework. Cut the new growth on all of these back by between one-half and two-thirds, always cutting to just above outward-facing buds. At the same time, prune back laterals on the inside of the tree to

about 10cm (4in), but leave laterals on the outside unpruned. Thereafter, pruning should be kept to an absolute minimum and the tree allowed to settle down to crop.

To train a fan, early in the first summer after planting a well feathered maiden (a young, untrained tree with several side-branches), cut out the main shoot at a point just above a pair of strong side-branches about 30cm (12in) above soil level. Tie these 'arms' on to diagonal canes attached to the main support wires. The following spring, cut back the two arms to points above a bud about 30cm (12in) from the main stem. Cut back shoots arising from the arms to three or four buds from their bases. The following spring, further shoots will have elongated from the arms. Two should be selected above and two below each of the initial shoots, tied in and shortened as before. Other shoots should be cut back to their bases. On a large wall, more arms can be created the following year, but stop once the allotted space is covered. Thereafter, annual maintenance pruning is required in spring. First cut out any shoots growing directly towards or away from the wall then, on each blossom-bearing side shoot, pinch out some of the leafy buds to leave one at the tip, one at the base and one in the middle. In early summer, pinch back each side-shoot to a point just above six leaves from the base. In late summer, cut back each fruited side-shoot to its junction with the new side-shoot and then tie in this new shoot.

## Fig

Figs are best grown as fans, trained initially as for plums (page 129). Thereafter, the pruning is dictated by the fact that, in cool climates, the fruit won't reach harvesting size within one season. The most important fruits are the pea-sized ones that appear in late summer at the tips of young shoots. If they survive the winter they should ripen by late summer or early autumn the following year. A second crop develops on new shoots in spring but fails to ripen, and should be removed in late autumn.

In early summer, pinch back to about five leaves from the base all of the

**below** All stone fruits are successful when fan trained. It is simple and much cheaper to do the whole operation yourself starting with a maiden plant (here in its third year after planting) rather than buy one 'ready-made'.

young shoots growing out of the ribs of the fan. These shoots will harden and produce embryo fruits in late summer. In midsummer, some old and unfruitful wood may be thinned out to let in more sunlight to ripen the fruit.

I find it best to do the majority of the pruning in spring, leaving on the old wood to give protection in winter. So, in spring, cut back to 2.5cm (1in) about half of the shoots that have borne fruit, in order to encourage new growth. The shoots that remain should be about 25-30cm (10-12in) apart, and should be tied in. Any other unwanted shoots should be removed completely and you should remove any shoots growing directly towards or away from the wall.

## Soft Fruit
### Training
The woody soft fruits are divided loosely into cane fruits (raspberries, blackberries and their relatives), bush fruit (gooseberries and currants) and the climbing grapevines and kiwi fruit. The bush fruits need no support but training is necessary. Cut out some shoots at an early stage to prevent overcrowding, the aim being to create a goblet-shaped plant with a fairly hollow central structure.

The best support for cane fruits is a system of horizontal wires between braced vertical posts. I use round, rustic, tannalised wooden posts, 3.5m (11ft) apart and sunk 45-60cm (1½-2ft) into the soil leaving a height of 1.8m (5ft 9in) above. Use plastic-coated 10-gauge or 3mm (⅛in) diameter wire. It can be twisted two or three times around each post or attached to bolts screwed through each post then pulled taut by hand. The wires are most usefully positioned at 60cm (2ft) above soil level. Individual canes should be tied to the wires with soft, degradable string in a figure-of-eight pattern.

The simplest training method is the Scottish stool system where the canes are allowed to emerge as a group from each stool and tied in a fan-pattern to the wires, any excess canes being cut out.

Blackberries and their hybrids have long flexible canes and, to cope with them, I favour the fan-training system which gives the highest yield although it is rather time-consuming. It is best employed on the single bay system where the new canes that will bear next season's fruit are tied up through the centre and then out along either side and over the top of the old canes that bear the current year's crop.

### Pruning
The canes of summer-fruiting raspberries, blackberries and all the hybrid berries should be pruned to soil level once the fruit has been picked, and the new canes then tied in. Cut or pull any canes emerging too far from the support wires and limit the number of new canes to eight or nine per metre (yard). Autumn-fruiting raspberry canes must be left until late winter and then pruned to soil level.

## Blackcurrants
### Training
After planting, cut back all shoots to just above two buds from the base. At the end of the first fruiting season, when the number of branches on the new plant should have at least doubled, cut back one or two to just above two buds from the base, and also cut out any weak shoots, cutting back to their junction with the parent branch.

## Pruning

In the second year, and in each subsequent year, cut back the oldest one-quarter or one-third of the shoots to just above the base, as well as any that are hanging very close to the ground. Also cut out any weak or damaged shoots. This may be done at any time between the ripening of the fruit and midwinter; some gardeners choose to do it when they are harvesting the crop.

## Red and White Currants
## Gooseberries
### Training and pruning

All three fruits are grown most conveniently as free-standing bushes, or as cordons against horizontal wires. Each method entails different training but essentially similar pruning.

With a bush, the aim is to produce a goblet-shaped plant with an open centre. In the first winter after planting, cut out any branches at the centre of the bush, and cut back the remaining branches by about one-third, to just above a bud. In the following winter, repeat the cutting back process; by now there should be eight to ten branches, which is the maximum number required. About six weeks after midsummer in every subsequent year, cut back the leading shoots of each branch by about one-third, and any side-shoots on them to just above six leaf-clusters from their base. And every winter, cut back the leading shoots of each branch again by a third, and all side-shoots to two buds from their base. Also remove any branches that grow up from the middle of the plant, and any suckers from below soil level. Occasionally you may need to train a new branch to replace one that is damaged.

Think of a cordon as one, two or three branches (single, double or triple cordons) trained vertically against a support; and remember that the pruning is essentially similar to that of a branch growing normally on a bush. In winter, after planting, select the strongest vertical branch(es) to tie in to the support wires, and cut out the remainder. About six weeks after midsummer in the following year, cut back all side-shoots to just above the sixth leaf-cluster from their bases, but leave the leading shoot untouched. In winter cut the side-shoots back again, to two buds from the base, and cut the leader back by approximately one-third. Continue this process until the leader reaches the top of the wires; from then on treat it in the same way as the side-shoots.

## Grapevines
## Kiwi Fruits
### Training and pruning

Immediately after planting in early winter, cut the main stem down to about 60-75cm (2-2½ft) above soil level, cutting to just above a bud. Support the stem, or 'rod', by tying it to a vertical cane. During the first summer, allow it to grow up to the topmost wire, and then pinch out its top. The strongest of the side-shoots should be tied in to the wires on either side of the rod, and pinched out just beyond five leaves from their base. Any other existing side-shoots should be pinched out altogether. In the following winter, cut back the rod by about half, and cut back the side-shoots to about 2-5cm (¾-2in) from their bases. During the second summer new side-shoots will grow out from these stubs: only one strong one should be allowed to develop and tied in to the support wires; weaker ones should be pinched out. In winter two years after planting, again cut back the rod, which will gradually be approaching the top of the wall, and cut back the side-shoots to leave 2-5cm (¾-2in) stubs.

Pinch out the laterals in summer at three leaves beyond the first flower-cluster in the first year, the second in the second year, and the third thereafter. Every winter the side-shoots should be cut back to leave short stubs; and when the rod has reached the top of the wires it should be treated like a side-shoot and cut back to the same point each year. Always remember that grapevines and kiwi fruits are big vigorous plants and if you are negligent in their pruning they will very soon become an unruly, unfruitful tangle.

**above** Grapevines are big, vigorous plants and require regular attention throughout the summer if they are to remain healthy and fruitful.

# Propagation

There are two ways of obtaining new plants. You can raise them yourself or obtain them from someone else. Buying plants from garden centres or nurseries offers you two big advantages. First, with annual bedding plants and vegetables especially, you will have been spared the time, trouble and expense involved in the sowing, germinating, pricking-on and hardening-off of a large number of plants. The downside to this is that you will pay proportionately very much more to offset the nursery's own costs and provide them with a profit. But, on balance, unless you are very enthusiastic and have a great deal of time to spare, buying the common bedding plants that are required in relatively large numbers makes a good deal of sense for many gardeners.

**below** This colourful summer planting contains a wide variety of hybrids and true species with single, semi-double or double flowers. Whilst some will readily set seed, there is no certainty that this will be either viable or true; and others will never set seed. The propagation of each type must therefore be judged individually.

For those plants required in small numbers and for uncommon types that are less likely to be stocked at garden centres, raising them from seeds represents a better if not the only option. The situation with vegetables is rather different, for most are sown directly outdoors and, in general, those few types that are better raised in pots for transplanting (runner beans, for instance) are required in small numbers that should be within most gardeners' production capabilities.

The second big advantage in buying plants is of special importance with perennials. Here, of course, the value of the 'head start' is much greater, but the choice in varieties is of even more significance. Many of the best types of herbaceous perennials and shrubs don't produce seeds; having double flowers (and hence no stamens), they have lost the ability to do so. Even those with single or semi-double flowers are generally complex hybrids and the offspring don't 'come true' from seed. Thus, all of these types must be propagated by vegetative means, generally by cuttings, and so buying plants initially is your only way of obtaining them.

But once you have bought a plant or even raised one from seed to maturity, vegetative methods can be used to multiply it further. All of these techniques make use of plants' natural abilities to regenerate roots or shoots. There are, however, significant biological and practical distinctions between the two reproductive methods. While a seed-raised plant can be very different in genetic make-up from its parents and so introduce variation, plants propagated by vegetative means, either naturally or using artificial techniques like division, cuttings and layering are genetically identical to the parent.

To introduce another term, they are clones. Both methods of propagation are important to commercial horticulture and to home gardeners.

## Raising plants from seed

Naturally, of course, all plants shed their seeds outdoors and it is there that they germinate, often following a period of dormancy or rest. In gardens, however, we can advance the season, give hardy plants a head start and extend their flowering or cropping by sowing their seeds indoors in warmth. Many garden plants, moreover, are native to climates warmer than ours and if they were to be sown directly outdoors, they wouldn't experience a long enough period of adequate warmth to enable them to germinate, mature, flower and/or fruit before low temperatures at the end of the season slowed them down or frost killed them. They must be sown under protection.

Plants that originate in warmer climates but can thrive perfectly well outdoors in cool areas in summer, although not in winter, are called half-hardy. Some of them are genuine annuals but most are really perennials. When grown in cool gardens for one season only, however, they all tend to be described as half-hardy annuals. The technique of sowing seeds in indoor warmth before moving the plants outdoors, once the danger of frost has passed, is called the half-hardy-annual technique.

## Sowing seed indoors

To raise seeds successfully indoors, some basic equipment is essential. Fresh compost, either a 'seed-and-cutting' or a 'multi-purpose' formulation, should be purchased each year. A propagator will be needed and there is a range of options from a simple plant-pot covered with a plastic bag to a purpose-made, electric thermostatically-controlled unit. To begin, I recommend you buy several standard plastic seed trays and one or more rigid plastic covers with adjustable manual vents. These are economical and versatile, as the seed trays can be used to hold smaller containers like half-trays or pots and the plastic covers can be easily moved from one seed tray to another.

Seeds require warmth to germinate rapidly and evenly. The ideal germination temperature varies for each species but, in practice, you should aim to provide three broad temperature

bands: low, less than 15.5°C (60°F), medium, 15.5-21.5°C (60-70°F) and high, above 21°C (70°F). A window ledge will suffice for seeds that require a medium temperature provided you move the propagator on to a nearby table before drawing the blinds or curtains at night, as the air temperature between the window and drawn curtains can drop dramatically. Seeds that need a high temperature can be placed in an airing cupboard for a brief period but remember to check daily and move the propagator into the light as soon as most of the seedlings have emerged.

You may prefer to have a heated propagator, but do choose one where the individual seed tray or pots can be removed from the warmth once the seedlings have germinated. Where there is no mains electricity supply nearby, use low voltage heating mats as a heat source under the seed trays. A transformer plugged into a mains socket in the house and a low-voltage wire run

**above** The seedlings in these seed trays will require pricking-on to further trays as they grow. This task could have been eliminated by using one-plant modular inserts.

**below** I find that a sand bench with thermostatically controlled heating cables offers the greatest versatility. I simply stand my covered propagator trays on the top.

**above** Seed tubes facilitate the sowing of very tiny seeds.

**below** If seedlings are transplanted, they must be handled extremely carefully.

to the greenhouse is all that is required. However, my ideal system for the greenhouse that does have mains electricity, is a heated sand bench: a large box, about 15cm (6in) deep and filled with sand in which a thermostatically controlled heating cable is buried. You can either make your own or purchase a kit. Take care to follow the instructions for calculating the area of bench needed for the lengths of cable. The cable should be laid in a regular pattern for uniform heating and no cable should cross over itself. A heated sand bench is very heavy, so make sure your staging is sturdy enough to cope with the extra weight.

The commonest mistakes made when sowing seeds are to have the compost too loose, too wet or too dry, or to sow the seeds at the incorrect depth. Fill the propagator tray with loose compost level with the top and then firm this down evenly (a small block of wood about 5 x 10cm/2 x 4in makes this very easy) so that its surface is approximately 1cm (½in) below the lip. Water the compost gently and leave the tray for about one hour to drain before sowing the seeds. There are several methods of sowing, dictated principally by seed size. Very small seeds sold loose in packets (lobelia or fibrous-rooted begonia, for instance) may be mixed with a small amount of inert, coloured 'filler' such as fine brick dust and scattered over the surface of the compost. Because of the difficulties of sowing these tiny seeds evenly, seed companies have tried various devices, such as supplying them in small, pencil-like tubes, in order to make the task easier, while proprietary sowing aids, including a useful suction device, are also available.

Most tiny seeds such as these should not be covered with compost because their food reserves are inadequate for the emerged seedling to reach the surface, but they can usefully be covered with finely sieved vermiculite to prevent drying-out. A few medium-sized seeds, such as those of primulas, must also be sown on the surface because darkness inhibits their germination. Almost invariably, you will be advised to sow seeds 'thinly' and, in general, this means that the space between individual seeds should be between 0.5 and 1cm (¼ and ½in), although you may well need to thin out the seedlings slightly after emergence. The distance between rows should be 2-3cm (¾-1¼in). After sowing, carefully push the compost back over the row and firm it with the wooden block as before.

Seeds, such as those of sweet peas, that are large enough to be picked up with forceps are best sown individually by pushing them into the compost to appropriate depth. With most very large seeds, the resulting seedlings are also large and the seeds are better sown directly into small pots of compost. This technique is also valuable with plants such as cauliflowers or aubergines that resent the disturbance brought about by pricking-on. Sow two seeds in each pot and, if both emerge, pull out the weaker.

Increasingly, gardeners are turning to individual 'modular' inserts comprising several small chambers to be filled with compost and placed within a seed tray, partly for the plants

that resent upheaval but also to cut down on the work involved in pricking-on generally.

Once the majority of the seedlings are showing their seed-leaves above the compost, some ventilation is required. Open the propagator vents half-way to increase ventilation as the seedlings elongate. By the time the first true leaves have expanded, the cover should be removed. At this stage the seedlings need regular attention: they need light but not direct hot sun and they need watering little and often.

Most bedding plants should be pricked out into a second tray where they should be spaced 3cm (1¼in) apart each way. A small dibber, pencil or plastic label is useful for making planting holes. Larger seedlings can be pricked out into small pots of potting or multi-purpose compost. When pricking-out take care not to damage the stems and roots; always provide support under the roots and compost.

### Hardening off

Perhaps the most critical stage of all is hardening-off, the process through which the plants are encouraged to produce more resistant tissue that will tolerate outdoor temperatures. This is most easily done by using a cold-frame (for more about these invaluable garden aids, see page 97). For the first week, leave the frame cover half open in the day time but closed at night and in the second week, keep the cover fully open during the day and half open at night. If you don't have a cold-frame, put the trays and pots outside during the day and bring them under cover at night. You need to take your local conditions into account, however, and it is also worth having some garden fleece and newspaper to provide protection if late frosts are forecast.

For many garden plants, sowing seed directly outdoors into the garden soil, in positions where they will grow (the hardy annual technique), makes more sense than using the half-hardy annual method. Many of those annuals that originated in cool climates will grow quickly enough to flower or crop satisfactorily within the season of sowing. A few types of plant are sown outdoors, but closely together into a seed bed from which they will be transplanted later; this is because they grow fairly slowly and would thus occupy valuable growing space for a long, unproductive period.

Whether seeds are to be sown directly into

their final growing positions or into a seed bed, the soil preparation is the same. The area will usually be roughly dug and organic matter incorporated in the autumn and then left with fairly large clods overwinter. By the spring, the winter rains and frost will have broken these down but the soil will still be in a lumpy and uneven state, almost certainly with some weed growth. It should then be dug again as soon as the land begins to dry out in the spring. About one week before sowing, the area should be raked to remove any remaining large clods and at the same time, an appropriate fertilizer should be scattered over the soil and incorporated into the upper few centimetres. Rake alternately in directions at 90 degrees to each other to obtain a level surface.

Spring sowings are invariably more successful if the soil is warmed gently beforehand. Cloches will do the job admirably, and can be replaced over the seeds after sowing. Their only drawback is they are easier to use with seeds sown in rows rather than broadcast and they need to be well secured against wind. An alternative is to use plastic sheeting over the surface of the soil before sowing, secured in place by digging it into a shallow trench. Use black or white, but not clear plastic as this will encourage weed growth.

Most vegetables are sown in rows, the spac-

**above** Rake in alternate directions to obtain a flat, fine surface for seed sowing outdoors.

**above** An improvised seed drill; the only important rule is to keep it straight.

**below** Only nick seeds on the side opposite the 'eye'.

ings and sowing depths varying slightly with each vegetable. Use a garden line to mark out a straight line, then carve out the seed drill with the end of a bamboo cane or the edge of a draw hoe. Sow thinly, either from the packet or from your hand, then cover the seed with soil and press down gently using the back of a rake. Summer-flowering annuals are usually sown in drifts or patches rather than in straight rows.

If you need to transplant seedlings from a seed bed to their final flowering positions, use a hand fork to remove the plants and a trowel for digging the planting hole. Plant at, or slightly greater than, the depth at which the plant was growing previously. Firm in with your hands and apply liquid fertilizer immediately afterwards.

## Special seed techniques

Most seed will germinate readily if sown correctly, but a few species are tricky as the seed has an in-built dormancy mechanism to help it survive through periods of adversity. I've listed below the commonest of the techniques that may help to overcome seed dormancy.

**Stratifying:** Often used for tree, shrub and alpine seeds. Place the ripe seeds (or fruits) in shallow pans of coarse sand, bury them about 2cm (¾in) below the surface and cover the pans with fine-mesh netting to exclude pests. Leave the pans outdoors in a sheltered place over winter. In spring, place them in the slightly warmer conditions of a cold-frame and germination should then begin slowly and erratically.

**Nicking:** Some seeds, like certain sweet pea varieties, have an exceptionally thick outer coat making it very difficult for seedlings to emerge. By nicking or cutting the seed coat with the tip of a sharp knife on the side opposite the 'eye' the seed coat can be encouraged to degrade quicker. Where the seed is too small for the seed coat to be cut by a knife, place the seeds in a screw-top jar with a cylinder of sandpaper and shake hard.

**Soaking:** Seed coats can often be softened by soaking. Try using warm water in a vacuum flask overnight. Seed that has sunk after soaking is more likely to be viable than any still floating on the surface.

**Firing:** For some plants from the tropics or subtropics, a high temperature is often needed to break dormancy. When seeds originate in areas where bush fires are common, germination may be induced by covering the seeds with dry straw and setting it aflame. If you want to try this do make sure you use a terracotta pot, not a plastic one.

## Collecting and storing seeds

There are advantages, apart from satisfaction, in collecting seed from plants in your own garden. With rare or unusual species, it may be impossible to obtain seed commercially and, if the plant happens to be an annual, saving the seed from existing plants provides you with the only way of perpetuating your stock. Many of the gardeners most successful at horticultural shows routinely save seed from strains of the particular vegetable specialities that they have kept season by season.

But against all of this there must be set some disadvantages. Many of today's garden plants are F1 hybrids and they certainly have many merits: they are vigorous, large, strong growing and ripen uniformly. But they are also expensive because of the labour-intensive method by which they are produced: a cross between parental plants must be made afresh each year. Seed saved from F1 hybrid varieties, therefore, is useless for the resulting offspring will be a complete and unpredictable hotchpotch.

Even with varieties that are not F1 hybrids, there is no guarantee that the seedlings you obtain will be identical to their parents. Plants that naturally are self-pollinating will almost invariably come true but those that naturally cross-pollinate may well have been fertilized by related plants growing nearby, although this in itself can offer the exciting prospect of something new and worthwhile turning up.

It's important to make preparations for collecting seed just before it ripens and spills on to the ground. Cut off the heads of plants such as lupins, poppies, peas and beans that produce dry seeds and hang them upside down in a warm but well ventilated and dry place, with a paper bag tied over them. The seeds should then fall naturally into the bag. Seeds, such as those of marrows and tomatoes that are produced within soft and fleshy fruits, should be separated from the surrounding tissues and washed thoroughly to remove any germination-inhibiting chemicals that may be present. Spread them to dry at room temperature before storing them in small paper envelopes.

Both for seeds that you have collected yourself and for commercial packeted seed (once the metal-foil packet has been opened), storage conditions are important if the viability is to be retained. The two factors that diminish the life of seeds are high temperature and high humidity. The ideal storage conditions, therefore, are provided by placing your seed packets inside a screw-top glass jar together with a small sachet of silica gel drying agent. The jar itself should then be placed in a refrigerator. Of course, even stored in this way, seeds will not last forever but, in general, small and fairly hard seeds such as those of brassicas, tomatoes or poppies will maintain their viability for several years. Larger and more fleshy seeds, such as peas and beans, may only last for two years at the most.

## Vegetative multiplication
### Division

The simplest method of multiplication is by division; an old gardening quip but a true one. Large clumps of almost all types of herbaceous perennials (but not woody plants) can physically be pulled apart and the smaller pieces replanted. The age at which they should be divided depends on their rate of growth but in most instances, once the crown reaches 12-15cm (5-6in) in diameter, it can be divided. The best times of year to do this are autumn or early spring, the latter being preferable for plants that are less hardy or that have large, fleshy tubers or rhizomes. The procedure is straightforward enough. Dig up the mature clump with a fork and pull it first into two, then more pieces; if possible, do this by hand, but if not, by inserting two forks, back to back, and levering them apart. Never use a spade for this will sever and damage the roots. From a clump of about 15cm (6in) diameter, it should be possible to obtain approximately ten new plants,

**above** Seed should always be collected in paper or cellophane bags, never plastic which will encourage rotting.

**above** Small plants are always best divided by pulling them apart by hand.

but always tear off and discard those parts that lay in the centre of the original crown; these will be degenerate and never give rise to vigorous new growth.

### Cuttings

After division, the most important method of vegetative propagation is taking cuttings and, in one form or another, this technique can be used with almost every type of plant, ranging from tiny alpines to forest trees. Very few species can't be induced fairly easily to form new root tissues, most of the exceptions being slow-growing plants with very close grained wood or those that produce copious amounts of latex.

Cuttings fall neatly into different categories, depending on the time of the year that they are taken and the part of the plant from which they are cut. A few general principles, however, apply to all.

Cuttings should almost always be removed from the parent plant with a clean cut made close to a bud. The exceptions are heeled cuttings and inter-nodal cuttings ( page 77). While

rooting powder containing growth-promoting hormones is not essential for all types of cutting, used correctly it never does any harm. And because the powder also generally contains a fungicide to prevent rotting, it is sensible to use it routinely. Moisten the freshly-cut end of the cutting, dip it in the powder (always buy fresh each season) and then knock off the excess.

All cuttings, with the exception of hardwood cuttings, should be rooted (or 'struck') in a covered chamber, either a propagator as used for seed sowing (page 71) or a covered cold-frame. It's very important to maintain a moist atmosphere around the cuttings for they will otherwise lose water through their leaves at a time when, lacking roots, they are unable to replace it from below. Even with a covered propagator, therefore, you should pay careful attention to the moisture content of the rooting medium and use a hand sprayer to mist over the cuttings regularly. The cold-frame can also be used for hardwood cuttings, although I prefer to root these in a sheltered spot in the open garden, inserting the shoots in a narrow V-shaped trench in which sand has been layered.

Inducing new roots to form on any type of cutting is always helped by good aeration in the rooting medium. For this reason, a soil-less compost alone is generally unsatisfactory and I almost always use a two-layered system, half-filling the propagator tray or pot with firmed soil-less potting compost and then topping up with a layer of horticultural sand. For leaf cuttings, the layer of sand may need to be shallower than the compost layer. Each cutting is pushed into the sand until its lower end is at the sand-compost junction. Thus, when the new roots form, they immediately have available a good supply of nutrient-rich growing medium.

### Principle types of cuttings

**Softwood cuttings:** These are cuttings taken early in the season, while the tissues are still soft and sappy. The ideal length is about 10cm (4in); they should always be handled carefully as the tissues, being soft, are readily damaged. Pipings are softwood cuttings 5-7cm (2-2¾in) long, taken from pinks and carnations where short lengths of stem tip are pulled away from the remainder, telescope fashion.

**Semi-ripe cuttings:** There's no strict definition of when a cutting is 'semi-ripe' but I think that the answer lies in the degree of springiness. If it bends readily when you twist it between your fingers, and then stays bent or oozes juice, it is still a softwood cutting. If it bends readily, but then springs back, it is semi-ripe. If you can't readily bend it by simple finger pressure, it is already hardwood. Most plants produce semi-ripe cuttings during the second half of summer and the ideal length is about 10cm (4in). There are two main ways of taking semi-ripe cuttings. The first is as normal stem cuttings, formed when a length of shoot is cut from the end of the stem and then cut off cleanly at a length of 10cm (4in). The second is as a basal cutting, where a side-shoot is selected that is already about 10cm (4in) in length and then pulled or torn from its parent stem to leave a small piece of the older stem at the base to form a 'heel'. When taking cuttings for the first time from a new plant, I take about half of each type, although there are some types of shrub that clearly are trying to tell you something, for it is almost impossible to pull away a basal heel; they simply snap off straight.

**Inter-nodal cuttings:** These are exceptions to the rule that cuttings should be taken close to a bud. They are used for a very few types of plant (clematis are the most important) which have their greatest concentration of natural root-promoting hormones between, rather than at, the nodes from which buds arise. The cuttings are, therefore, severed midway between the nodes although they should still be pushed into the compost up to the level of the bud.

**Hardwood cuttings:** These are cuttings taken of wood that has already become fairly tough and woody; ideally during the current year. It's a mistake, however, to imagine that tough old wood from ancient branches can form hardwood cuttings. Timing is less critical and they can be taken at any time between autumn and winter. The shoot should be cut to a length of about 25cm (10in) and inserted to about two thirds of its length in either a cold frame or a V-shaped trench lined with sand in a sheltered spot in the open garden.

**Leaf-bud cuttings:** There is a limited range of shrubs that can successfully be propagated from single buds but they do include some very

**above** Hormone rooting powder is invaluable; but be aware that using too much can be counter-productive and may *suppress* growth.

**left** Softwood cuttings are taken in the early part of the season while the shoots are still soft and green.

important ones: camellias, roses, grapevines, clematis, ivy and mahonias. Early spring and autumn are the best times for leaf-bud cuttings although, of course, cuttings taken in spring make use of last year's buds; summer and autumn cuttings make use of those of the current season. The bud must be mature and healthy and the cuttings should be trimmed to leave approximately 1cm (½in) below each bud and about 25mm (⅛in) above it. The lower part of the stem and the lower half of the bud itself should be buried in the rooting compost. I find that bud cuttings are best with little or no bottom heat. They should be covered but kept ventilated and placed somewhere sheltered.

**above** Semi-ripe cuttings are taken during the summer. They are often, as here, taken with a 'heel': a small portion of the older parent shoot still attached to the base.

**below** Hardwood cuttings are taken in late autumn.

**Root cuttings:** Herbaceous perennials with thick storage roots are especially amenable to being propagated by root cuttings. Much the best way is to dig up the parent plant, wash off the soil and select healthy, white roots from close to the main crown. Cut the roots into pieces about 3cm (1¼in) long but make a straight cut across the top (the plant end) and a sloping cut across the bottom to help distinguish which is which. Push them into pots of compost such that the top of each cutting is flush with or just below the surface. Cover them in the usual way and incubate them, ideally with a little bottom heat. They should root within about six weeks and should be grown on until stems and leaves have formed.

**Bulbs**

Bulbs can be propagated in a number of ways. Division can be used for bulbs or corms that grow in clumps, and spring-flowering bulbs, such as snowdrops, are best divided while still in full growth after flowering. Daffodil bulbs and crocus corms often have small bulblets or cormlets forming around their base. The largest ones are worth detaching and growing on, allowing between one and three years before they reach flowering size.

**Bulbils:** Some lilies form little bulbs called bulbils on their stems, and these can be removed

and sown like seeds. Remove them from the plant about a fortnight after flowering has finished. Plant in a partially shaded spot with the tips just below the soil. You can expect a flowering plant within two to three years.

**Bulb scaling:** This is a useful method of multiplying lilies as you can obtain several plants from just one expensive bulb. Carefully pull away up to six of the fleshy outer scales and place them in a plastic bag containing multipurpose compost. Close the bag and hang it up in a warm place such as an airing cupboard. After three weeks, roots should have formed on the scales. Each rooted scale can be potted up and grown on; such plants should flower within two or three years.

## Using 'ready-made' plants

Sometimes, the process of obtaining new plants can be speeded up compared with the conventional cutting technique, by making use of the 'ready-made' offspring that some plants produce. The most important among these are runners which are especially significant on strawberries, but I must emphasise that strawberries are also among the plants that soon accumulate virus contamination and taking runners from existing old stock will be self-defeating. This is an instance where you will do well to buy fresh stock. The second common type of ready-made plant is the offset. These are familiar as miniature plants growing from the base of many species of *Agave*, *Aloe* and other succulents. When removing offsets from parent plants, I prefer first to sever the connection between parent and offspring and then allow the young plant some weeks of independent existence to build up its own root system *in situ* before it is transplanted.

## Layering

Some shrubs root poorly from cuttings, commonly because evergreen cuttings lose too much water through their leaves before they have had a chance to root. Layering is a successful alternative technique for such plants. Select a low-growing branch and strip off a section of leaves, starting about 20cm (8in) from the tip. Cut a shallow nick on the underside of the stem and pin the branch down into a shallow trench (if your soil is poor, use a hand fork to dig in some soil amendment or fresh topsoil). Cover the branch with soil. Stake the

upright portion of the stem and leave the plant for between six months and two years to develop roots.

## Air layering

This is a technique used on large-leaved evergreens that lack low-hanging branches and an area of bare soil in which to peg them down. Air layering is often used to improve the shape of houseplants such as rubber plants, that have lost a number of their lower leaves. A small cut is made on the main stem and wedged open with a match stick. Moist peat or sphagnum moss is packed around the wound and enclosed in black plastic to retain moisture and keep out the light. The plastic is held in place with sticky tape. The layered stem could take between two months and a year to root, when you should remove the moss and plastic, sever the stem just below the layer and pot up the new plant.

**above** Removing the fleshy scales from lily bulbs and using them as cuttings is a simple and inexpensive way of propagating these costly plants.

**below** Layering is a valuable technique for plants such as many evergreens that are reluctant to strike from cuttings.

# Organic Gardening and Composting

For many traditional gardeners, the recent increase in the popularity of 'organic' gardening appears to have brought with it some rather extreme notions; it would be easy to believe that to garden organically, your garden has to resemble a municipal dump. Let me assure you otherwise. For me, organic gardening is simply gardening the way that nature intended; where natural processes are adapted to garden use and as much natural material as possible is reused or recycled. I believe that I garden organically and yet, in my own garden, there is not a car tyre or roll of old carpet in sight. In truth, all good gardeners have always been organic in their methods, and much of the current misconception and misunderstanding seems to stem simply from too rigid an adherence to definitions. I don't mind what name you give to it, I simply hope that you will garden with common sense.

**above** Manure forked onto the surface of the soil in autumn will be dragged down by earthworms.

**below** Always be very careful when using any garden sprays in the vicinity of a pool.

It seems easy enough to define as organic any material 'derived from plants or animals'. Composts and manures are, by definition, of plant and animal origin and they are vital to a well functioning garden for their role as physical soil amendments. So everyone who makes their own garden compost or digs in manure in the autumn is certainly gardening organically in one sense. That much is straightforward. Where matters become confused is in the consideration of the rather more refined materials that constitute fertilizers and garden pesticides. General advice on their use is given elsewhere in the book but I feel it is appropriate for me to consider here the organic considerations that may be involved in your choice.

People who have a practical or emotive aversion to using synthetic chemicals turn instead to 'natural' products; using fish, blood and bone as a general fertilizer instead of Growmore, for example, and pyrethrum instead of malathion as an insecticide. I offer no dogma on the subject but would simply like to draw your attention to some less obvious facts that you might wish to consider.

When selecting fertilizers, remember that they all break down in the soil into much more basic components. Plants absorb nitrogen, not dried blood or ammonium sulphate; and chemically, there is no distinction between nitrogen from one or other source.

Many animals are raised by intensive-farming techniques and fed synthetic foods and medicines during their lives, so does this render their by-products, such as bone meal or dried blood, unacceptable for use in the garden? And while it must be accepted that the manufacture of synthetic chemicals can be despoiling to the environment and inefficient in terms of energy use, it is only fair to ask if this is more or less acceptable than the despoiling of the environment that occurs in the extraction of such natural products as guano or limestone.

In choosing an insecticide of natural origin such as derris, do be aware that some of the most toxic chemicals known to man are similarly of natural origin, that materials like derris occur naturally in immeasurably lower concentrations than you are applying to your plants (with consequently very different effects), that derris is undiscriminating in its action, killing good and harmful insects with equal efficiency, and it is very poisonous to fish. As I have said, I offer no dogma and where you choose to draw the line on what is and isn't acceptable to you is a matter of individual choice. But make sure that you are in possession of all the facts.

## Compost and compost making

I consider a functioning compost heap to be at the heart of any well-managed garden. The process of composting transforms garden waste into a valuable material that can be returned to the soil again. And on a purely pragmatic level, composting reduces the need to dispose of rubbish in dustbins or by visits to the local tip and is, of course, more 'friendly' both to the environment and to neighbours than a bonfire.

But rather than simply returning fresh organic matter straight back to the soil, it is better to allow it to undergo the first stages of decomposition in the controlled conditions of a compost bin. By isolating the material at this stage, when the decomposition bacteria require a boost of nitrogen in order to function, the soil is protected from the risk of nitrogen there being temporarily depleted.

There are a number of designs of compost bin, but I prefer the traditional wooden type with slatted sides to allow adequate aeration, which is the key to successful compost making. Don't be tempted to buy the smallest bin available; within limits, the larger the mass of material, the more it will retain the heat required for decomposition. I recommend a wooden, slatted compost bin of about 1.2m (4ft). If space permits, choose a double bin; as one container is being filled, the other is maturing for use.

Most organic waste from the garden and much from the house can be added but among the few substances that are best avoided are

those materials that will not break down, such as plastic, metals or minerals, and glossy, plasticised paper. It is said that animal remains such as chicken carcasses might attract vermin, but I bury them in the centre of the heap, among lawn mowings for instance, and have experienced no problems. Large quantities of leaves break down more slowly than most organic matter and are best stacked separately in a wire-netting leaf mould cage, also of about 1.2m (4ft) to make mulching material. Newspaper and woody materials, such as prunings, should be shredded first to aid decomposition, while lawn mowings are best mixed with coarser material; and compost made from them shouldn't be used within two months of applying lawn weedkiller.

A proprietary compost 'accelerator' or fresh manure will provide the initial supply of nitrogen that the bacteria require, and should be applied after every 15-20cm (6-8in) layer of organic matter has been added. The material should be kept moist but not waterlogged and natural rainfall should provide enough moisture, but it may need to be supplemented during dry spells. During periods of heavy rain, a plastic sheeting top will prevent water-

**above** Slatted wooden compost bins allow good aeration and help decomposition. And several bins are always better than one.

**above** My compost shredder is invaluable in ensuring that almost all organic waste is composted. But I am always careful to use gloves and eye protection.

| Organic material | Practical considerations and approximate N:P:K nutrient values |
|---|---|
| **Manures** | |
| Fresh farmyard | May be added to the soil in autumn: otherwise should be stacked or composted before use. 1.2:0.4:0.5 |
| Rotted farmyard | May be applied safely to the soil in spring. 0.4:0.2:0.6 |
| Stable | Lower moisture content than farmyard; easier and generally more pleasant to handle. 0.7:0.5:0.6 |
| Pig | Strong smell, unpleasant and antisocial. 0.6:0.6:0.4 |
| Sheep | Similar to stable manure but rarely available in large quantities. 0.8:0.5:0.4 |
| Rabbit | Fairly high in phosphate but rarely available in large quantities. 0.5:1.2:0.5 |
| Chicken | High in nutrients but can cause imbalance between nitrogen and potash; compost before using to avoid ammonia smell. 2.0:1.8:1.0 |
| **Other materials** | |
| Bark | Various grades available, stack before use to reduce toxins, although bagged products should be ready to use; almost no nutrients. |
| Cocoa shells | Attractive, easy to handle and sweet smelling mulch for small beds; not as long-lasting as bark chips. 3:1:3 |
| Garden compost | Weeds can be a problem if bin is not sufficiently hot. 0.7:0.4:0.4 |
| Leaf mould | Rots slowly, different types of leaf break down at different rates and large leaves are best shredded first. 0.4:0.2:0.3 |
| Spent mushroom compost | Principally peat with added lime; may contain insecticide residues and will raise soil alkalinity. 0.6:0.5:0.9 |
| Sawdust | Rots very slowly and may be toxic to some plants; valuable for mulching blueberries. 0.2:0.1:0.1 |
| Seaweed | Best composted before use, can attract flies; do not harvest from beaches without permission. 0.6:0.3:1.0 |
| Soot | Compost before use and mix with other materials to dilute possible toxins. 3.6:0.1:0.1 |
| Spent hops | Compost before use. 1.1:0.3:0.9 |
| Straw | Compost before use if using as a soil amendment; can be used to protect plants over winter or to protect strawberry fruit from contact with soil. 0.5:0.2:0.9 |

logging. I have never found it necessary to add soil or lime to a compost bin but the contents of the bin should ideally be turned at least once. In practice, it's easiest to turn the material about three weeks after it has been added. Compost should be ready to use after about six months, but the speed of decomposition is temperature-dependent so it varies both with the time of year and type of material.

## Other soil amendments

Even the keenest re-user of waste material will find it difficult to make enough garden compost for all of their mulching and soil-improving needs, so most of us require some additional materials. In making your choice, however, whether from a local source, branded products from a garden centre or by mail order, choose wisely. Don't be swayed by claims of 'essential plant foods' and 'enriching the earth'. What you require is an economical, bulky product that will open up the soil and provide a source of humus (and ideally, a small amount of nutrient). Be wary of products that recommend very low application rates; all proven, practical soil amendments for garden use work properly only if added in fairly large quantities.

I have summarised the salient features of the commonest organic materials in the Table (opposite) to assist you in making your choice. The significance of the nutrient content should be read in conjunction with my comments on fertilizer usage in the next section of the book.

## Mulches and mulching

Mulching offers a method of weed control that doesn't rely on chemicals, a way of retaining moisture within the soil, a protection for plants against penetrating frost, and, if organic mulches are used, a convenient method of applying bulky organic matter with minimal labour. A mulch is simply a layer of material placed over the surface of the soil. The material can either be loose, garden compost, leaf mould or manure, for example, or, like paper or plastic, laid in sheets. A loose mulch should be applied in a layer at least 5cm (2in) thick and will need replacing twice a year as it breaks down. The ideal times to apply mulches are in early spring, when the soil should still be wet with winter rains yet has started to warm up, and in autumn when rain will again will have

soaked the soil yet winter cold will not have begun to penetrate.

The so-called no-dig system is becoming popular amongst some vegetable growers and, in one of its manifestations, depends heavily on organic mulching. The essence of the operation is to walk as little as possible over the soil surface, minimising compaction and removing the necessity for regular digging. Organic matter is applied either by mulching and allowing earthworms to incorporate it in the soil or by occasional double digging (page 56). I don't believe that plastic-sheet mulching, an unsightly, environmentally unfriendly activity, is justified other than for the control of persistent deep-seated weeds. For every other use of a plastic mulch, an organic blanket will serve equally.

**above** Leaf mould is best stacked in a simple cage as leaves decompose slowly.

**below** Organic mulch is invaluable in helping to retain soil moisture.

# Fertilizers and Feeding

A fertilizer adds one or more essential plant nutrients to the soil. Unlike soil amendments, which add bulk to improve the physical structure of soil, they are both more concentrated and simpler chemically. Manufacturers often confuse gardeners by using general terms such as 'feeding the soil' and 'enrichment' for both products but their roles are quite separate. Whereas soil amendments are added in generous amounts before, at or after planting and precise quantities are not too critical, fertilizers should be added more carefully. Apply too little fertilizer and the objective will not be achieved; apply too much and this can adversely affect plant growth or even have an environmental impact, for example, by permitting excess nitrogen to leach into water courses. For optimum results, fertilizer should always be added at the rates and at the times recommended on the packaging.

**above** Wild flowers look attractive for a limited period; for long displays in the garden, additional feeding is essential.

**below** Fertilisers can encourage foliage or flowers, so choose an appropriate blend.

## Why plants need feeding

Although plants manufacture organic nutrients within their green tissues by photosynthesis, they obtain virtually all their mineral nutrient requirements from the soil. In a natural habitat, where native plants grow at natural spacings and aren't interfered with or removed from the site when they mature or die, a nutritional balance is maintained. Sufficient nutrient is returned to the soil through the decomposition of dead plants to satisfy the needs of those still growing. This is far from the case in gardens, especially in vegetable gardens and annual beds, where we grow largely non-native plants, grow them in unnatural ways (confined in containers for example), grow them much closer together than actually happens in nature, remove them at the end of the season and replant the same site very soon afterwards. Without the use of supplementary feeding, the plants would fall far short of our needs and expectations.

## Plant nutrients

There are three major elements needed by plants: nitrogen, phosphorus (generally referred to as phosphate) and potassium (generally referred to as potash). Of these, nitrogen is most likely to be in short supply at any time as it is easily washed out of soils by rain, especially during the winter. In addition, there are minor elements – calcium, magnesium and sulphur – which are also important but needed in smaller quantities. Finally, there are elements needed in extremely small amounts, referred to as trace elements. These are iron, manganese, boron, copper, molybdenum, zinc, sodium and chlorine. Most British soils contain adequate supplies of minor and trace elements, even for the added demands of garden plants, so the majority of garden fertilizers are blended to supply the three major nutrients, particularly nitrogen.

## Main types of garden fertilizer

Although it's possible to supply one or two elements at a time by the use of so-called straight fertilizers like potassium sulphate, most gardeners find it easier to use compound mixtures.

## Major elements and their role in plant growth

| Element | Role |
|---------|------|
| Nitrogen | A major constituent of protein and essential for many aspects of plant growth. Especially important for leafy, as opposed to flower and fruit growth. |
| Phosphorus | A constituent of many proteins, fats and carbohydrates. Especially important in the ripening of fruits, the maturation and germination of seeds and root growth. |
| Potassium | Essential for good flower and fruit formation. Probably involved with aspects of photosynthesis and with the control of water loss from plants. |

These are balanced blends of different chemicals, formulated principally on the basis of plant's nitrogen requirements, with the amounts of phosphorus and potassium balanced accordingly. Fertilizer packaging is required by law to state the proportions by weight of the three major plant nutrients in a formula usually expressed as N:P:K. It's important to remember, however, that these are relative proportions, not the absolute amounts. A fertilizer with an N:P:K content of 3:3:5, for instance, is relatively just as potassium rich as one of 6:6:10.

## Recommended essential garden fertilizers
### 1. A balanced general purpose solid fertilizer
This type of fertilizer is particularly valuable for use among vegetables and other plants at or just before the start of the growing season. The commonest artificial blend available in the UK is the granular mixture called Growmore which contains N:P:K at 7:7:7.

The principal organically based compound fertilizer is fish, blood and bone, a blend of dried blood, finely ground bone meal and sulphate of potash (not, of course, organic). Like

all organically based fertilizers, its composition is variable but is approximately 5.1:5.:6.5. The nitrogen from the dried blood tends to be more slowly available than that from the ammonium sulphate in artificial mixtures and the phosphorus is released more slowly from the bone meal.

### 2. A general purpose liquid fertilizer, relatively high in potassium
A fertilizer of this type should be the mainstay of most gardeners' fertilizer usage during the height of the season. There are several branded liquid products of this nature, varying in their relative nutrient contents and most containing additional minor and trace elements, since they tend to be used extensively for plants growing in soil-less composts. The concentrated liquid tomato fertilizers, for instance, generally with a composition of around 5:5:9 derived from inorganic components, are of this type. Most of the soluble fertilizers purchased in the form of powders or crystals also fall into this category, having nutrient ratios of about 15:5:20.

### 3. Bone meal (organic) or superphosphate (artificial)
These slow-release sources of phosphorus should be used routinely in the planting of trees, shrubs, perennials and bulbs.

**left** It's essential to give fertiliser sequentially to fast growing plants like vegetables.

**below** Long-term plants such as roses benefit from being fertilized twice a year; once at the start of the season and again after flowering.

**above** My hose-end dilutor has become an indispensable aid for applying liquid fertiliser.

**below** Abnormal leaf colouration will soon indicate if plants are short of particular nutrients.

### 4. Two lawn fertilizers
Lawns should normally be fed twice a year, in spring and in autumn, but the nutrient requirements are different at these times. I discuss lawn feeding and lawn management elsewhere (page 164) but you should have two powder-formulated lawn fertilizers; one with a relatively high nitrogen content for spring and summer use and one relatively lower in nitrogen for autumn and winter application. The latter is also the fertilizer I recommend for use before seeding or turfing.

### 5. Rose fertilizer
Fertilizers formulated for roses contain a blend of the major nutrients but with special emphasis on potassium to encourage flowering. Most branded products also contain additional magnesium because roses are especially prone to deficiency of this element. I apply rose fertil-izer following the spring pruning and again after the first flush of early-summer flowers. Although formulated specifically for roses, these fertilizers also provide an ideal balanced feed for other flowering shrubs and I feed them all at the same time.

### 6. Sequestered iron
Although most soils have enough trace elements for plant growth, and fertilizers often contain them as impurities, one minor nutrient that some plants can't easily absorb from an alkaline soil is iron. Additional iron should be supplied in a form known as sequestered iron, which can be taken up readily.

## When and how to feed plants
Rapidity of action is important in choosing a fertilizer. Slow-release products will break down in the soil over a long period to release nutrients, so products such as coarse-grade bone meal are often recommended when planting permanent plants such as trees, shrubs or perennials. For a quicker-acting feed at the start of a growing season, fish, blood and bone or Growmore are useful.

For the quickest results during the height of the summer when fast-growing crops are putting on new foliage, flowers and fruit, you need a liquid fertilizer. At these times it can be usefully applied as a foliar spray using a hose-end dilutor. The leaves absorb the nutrients directly rather than via the normal pathway of the roots and this can be conveniently quicker in the summer months.

## Nutrient deficiencies and their recognition
Although genuine deficiencies are rarely serious in British gardens, alkaline soils can make many nutrients unavailable to plants and where heavy cropping takes place, such as in a fruit or vegetable garden, deficiency effects can be seen. Plants growing in soil-less composts can also be at risk from nutrient deficiencies unless supplementary feeding takes place after about six weeks.

## Fertilizer application
Whether fertilizers are applied as liquids, granules or powders, it is very important that they are spread as uniformly as possible in the area where they are needed. Powders and gran-

| Element | Indicator plant | Symptoms | Treatment |
|---|---|---|---|
| Nitrogen | Brassicas. Also common on other leafy vegetables | Plants and leaves small, with purple, red or yellow foliage tints | Apply N fertilizer at the start of each growing season and top up while growth continues |
| Phosphorus | Currants | Dull bronzing of the leaves with brownish spots. All growth weak, flowering and fruiting delayed | For specific P deficiency, apply superphosphate or bonemeal close to plant roots |
| Potassium | Tomatoes. Other flowering and fruiting plants | Undersized fruit, often uneven ripening, some scorching of leaf margins. Often weak general growth | For specific K deficiency, apply potassium sulphate in advance of sowing or planting |
| Calcium | Tomatoes. Many other fruit and vegetables | Dark lesions at the blossom end of tomatoes (known as 'blossom-end rot'). Leaf tips and growing points blackened ('tip burn' of lettuce) | Apply lime or spray with calcium chloride |
| Magnesium | Lettuces. Also roses, tomatoes | Yellowish marbling on the leaves and bedding plants | Use magnesian limestone or a rose fertilizer |
| Iron | Raspberries. Also azaleas, camellias, hydrangeas, roses | Pale or yellow leaves with darker veins | Sequestered iron |
| Manganese | Peas. Also other fruit and vegetables | Dark lesions in the pea cotyledons when the seeds are pulled apart (called 'marsh spot'). Inter-veinal yellowing, often with dead patches | Avoid over-liming. Spray affected plants with manganese sulphate (1.5g/litre) |
| Boron | Sweetcorn. Also apples, lettuces | Pale stripes on leaves and cobs fail to form properly. Corky patches in apples | Rake in borax at planting time at 3g/square metre |
| Molybdenum | Cauliflowers | Leaf blade is markedly narrowed (called 'whip-tail') | Use lime to raise pH on acid sites |

ules applied to individual plants or to rows of vegetables are almost always spread by hand and, with practice, it is fairly easy to obtain even coverage. Nonetheless, dosage should be judged carefully and handfuls of fertilizer not just thrown around indiscriminately. Modern fertilizer packet labels generally bear dosing instructions in g/square metre (and sometimes in oz/square yard too). With a set of scales, therefore, determine the weight of one of your own handfuls of each fertilizer you use and then write this either on the packet or on a card pinned up in your garden shed. And always remember to wear gloves and wash your hands after handling any fertilizer.

For lawn fertilizers, use a small wheeled spreader for uniform dosing. It's wise to buy a spreader that can be calibrated variously so that it may be used with products from different manufacturers that may need slightly differing dose rates.

On a small scale, liquid fertilizers can be applied by sprayer or, especially on a lawn, by watering can, but for large areas of garden, use a hose-end dilutor, which is a container that can be fitted to the delivery end of a hose-pipe. The container is filled with a concentrated fertilizer solution and the flow of water through the hose draws out concentrate to deliver diluted liquid feed.

# Water and Watering

Water is essential for plant growth, because not only is it the main constituent of the protoplasm of plant cells, but because there must be sufficient moisture in the soil for plants to maintain a through-flow of water and the nutrients dissolved in it. While much research has been performed on the amount of water required to produce commercial crops, until recently little thought was paid to the needs of the amateur gardener. Now gardeners find their watering habits coming under close scrutiny as water charging through metering becomes more widespread and water shortages are experienced in many parts of the world. As a result, the benefits of research for commercial growers are becoming more widely available to gardeners.

**above** Plants for use in hot, dry spots must be chosen carefully for their ability to tolerate lack of moisture.

**below** A weedy bed loses valuable moisture through the weed foliage.

Watering can be a chore, so even if water is in plentiful supply, it is still worth assessing how you water your plants to see if the task can be done more efficiently and if new watering equipment could make your life easier. You should aim for the majority of your established garden plants to obtain most of their moisture from the soil with only some supplementary watering during dry spells in the growing season. But to achieve this, you need to determine which plants will benefit most from extra water, when to apply it and how much to give.

If you live in a low-rainfall area or you have a soil that is light and free draining, drought problems are likely to be frequent. In the medium to long-term, you should set about systematically improving the soil's moisture retentiveness by adding organic matter regularly (see page 83). In the shorter term, applying the organic matter as a mulch (provided this is done when the soil is already moist) will help. But even more immediate benefit can be achieved by growing plants better able to tolerate dry conditions. Species from the Mediterranean (such as many herbs) or South Africa (many summer annuals and tender perennials, like pelargoniums) make good choices. And any plants with grey or silvery foliage are drought tolerant, the colour being due to numerous tiny hairs that restrict water loss from the leaf surface.

Keeping down weed growth can ensure that more water in the soil is available for your plants, and only grow as many vegetables as you really need because much water is wasted by loss through their foliage.

## How much water and when

Although all plants need water, it's only at certain stages of growth that their water demand is

**left** Always water carefully; using a rose on a watering can helps ensure that valuable soil isn't washed away from the base of plants.

critical. As a general guideline, I suggest that you concentrate first on annuals, such as bedding plants and vegetables and then on fairly shallow-rooted perennials like rhododendrons and soft fruit. Apply water when the object of their cultivation is beginning to mature: lettuces as they begin to heart up, potatoes at flowering time (when their tubers start to swell) and flowers as buds burst, for example. During these periods, you should aim to supply about 25 litres of water per square metre (5gal./yd²). Or, alternatively, apply 15 litres per square metre (3½gal./yd²) once a month or 10 litres per square metre (2¼gal./yd²) once a fortnight. New plants will need watering until their root systems are established and they can obtain moisture from further down in the soil. Plants in containers will always need regular watering, the smaller and more exposed the container, the more it will lose water and hanging baskets may need watering twice a day in summer. Many gardeners spend much time, effort and expense in watering their lawns but despite turning brown in periods of drought, grass has remarkable powers of recovery so, with the exception of newly-laid or sown lawns,

lawn watering in most years is in fact wasteful.

Where it is practicable, try to water plants in the evening as this gives the moisture a chance to soak into the soil surrounding the roots before the sun's heat evaporates it. When pouring water from a watering can or hose, allow water to soak into the soil before adding more. Simply flooding water around the base of a plant will cause water to run off away from the plant and can wash away soil and expose surface roots.

## Garden watering systems

While watering cans still look familiar, other garden watering equipment has changed beyond recognition in recent years. But before investing in expensive watering equipment, check with your local water company for any regulations or restrictions relating to their use. Unattended watering equipment, in particular, is regulated in some areas and, to use it, you may need a permit or licence or be required to have your domestic water supply metered. And in times of water shortage there may be additional restrictions on the use of hose pipes and sprinklers. The mains water pressure in your

Of the many attachments available at the delivery end, I find you really need one good, adjustable sprayer that offers a gentle spray as well as a strong jet, and a comparable, adjustable pattern sprinkler. Choose a sprinkler that will be appropriate to the size and shape of your garden; nothing is more wasteful or annoying than watering neighbours' gardens as well as your own. In a large garden, it makes sense to fit a hose-end connector that automatically shuts off the water supply when you change hose-end appliances, so avoiding a long walk back to the tap. Where watering restrictions are in place, use a watering can to supply water to the plants that need most, and direct the water close to the plant root zone.

### Greenhouse watering systems

Watering in the greenhouse has its own particular problems, the extra warmth combined with plants in small pots mean that watering must be done frequently, and a watering can may be hard to manoeuvre in confined space. The following types of irrigation system, ideally controlled from the mains by a 'watering computer', are worth considering if you are regularly away from home:

**above** Use an adjustable sprinkler to ensure that water is only delivered where it is most needed.

**below** Modern drip irrigation systems are invaluable in a greenhouse; especially one that must be left unattended for long periods.

area can affect the functioning of certain types of sprinkler and in high-pressure areas, less well made types of tap and hose connector can leak or burst. In Britain, the mains pressure varies from 30 lb/square in (211 kg/square cm) to about 130 lb/square in (914 kg/square cm). All watering systems are immeasurably easier to use if you have an outside tap with a screw thread but, by law, they must be fitted with a back-flow prevention valve to avoid contamination of the water supply.

When purchasing a hose, opt for a double-wall, knitted type on a through-flow hose reel with snap-fit connectors. Consider an automatic metering device (attached to your tap) which will turn off the flow after a predetermined length of time or, more usefully, after a predetermined volume of water has been delivered. More sophisticated 'watering computers' are also available which enable you to programme your watering to turn on and

**Trickle (or drip) irrigation:** Water, from the mains or from a reservoir, is carried along a series of narrow plastic tubes, each ending in a nozzle through which water drips. Each drip-nozzle supplies one plant pot. These systems can be tricky to assemble and need time and patience to set up but, once established, are useful for not only greenhouses but for containers on patios or for hanging baskets. They also are very precise, with water being directly delivered to each pot.

**Overhead (or mist) irrigation:** These have similar water supply systems to trickle irrigation, but water is sprayed downwards from nozzles attached to the greenhouse roof. They are useful for propagation and are often installed over a sand propagating bench but great care is needed in greenhouses with mains electricity.

**Capillary Watering:** This depends on the ability of the compost in a pot to act as a wick, drawing up moisture from wet matting through

the pot's drainage holes. The plant pots are set out on capillary matting contained in shallow metal trays, the matting being kept moist by contact with a water reservoir. I have found polyester matting 2-3mm (⅛in) thick gives the best results for 9cm (3½in) diameter pots of soil-less compost but pot size and compost type will affect the results. This is a simpler system than trickle or mist irrigation but it has its limitations. Using pots of different sizes or with different plants or composts can result in uneven watering and there must be good contact between the base of the pot and the matting. Algal growth on matting can be unsightly so an algicide may have to be used twice a year. Because there is restricted drainage, fertilizers (which still need to be applied by watering from above) can build up in the pots to damaging levels. As a precaution, an occasional thorough watering from above to flush out any build up of salts is advisable.

## Water conservation

Rainwater can and should be stored whenever possible. One or more water butts can be positioned to collect water from buildings. Use this collected water for outdoor plants in beds and borders, but not for greenhouse plants as the algal and fungal spores and 'wildlife' that it con-

tains may result in damage to young seedlings. During periods of water restriction, domestic waste water from washing up bowls and baths should be used in the garden although water containing bleach, chemical disinfectants or grease is best not used.

Increasingly, gardeners are turning again to the underground storage tanks, popular in Victorian gardens, and a number of systems are now available, including the use of permeable paving blocks to collect water falling onto driveways. Inevitably, these are costly to install but worth considering for their long-term value.

## Types of water

Tap water can be used for all plants as the chlorine in it does not affect plant life. Soft water has very few mineral impurities whereas hard water contains large quantities of calcium or magnesium salts. In an outdoor border or bed, hard water is unlikely to be problem for lime-hating plants but such salts can build up when plants are grown in containers. The result can be yellowing of the foliage and poor growth so to avoid this, use rainwater for lime-hating species. Chemically softened water has caused harm to some types of plant so should be tested on a few samples first.

**left** Rainwater is a very valuable resource; but can contain spores and pests so I don't use water from a rain butt in the greenhouse.

# Greenhouses and Cold-frames

A greenhouse allows you to grow plants in conditions of enhanced solar radiation, so extending both the seasons and the range of types that can be grown. But with careful planning, your greenhouse can offer you numerous options: a facility for raising hardy and half-hardy plants to transplant outdoors, space for overwintering tender plants either in a dormant or an actively growing state, an unrivalled opportunity to produce both summer and winter salad crops, protection for a grapevine, peach or other marginally hardy fruit plant, scope for raising and maintaining house plants or even, if you wish, an area that can be converted into conditions suitable for tender orchids and other tropical species.

**below** A dome shaped greenhouse is very efficient at light capture but inefficient in its use of space.

Initially, you have three main considerations: the style, size and siting of your greenhouse.

### Greenhouse styles

When choosing a greenhouse, there are two main factors to consider besides appearance: the influence the shape has on the usable internal space and the effect that the angle of the translucent surfaces has on light transmission. While time of day and season of the year are obvious variables, a sheet of glass at right-angles to the sun's rays will always allow through approximately 90 per cent of the light striking it whereas, at an angle of incidence of more than 40 degrees, the percentage transmission falls off rapidly. So the most efficient greenhouse shape is in fact a dome; but this is scarcely practicable other than on a small novelty scale. Next best is a square house with four roofs of equal size, or house with a semi-circular roof and vertical ends. Although ideally such a house should be as high as it is wide, the design is made more practical by flattening the profile and by using plastic instead of glass; the principle behind the 'polythene tunnel'. The next preference is a structure with a straight roof and sides 60-70 degrees from the horizon-

**above** The 'span' house, with or without glass to ground level is the most popular and practical type.

tal, while the least effective is the commonest shape: a straight roof and vertical sides. A lean-to greenhouse is usually half the latter pattern built against a vertical house wall, often painted white. There is merit here in that heat from the adjoining building will help retain warmth in winter but there will be a lack of light from one side. Nonetheless, a lean-to can be an attractive option for a small garden.

Most modern greenhouse frames are aluminium although wooden ones (either deal or the much more durable softwood, western red cedar) are still available. Maintenance is certainly greater with a wooden frame; deal should be painted or treated with preservative annually and even red cedar should be treated every two or three years. While aluminium will, therefore, be the more popular option, I must point out the advantages that a wooden greenhouse confers. Heat loss is less through a wooden frame, the fixing of insulation and

other attachments within is usually easier, the structure is generally more resilient when subjected to gales and, in many gardens, especially of old houses, a wooden building blends in in a way that an aluminium one never can. But whatever the material, every greenhouse should be firmly anchored to the ground and preferably erected on 20cm (8in) deep concrete foundations. Easily the best floor for a greenhouse is gravel over firmed soil; this permits water to drain away freely and an annual treatment with a garden disinfectant will eliminate any pests, disease organisms or weeds.

Although most conventional greenhouses are made with glass held in frames, much cheaper structures are available using one or other forms of clear plastic. While providing useful additional space for protecting plants, they have several drawbacks and cannot really be considered a substitute for a glazed greenhouse. All plastic sheet has a limited life and

**above** Try to choose a greenhouse style appropriate to your house and garden.

**below** Purpose-made bubble film insulation is essential to retain warmth and cut down on your heating costs.

will need replacing after two or three years as it becomes torn by the wind, attracts dirt by static electricity and is rendered more or less brittle by the ultra-violet radiation in sunlight. Moreover, while plastic more readily transmits light and heat than glass, this is a two-edged attribute, for as a plastic structure will warm up more quickly so it will cool down more quickly too. The surfaces need to be kept clean, even a moderate amount of dirt can impair the transmission of light by up to 40 per cent. Plastics can be harder to clean than glass, they often leave gaps where they join the frame, and are prone to tears or damage. Plastics can be degraded by ultra-violet light though for garden use they should have been treated. Glass still has a lot to offer but the safety aspects should be considered carefully. This applies not only to young children but older people as well.

## Greenhouse size

Larger greenhouses cost more to buy and to heat; a 3 x 2.5m (10 x 8ft) structure will be about 25 per cent more costly to heat than a house of 1.8 x 2.5 m (6 x 8 ft). For a garden up to about one-third of an acre, I suggest you choose a 3.6 x 2.5m (12 x 8ft) greenhouse with a rigid internal frame partition and a door, dividing it into two 1.8 x 2.4m (6 x 8ft) units. One, with removable staging, can be used for summer tomatoes, overwintering fuchsias, pelargoniums and other tender perennials or growing winter lettuce. The other unit has permanent staging with a propagating sand bench. It is also heated to overwinter tender subjects and for early and late-season plant raising.

## Greenhouse siting

Few gardens have a spot that satisfies all the desirable criteria for siting a greenhouse. It should be close to electricity and water supplies, in a level, open yet sheltered position, away from deciduous trees if possible. Ideally, an oblong greenhouse should be positioned with its long axis east-west for the most uniform illumination.

## Greenhouse staging

Most staging is either wood or aluminium and is usually purchased from the greenhouse manufacturer. A mixture of fixed and removable staging allows you to adapt the greenhouse to the needs of different plants through the growing season. The working height of the staging is usually dictated by the manufacturer and by the height and form of the greenhouse sides, but I've found it worth installing a short length of staging at a height of 75cm (30in) for potting and pricking-out from a sitting or standing position.

## Greenhouse heating

Although all greenhouses are warmed by the sun, they are usually called 'unheated' unless additional heating has been supplied artificially. Extra heating will enable you to grow a wider range of plants and possibly to grow crops out of season, but heating costs must be taken into account.

There are four main ways of heating a greenhouse: electricity, paraffin, solid fuel and gas. There are advantages and disadvantages for each heat source but I believe the benefits of electricity with its versatility, reliability and lack of maintenance make it easily the first choice. A thermostatically-controlled, electric

**left** Modern, thermostatically controlled electric fan heaters are my preferred option for greenhouse heating.

fan heater is a cheap, simple heat source with the bonus of encouraging air circulation, which can help minimise diseases. The fans can also be used in summer to help cooling. Check the temperature inside the greenhouse with a maximum and minimum thermometer. Every 2.8°C (5°F) rise in temperature roughly doubles the amount of heat required (and hence the cost), so choose very carefully the minimum temperature necessary for your plants. For example, a night-time minimum of 2°C (36°F) will keep overwintered plants, like pelargoniums, fuchsias and dahlia tubers alive, but nothing will grow. A night-time minimum of 7°C (45°F) will allow you to grow winter lettuce as well as cuttings and young plants. A minimum temperature of 15°C (59°F) and additional lighting will be needed to grow winter salad crops like tomatoes and cucumber.

On balance, I recommend a winter minimum of 7°C (45°F); then, from late winter onwards the warming effect of the sun during the day should raise the temperature, so sowing and pricking-out can commence. And of course, the greenhouse makes a welcome winter retreat for a gardener too.

## Temperature management in greenhouses

Insulating the greenhouse will help cut fuel costs. Double skin, bubble polythene film is

**below** Bottled gas heaters are efficient but don't offer the useful air movement that an electric fan provides.

are sold with insufficient vents but it is worth choosing a greenhouse with additional ones at the time of purchase; they are much more tricky to add later. There are three functions of ventilation: to restrict the rises in air temperature as a result of the sun's heat, to restrict the rise in humidity, and to admit air that can supply carbon dioxide needed for photosynthesis. You should aim to have vents both in the roof and in the sides and they should be equal to at least 15 per cent of the floor area to work effectively. Automatic venting systems, which require no electricity are extremely valuable, particularly if, like most gardeners, you are out for much of the day.

## Management

Between the removal of summer crops and preparation of the greenhouse for winter, the whole interior should be cleared of plants and scrubbed inside with a garden disinfectant. Finish by washing surfaces down with clean tap water and fumigate with a fungicide and insecticide 'smoke'.

## Greenhouse watering

Watering in a greenhouse is a perpetual problem and much time will be saved in the summer months by planning, at the outset, how your plants can be watered most efficiently. I have discussed the use of automatic watering systems elsewhere (page 90) but the biggest consumers of water in most gardeners' greenhouses in summer are tomatoes.

Ring Culture: I have described the various ways of growing tomatoes elsewhere (page 156), but it's appropriate to discuss here the ring culture technique as this can be set up when the greenhouse is constructed. A trench, 30-35cm (12-14in) deep and 35-40cm (14-16in) wide, should be dug along one side of the greenhouse. The trench should then be lined with heavy-gauge plastic sheet and filled with pea gravel. Bottomless pots containing tomato plants in soil-based compost stand on this gravel. Liquid feed is applied to the compost in the pot but the plants' water needs come from a second root system that develops in the gravel bed. The gravel reservoir need only be filled once a week, compared with the need for more frequent, if not daily, watering of growing bags or conventional pots.

**above** Automatic vent openers operate by the simple expansion of a column of wax.

**below** Greenhouse lighting isn't essential; but if you do use it, be sure that its output really is adequate to make a significant improvement.

popular, but do choose one specifically for greenhouse use, as apparently similar materials sold for packaging may not be ultra-violet stable. It is possible to cut down heat loss by 40 per cent using insulation; there will be some loss of light transmission but this makes little difference to crop yields in practice. Insulating film is usually removed in spring, but I find it more convenient to leave it in place and so dispense with the need for summer shading.

In summer, greenhouses become very hot and ventilation is essential. Many greenhouses

## Greenhouse lighting

Most gardeners manage without using supplementary greenhouse lighting, but it has its uses if your greenhouse is heated to high levels to grow plants over the winter or you wish to obtain good seedling growth in late winter or early spring. There are a number of important considerations in choosing a lighting system but essentially you require one that offers the maximum amount of light output within the wavelengths required for photosynthesis while having low installation and running costs. Much the most efficient are low-pressure sodium lamps but they are among the most expensive to install and most gardeners opt for the relatively inefficient but cheap low-pressure mercury discharge fluorescent tubes. Whichever system you select, however, do check carefully that its output really will be cost-effective.

## Propagating benches

Not to use a greenhouse for plant propagation is a fearful waste of resources and I consider a sand propagation bench to be essential. It is an important consideration when you are planning a greenhouse and deciding on the type of staging; I have discussed it in detail on page 71.

## Cold-frames

Anyone who has a greenhouse for raising young plants for use outdoors will need a cold-frame as a halfway-house for hardening them off. A cold-frame is also required for raising hardy seedlings and cuttings, it can be used for winter salads and during the summer it can be used for growing cucumbers, melons or other tender crops. A well-made, insulated and correctly-sited cold-frame should elevate the temperature by at least 7°C (12°F) above the outside ambient.

Cold-frames are available in the same materials as greenhouses, but being smaller structures, the better heat-retaining properties of glass and wood are even more important. Where young children use the garden, however, a covering of plastic will be safer. The commonest size of frame is about 60cm x 1.2m (2ft x 4ft), which should hold about eight standard-sized seed trays full of young plants, but is too small for crop raising. A height of at least 30cm (12in) at the front and 45cm (18 in) at the back is essential for hardening-off taller bedding plants. The lid should be easily removable and able to provide ventilation, although the whole structure should be draught-proof when required. Damage from winds is a serious problem so it should be sited in a sheltered position and anchored firmly.

There is much to be gained from making your own from a wooden window frame, or buying a large commercial wooden Dutch-light pattern frame (with glazed covers but solid sides). Site the frame near the greenhouse, in a sunny sheltered aspect if possible. Fit bubble insulation to the frame in winter. In summer, shading material may be needed if you use it for rooting cuttings.

**below** Cold-frames are most usefully sited close to the greenhouse for the easy transfer of young plants for hardening off.

# Pests and Diseases

Like people and animals, plants are affected by pests and diseases. Garden plants aren't peculiar in this respect; wild plants too are attacked although the impact on them is seldom noticed. Wild plants have had hundreds if not thousands of years to adapt to their environment. Natural selection among populations has meant that neither extremely vulnerable nor extremely resistant plants remain. Very vulnerable ones would be wiped out in a short time; extremely resistant ones would result in the pest or disease itself being eliminated.

**above** Powdery mildew is probably the commonest type of fungal disease in gardens.

**below** Sap-sucking aphids achieve their debilitating effects through force of numbers.

Garden plants have had inadequate time to adapt to their surroundings; most are exotic species and most are artificially raised or selected varieties. A plant from South Africa or China may have little or no resistance to the diseases or pests that it will encounter in a European garden. The processes of plant breeding and selection themselves can play a part, for in selecting for some horticulturally desirable feature such as large flowers or early maturity, plant breeders may inadvertently have bred out what natural resistance to diseases and pests the plant did originally possess.

If we compare plant diseases with human diseases, one big difference becomes apparent. In humans, bacteria and viruses are the most important causes. Sore throats, septicemia, measles, chicken pox – all have a viral or bacterial origin. Diseases in humans caused by fungi are less common; ringworm, athletes foot and thrush are among the few likely to be encountered. With plants, the situation is reversed. Fungi, usually microscopic moulds, account for the bulk of common garden diseases, like mildew, rust, canker, blight, Dutch elm disease. Bacterial diseases are rarely as important – fireblight is the disease which most gardeners will have heard of. Viruses and other sub-microscopic organisms are important but generally less obvious for, although some do produce distinctive symptoms such as mosaic patterns on leaves, their effect is generally more insidious, bringing about an overall decline in vigour or crop yield.

All pests are animals; most major groups within the animal kingdom include a few species that can cause problems in gardens. At one extreme are mammals and birds; sparrows, bullfinches, rabbits and deer can, in their way, be extremely troublesome. At the other end of the size spectrum are eelworms, microscopic soil-inhabiting creatures barely 2mm (⅛in) in length. In between come creatures such as mites, myriapods, molluscs and crustaceans. Outweighing all others, however, are insects. Aphids, beetles, bugs, scales, sawflies whiteflies, and the larvae of butterflies and moths are just some of the most important.

Unlike diseases, some pest activity is indirect but still troublesome. Ants can undermine plants through their tunnelling activities in soil, for instance, but most pests cause harm by feeding on plants. And there is a broad but useful subdivision into those that are sap suckers, like aphids and whiteflies, and those that are chewers and eat pieces of plant tissue wholesale, like caterpillars and rabbits.

Some fungi and bacteria feed solely on dead matter. They are called saprobes and are very important in the breakdown of organic matter in the soil and in a compost bin. Those that feed on living matter are called parasites. When a parasite causes a disease, it's called a pathogen; the plant attacked is called its host.

The division into saprobe and parasite isn't, however, a rigid one. Some pathogens can live in innocuous fashion on dead organic matter and then turn their attention to living tissue. *Botrytis* grey mould is a very important example of this condition and is as much at home on piles of dead vegetation as it is on living plants. By contrast, there are some fungi and bacteria that simply can't survive in the absence of a living plant and very familiar examples of this group include rusts and mildews.

Fungi can be seen *en masse* in the form of mould or sometimes as much larger, distinct individuals, like toadstools. Even bacteria, which individually are microscopic, can often be seen as coloured droplets, each containing millions of separate cells. Viruses, however, which can exist only within the living cells of another organism can be seen only with powerful electron microscopes. Fungi are very susceptible to damage caused by drying out and, by and large, they are unable to grow and feed at low temperatures, a feature of temperate-climate winters. This is a problem compounded for parasites by the fact that their host plant has very probably itself died down to survive only as a rootstock, corm or seed.

During the winter, therefore, fungi are in a vulnerable condition and unable to disperse rapidly. The converse is that, during the summer, they are able to multiply and disperse very rapidly indeed. They do this by virtue of their method of reproduction which produces, not seeds, but spores; much smaller, relatively fragile bodies that are easily blown by the wind, germinate and grow into new organisms very quickly. Much of plant disease control and avoidance is directed towards preventing the formation and dispersal of these spores.

Pests too can be vulnerable in the winter. Being cold blooded, their activity tends to be related directly to temperature and they pass the cold months either as adults in a torpid, hibernating state, or as eggs, larvae or other immature forms. And, like fungi, they too are disadvantaged when their host plants die down. Let's then see how this knowledge of pest and disease behaviour enables us to control them most effectively.

## Healthy plants

One common way for pests and diseases to be introduced into a garden is on planting material. When establishing a new planting, therefore, it's essential to obtain your plants, seeds, bulbs and all other planting material from a reputable supplier.

Newly purchased plants in the form of transplant sized individuals, crowns, rootstocks or young trees or shrubs should be inspected carefully and any obviously damaged or diseased parts cut away.

Seeds don't usually show visible signs of any diseases that they may be carrying and, in any event, it's highly improbable that you will find particles of soil or plant debris with the seed in a packet. Nonetheless, many gardeners save their own seed; I encourage them to do it as it is highly satisfying but you should always try to emulate commercial quality standards and, above all, only save seed from plants that are themselves vigorous and healthy.

By contrast, it's still possible to buy poor quality ornamental bulbs. If you examine them, you will see many that are undersized compared with those from a reputable source; many will have small surface lesions, indicative of a disease problem and may also have scarring or erosion of the surface as evidence of a pest attack. When lifting bulbs yourself, throw away any showing signs of disease.

Where seeds or bulbs, corms and tubers have been collected or lifted from the garden, there's a further factor to be considered; while they may be perfectly healthy at the time of lifting, they can deteriorate during storage. Cool, dry, well ventilated conditions are needed for bulbs and these are best supplemented by a dusting with one of the combined fungicide and insecticide dressings now available.

Virus contamination is much less obvious, and because it is present throughout the plant's tissues, it is passed from parent to offspring when plants are propagated vegetatively. This is why 'seed' potato tubers are best bought afresh each season and why plants such as dahlias, carnations and chrysanthemums should be examined carefully before they are used for new plantings. With longer term crops such as fruit bushes and trees, ensuring that healthy stock is obtained is even more important. Always buy only certified virus-free plants from reputable suppliers.

**above** *Botrytis* grey mould attacks dead plant material but spreads easily to living tissues also.

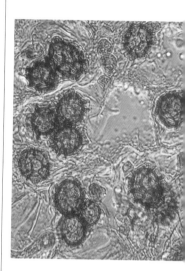

**above** Fungal spores are the means by which diseases spread; here they are buried in

**above** Insects eggs are often overlooked on the underside of leaves.

**above** By rigorously discarding diseased bulbs or other planting material, many problems can be avoided.

**below** The effects of virus are often insidious and easily overlooked; like these pale streaks on the foliage.

## Resistance to pests and diseases

You will sometimes hear of plants that have some inbuilt resistance to pests and diseases and must wonder why these aren't more widely available. The explanation is that plant breeders can only make use of such resistance as occurs naturally in wild plants. Where these are significantly different from the cultivated forms, it may be impossible to breed the resistance into the cultivated plants without losing some other desirable features. And because the process will, in any event, be long and costly, it is only really worthwhile with major commercial crops such as cereals.

## Garden hygiene

A neat and tidy garden is much more likely to be healthy than one that is cluttered with rubbish, debris and the remains of old plants. There are two main reasons for this: rubbish creates hiding places for pests such as woodlice and snails, and as some fungi can live equally satisfactorily on dead and living plant material, they can perpetuate on debris and spread from there to attack living plants.

## Traps and barriers

Although you can't trap plant diseases, you can catch some pests. At their simplest, these traps can be sticky cards to enmesh whitefly, while at their most advanced, they can be pheromone-baited devices to lure and ensnare male fruit moths. Barriers can range from fencing to keep out deer or rabbits to netting over or around soft fruit to keep out birds, lightweight fleece over vegetables to protect them from egg-laying flies or caterpillars, to prickly twigs around soft plants to deter slugs.

## Biological control

The use of natural parasites and predators to control pests certainly isn't new. Farmers in China were doing it in the 13th century by putting ants into their litchi and citrus trees with the objective of protecting them from pest attack. Recently, the use of parasites and predators has been very valuable in the control of pests in greenhouses where the restricted environment is particularly favourable for their use. The greenhouse being enclosed, the predators are unlikely to fly away and, being warm, the environment offers them no incentive to venture outside. Only over the past few years, however, have production, marketing and packaging methods been developed to allow some biological control methods to become available to amateur gardeners. One or two more become available each season

## Encouraging natural biological control

Because a number of biological control methods are now available to gardeners, there's a tendency to forget that comparable phenomena do already occur and operate in gardens. You can do a good deal towards helping pest control by encouraging these natural systems. Among many groups of beneficial garden insects are various species of ground beetle, hoverflies, lacewings, ladybirds, and many groups of flies, among which the ichneumonids that parasitise caterpillars are the best known. Try to keep garden pesticide use to a minimum so as not to harm these creatures, and particularly avoid chemicals that persist in the environment for some time. Quite often, and understandably, gardeners tend to use pesticides most when they see the most pests. In reality, the bulk of the damage to plants may by then already have been done, and the pest populations could be about to collapse as predators build up. Thus, by using pesticides then, you may be doing more harm than good.

## The advantages and disadvantages of biological control

### Advantages

• No chemicals are involved, an attraction for gardeners who prefer to avoid chemical use.

• The methods are natural in that they make use of a preference that a creature displays in the wild; although not necessarily in the same country.

• Treatments are often fairly specific, in that a particular control agent will only affect one type of pest or group of pests. This is rarely the case with chemicals.

• There is no possibility of damage being caused to the plants; some plant species, for instance, may be susceptible to chemical scorching.

### Disadvantages

• The methods are relatively expensive compared with most chemicals.

• Few methods are suitable for use outdoors.

• No chemicals or general traps (such as sticky

yellow cards) may be used to control other pests affecting the same plants, as these will also kill the predators.

• In small greenhouses, such as those in gardens, the predator or parasite may rapidly eliminate the pest and then itself die out. Repeat applications (and therefore repeat purchases) may be necessary. In commercial greenhouses, there will always be sufficient pests remaining for the predator to continue.

• It may be necessary to predict the occurrence of a pest problem some time in advance because few control agents are available off the shelf; they must be ordered from the suppliers.

• There are no biological control methods available for gardeners to use against plant diseases.

### Notes on biological controls

• The ways in which the different methods act vary. The bacterial spray for caterpillars and also the nematode-based controls all depend on bacteria to attack and degrade the target pest, so bringing about its death. The parasitic wasps and gall midges act by laying their eggs into the pest. These then hatch and the resulting larvae feed on the pest. The ladybird beetles, in larval and/or adult form feed wholesale on the pests.

• The recommended minimum temperatures vary slightly between the companies marketing the controls but, within defined limits, all work better as temperature rises.

• Always check the directions carefully with regard to the method of application and for details of how long and under what conditions the organisms will remain effective after you receive them.

• And finally, it should be added that none of these biological control organisms is in any way harmful to humans.

### Chemical remedies

#### Use of chemicals

Chemicals on sale through garden centres and shops, must, by law, have been cleared for use by the Ministry of Agriculture. The Ministry will have been satisfied that thorough evidence has demonstrated both the effectiveness and the safety of a product, used for the purpose described and in the manner directed. You must, however, follow the manufacturers' guidelines as given on the product labels.

It's most important only to use chemicals sold specifically for garden use. You must not use household chemicals in the garden and nor should you turn for your supply to commercial plant-growers and farmers. They use far more of a far greater range of products than any gardener and quite different criteria apply to commercial situations.

### Insecticides and fungicides

Insecticides are chemicals to kill insects, whereas fungicides are chemicals used to kill fungi. But the spectrum of pest and disease-causing species extends, of course, beyond insects and fungi, so what is to be done about bacteria and viruses, invertebrates other than insects, and birds and mammals? Most insecticides will have some effect on other living creatures, which is precisely why we have to take precautions when handling them. Several insecticides will have some controlling effect on pests such as woodlice and millipedes but almost none will have any impact on mites or

**above** *Rosa rugosa* is a disease and pest resistant rose but it's rather rarely that resistance provides the total answer to a problem.

### Principal biological control methods available for garden use

| Pest | Biological control organism | Notes |
|---|---|---|
| Aphids | *Aphidoletes aphidimyza* [Predatory gall midge] | Greenhouse; minimum air temperature 10°C (50°F) |
| Aphids | *Aphidius matricariae* [Parasitic wasp] | Greenhouse; minimum air temperature 18°C (64°F) |
| Caterpillars | *Bacillus thuringiensis* [Bacterium] | Greenhouse/outdoors; applied as a spray |
| Mealy bugs | *Cryptoleamus montrouzieri* [Predatory ladybird beetle] | Greenhouse; minimum air temperature 20°C (68°F) |
| Red spider mites | *Phytoseiulus persimilis* [Predatory mite] | Best in greenhouse; minimum air temperature 16C (61°F) |
| Scale insects (soft scale only) | *Metaphycus helvolus* [Parasitic wasp] | Greenhouse; minimum air temperature 22°C (72°F) |
| Slugs | *Phasmarhabditis hermaphroditica* [Nematode carrying bacteria] | Outdoors; minimum soil temperature 5°C (41°F) |
| Soil pests (some) | *Steinernema carpocapsae* [Nematode carrying bacteria] | Outdoors; minimum soil temperature 14°C (57°F) |
| Vine weevils (larvae) | *Heterorhabditis megadis* [Nematode carrying bacteria] | Outdoors; minimum soil temperature 12°C (54°F) |
| Vine weevils (larvae) | *Steinernema carpocapsae* [Nematode carrying bacteria] | Outdoors; minimum soil temperature 14°C (57°F) |
| Whiteflies | *Delphastus pusillus* [Predatory ladybird beetle] | Greenhouse; minimum air temperature 20°C (68°F) |
| Whiteflies | *Encarsia formosa* [Parasitic wasp] | Greenhouse; minimum air temperature 18°C (64°F) |

**above** Sticky yellow cards easily and simply trap whiteflies and other pests.

**below** The black spots on this leaf are whiteflies that have been parasitised by *Encarsia*.

eelworms or slugs and snails. The latter are, however, effectively combated with specific molluscicides, of which two are available to gardeners. Some fungicides will effect some control of bacteria but not very efficiently. No chemical has any direct effect on viruses but the impact of viruses can be lessened by control of the aphids or other creatures which introduce them into plant tissue.

### Choice of chemicals

If you walk into a garden centre or garden shop, you will see a very large display of both insecticides and fungicides on sale. How do you make a choice from the many that are available? First, you should appreciate that the number of chemical ingredients is only a small fraction of this total and the same substances are sold under several different brand names. Most advisory literature and radio and television guidance refers to the materials by their chemical, not their brand names. I've followed the same maxim in this book and you should therefore look for the chemical name or 'active ingredient' on the product label. It will generally be in smaller-sized print than the brand name but it must, by law, be there.

It's important to understand that not all fungicides or insecticides control all types of disease or pest with equal efficiency. Unless you have a very serious problem with one specific or unusual problem and must therefore use a very specific chemical, try to buy those products that will treat a wide range of problems. Many products contain a blend of chemicals specifically to enhance this range; many proprietary rose treatments for instance include both a fungicide to control mildew,

black spot and rust, while also containing an insecticide to combat aphids. You must not, however, yourself mix together two different products unless the manufacturers state specifically that this is permissible. You may reduce the overall effectiveness and/or damage your plants. And do check also that your chosen product may be used on your particular plant. Some plants (ferns and fuchsias are common examples) may be harmed by products even such as those based on natural soaps that are otherwise perfectly safe.

### Systemic and non-systemic compounds

You will sometimes see the word systemic on packaging of garden chemicals. A systemic chemical is one that is absorbed by the plant and moved in the sap from one part of the plant to another. By contrast, a non-systemic or contact product remains on the surface of the plant and kills pathogen or pest as the two come into direct contact there. There are advantages and disadvantages with both. The systemic product is required in smaller quantities, can be sprayed with much less accuracy, is not liable to be washed off by rain and have its effectiveness diminished, and is able to penetrate and eradicate pests or pathogens that are concealed and protected from more direct action. There are, nonetheless, certain disadvantages with edible produce, for the fact that systemic chemicals are taken up into the plant's tissues and have a long-lasting effect means also that the safe interval between time of application and the time that the produce may be eaten is correspondingly longer. In the kitchen garden, therefore, a contact chemical is often the best choice.

## Trouble-shooting Charts

| Problem | Detail | Probable cause | Problem | Detail | Probable cause |
|---------|--------|----------------|---------|--------|----------------|
| Symptoms on LEAVES | | | | Fairly large holes, over entire leaf or confined to edges | Caterpillars Beetles |
| 1. Wilting | General | Short of water Root pest Wilt disease | | Semi-circular pieces taken from edges | Leaf cutter bees |
| 2. Holed | Generally ragged | Small pests (millipedes, flea beetle, woodlice) Capsid bugs | 3. Discoloured | Black | Sooty mould |
| | | | | Predominantly red | Short of water |
| | Elongate holes; usually with slime present | Slugs or snails | | More or less bleached | Nutrient deficiency Short of water Too much water |

## Trouble-shooting Charts (continued)

| Problem | Detail | Probable cause |
|---|---|---|
|  | Silvery (plums and cherries) | Silver Leaf |
|  | Irregular yellowish patterns | Virus |
|  | Irregular tunnels | Leaf miner |
|  | Surface flecking | Leafhopper |
|  | Brown (scorched) in spring | Frost |
| 4. Spotted | Brownish, angular, with mould beneath | Downy mildew |
|  | Brownish, irregular or rounded; no mould | Leaf spot |
|  | Dark brown or black; not dusty | Scab |
|  | Small, dusty, brown, black or brightly coloured | Rust |
| 5. Mouldy | Black | Sooty mould |
|  | Grey, fluffy | Grey mould |
|  | White, velvety | Mildew |
|  | Brown (tomatoes) | Leaf mould |
|  | White, beneath leaves (potatoes) | Blight |
| 6. Infested with insects | White, moth-like, tiny | Whiteflies |
|  | Green, grey, black or other colour | Aphids |
|  | White, woolly (greenhouse) | Mealy bug |
|  | Flat, encrusted, like limpets | Scale insects |
|  | Large, six legs, worm-like | Caterpillars |
| 7. Curling | Insects present also | See 6 |
|  | Tightly rolled in spring | Sawfly |
|  | Puckered, reddish (peaches and almonds) | Peach leaf curl |
|  | Puckered, yellowish (pears) | Pear leaf blister mite |
| 8. Cobwebs present | Plant wilting | Red spider mite |

### Symptoms on FRUIT

| Problem | Detail | Probable cause |
|---|---|---|
| 1. Pieces eaten away | Fruit close to ground | Slugs |
|  |  | Mice |
|  | Tree fruits | Birds |
|  |  | Wasps |
| 2. Distorted | With rounded bumps (apples) | Capsid bugs |
|  | Black powder within (sweet corn) | Smut |
|  | Ribbon-like scars (apples) | Sawfly |
|  | Split (tomatoes) | Short of water |
| 3. Discoloured | Uneven ripening (tomato) | Virus |
|  |  | Nutrient deficiency |
| 4. Mouldy | While on plant (tomato) | Grey mould |
|  |  | Blight |
|  | While on plant (tree fruit) | Brown rot |
|  | In store | Fungal decay |
| 5. Spotted | Tree fruit | Scab |
|  | Tomato | Ghost spot |
| 6. Maggoty | Tree fruits | Caterpillars (Codling moth) |
|  | Peas | Caterpillars (Pea moth) |

| Problem | Detail | Probable cause |
|---|---|---|
|  | Raspberries | Beetle |
| 7. Dropping prematurely | Pears | Pear midge |
|  | Apples (in early summer) | June drop (normal; not a pest or disease) |

### Symptoms on FLOWERS

| Problem | Detail | Probable cause |
|---|---|---|
| 1. Drooping | General | Short of water |
|  |  | End of flowering period |
| 2. Tattered | Masses of tiny holes | Caterpillars |
|  | Large pieces torn away | Birds |
| 3. Removed | Usually discarded nearby | Birds |
| 4. Distorted | Usually only a few plants affected in a bed | Virus |
| 5. Discoloured | Powdery white covering | Powdery mildew |
| 6. Mouldy | Fluffy, grey mould | Botrytis grey mould |

### Symptoms on STEMS

| Problem | Detail | Probable cause |
|---|---|---|
| 1. Eaten through | On young plants | Slugs or snails |
|  | On older plants | Mice or rabbits |
|  | On young trees | Rabbits or deer |
| 2. Infested with insects | Green, grey, black or other colour | Aphids |
|  | White, woolly, on bark | Woolly aphid |
|  | Flat, encrusted; like limpets | Scale insects |
|  | Large, six legs, worm-like | Caterpillars |
| 3. Rotten | At base; young plants | Stem and foot rot |
|  | On trees and shrubs | Decay fungus |
| 4. Blister on bark of trees | More or less spherical | Gall |
|  | Target-like | Canker |
| 5. Dying back | General | Short of water |
|  |  | Canker or coral spot |
|  |  | Root pest or disease |
|  |  | See p. 000 |
|  | Raspberries |  |
| 6. Abnormal growth | Like bird's nests | Witches' broom |
|  | Leafy plant | Mistletoe |
|  | Buds swollen (blackcurrants) | Big bud |

### Symptoms on ROOTS and BULBS

| Problem | Detail | Probable cause |
|---|---|---|
| 1. Decayed | General | Decay fungi |
| 2. Parts eaten away | General | Small soil pests (millipedes, wireworms, leatherjackets) |
|  | Corms and bulbs | Vine weevil |
| 3. With irregular swellings | Brassicas and wallflowers | Clubroot |
|  | Potatoes | Eelworm |
|  | Peas and beans | Root nodules |
| 4. Maggoty | General | Fly larvae |
| 5. With warty spots | Root vegetables | Scab |

above The appearance of fungal fruit-bodies on a tree trunk betrays the presence of decay within.

## Safe use of garden chemicals

• Read the label carefully and use the product only in the way and for the purpose described.
• Don't use any chemicals that have lost their labels and don't decant chemicals from a large pack into a smaller one. Garden chemicals must only be kept in their original packaging.
• Don't mix or prepare garden chemicals in the kitchen, and keep sprayers, watering cans or other equipment specifically for pest and disease control. Don't use the same equipment for fertilizers or weedkillers.
• Wash out equipment thoroughly after use and pour excess diluted product on to an area of waste ground. Waste concentrated products should be disposed of according to the advice offered by your local authority.
• Store all chemicals out of reach of children and pets, preferably in a locked cupboard and away from extremes of temperature.
• Don't spray plants in strong wind, in bright sunlight or when flowers are fully open. The best time is the early morning or late evening.

## Identifying pests and diseases

Correct identification is the prelude to effective control. By using the key, you should be able to place your particular problem in its group.

## Chemicals available for garden pest and disease control

The following lists indicate the principal chemicals available for gardeners to use. But it's important to realise that these change annually as chemical ingredients or products are withdrawn, the permitted uses alter, formulations are varied or, very occasionally, an entirely new chemical is introduced. You must check the label recommendations carefully therefore before you buy and before you use any particular product for a particular purpose.

## Fungicides (chemicals to control diseases)

| Chemical | Mode of action | Notes | Uses |
|---|---|---|---|
| Ammonium carbonate | Contact | Only in mixture with copper sulphate | See copper sulphate |
| Ammonium hydroxide | Contact | Only in mixture with copper sulphate | See copper sulphate |
| Bupirimate | Systemic | Only in mixture with triforine | See triforine |
| Captan | Contact | Only in hormone rooting powders | To protect cuttings from rotting |
| Carbendazim | Systemic | The most widely used systemic fungicide, taking the place of the now-withdrawn benomyl | A very wide range of diseases of edible and ornamental plants and lawns. |
| Copper oxychloride | Contact | | See copper sulphate |
| Copper sulphate | Contact | Only in mixture with ammonium hydroxide as Bordeaux Mixture and ammonium carbonate as Cheshunt Compound | A wide range of diseases on edible and ornamental plants. Especially useful against blight and rusts |
| Dichlorophen | Contact | As a fungicide, only in hormone rooting powder. (But also widely used as a moss killer) | To protect cuttings from rotting |
| Mancozeb | Contact | | Especially useful against blight and rusts |
| Myclobutanil | Systemic | | Especially against rose diseases and apple scab |
| Penconazole | Systemic | | Especially against rust diseases on ornamental plants |
| Sulphur | Contact | Alone as liquid or powder and also in combination with other chemicals | Especially useful against mildew and as protection for stored ornamental bulbs |
| Thiophanate-methyl | Systemic | As a root dip formulation for brassica transplants | Only for clubroot control |
| Triforine | Systemic | Only in mixtures, either with bupirimate or with sulphur and insecticide | Especially for rose diseases; also fruit but not vegetables |

## Insecticides (chemicals to control pests, especially insects)

| Chemical | Mode of action | Notes | Uses |
|---|---|---|---|
| Bendiocarb | Contact/systemic | | Ant and other crawling pest control |
| Bifenthrin | Contact | | Most pests on edible and ornamental plants |
| Bioallethrin | Contact | Only in mixture with permethrin | See permethrin |
| Borax | Contact | | As ant bait |
| Butoxycarboxim | Systemic | Formulated on impregnated cardboard 'pins' for insertion into compost in pots | |
| Chlorpyrifos | Contact/Systemic | | Ant and other crawling pest control |
| Cypermethrin | Contact | | To control ants and other crawling insects |
| Deltamethrin | Contact | | To control ants and other crawling insects |
| Fenitrothion | Contact | | |
| Heptenophos | Systemic | Only in mixture with permethrin | See permethrin |
| Horticultural soaps (natural fatty acids) | Contact | | Aphids, whitefly, red spider mite and soft scale on edible and ornamental plants |
| Lindane | Contact | | For control of soil pests |
| Malathion | Contact | Alone and in mixture with permethrin | A wide range of pests, especially sap-sucking types on edible and ornamental plants |
| Permethrin | Contact | The most widely used modern garden insecticide; alone and with other chemicals. Also available as smoke formulation for greenhouse whitefly control | Most pests on edible and ornamental plants |
| Piperonyl butoxide | Contact | Only in mixture with permethrin | A wide range of pests on edible and ornamental plants |
| Pirimicarb | Contact/Systemic | Available alone and in mixture with fungicides | Almost specific to aphids |
| Pirimiphos-methyl | Contact | | A wide range of pests on edible and ornamental plants |
| Pyrethrins | Contact | General name for a group of chemically similar substances | See permethrin |
| Pyrethrum | Contact | | A wide range of pests on edible and ornamental plants |
| Quassia | Contact | Only in mixture with rotenone | See rotenone |
| Resmethrin | Contact | Only in combination with pyrethrins | See permethrin |
| Rotenone (derris) | Contact | As liquid or powder, also in combination with quassia | A wide range of pests on edible and ornamental plants |
| Tar oils | Contact | | Control of overwintering pests on deciduous trees and shrubs in the dormant season |
| Tetramethrin | Contact | Only in mixture with permethrin | See permethrin |

## Molluscides (chemicals to control slugs and snails)

| Chemical | Mode of action | Notes | Uses |
|---|---|---|---|
| Metaldehyde | Anaesthetic | As liquid and pellets | Slugs and snails |
| Methiocarb | Gastric action | Only as pellets | Slugs and snails |

# Weeds

Weeds are native plants in direct competition with cultivated vegetation for the same basic essentials of light, water and nutrients. Native plants growing in the fields and hedgerows are admired, protected and called wild flowers. A rather different attitude exists in gardens and with some justification for if you don't exercise some form of weed control, your garden will inevitably suffer. With a few exceptions, native plants are better adapted to the local climatic and other conditions than any alien that you may grow in your garden. By virtue of their greater hardiness, faster reproductive rate or other reasons, they are quite simply more efficient competitors. Much as you may like and admire them in their wild habitat, native plants must be controlled if your garden is to realise its full potential.

**above** Groundsel is a common annual weed that will continue to set seed even after it is chopped down.

**below** Some perennial weeds, like dandelion, spread rapidly by seed and also have persistent roots.

Perhaps 50 or 60 different plant species are of major importance in Britain as garden weeds. Their relative effects on your gardening activities will vary depending on the area in which you live, the type of soil in your garden and the types of plant that you cultivate. Nonetheless, weed species can be grouped into two major categories on the basis of the way they grow and reproduce, and these groupings largely dictate their efficiency as competitors and the control measures that are likely to be effective against them.

### Types of weed

Successful weeds have individual attributes that set them apart, not just from garden plants, but also from many other native species. An understanding of these attributes is important in each instance to help you select an appropriate control method.

Most numerous in terms of species and individuals are annual weeds, which produce flowers and set seed within a single year. The seeds of some annual weed species require no period of cold or enforced dormancy before they can germinate and if, as with groundsel (*Senecio vulgaris*), this is combined with the ability to produce flowers and seeds very early in life, more than one generation may occur within the course of a single season. A few species, like the annual meadow grass (*Poa annua*) can germinate in every month of the year. A short generation time is combined in most annual weeds with the ability to produce vast numbers of seeds. This can vary from less than 100 seeds per plant in cleavers (*Galium aparine*) to over 18,000 for some sow thistles (*Sonchus* spp.). Once in the soil, the seeds of most annual weeds have the potential to

survive for at least 10 years; although some, such as black nightshade (*Solanum nigrum*) can survive for four times this long, while field poppy seed (*Papaver rhoeas*) famously persists in a viable state for at least 80 years. It's evident, therefore, that the key to keeping control of annual weeds lies in using a method that eliminates the plants *before* they set seed.

There are a few shallowly rooted perennial weeds, such as daisies (*Bellis perennis*), that behave in beds and borders in much the same way as annuals, although in lawns and paths, they assume a rather different status that I shall come to shortly. For the present, however, my concern is a much more important group that, for simplicity, I call persistent perennials.

All perennials differ from annuals, of course, in that each individual lives for longer than one season (although not, in a literal sense, forever; perennial doesn't equate with immortal). While they too produce seeds, sometimes in large numbers, their importance as garden weeds derives much more from vegetative methods of spread, such as creeping roots, spreading rhizomes or bulbils. Some plants can even regenerate from small parts of

**above** Bindweed is an example of those perennial weeds that spread little by seed but have very deep and far-reaching roots.

## Method of spread of some important British perennial garden weeds

| Species | Common Name | Method of Spread |
|---|---|---|
| *Achillea millefolium* | Yarrow | Rhizomes, some seeds |
| *Aegopodium podagraria* | Ground elder | Rhizomes, some seeds |
| *Agropyron repens* | Couch grass | Rhizomes, few seeds |
| *Bellis perennis* | Daisy | Seeds, short creeping stems |
| *Calystegia sepium* | Hedge bindweed | Rhizomes, creeping stems |
| *Cirsium arvense* | Creeping thistle | Creeping roots |
| *Convolvulus arvensis* | Field bindweed | Creeping roots, some seeds |
| *Epilobium angustifolium* | Rosebay willowherb | Seeds |
| *Epilobium montanum* | Broad-leaved willowherb | Seeds |
| *Equisetum arvense* | Field horsetail | Rhizomes |
| *Lamium album* | White dead-nettle | Rhizomes |
| *Oxalis* spp. | Pink-flowered oxalis | Bulbils |
| *Ranunculus ficaria* | Lesser celandine | Bulbils, seeds, root tubers |
| *Ranunculus repens* | Creeping buttercup | Creeping stems, some seeds |
| *Fallopia japonica* | Japanese knotweed | Rhizomes, some seeds |
| *Sagina* spp. | Pearlworts | Seeds |
| *Taraxacum officinale* | Dandelion | Seeds, pieces of root |
| *Trifolium repens* | White clover | Creeping stems, seeds |
| *Urtica dioica* | Stinging nettle | Creeping stems, seeds |
| *Veronica filiformis* | Creeping speedwell | Creeping stems |

**above** The lesser celandine is well equipped to spread, producing seeds, tiny, easily detached tubers and also bulbils.

**below** The old-fashioned daisy grubber still provides a very effective way of removing individual weeds that don't have persistent roots.

stem or roots left behind in the soil. Different weed species vary in this ability; for example, dandelion (*Taraxacum officinale*) can produce new plants from any part of its tap root, but docks (*Rumex* spp.) can only regenerate from the top 7-10cm (2¾-4in). Plants like ground elder (*Aegopodium podagraria*), couch grass (*Agropyron repens*), or horsetail (*Equisetum arvense*) have creeping rhizomes with frequent nodes bearing buds. If the rhizome is severed or otherwise disturbed, these buds are stimulated to grow.

The physical eradication of perennial weeds can be exceedingly difficult for, not only is finding the roots and removing them from the soil hard work, but if a portion can break off and regenerate the problem can be almost insurmountable. Perhaps in a league of their own are weeds that produce bulbils (small bulbs that break off from their parent) for these cannot be controlled by physical means and, in the case of the pink-flowered *Oxalis* spp., this attribute is combined with almost total resistance to available weedkillers.

## Non-chemical weed control

The most straightforward way of controlling annual or shallow-rooted perennial weeds is by digging or pulling them up by hand or with a hand fork or by cutting them down with a hoe. Hoeing is best done on a warm, dry day so the cut plants will shrivel quickly, although groundsel and annual meadow grass can continue to mature their seeds if they are hoed down during flowering so they should be raked up for disposal. If the weather and soil are moist when weeds are hoed, however, some weeds may produce new roots in response to wounding and end up, in effect, merely having been transplanted. When you are clearing new ground, regular digging with a fork has a role even for perennial weeds such as couch grass, nettles and thistles, but I advise against using a spade or rotary cultivator which will chop up and disperse them further.

On lawns, it's often possible to remove small numbers of daisies, dandelions and other rosette-forming perennials by means of a small, two-pronged digging tool called a daisy grubber. However, care must be taken to remove all the root as simply snapping off a portion may encourage re-growth. Long-handled 'weed keys' are also available for removing weeds from lawns, while a path weeder, a small hook-like tool, can be used for cutting and hooking out weeds from between paving slabs.

Hoeing and digging are, at best, curative methods of weed control; how much better to prevent weeds from emerging. By adding material over the soil surface we may not prevent weed seeds from germinating but, starved of light, the seedlings will be unable to survive. The simplest way to do this is to apply a loose mulch of garden compost, leaf mould, well rotted manure, bark chips or similar organic matter. A 5cm (2in) thick layer is needed to prevent annual weed seedlings from reaching the surface and this will need to be topped up at least once a year. In the vegetable and fruit garden, black plastic sheeting can be used to suppress weeds, although this is not an attractive option in more ornamental parts of the garden unless the sheeting is covered with a layer of loose mulch. It's almost impossible to eradicate perennial weeds by mulching, however, although plastic sheet mulching will achieve a significant reduction if left in place for one season. It is, however, unsightly.

Most annual weeds have a high demand for light, so garden plants with large leaves that grow rapidly can soon create a canopy over the soil and prevent the weeds from emerging and growing. These so-called ground-cover plants are often widely promoted as ideal for 'low-maintenance' gardening. If you choose the right plants and plant at realistic spacings, this can work well in large gardens, but the ground must first be clear of perennial weeds.

## Chemical weed control

It will be apparent from what I have said already that physical methods of control have serious limitations with persistent perennial weeds in beds and borders. On lawns and paths, too, it's virtually impossible to control all weed growth physically. But there will also be occasions when it's difficult to keep on top of an annual weed problem in this way.

It is not always practicable to mulch all parts of the garden. Soil being prepared for seed sowing, for example, and in the spring especially, with weed seedlings emerging at a prodigious rate and the land too wet for hoeing, even annual weed growth can soon become out of hand. This is why I doubt if many gardeners could manage totally without resorting to a weedkiller. However, choosing an appropriate weedkiller is critically important. Using the wrong weedkiller can have disastrous consequences, worse than with any other type of garden chemical.

We need to consider five principle types of product although, as will be apparent, these categories are not all mutually exclusive. It is important to remember first that only you know the difference between a weed and a garden plant; in other words, it is you as a gardener who must play the major part in deciding how effective and safe a weedkiller is to be by using it appropriately.

Total weedkillers kill all vegetation with which they come into contact. By contrast, selective weedkillers only kill certain types of plant; the only type presently available to gardeners are those that kill only broad-leaved weeds and can therefore be used safely on lawns. Some other weedkillers are selective in the sense that they can only kill seedlings and are safe to use, therefore, among established plants, but would be devastating in a seedbed. Some weedkillers work by contact, killing

**above** Annual weed growth is readily suppressed with an organic mulch.

green tissues more or less through surface action; others are absorbed and then translocated within the plant, and these are obviously of special value for deep-rooted persistent perennial weeds. Residual weedkillers (which are also usually total weedkillers) persist in the soil for some weeks or months to kill seeds or freshly germinated seedlings. Clearly, a residual total weedkiller will render an area bereft of plant life for some time, a season or more, so such products should only be used on paths or other unplanted areas. Non-residual total weedkillers kill all existing vegetation but are rendered inactive in the soil so replanting or sowing can, therefore, proceed very soon afterwards.

I have listed the weedkillers that are currently available to gardeners and indicated their modes of action and garden uses (see page 111). Most are sold in proprietary mixtures for particular purposes, but it's very important that you don't attempt to make up mixtures yourself; two incompatible chemicals could produce a very harmful cocktail. Weedkillers are usually applied as a diluted liquid, made up from a powder or liquid

**right** It makes sense to shield
valuable plants against
weedkiller splash; and always
label the can so it isn't used
for any other purpose.

**right** It makes sense to shield valuable plants against weedkiller splash; and always label the can so it isn't used for any other purpose.

**below** If weedkiller is applied
with a sprayer, be sure to use
a protective cone around the
nozzle.

concentrate, using a watering can (especially on lawns or paths) or a sprayer. Never spray in windy weather and take care to ensure that the chemical is applied only to the target plants. Always wash out watering cans and sprayers thoroughly after use and as an added precaution, never use weed-killer containers for applying any other type of chemical.

Sometimes, weedkillers can be applied as granules or as powders – some powdered lawn fertilizers have a selective weedkiller incorporated with them – and at least one translocated weedkiller is available as a gel formulation for painting on to individual plants. I have never found this gel to be effective, however, and prefer to obtain localised activity by using a liquid formulation in a small sprayer and shielding nearby plants with a piece of card.

When spraying, remember that, in general, the finer the droplets, the more effective the coverage. And remember, too, that more than with any other type of garden chemical, weedkiller effectiveness is closely allied to climatic conditions. Warm dry weather, combined with a moist soil, is ideal, although the special conditions necessary for each product should be checked carefully on the label; the very useful translocated weedkiller glyphosate, for example, requires six hours without rain after application if it is to be fully absorbed into the plants' tissues.

And finally, remember that you may need to apply a chemical weed treatment more than once during the season to keep the weeds under control.

New active weedkiller ingredients haven't yet been developed for amateur use, and the costs are prohibitive, but there are new developments in the way weedkillers are applied. Ready-to-use products which do not need to be diluted are becoming more popular, often sold either as hand-held sprays, as gels or solid sticks that are painted on. The advantage with these methods is that small areas of weed can be dealt with quickly. However, they have their drawbacks – they are expensive for treating large areas and nozzles may become blocked on ready-to-use sprayers.

## Moss

Moss is one of the major weeds affecting lawns and, for many gardeners, applying a moss killer is an annual ritual. The growth of moss on lawns is an indication that the lawn needs a change in its management so the grass can compete more effectively; simply applying a moss killer won't change that fact. In particular, moss will become a serious problem if the grass is mown too short, if it is shaded, under-fed or the soil is water-logged and compacted. I discuss this, along with other aspects of lawn care, on page 164.

## Disposal of weeds

When weeds are controlled with a weedkiller, the dead plants tend to shrivel away. When weeds are controlled physically, however, by hoeing or digging, they may be disposed of safely in a properly functioning compost bin. The temperature in the bin should attain at least 70°C (158°F) and this will be adequate to kill almost all seeds. In practice, I can say that I have never known weed seeds of any type to survive my own compost heap; no seedlings have ever emerged from compost subsequently spread as a soil mulch, at least. My only reservation is with rhizomes of couch grass. I don't know the temperature necessary nor the period over which it must be maintained to kill these rhizomes, and as the consequences of spreading couch further are so serious, I feel that the rhizomes are better bagged up and removed to a public refuse tip.

**above** Only rake out moss after a moss-killer has been applied or you will simply spread it further.

## Chemical weedkillers available to gardeners

| Chemical | Mode of Action | Garden Use |
| --- | --- | --- |
| Amitrole (Aminotriazole) | Translocated | Total |
| Atrazine | Contact/residual | Total |
| 2,4-D | Translocated | Selective against broad-leaved plants |
| Dicamba | Translocated | Selective against broad-leaved plants |
| Dichlobenil | Residual | Selective against seedlings and young plants |
| Dichlorophen | Contact | Selective against moss |
| Dichlorprop | Translocated | Selective against broad-leaved plants |
| Diquat | Contact | Total |
| Diuron | Residual | Total |
| Ferrous sulphate | Contact | Selective against moss |
| Glyphosate | Translocated | Total |
| MCPA | Translocated | Selective against broad-leaved plants |
| Mecoprop | Contact | Selective against broad-leaved plants |
| Paraquat | Contact | Total |
| Simazine | Residual | Total |
| Sodium chlorate | Residual | Total |

# Container gardening

Container gardening is presently very fashionable but it is nothing new; it has a history stretching back to Classical times and the earliest days of horticulture. It still offers a very versatile way of growing plants, for almost any type can be grown in a container if the correct planting medium is used. On the one hand, containers may constitute almost the entire garden for those with very confined space, and on the other, they can be used instantly to change the appearance of a much larger area. Nonetheless, the choice, handling and indeed the limitations of containers are the same. Plant roots are restricted to the moisture and nutrients they can obtain from the small volume of compost, so more care in watering and feeding is needed.

**above** Grow a slightly tender small tree or shrub in a container and you can easily move it to a sheltered spot.

**below** Flat-backed wall pots may look attractive but dry out so rapidly that I find them rather impractical.

And as container gardening involves more work, it is usually reserved for plants that have particular merit – unusual foliage or a very long flowering season, for instance.

Some of the principles of container gardening are also applicable to small raised beds, table beds and peat beds, but I discuss these in detail in the chapter on alpine plants (see page 196).

## Size and shape of containers

A visit to any garden centre will reveal a huge array of containers, varying in size and shape, and manufactured from a wide range of materials including terracotta, wood, concrete, reconstituted stone and various types of plastic. Aesthetic considerations and cost will play a major part in dictating your choice although, in general, plastic is the cheapest, least attractive and functionally has perhaps the greatest drawbacks.

There are certain features that are important when containers are being used. First, therefore, I shall consider free-standing containers and will suggest some of the aspects that you should take into account when making your choice.

A cubic metre (cubic yard) of potting compost weighs approximately 1 tonne (1 ton). If you plan to move full containers, therefore, the size of the container and the volume of compost it will contain become very important considerations. I find that a terracotta tub about 40cm (16in) tall and 36cm (14½in) in diameter is the maximum that I can move comfortably. Concrete containers of the same size will, of course, be proportionately heavier. Conversely, many containers, although superficially attractive, are too small or shaped such that they contain too small a volume of compost to be functionally effective. They fail partly because they require watering unrealisti-

cally often and also because there is insufficient space for the roots of a plant with large enough leaf and flower growth to be attractive. Some concrete containers, for instance, appear fairly large externally but have very thick walls and a limited internal space. Some of the containers sold for attaching to walls also contain very small volumes of compost and flat-backed wall pots are, in my experience, particularly troublesome. In general, I would advise against choosing any container that had an internal volume less than that of a conventional plant pot, 20cm (8in) in diameter.

Stability of free-standing pots is another important consideration and is a function of several features: height, the ratio of height to diameter, volume of compost, type of compost (a soil-based compost is very much heavier than the equivalent volume of a soil-less one), size of plant and relative exposure and windiness of the site. Again, I can only advise on the results of my own experience and suggest that the most important feature when choosing a stable container is to avoid those that taper sharply downwards and have a basal diameter less than about two thirds that of the top; the taller the container, the more important this ratio becomes.

## Container materials

I have already mentioned that I would never, for preference, choose a plastic container; they will always look like plastic containers and thus inferior, they are easily damaged if moved when full, many types discolour and become more brittle with age and they suffer from the important drawback of being impermeable to water and air. Any plants grown in them are likely to suffer from water logging and consequent root damage. They do, of course, have the advantage of being relatively cheap, so you can certainly buy a large number and so immediately colour a new garden at a time when there will certainly be more pressing demands on your funds. I suggest, therefore, that if you must begin your container gardening life with plastic pots (or even with really make-do vessels such as old paint cans), you should gradually replace them, one or two per year, with more attractive and traditional types.

Unglazed earthenware called terracotta has been used to make plant containers for centuries and is undeniably lovely, if expensive.

But choose carefully; there are some very attractive pots imported from warm countries that cannot tolerate even a slight degree of frost without flaking or cracking. These must, therefore, be taken under cover in the winter. The frost tolerance of terracotta depends on the nature of the clay used and the way that it is fired. Some manufacturers are now so confident of their materials that they offer a 10-year guarantee of frost resistance so their pots can safely be planted with perennials and left outdoors permanently. Use your non-hardy terracotta pots for plants, such as specimen fuchsias, that must themselves be taken into the protection of greenhouse or conservatory in the winter.

Troughs or other containers hewn from natural stone are beautiful but now extremely scarce and prohibitively expensive. Their place has been taken by moulded concrete and reconstituted stone vessels, some of which are very difficult to distinguish from the real thing. Check that these containers too are frost tolerant and that they don't contain a chemical setting or hardening agent that is toxic to plants

**above** By growing a non-hardy plant in a container, it can be kept in a greenhouse or other protection until the weather is warm enough and then brought out in its full glory.

treated with non-toxic preservative inside and lined with plastic sheet also pierced with drainage holes. Within this wooden frame, you may then place plastic troughs and pots containing the plants. This arrangement allows you to plant up the containers (and even allow the plants to mature) before placing them on view and also gives you the flexibility of replacing individual pots or troughs during the summer.

Hanging baskets present special difficulties. Their weight when full and wet should be a major consideration and support brackets must be strongly anchored. For reasons of weight if none other, soil-less compost is much to be preferred and drainage should be free but not so liberal that the whole requires watering more than once each day. Composts are now available that incorporate moisture-retaining gels in order to cut down still further the frequency of watering. Some restrictive liner is necessary in any hanging basket to prevent the compost from falling out, and, while the natural sponginess of sphagnum moss is ideal, it is now difficult or costly to obtain and the easiest method for the modern gardener is to buy wool or similar fibre-based alternatives. Many modern baskets are too shallow to be effective and the compost inevitably dries out very rapidly; a basket should be at least 30cm (12in) in diameter and at least 18cm (7in) deep.

## Compost

The choice of compost for containers (apart from hanging baskets) is relatively straightforward. If the plants are to be grown at least semi-perennially, by which I mean for more than one season, use a soil-based potting compost such as John Innes No. 3, although for alpines, a more gritty mixture is preferable (page 198). If they are to be grown as annuals for one season only, use a soil-less potting compost. But always remember that the nutrient reserves of a soil-less compost are less than those of a soil-based type and that the liquid feeding which is essential for all plants in containers should begin for them after about 3 weeks, whereas a soil-based compost should be adequate for twice this long before a supplement is needed.

And once the plants are established, bear in mind that with no water reserves to tap at

**above** Grow plants in separate pots and group them together in a window box.

**below** Hanging baskets are undeniably pretty when well planted; but never forget that they need almost constant attention.

until they are well weathered. The easiest way to encourage the growth of lichen and algae, and so simulate more closely a genuine old stone container, is occasionally to paint the concrete with milk or liquid cow manure.

Wooden half-barrels offer easily the cheapest way of obtaining really large containers but should be painted inside and out with a nontoxic preservative before use. Also, remember to drill several drainage holes in the barrel before they are filled with compost. It's very difficult to move a half barrel full of compost but, if it must be done, try using three rollers cut from lengths of old scaffolding pipe.

And so to types of container other than those free-standing in the garden. Window boxes are a special delight in inner city gardens (provided they are out of reach of vandals) and for apartment dwellers. Much the best system is to invest in wooden boxes – which may have to be specially made – of the exact size and shape of your window ledge

depth, watering at least once and preferably twice a week (with a once-a-week feed) is essential for tubs; and watering once a day with twice weekly feeding is the regime for hanging baskets.

Growing-bags are discussed again under the subject of vegetables (page 135) but although popular to some extent for annual ornamentals, they have serious limitations. In a greenhouse, I much prefer the ring-culture system (page 96) of raising tomatoes and similar plants and urge all greenhouse tomato growers to consider this very seriously. Growing-bags are useful, however, for tomatoes, cucumbers and similar crops outdoors on paved areas where there is no access to bare soil and there are now several proprietary ways of overcoming the difficulty of providing staked support for plants raised in this way. Apart from this, the plastic growing-bag has for long had a major drawback in that watering is very hard to regulate. It is impossible to see if the compost is wet or dry and plants can easily suffer from both extremes.

Recently a number of ingenious ways have been devised to overcome the problem of watering. The most effective of those that I have tried entails using a small transparent water reservoir with a tube that is pushed into the side of the bag. It will keep the compost fairly uniformly moist for several days and it is easy to see when the reservoir itself needs replenishing.

### Planting containers

Containers need drainage holes at the bottom, so you should place a few stones, or old crocks if you have them, over the top of the holes. Add the compost, breaking it up if it has become compressed in the bag. Water the plants in their original pot and leave them to drain before planting. After planting, press down the compost so the level is 3-4cm (1¼-1½in) below the rim of the container, otherwise water will run off the compost. Large containers can be mulched. Small 'feet' for holding the pots off the ground are worthwhile when containers are on paved areas: they assist drainage, prevent staining of the underlying surface and help to discourage slugs and snails

Hanging baskets should be planted up as they are filled with compost. After lining the basket, place a small volume of compost in the base and feed any trailing plants carefully

through the sides of the basket from within. You risk damaging the plants if you attempt to push them through from the outside. Gradually fill the container with more compost. Once the basket is about three quarters full, position the top plants starting with the central specimen and working outwards. Strawberry and parsley pots are filled along much the same lines as hanging baskets, but as it is hard to water these evenly, do make sure that the roots are firmly in contact with the compost from the outset.

Winter container plants are becoming ever more popular, but it is important to remember that even hardy plants can suffer if their root-ball is frozen over winter, something that can happen in the small volume of compost offered by a hanging basket. Plants grow very little during the winter months and small plants won't fill out the basket as they will in summer, so use more mature plants; winter-flowering pansies, for example, should already be in flower when they are planted.

**below** I have grown my greenhouse tomatoes by ring culture for many years; and am rather pleased with the results.

**above** The trick to planting a container such as a strawberry pot is to pass the plants through from the inside and then gradually pack in the compost around them.

## Aftercare

Once containers are planted, you will need to water and feed the plants regularly throughout the growing season. All annuals in containers should be watered at least twice a week and summer hanging baskets will need watering daily.

A spray lance attachment to a hose can make watering easier although an alternative, if you have several hanging baskets, is to install an automatic watering system. Long-term container plants will be in a bigger volume of compost and watering need not be so frequent, although a mulch in early spring can also help reduce watering.

Short-term plants like bedding and tender perennials grow rapidly and should be fed with a liquid feed around six weeks after planting and this should then continue every week until growth slows down. Slow-release tablets or granules that are inserted in the compost at planting time are popular for container plants but extra feeding with liquid fertilizer is often still needed later in the season. For flowering plants, a fertilizer with a high potash content, like a tomato feed, is suitable.

Summer vegetables grown for their leaves may be fed with a balanced liquid fertilizer, like liquid Growmore, although fruiting crops need a special tomato feed. Again, once a week should be sufficient at first, increasing to twice a week when growth is very rapid. For permanent plants in larger containers of soil-based compost, it should be sufficient to replace the top few centimetres of compost. And always remember that every plant in a container must look its best when on display, so regular deadheading and removing of faded foliage is important.

## Using containers in the garden

The really big advantage of growing plants in containers is the degree of control that you can exercise over them and their environment. Whereas a poor soil takes many years to improve, you can plant up containers with good quality compost and obtain fine and rewarding results within a season. Dull corners can be brightened even where there may be no soil as in a balcony garden or a courtyard. You can position plants where the conditions are ideal for them: those that suffer from exposure can be given shelter, while those that prefer dappled shade can also be accommodated, and so on. Plants can be brought on show when they are at their peak and moved out of the way when they fade.

Gardening with containers allows you to grow and enjoy plants that are wholly unsuited to the type of soil occurring naturally in your garden. By selecting an appropriate compost, you may have acid-loving plants in an alkaline garden or plants that need a free-draining, sandy loam even if your garden soil is wet, heavy clay. And, as you can control the soil or compost within the container, soil-borne pests and disease are not usually a problem although temporary plants should be planted in fresh compost in clean pots each year.

To integrate them into your overall garden, choose containers that will work harmoniously with your garden style. Rustic or informal containers will enhance a cottage garden but not a formal area. If in doubt, choose a selection of plain terracotta pots, the largest you can afford, which will suit most gardens and planting schemes. A group of containers can be used to soften hard surfaces, such as an area of gravel, paving or concrete and a climber in a container can break the bleakness so often found where a wall meets a horizontal hard surface.

While a container can provide much-needed vertical elements in flat gardens, you need to be bold with both your choice of pot size and plants to make an impression. For example, use a collection of small pots with the same repeated planting to create an impact. Small pots, each planted with a bright red pelargonium, positioned one on each of a flight of steps produces a band of colour and also invites the visitor to walk up the steps to explore the rest of the garden.

In a formal garden, try a container-grown specimen of topiary to provide year-round structure. Grow a fruit tree on a dwarfing rootstock in a large tub in order to obtain fruit from a courtyard garden; use tubs for growing bulbs, (either, as with lilies in the form of a permanent planting or as with daffodils and tulips, to

provide colour before summer annuals take over); and plant a small selection of pots with herbs to be positioned close to the kitchen. Use tubs or hanging baskets to brighten up your front door; again choose subjects that will work in harmony with your style of entrance. A pair of trimmed container-grown evergreens on either side of the front door can look very stylish and they are easy to maintain.

A tree in a container is a long-term feature that will act as a foçal point in the garden, so it is important to choose carefully. It should be slow growing and have something to offer throughout the year.

You are unlikely to become self-sufficient by relying on vegetables from containers, but it is often useful to have crops close at hand on the patio or by the front door if most of your vegetables are grown on an allotment. I would not trouble with most brassicas, sweet corn or globe artichokes; the plants are too big for their yield. Potatoes in dustbins in an unheated greenhouse can provide clean, early crops but if you want your containers to be attractive as well as productive, use vegetables like carrots and beetroot that have attractive foliage. Tomatoes are a well tried crop for containers and miniature, small-fruited bush varieties like 'Tumbler' can be grown in a hanging basket with basil. Peppers look attractive in large pots on the patio but they need staking. Lettuces are quick-growing and work well, especially where they can be grown alongside herbs.

Using containers to conceal unsightly features can be very effective, but if used to disguise a drain or man-hole cover, it makes sense to support the tub or other vessel on wooden battens placed either side of the offending object. It will then be easier to move and will not damage the cover.

Finally, a word of caution for those who container garden in high-rise city apartments. Do ascertain the weight restrictions imposed on your floor; remember that statistic of 1 cubic metre of compost weighing 1 tonne (1 ton).

# Plants & gardens

In this part of the book, I have described all of the possible groups of plants that you might wish to have in your garden and the garden situations in which they might be grown. Very few gardens contain all possible components. Even the most popular overall feature, the lawn, is lacking from small courtyard gardens while many others, for reasons of personal choice or unsuitability of site and soil will for instance have no pool, kitchen garden or shrubbery.

My main concern here has been to explain how each broad type or group of plants should be grown. I have given a selection of varieties within each broad heading but have given little information about the special characteristics and merits of each. For more information on individual plants and on the range of species and varieties available for particular roles, you should refer to 'Stefan Buczacki's Plant Dictionary'.

# The Fruit Garden

The division of the fruit garden into soft fruit and tree fruit may seem an odd one, but there are valid and practical distinctions between the fruits that grow on trees and those that grow on bushes or canes. Most importantly, tree fruits are long-lived plants whereas canes and bushes need replacing after relatively few years. Their pruning is quite different, their cultivation is different, mainly because of their difference in size and, unlike many tree fruits, soft fruits are self-fertile, so only one variety is needed to obtain a crop.

### Planning a fruit garden

Even some soft fruit plants will last for up to 10 years, so it is worth planning a fruit-growing area as a long-term feature. It's important to check relative spacings and remember to allow room for the paths that you will need for access. Where only a small area can be given over to fruit, choose varieties with the longest cropping times, and consider restricting their size by training them as cordons or fans.

### Soft Fruit
#### Site and soil

In general, soft fruit are slightly more shade tolerant than most tree fruit, but it is still important to plant them in the sunniest available area of the garden. Most require similar cultural treatment and similar protection, so it is sensible to group them all together in a fruit cage.

A fruit cage can produce dramatic improvements in the quality and quantity of the crop and should be considered by anyone who is planning a fruit garden. It shelters fruit from wind, so encouraging pollination and reduces bird damage more effectively than merely draping the plants with netting. Fruit cages can be made with rustic wooden poles, or proprietary models can be purchased with light tubular aluminium frames. Frames should be at least 1.8m (5ft 9in) tall, and the netting should have a mesh size of around 18mm (¾in). For a very robust structure, a wooden-framed cage can be made with galvanized chicken wire on the sides and lightweight plastic netting on top.

The ideal soil is a moisture-retentive loam with a pH of about 6.5, with organic matter incorporated before planting – it's impossible to place compost or manure in the vicinity of the plants' roots once they are established. If at all possible, don't attempt to establish soft fruit on a site from which old fruit bushes or canes have been removed recently, because there may be some carry over of viruses in the soil.

Where shortage of space does make such an arrangement necessary, it is sensible to remove the soil from each planting position and swap it for fresh soil taken from elsewhere in the garden. On alkaline soil, raspberries and strawberries especially may be deficient in iron, resulting in poor growth and yellowing foliage. However, many gardeners do obtain reasonable crops from alkaline soils, even if the plants appear rather chlorotic. Ideally, they should be given an application of sequestered iron in spring on this type of site (see page 86).

The exceptions to the general site requirements are for blueberries and cranberries, which are called acid soil fruits because they need a pH as low as 4.0 or even 3.5. If your garden, like most gardens, is unable to offer these conditions, try growing them in large containers. You may not obtain a huge crop but they are satisfying to grow

**below** There is an obvious and important division of a fruit garden into the soft fruit that require protection from birds, and tree fruit that can be grown in the open.

### Planting

Bare-rooted plants typically available by mail order from specialist fruit suppliers and delivered in late autumn, must be planted promptly. Container-grown plants may be bought from garden centres at all times of the year, but they too will establish much better from autumn planting.

Use well rotted organic matter and a handful of bone meal in each planting hole and after planting, water in with a dilute solution of liquid fertilizer and top up with an organic mulch.

### Feeding and watering

Over the years, I have found that my soft fruit garden's needs are satisfied by two main fertilizers. The first is a balanced general fertilizer, applied once a year; I use fish, blood, and bone but Growmore is an artificial alternative. The second, which I apply every third year, or if fruiting has been poor, is a further dressing with potassium sulphate.

An adequate supply of moisture is very important for fruit quality. Even after mulching, you should water with a seeping hose, watering can or sprinkler if there is a dry spell when the fruit is beginning to swell.

### Weeding

Weed control is important when growing soft fruit, but not difficult. Close to the plants, annual weed growth, at least, will be kept in check by the moisture-retaining mulch. Between the rows, an organic matter mulch may also be laid to suppress annual weeds, if sufficient mulching material is available. Failing this, use a contact weedkiller or rely on regular hand weeding; hoeing will damage the shallow roots.

### Problems

A build-up of viruses will inevitably occur in soft fruit plants after a few years although gooseberries are usually free from them. Viruses reduce vigour and fruit production and, even though you should always start with virus-free stock, eelworms in the soil or aphids will transmit virus to your plants. There is no chemical control for virus, and affected stock should be replaced.

Powdery mildew and grey mould (*Botrytis*) are the main fungal diseases but they are rela-

tively easily controlled (page 98). The most important pests of soft fruit are aphids but a tar-oil winter wash will usually keep them in check (page 101).

### Propagation

Although it is possible to propagate soft fruit yourself by cuttings, layers or runners, I do not advise this. By the time that soft-fruit plants are in need of replacement, they will almost certainly be contaminated with virus and new, certified virus-free stock should be obtained from a reputable supplier.

### Training and pruning

In the individual plant entries, I have indicated if training or other support is needed and also indicated the optimum time for pruning. Details of both operations are described in the appropriate sections in the first part of the book (page 60).

### Harvesting and storing

Even though careful choice of varieties will extend the season, there's no denying that soft fruit do all ripen within a fairly short space of time. Fortunately, all types

**above** Modern fruit cages of lightweight aluminium construction are readily available but for robustness, you need wooden posts and wire netting.

**below** The best time to plant fruit is in late autumn when mail-order nurseries send out stock bare-rooted and carefully packed.

**above** Weed control is essential in the soft fruit garden and here both plastic sheet and organic matter are being used.

can be frozen, although strawberries give the least satisfactory results. Most of them can also be made into jams or other preserves.

## Bush Fruit
### Blackcurrant
### *Ribes nigrum*
### Grossulariaceae

This is an easy fruit to grow, as it is more tolerant than many soft fruit of heavier, wetter soils but the plants need a sheltered position and most varieties require considerable space. My main concern is that most modern varieties are barely sweet enough to eat without added sugar, although they do have an extremely high vitamin C content.

**Planting:** two-year-old bushes will establish better than one- or three-year-old plants. Plant before midwinter, and plant deeply so the soil just covers the basal fork where the lowest branches arise. After planting, cut back all the shoots to a point just above two buds from the base. This will encourage the essential branching at or just below soil level.

**Spacing:** 1.5-1.8m (5ft-5ft 9in) except for the variety 'Ben Sarek' which should be planted at 1-1.2 m (3-4ft).

**Care:** no support needed and cannot be grown as cordons; normal feeding and watering although they respond particularly well to additional nitrogen. Prune immediately after picking or in winter.

**Problems:** American mildew, aphids, capsid bug, gall mite, grey mould, leaf midge, reversion, rust, virus.

**Harvesting:** wait until all the fruit on each bush is ripe, pick the entire strigs and then strip them in the kitchen, or try shaking the bushes so fruit falls on to old sheets.

**Storing:** will keep fresh for a week in a refrigerator; good for jam, also bottles and freezes well.

**Varieties:** 'Wellington XXX', early to mid-season, big, spreading; 'Ben Sarek', mid-season, heavy cropping, small, compact; 'Ben Lomond', mid to late-season, upright, large fruit.

## Gooseberry
### *Ribes uva-crispa* var. *reclinatum*
### Grossulariaceae

The fruit is rather sour for most modern tastes and the thorns make for difficulty in picking, although training the plants as cordons makes picking and pruning much less hazardous. Gooseberries are slightly more shade tolerant than most soft fruit, but the dessert varieties will remain sour unless in full sun.

**Planting:** buy two or three-year-old bushes and plant in early winter. Even if growing in a row as cordons, dig individual planting holes.

**Spacing:** free-standing bushes 1.5-1.8m (5ft-5ft 9in); single cordons 30cm (12in), double cordons 60cm (24in) with 1.2m (4ft) between rows.

**Care:** no support for bushes; cordons need a system of posts and wires for support similar to raspberries but with three wires spaced at 60cm (2ft), 90cm (2ft 11in) and 1.2m (4ft) apart. Normal feeding and watering, although they are responsive to additional potash. Prune soon after midsummer and again in early winter.

**Problems:** American mildew, aphids, capsid bug, grey mould, leaf spot, magpie moth, rust, sawflies.

**Harvesting:** pick fruit as it ripens, when it detaches easily from the stalk.

**Storing:** will keep fresh for around three weeks in a refrigerator, also freezes well.

**Varieties:** 'Careless', early to mid-season, spreading; 'Invicta', early to mid-season, upright, mildew resistant; 'Lord Derby', late, dark red sweet fruit, big, spreading.

## Redcurrant and Whitecurrant
### *Ribes rubrum* Grossulariaceae

These are easy and rewarding plants that deserve to be more widely grown. Both have a flavour similar to each other, but different from that of blackcurrants. They are very heavy cropping, so can be successful even in the smallest fruit garden.

**Planting:** as for gooseberries.
**Spacing:** as for gooseberries.
**Care:** as for gooseberries.
**Problems:** gooseberry sawfly, leaf spot, red currant blister aphid.

**below** Immediately after planting, blackcurrants should be cut back to just above soil level.

**Harvesting:** pick the fruit on the strig and separate them later if needed.

**Storing:** can be stored fresh for several days in refrigerator, frozen, made into jelly or juice.

**Varieties: Red:** 'Red Lake'; **White:** 'Versailles Blanche'.

## Cane Fruit

### Blackberry *Rubus fruticosus* Rosaceae

Most gardeners are familiar with the wild bramble and the exquisite taste of its fruit, but are understandably wary of the tangled invasion that would result if it were to be introduced into a well ordered fruit garden. There are more manageable varieties, however, and although their flexible canes may be more fiddling to train than the stiff ones of raspberries, the fruit is a passable imitation of that of their wild relative. They have some shade tolerance but are seldom successful on thin, chalky soil or in frost pockets.

**Planting:** plant in early winter with no more than 8cm (3¼in) of soil covering the roots. After planting, cut the canes back to just above a bud about 25cm (10in) above soil level.

**Spacing:** usually a single plant is sufficient. Less vigorous varieties should be 2.5m (8ft) apart with 2m (6½ft) between rows. More vigorous types need 3.5-4.5m (11ft-14¾ft) apart and 2.5m (8ft) between rows. The recent variety 'Loch Ness' is smaller and more manageable and can be planted at 1m (3ft) each way.

**Care:** needs careful support and training with four wires spaced 30cm (12in) apart, with the lowest 90cm (3ft) above soil level. Train by the fan system on either single or alternate bays. Prune immediately after fruiting. Feeding and watering is similar to that of raspberries.

**Problems:** cane spot, capsid bug, crown gall, grey mould, leaf hopper, raspberry beetle, rust.

**Harvesting:** as soon as the fruit attain full colour. The fruit doesn't separate from the stalks or plugs and should be picked with them; the plugs are soft and don't detract from the flavour and disintegrate when the fruit are cooked.

**Storing:** fresh in a refrigerator for about a week or freeze.

**Varieties:** 'Loch Ness', early to mid-season, short upright growth, thornless; 'Ashton Cross', mid-season, vigorous, probably the best flavoured.

### Hybrid berries

Numerous hybrids, most with elongated red fruit have been found or bred between blackberries, raspberries and other *Rubus* species. Many are little more than curiosities but a few have outstanding flavour and are certainly worth growing. All of the following are cultivated in the same way as blackberries, but crop earlier unless otherwise stated:

### Boysenberry

Derived from 'Himalayan Giant' blackberry. Large, purple fruit, like an elongated raspberry. Early, vigorous, thorny, drought tolerant and a good plant for light, free-draining soils where other cane fruits fail. A thornless variety also exists.

### Hildaberry

Tayberry and boysenberry hybrid. Very large, red fruit. Very early, vigorous, thorny.

### Japanese Wineberry

A true species, *Rubus phoenicolasius*. Small, very pretty bright orange fruit. Early, fairly vigorous, very attractive with masses of soft prickles.

### King's Acre Berry

Raspberry and blackberry hybrid. Medium, very dark red to black fruit, flavour good. Early, fairly vigorous, thorny.

### Loganberry

Raspberry and blackberry hybrid. Large, dark red fruit, flavour very good. Early, fairly vigorous, the selection 'LY 59' is thorny but there is a thornless variant called 'LY 654'.

### Marionberry

Possibly a raspberry and blackberry hybrid or a distinct species. Huge, dark red to black fruit. Early to mid-season, very vigorous, very thorny.

**above** Gloves are seldom essential in the garden but gooseberry pruning is one of those occasions.

### Phenomenal berry

Hybrid between two American raspberries. Large, dark red fruit.

### Silvanberry

Hybrid involving boysenberry, youngberry, loganberry and marionberry. Large, dark red fruit. Early to mid-season, very vigorous, thorny, claimed to be suitable for exposed, windy positions.

### Sunberry

Raspberry and blackberry hybrid. Medium, dark red fruit. Early to mid-season, very vigorous, thorny.

### Tayberry

Raspberry and blackberry hybrid. Large, dark red fruit, generally reckoned the best of the raspberry-blackberry hybrids. Early, moderately vigorous, thorny, not very hardy and less good for exposed gardens; always choose the certified virus-free 'Medana' strain.

### Tummelberry

Hybrid between two tayberries. Large, dark red fruit, flavour moderate. Early, but slightly later than tayberry, moderately vigorous, thorny, hardier than tayberry so better for more exposed gardens.

### Veitchberry

Raspberry and blackberry hybrid. Large, dark red fruit. Mid-season, moderately vigorous, thorny.

### Youngberry

Loganberry and dewberry (*Rubus caesius*) hybrid. Large, dark red-purple fruit. Early to mid-season, moderately vigorous, thorny but there is a thornless variety.

### Raspberry *Rubus idaeus* Rosaceae

Grown well, raspberries offer a large crop from a small area, pruning is simple and, by careful choice of varieties, fresh fruit can be picked from summer into the early autumn. They will benefit from having plenty of organic matter added to the soil as the shallow roots are prone to drying out. Light shade can be tolerated, as can spring frost, but they must have shelter from strong wind.

**Planting:** buy bare-rooted stock and plant in early winter. As raspberries are usually grown in rows, take out a trench at least 45cm (18in) deep and plant the canes shallowly with the upper part of the roots 5cm (2in) deep on top of the carefully firmed contents of the trench. Water well, mulch and cut back the canes to just above a bud about 25cm (10in) above soil level.

**Spacing:** 70cm (27in) if you follow the Scottish stool training system. For most varieties, the distance between rows is 1.2-1.5m (4-5ft) but more vigorous types are better 1.8m (5ft 9in) apart.

**Care:** support essential except for a few short-caned black- and purple-fruited varieties, and possibly autumn-fruiting varieties in sheltered areas. Horizontal wires trained between vertical posts offer the easiest method and the wires should be 60cm (24in) and 1.2m (4ft) above soil level, with an additional one at 1.5m (5ft) for tall varieties. Prune summer-fruiting varieties immediately after fruiting; autumn- fruiting (primocane) varieties in late winter. Hoe or pull off unwanted suckers.

**Problems:** cane blight, cane midge, cane and leaf spot, capsid bug, caterpillars, grey mould, iron deficiency, leaf hopper, powdery mildew, raspberry aphids, raspberry moth, rust, sawflies, spur blight, virus, wilt.

**Harvesting:** pick as soon as the fruit parts easily from the core.

**below** After fruiting, the old canes of blackberries and related fruits should be cut back to soil level.

**Storing:** will remain fresh in refrigerator for a few days; freezes well and can be made into jam.

**Varieties:** 'Glen Moy', early, no prickles; 'Glen Prosen', mid-season; 'Malling Admiral', late; 'Autumn Bliss', autumn, very vigorous, the only good autumn variety.

### Acid-soil Fruit
### Blueberry *Vaccinium corymbosum*
### Ericaceae

If you have room and patience for blueberries you will be rewarded with a rather special-tasting fruit that combines sweetness and acidity. A strongly acidic soil is needed, or containers of ericaceous compost at least 45cm (18in) deep and wide. They also require a very sunny position with shelter from cold winds and late frosts but don't need protection from birds.

**Planting:** buy two-year-old, container-grown plants and plant in winter, but no deeper than the soil mark on the stem.

**Spacing:** 1.2-1.5m (4-5ft) between plants, 1.5-1.8m (5ft-5ft 9in) between rows.

**Care:** no support or training is needed, mulch with coniferous sawdust to a depth of 15cm (6in). Very light feeding in early spring but keep the soil moist during dry spells. The roots resent disturbance, so hand weed only. Prune as for blackcurrants.

**Problems:** leaf yellowing, canker, grey mould.

**Harvesting:** place a hand under each cluster of berries and roll them in the palm. They are slow to start fruiting, taking around six years, but will crop for 20 years or more.

**Storing:** will keep fresh for three weeks in a refrigerator, also freezes well.

**Varieties:** 'Bluetta', early; 'Blue Crop', early to mid-season.

### Cranberry *Vaccinium macrocarpon*
### Ericaceae

This is a pretty little plant when in fruit, its wiry stems creeping over the soil and bearing jewel-like berries. The soil must be very acidic, as low as pH 3.5, organic, wet but free-draining.

**Planting:** buy container-grown plants and don't let them dry out before planting. Plant in winter, no deeper than the soil mark on the stem. Spread a 2.5cm (1in) layer of lime-free sand over the bed after planting.

**left** Blackberries and similar fruit plants with flexible canes are most readily trained in fan pattern.

**below** Raspberries produce their new shoots as suckers and these must be thinned out carefully in order to obtain the best from the plants.

above **above** Blueberries aren't often grown in gardens and they have the unusual requirement of a deep, acidic mulch of sawdust.

**below** Cape gooseberries are readily grown as annuals in growing bags or other containers in a greenhouse.

**Spacing:** 30cm (1ft).
**Care:** No feeding is normally necessary but a light dressing with nitrogen should be given if growth the previous season has been poor. No training and pruning except for trimming aerial shoots in spring.
**Problem:** aphids.
**Harvesting:** fiddly to pick so wait until most of the fruit is ripe before harvesting all together.
**Storing:** will keep for up to two months in a refrigerator, also good frozen or as jelly or juice.
**Varieties:** 'CN'; 'Hamilton'.

### Herbaceous Fruit
### Cape gooseberry *Physalis peruviana* Solanaceae

This is an unusual choice of fruit, but one I have grown successfully many times. It makes a useful addition to the limited number of half-hardy fruit crops, being easy to grow annually from seed or maintain as a greenhouse perennial. The small orange cherry fruits are encased in papery calyx like those of its ornamental relative, the Chinese lantern, *P. alkekengi*.

**Sowing:** start six weeks before you intend to plant out, although if growing in a greenhouse with a minimum temperature of 7°C (45°F), you can plant out four to six weeks earlier. Sow two seeds to each 9cm (3½in) pot of soil-based compost and pull out the weaker seedling if both germinate.
**Planting:** when growing outdoors, prepare a well manured bed and rake in a general fertilizer one week before planting, then plant out after the last frost, putting cloches over the young plants at first. In the greenhouse, plant in growing bags or 20cm (8in) diameter pots of John Innes No 2 Potting Compost.
**Spacing:** 45cm (1½ft).
**Care:** insert a stout cane close to each plant and tie-in as the plant grows. Pinch out growing tips when the plants reach 45cm (1½ft); no need to remove side shoots. Keep compost or soil moist and apply a tomato

feed weekly after the first fruit has set.
**Problems:** aphids, whitefly.
**Harvesting:** pick when the calyx becomes very papery and the fruit inside is a rich colour.
**Storing:** will keep for several weeks and may be eaten fresh by peeling back the calyx, or made into jam.
**Varieties:** no named varieties

### Strawberry *Fragaria* x *ananassa* Rosaceae

This remains a great favourite even though commercially grown fruit has little taste. The varieties with the finest flavour tend to crop for only a short time, although the most recent developments have been with 'everlasting' and annual 'day-neutral' varieties that crop for longer. Strawberries are best treated like vegetables, for their cultivation and habit is quite different from that of other soft fruit.

They are not long-term plants; three or four years is the effective productive life of many varieties and some are better grown as biennials or annuals. They also take up a considerable area, with 25-30m$^2$ (80-100ft$^2$) a typical bed; remember that, as with vegetables, you must rotate the plot so you will need to devote two or three times this area to strawberries at some time. The soil should be prepared as for a vegetable crop but protection from birds is essential and best provided by wire netting covers or conventional cloches, which have the added advantage of encouraging earlier ripening. Strawberries can be grown in containers in John Innes No.2 Potting Compost, but it is a fiddly task and yields are low.

**Planting:** start with certified virus-free plants. Pot-grown plants in bio-degradable pots establish best when planted from midsummer to autumn. Bare-rooted runners are cheaper and freshly lifted plants should be planted from late autumn to early spring, cold-stored ones in spring or late summer.
**Spacing:** 30-45cm (1-1½ft) between plants, 70-90cm (2¼-3ft) between rows.
**Care:** feed in early spring with potash. As the fruit starts to swell, water plants well then tuck straw between the soil and fruit to keep the fruit clean (or lay down black plastic sheeting before planting). Cut off the runners as they grow. Cut off old foliage after harvesting the fruit and clear away the straw.

**Problems:** aphids, birds, grey mould, iron deficiency, leaf spot, powdery mildew, red spider mite, slugs, strawberry beetle, strawberry mite, virus, weevil.

**Harvesting:** pick complete with the calyx when uniformly red.

**Storing:** best eaten fresh within a few hours of picking, or used for jam. Freezing alters shape, texture and flavour so frozen fruit is best used for cooking.

**Varieties:** 'Aromel', autumn, easily the best 'perpetual' strawberry; 'Cambridge Favourite', mid-season, the best all-round variety; 'Pegasus', late.

## Tree Fruit
### Site and soil

Most gardens can grow some tree fruit, apples and damsons being the most suitable for cold, exposed areas. With the exception of figs, the best crops will be obtained from fertile loam with a pH around 6.5, but adding organic matter, mulching, watering and feeding fruit trees will help on less than ideal soils. It is unwise to plant new fruit trees in gardens where old trees have canker or where honey fungus is present. When planting fruit trees in grass, an area about 1m (3ft) in diameter around the trunk should be kept clear of weeds and grass.

### Spacing

The number of fruit trees you can accommodate in a given space depends, to some extent, on the rootstock on which they are grafted; apple trees offer the widest choice. Do be aware, however, that the more dwarfing the rootstock, the better must be the growing conditions and aftercare. Growth can also be restricted by training trees as cordons or fans. With apples, another option is to buy a so-called family tree, where several different varieties have been grafted on to the same roots. This neatly circumvents another complication, for apples and pears are not self-fertile, i.e. another, compatible variety (or, in some cases, two additional varieties) are needed in order for pollination and fruit-set to occur.

### Problems

Some varieties are inherently prone to biennial bearing, producing a worthwhile crop only every alternate year, and trees under stress can sometimes switch to a biennial state. The

process may sometimes be reversed by careful feeding, watering and light pruning.

Fruit trees are subject to many pests and diseases, but once mature, few control measures are realistic. A tar-oil winter spray and the use of biological control to limit codling moth are among the few routine measures that I consider worthwhile. Removing and destroying diseased fruit will have some impact on limiting damage in the following year.

### Training and pruning

Early training then, in later years, routine pruning is important with most types of tree fruit. Details are given on page 60.

## Apple *Malus* spp. and hybrids
### Rosaceae

Garden apple trees fall roughly into three main types: the crab, the dessert or eating apple, and the more acid culinary apple or cooker (a fourth group, the very acid cider apple, is rarely grown in gardens). Some varieties are described as dual purpose and are useful in limited space, for they cook well but are not so acidic that they cannot be eaten fresh. Apples can be trained in a number of ways, generally

**above** Don't under-estimate the area needed to grow a productive bed of strawberries; remember that they will need to be rotated every few years.

**above** A double row of apples trained into a tunnel is both attractive and an efficient way of having many varieties in a small area.

**below** The range in size of apple trees obtainable by choice of rootstocks is remarkable. These are mature trees of the same variety; that on the left is grafted on M.106, that on the right on M.27.

produce a good or even prolific crop with the minimum of attention, are available on a good range of rootstocks and are also the most versatile of all tree fruit.

**Planting:** in late autumn.
**Spacing:** depends on rootstock (see chart) and training method.
**Care:** stake young trees and those on dwarfing rootstocks. Feed and mulch in early spring. Prune cordons and espaliers in summer ,and free-standing trees in winter; old trees should only have damaged branches removed.
**Problems:** aphids, bitter pit, codling moth, canker, fruit rot, honey fungus, powdery mildew, scab, winter moth, woolly aphids.
**Harvesting:** when the fruit parts readily from the branch if lifted and twisted; fruit colour as a sign of ripeness can be misleading.
**Storing:** fresh in cool, dry room with good air circulation. Put fruit in slatted boxes or pack in clean, plastic bags with ventilation holes. Late-maturing varieties can be left on the tree; generally the later maturing the variety, the better it keeps in store.
**Varieties:** check when buying that you have varieties that will pollinate each other. Generally, those that flower at the same time will be suitable.
**Dessert varieties (in order of maturing):** 'Beauty of Bath'; 'Discovery'; 'Redsleeves'; 'Fortune'; 'James Grieve', dual purpose;

'Greensleeves'; 'Ellison's Orange'; 'Sunset'; 'Blenheim Orange', dual purpose; 'Jupiter', triploid, requiring two other pollinators; 'Spartan'; 'Worcester Pearmain'; 'Crispin', triploid, requiring two other pollinators; 'Idared'; 'Tydeman's Late Orange'; 'Kent'; 'Golden Delicious'.
**Cooking varieties:** 'Bramley's Seedling', triploid, requiring two other pollinators; 'Howgate Wonder'.

### Pear *Pyrus communis* Rosaceae

Pears are more difficult to grow than apples, being slower to mature and less hardy. Your best chance of success is to grow a cordon or espalier against a warm wall. There is little choice of rootstock and most are grafted on to the moderately growth restricting 'Quince C'.

### Effects of growth restricting apple rootstocks

| Rootstock | M.27 | M.9 | M.26 | M.106 | M.111 |
|---|---|---|---|---|---|
| Height of free-standing tree after 10 years (m) | 1.5 | 2 | 2.5 | 3-4 | 5 |

| Spacing (m) | Free-standing | Cordon | Espalier |
|---|---|---|---|
| | 1.5 | 0.75 | N/A |
| | 3 | 0.75 | 3 |
| | 3.5 | 1 | 3.5 |
| | 4.5 | 1 | 4 |
| | 6 | N/A | 5 |

**Planting:** in late autumn.
**Spacing:** cordons 1m (3ft) between plants, espaliers 4m (13ft), free-standing trees 4.5m (14ft 8in).
**Care:** feed and mulch in early spring. Prune cordons or espaliers in summer and winter, free-standing trees in winter.
**Problems:** aphids, canker, fireblight, fruit rots, leaf blister mite, pear midge, powdery mildew, scab, winter moth.
**Harvesting:** pick slightly under-ripe when the fruit parts readily from the branch.
**Storing:** fresh, but arrange them individually, inspect regularly and remove them as they ripen. Hard, cooking varieties can be left on the tree until needed.
**Varieties:** 'Conference', 'Beurre Hardy', 'Williams Bon Chrétien', 'Doyenné du Comice'.

## Quince *Cydonia oblonga* Rosaceae

Quince make attractive, self-fertile trees around 3m (10ft) or more tall but are slow in starting to fruit. The blossom is especially beautiful and the large fruits are aromatic but too acidic to be eaten fresh, so are used for making jelly or pies. The trees require a sunny, sheltered site and, in cold areas, they need the protection of a warm wall. Soil should be moist and preferably slightly acidic.

**Planting:** bare-rooted two to four-year-old plants in autumn or winter.
**Spacing:** 4-4.5m (13ft-14¾ft).
**Care:** young plants benefit from watering and mulching, established plants need little attention but remove suckers if they appear. Prune young quinces as you would apple trees; mature plants require only the removal of dead or crossing branches in winter.
**Problem:** leaf spot.
**Harvesting:** pick in late autumn when skins have turned from green to gold; or pick before first frosts when green; they turn yellow when stored.
**Storing:** store in cool, dark place with good air circulation but do not wrap or store in plastic bags because the flesh will discolour. Store away from other fruits as they have a strong aroma. Use in cooking or for jam.
**Varieties:** 'Vranja'

## Medlar *Mespilus germanica* Rosaceae

An attractive, self-fertile tree, offering spring blossom and red/gold autumn foliage colours, in addition to the fruit which look like large rose hips. A sunny, sheltered site is ideal although some shade is tolerated and they are hardier than quinces. Moist garden soil is suitable unless very alkaline or water-logged. Trees are usually grafted on to 'Quince A' rootstock.

**Planting:** late autumn to winter.
**Spacing:** 4.5m (14ft 8in) for bushes, 8m (25ft) for half-standards.
**Care:** cultivation is as for apple but little pruning other than initial shaping is needed.
**Problems:** caterpillars, leaf spot.
**Harvesting:** for the best-flavoured fruit, leave on the tree for as long as possible, preferably until late autumn. Pick when the stalk parts easily from the tree.
**Storing:** fruit must be stored to soften them

after picking by a method called bletting. Dip the stalks in strong salt solution to prevent rotting and store, stalks upwards, on slatted trays. Use when flesh is soft and brown, to make jelly.
**Variety:** 'Nottingham'.

## Plum, Gage *Prunus domestica*
## Damson *Prunus insititia*
## Rosaceae

If you have the space and a favourable site, a free-standing plum tree will crop with very little pruning. For the best fruit, the trees require a warm position; fan-training against a warm wall works well but requires more attention. Plums suffer in colder areas, as their blossom opens early and is prone to late frost damage. Most soils are suitable, except very dry or very water-logged sites. Most of the popular plum varieties are self-fertile but there is no true dwarfing rootstock.

Gages are small, usually green or yellow types of plum, often considered to be the finest of dessert plums but needing more favourable growing conditions. Damsons are small plums and are hardier, but the fruit is astringent and should be cooked with plenty of sugar.

**above** Pears are ideally grown as espaliers against a wall where they will benefit from the reflected warmth.

**below** Rather like quinces, medlars are fruit trees with a long history of cultivation and a recent history of being ignored.

**Planting:** in late autumn.

**Spacing:** 5m (16ft) for tree or fan on 'St Julien A' rootstock, 3m (10ft) for tree or fan on 'Pixy' rootstock.

**Care:** feed and mulch young plants in early spring. Prune fan-trained plants in spring, and pinch back side-shoots in summer. Established plum trees need little pruning, but damaged growth should be cut out in spring rather than winter. Suckers should be pulled out promptly.

**Problems:** aphids, brown rot, bacterial canker, honey fungus, plum fruit moth, rust, silver leaf disease.

**Harvesting:** pick slightly before the fruit is ripe to avoid losing the crop to birds, wasps or brown rot.

**Storing:** not satisfactory fresh but may be frozen if the stones are removed or made into jam, bottled or stewed.

**Varieties:** (all self-fertile) **Plums:** 'Victoria', mid-season, easily the best all-round variety for dessert and culinary use; 'Marjorie's Seedling', late, a very useful, heavy-cropping, all-round variety to follow on from 'Victoria'; **Gage:** 'Oulin's Golden Gage', early, the best of the widely available dessert gages. **Damson:** 'Merryweather'.

**below** The scourge of plum trees is silver leaf disease, encouraged by pruning in autumn instead of spring.

## Peach and Nectarine
### *Prunus persica*
### Rosaceae

Often thought of as warm-climate crops, they are fairly hardy, the only limiting factor being leaf curl disease. They will crop well in cool climates with shelter, but problems will arise on sites with cold springs. Even in mild areas, I suggest growing them fan-trained against a wall. The nectarine is a smooth-skinned variety of peach and its requirements are identical. The ideal soil is moist and slightly acidic, although it must not be deficient in calcium.

**Planting:** in late autumn.

**Spacing:** 4m (13ft) for fan-trained plants on 'St Julien A' rootstock.

**Care:** feed and mulch in early spring. Hand-pollinate blossom in spring. Prune established fan-trained plants in spring, pinch back side-shoots in early summer. When the fruit starts to colour, peg back the foliage to expose it to the sun.

**Problems:** aphids, bacterial canker, brown rot, fruit rots, peach leaf curl, silver leaf.

**Harvesting:** gently feel the fruit for signs of softness close to the stalk. Handle gently to prevent bruising.

**Storing:** for short periods only in a refrigerator but may be bottled after the stones are removed.

**Varieties:** Peach: 'Peregrine'; 'Rochester'. **Nectarine:** 'Lord Napier'.

## Apricot *Prunus armeniaca*
### Rosaceae

Contrary to popular belief, apricots are hardier than peaches although earlier in blossoming, so they may need protection in early spring. They may be grown free-standing but generally are best fan-trained against a warm, sunny, sheltered wall.

**Planting:** in late autumn.

**Spacing:** 4m (13ft) for fan-trained plants on 'St Julien A' rootstock.

**Care:** feed and mulch in early spring. Check pH of acidic soils and, if necessary, add lime in autumn to raise to pH 6.5. Provide removable screen of fleece or plastic sheets to place in front of plants when blossom appears. Hand-pollinate in spring. Prune in spring and summer.

**Problems:** as for peaches and nectarines.
**Harvesting:** as for peaches
**Storing:** as for peaches.
**Variety:** 'Moorpark'.

## Sweet cherry *Prunus avium* Rosaceae

For fresh, dessert cherries, you need a sweet cherry. Unfortunately, there is only one self-fertile variety, they are very frustrating to grow, romping away to form a large tree, and birds take all the fruit. I recommend fan-training against a warm wall to make netting easier or growing the self-fertile variety in a large fruit cage. There is one moderately growth-restricting rootstock in 'Colt', others like 'Inmil' that showed promise have proved unsatisfactory.

**Planting:** in late autumn.
**Spacing:** 5m (6ft) if fan-trained on the rootstock 'Colt'.
**Care:** feed and mulch in early spring. Check pH of acidic soil and lime in autumn, if necessary, to raise the pH to 6.5. Use netting as fruit starts to ripen. Prune in spring and summer, pull away suckers as they arise.
**Problems:** aphids, bacterial canker, birds, silver leaf.
**Harvesting:** when fully coloured, cut the stalks with scissors.
**Storing:** eat fresh.
**Variety:** 'Stella' (self-fertile).

## Bitter cherry *Prunus cerasus* Rosaceae

This is also known as the Morello, sour or acid cherry, names that indicate it is suitable only for cooking. It is easier to grow than the sweet cherry, producing a smaller tree, and most varieties are self-fertile but, again, I recommend fan-training and they are successful even against a cool, shady wall.

**Planting:** in late autumn.
**Spacing:** 4m (13ft) if fan-trained on the rootstock 'Colt'.
**Care:** as for sweet cherries, but acid cherries are pruned on a renewal system to encourage the production of one-year-old wood which bears the fruit.
**Problems:** as for sweet cherries.
**Harvesting:** as for sweet cherries.
**Storing:** freeze if not used fresh for cooking.
**Variety:** 'Morello' (self-fertile).

## Mulberry *Morus nigra* Moraceae

The black mulberry is a wonderful-looking tree with superb-tasting fruit. It can reach a height of 6-10m (20-33ft), and is usually grown as a half-standard or standard. Prune simply to establish a strong and solid framework, and only prune in winter since it can bleed sap rapidly. A moist, slightly acid soil is preferred. Mulberries are grown on their own roots and are self-fertile.

**Planting:** late autumn to winter except in cold areas when spring planting is safer.
**Spacing:** 8-10m (25-33ft)
**Care:** similar to apples but only needs training to produce a strong framework; little or no maintenance pruning is required.
**Problems:** generally trouble-free although a canker disease may be seen occasionally.
**Harvesting:** when fully ripe in late summer.
**Storing:** freeze.
**Varieties:** normally sold as un-named varieties.

**above** Early blossoming trees such as peaches will always benefit from some temporary frost protection.

**below** Cherries are most simply grown fan-trained against a wall.

above The cropping of nut trees is encouraged by partially breaking the side-shoots in summer.

below These fig fruits will drop from the plant in late autumn or winter. The embryo fruits that will form the next year's crop are barely visible at the shoot tips.

### Cobnut *Corylus avellana* Filbert *Corylus maxima* Betulaceae

The cultivated cobnut is a relative of the wild hazel-nut; the filbert, with its shaggy husk, is a distinct European species. Both are suitable for the wilder, wooded garden as they need considerable room to grow, and conditions of light shade and shelter. Many are self-fertile, but as the male and female flowers don't always open simultaneously, it makes sense to grow a mixture of varieties. Expect to harvest nuts after three or four years.

**Planting:** in late autumn.
**Spacing:** 5m (16ft).
**Care:** feed and mulch in early spring. Train as for a free-standing apple tree then, in late summer, use your hands to break all strong side-shoots growing from the main branches and leave them hanging. Cut the broken shoots back to 5-8cm (2-3¼in) in late winter or early spring.
**Problems:** powdery mildew, squirrels, nut weevil.
**Harvesting:** when the husks start to turn pale.
**Storing:** dry before storing.
**Varieties:** Cobnut: 'Nottingham Cob'; Filbert: 'Kentish Cob'.

### Walnut *Juglans regia* Juglandaceae

Although only suitable for large gardens, I wish that more gardeners would take a long-term perspective and plant a walnut tree.

**Planting:** late autumn.
**Spacing:** 5m (16ft), plant a small copse of trees to ensure pollination.
**Care:** feed and mulch in early spring for the first few years. Regularly pinch back shoot tips to about six leaves, avoiding the shoots bearing male flowers; this will help induce fruiting earlier than the usual 10-15 years. Do not attempt to prune mature trees.
**Problems:** leaf blight, leaf spot, nut rot.
**Harvesting:** for pickling, collect in summer while shells are still soft. For eating fresh, wait until nuts drop.
**Storing:** clean, dry gently and store.

**Varieties:** there are named varieties of walnut, but trees hardly ever seem to be named when they are offered for sale. It is more important that you buy from an experienced fruit nursery and obtain grafted plants, with the scion taken from a parent tree known to be freely fruiting.

### Fig *Ficus carica* Moraceae

The plants are self-fertile and hardy, but in cool climates they will only reliably produce edible fruit if fan-trained against a warm, sheltered wall. They differ from other fruit trees in two respects: they must have poor soil, and the small embryo fruits formed towards the end of one season are those that mature and ripen the following year. The best way to grow them is in a mixture of soil and limy rubble with the roots confined by putting 60cm (2ft)concrete slabs around the planting hole. Figs can also be grown in containers but will need plenty of water in summer and should be brought into a frost-free greenhouse overwinter.

**Planting:** in spring.
**Spacing:** one fan-trained plant on a wall at least 3m (10ft) wide and 2m (6½ft) high.
**Care:** mulch well, no feeding required except in containers. Water well as fruit swells. Prune wall-trained plants in spring.
**Problem:** coral spot.
**Harvesting:** wait until fruit hangs down and is soft with the skin just starting to split.
**Storing:** best eaten fresh.
**Variety:** 'Brown Turkey'.

### Climbing Fruit
### Grapevine *Vitis vinifera* Vitaceae

Although fruiting outdoor vines are found in gardens, for a reliable crop in cool climates, I would always cultivate them in an unheated greenhouse.

**Planting:** in early spring or late autumn. Plant just outside the greenhouse then pass the main shoot in through a hole close to the base of the greenhouse wall. Prepare the planting position with liberal amounts of compost, broken bricks to improve drainage and 2.5-3kg (5-5½lbs) of John Innes Base fertilizer.
**Spacing:** 2m (6½ft) but one plant is enough.
**Care:** feed with general fertilizer in spring and mulch well. Water copiously when fruit is

swelling and give a liquid high potash feed every two weeks in summer. Train carefully; prune established plants in winter and spring.

**Problems:** downy mildew, grey mould, powdery mildew, red spider mite, scale insects.

**Harvesting:** as the fruits change colour, taste to check for sweetness, then cut off in bunches with scissors.

**Storing:** for short periods at room temperature or in a refrigerator.

**Varieties:** 'Black Hamburgh'; 'Siegerrebe'.

### Kiwi fruit *Actinidia deliciosa* Actinidiaceae

Once known as the Chinese gooseberry, this fruit has been renamed and is now widely available in supermarkets; although the flavour is bland, it has a high vitamin C content. It is hardier than the grapevine, which is fortunate as it is too vigorous for most greenhouses, and should be grown against a tall, warm wall.

**Planting:** mid-spring or early autumn. Plant 20-25cm (8-10in) away from a wall and add well rotted organic matter if the soil is poor.

**Spacing:** 6m (20ft), female and male plants are often sold together in the same container for good pollination and should be treated as one plant for planting and spacing purposes, but trained in opposite directions.

**Care:** feed and mulch in early spring. Water

well as fruit starts to swell. Prune as for a grapevine.

**Problems:** aphids, red spider mite.

**Harvesting:** pick as the fruit attains full colour and feels slightly soft to the touch.

**Storing:** for several weeks in refrigerator.

**Varieties:** 'Hayward', female; 'Tomuri', male.

**above** In order to obtain adequate water and nutrients, a grapevine should be rooted outside the greenhouse and the main shoot passed in through a hole.

**left** Kiwi fruits are very vigorous plants and you will need a male and female in order to obtain a crop.

# The Vegetable Garden

Vegetables are a diverse collection of plants, mostly annuals or biennials, grown for their edible parts. Almost by definition, they are usually eaten cooked, although a group, commonly distinguished as salad crops, is eaten raw. The name vegetable, although implying some vegetative (non-flowering) part of the plant, is a loose term and many of the crops that are eaten as vegetables (peas, beans, tomatoes, egg plants, peppers and the many members of the cucumber family, for instance) are botanically fruits while some, such as cauliflower and globe artichoke, are immature flowerheads. There are relatively few perennial vegetable crops; the most important are asparagus and rhubarb (which, ironically, is sometimes considered a fruit, although here it is a true vegetative part, the stem, that is eaten). A large group of unrelated crops – turnips, onions, potatoes and Jerusalem artichokes among them – are grown for their edible roots or other underground parts.

**above** An open and sunny position will always give the best results and ensure that a vegetable plot is both productive and attractive.

## Site and soil

The ideal position for vegetables is in an open spot that attracts maximum sunlight, but is sheltered from the most severe weather. Frost-pockets should be avoided and, in exposed areas, some shelter in the form of a hedge or windbreak is advantageous. Few gardens have the deep, rich, yet free-draining soils described as prerequisites for vegetable growing in old gardening books. But fortunately almost all soil types can be improved by good cultivation and the addition of bulky organic matter, especially animal manure or well-made garden compost. If your soil is shallow, root-crop growing will be especially difficult but raised beds contained with boards and filled with well manured soil will allow most types to be grown successfully. A pH of around 6.5 (slightly acidic) is ideal. Soils that are more acidic than this can be improved by the addition of garden lime.

## Space required

A standard allotment garden, of roughly 250m² (300 sq yds) was once regarded as the minimum that could keep an average family self-sufficient in vegetables. But few gardeners today either can or would wish to devote this amount of space to vegetable growing. If you buy, rather than grow, bulky crops such as potatoes (especially main crop potatoes) and cabbages, and concentrate instead on high-value and high-yielding crops, a plot of roughly 100m² (120sq yds) should make a significant contribution to your home's vegetable requirements. Plots smaller than this are still valuable, but here it is advisable to concentrate on those vegetables and salad crops that really are best when harvested fresh.

## Sowing and planting

Almost all vegetables may be sown directly into the position where they are to grow, using the technique described on page 73 for hardy or half-hardy annuals. Early in the season, or on cold wet soils or in exposed areas, there are distinct advantages in sowing hardy vegetables under protection (in a greenhouse or cold frame) into 8cm (3½in) pots and transplanting the young plants four or six weeks later. With half-hardy vegetables such as runner beans, sweet corn and courgettes, for instance, you can gain many precious weeks by starting the seed in warmth. A few vegetables, most notably root crops like carrots, parsnips and beetroot, can't be successfully transplanted but a comparable advantage may be gained by covering the newly-sown seeds with cloches.

## Rotation

The theory of crop rotation, whereby related plants are grown together but on a different part of the vegetable plot each year over a three year cycle (right), is based on sound scientific principles. It is designed to ensure that the soil's nutrient reserves are used to the full and to help prevent serious pest or disease problems building up in the soil. But the principle was designed for commercial practice; I have reservations about the usefulness of such a system on a small home garden plot. Moreover, many gardeners don't want to devote equal areas to peas and beans, root crops or brassicas and may prefer to grow more of the crops such as lettuce, spinach and courgettes that fall outside the conventional rotation groups. My advice is to use a rotation scheme in so far as it fits in with other constraints, but not to consider it a Holy Grail.

## Problems

Like all plants, vegetables suffer from pests and diseases. Most are minor nuisances, however, and their effects merely cosmetic. Many problems can be avoided by a combination of garden hygiene, healthy seed stock and non-chemical preventive measures. For example, garden mesh will protect many crops from airborne pests. Among the problems that can cause significant loss of yield are potato blight, cabbage root fly, fruit rots and carrot fly, while white rot of onions, club-root of brassicas and some nematodes are particularly insidious by virtue of their long persistence in the soil.

## Feeding and watering

Without feeding, most crops will be disappointingly small. Each vegetable has different requirements and, for the sake of simplicity, I have divided them very roughly into three groups: those requiring low, medium and high levels of a general-purpose fertilizer. These equate approximately as follows:

## Growmore or Fish, blood and bone

**Low**      <130g2/m (<4oz/sq yd)
**Medium**    130-275g/m2 (4-8oz/sq yd]
**High**     >275g/m² (>8oz/sq yd]

## Crop Rotation

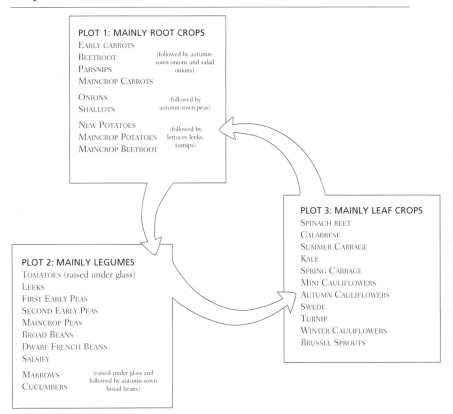

PLOT 1: MAINLY ROOT CROPS
EARLY CARROTS
BEETROOT    (followed by autumn-sown onions and salad onions)
PARSNIPS
MAINCROP CARROTS

ONIONS    (followed by autumn-sown peas)
SHALLOTS

NEW POTATOES    (followed by lettuces leeks, turnips)
MAINCROP POTATOES
MAINCROP BEETROOT

PLOT 2: MAINLY LEGUMES
TOMATOES (raised under glass)
LEEKS
FIRST EARLY PEAS
SECOND EARLY PEAS
MAINCROP PEAS
BROAD BEANS
DWARF FRENCH BEANS
SALSIFY
MARROWS    (raised under glass and followed by autumn-sown broad beans)
CUCUMBERS

PLOT 3: MAINLY LEAF CROPS
SPINACH BEET
CALABRESE
SUMMER CABBAGE
KALE
SPRING CABBAGE
MINI CAULIFLOWERS
AUTUMN CAULIFLOWERS
SWEDE
TURNIP
WINTER CAULIFLOWERS
BRUSSEL SPROUTS

My preference is for the organic-based fish, blood and bone, though the artificial Growmore will give equally good results. Some gardeners who opt for the completely organic approach attempt to rely entirely on bulky organic matter such as well rotted manure or garden compost but very large quantities are needed to satisfy the crops' entire nutrient requirements in this way.

Water should be used economically. Always sow into moist soil and water in transplanted crops thoroughly. Thereafter a simple rule is only to water when the edible part of a crop is maturing. Therefore, water beans when the pods are setting, potatoes when the tubers are swelling and cabbages when the hearts are forming.

## Harvesting

The main advantage of growing your own vegetables is that you can harvest

**below** It's important to apply appropriate fertilizer to vegetable crops; but not all at once. Some must be given at planting time and some whilst the crop is growing.

**above** Straw is invaluable as protection in the vegetable garden, either for root crops being stored in the ground or, as here, for the crowns of globe artichokes.

**below** The ranges of leaf form and colour now available ensure that lettuces provide the ornamental back bone to any kitchen garden plantings.

each at its peak and eat it immediately. In the descriptions below I have indicated the age at which each type of crop can be expected to mature. In mild areas or abnormally favourable conditions these periods may be shortened.

### Storing

Some vegetables are worth growing not just to be eaten fresh, but to supplement shop-bought produce during the winter months. The simplest and most economical method of storage is to leave the produce in the ground, and a surprising number of crops respond well to this. A few vegetables are worth freezing (sometimes after blanching) and several more can be successfully stored dry in a cool outbuilding.

### Leafy Salad Crops
### Endive *Cichorium endivia* Asteraceae
The endive is related to the lettuce but differs in some important ways. Because it is hardier than most lettuces, it can be cut during the winter but, conversely, it is slower growing and some must be blanched to eliminate bitterness. There are curled and plain-leaved varieties; all require a sunny position and rich moist soil. It runs to flower fairly quickly in the second year when it is most attractive.

**Sowing:** half-hardy annual technique sequentially from mid-spring to early autumn; don't sow broad-leaved varieties before midsummer.
**Base fertilizer:** medium.
**Spacing:** 20 x 20cm (8 x 8in).
**Care:** don't allow the soil to dry out. Blanch the hearts by covering the plant with clay plant pots that have had the holes sealed.
**Problems:** slugs.
**Harvesting:** 15 weeks (early sowings); 20 weeks (autumn sowings).
**Yield:** 4 plants per metre (yard) of row.
**Storing:** not satisfactory.
**Varieties:** 'Batavian Broad-Leaved' (broad-leaved); 'Ione' (curled).

### Lettuce *Lactuca sativa* Asteraceae
Although shop-bought lettuce has improved greatly in recent years, I still find it falls short of the flavour of the garden-fresh crop. Lettuce will grow on most soils, though it is best in full sun. However, the secret of good, tender lettuce is to grow it quickly, on rich soil and with plenty of water. By choosing varieties carefully and using cloches and a frost-free greenhouse, it is possible to have fresh lettuce all through the year, although I prefer to switch to endive in the autumn.

There are four main types of lettuce: the smooth-leaved butterhead or cabbage varieties; the curly-leaved crispheads; the upright, rather Chinese cabbage-like cos; and the heartless loose-leaved varieties. There are also red or purple-leaved forms of some of them.

**Sowing:** hardy annual technique, but choose method appropriate to time of crop maturity: for summer and early autumn crops, raise young plants in greenhouse for transplanting outdoors in spring and/or sow in growing positions from spring to summer, using cloches for the earliest sowings. For a successional crop all summer, sow a new row as the seedlings emerge from the previous row. For early winter crops, sow in growing positions in summer and cover with cloches from early autumn. For mid-winter crops, sow or plant in border or growing bags in a frost-free greenhouse or outdoors under cloches. For early spring crops, sow in growing positions in late summer under cloches or in a cold-frame.
**Base fertilizer:** medium.
**Spacing:** 25 x 25cm (10 x 10in) or for smaller varieties 15 x 15cm (6 x 6in).
**Care:** water regularly.
**Problems:** downy mildew, grey mould, root aphid, slugs.
**Harvesting:** 6-15 weeks, when hearts are firm. With loose-leaved varieties, simply remove leaves as required.
**Yield:** 3-6 lettuces per metre (yard) of row.
**Storing:** not satisfactory.

**Varieties:** 'Tom Thumb' (small butterhead); 'Webb's Wonderful' (crisphead); 'Little Gem' (small cos); 'Winter Density' (winter-hardy cos); 'Salad Bowl' and 'Red Salad Bowl' (leaf).

## Rocket *Eruca vesicaria sativa* Brassicaceae

A very old salad plant that has recently become fashionable once again. The young leaves have a spicy flavour, though older leaves can taste very hot. Rocket grows best in a rich, moist soil but is useful as it will tolerate partial shade. In an open position in hot summers it has a tendency to run to seed very rapidly.

**Sowing:** hardy annual technique in succession from early spring to early summer.
**Base fertilizer:** low.
**Spacing:** 7.5 x 7.5cm (3 x 3in).
**Care:** maintain soil moisture to help minimise running to seed.
**Problems:** flea beetle.
**Harvesting:** 6-8 weeks; pick individual leaves as required, or cut just above soil level and allow to re-grow.
**Yield:** 8-10 plants per metre (yard) of row.
**Storing:** not satisfactory.
**Varieties:** no named varieties.

## Land cress *Barbarea verna* Brassicaceae

Land cress is an easily grown substitute for watercress. It is very hardy with a hot taste and will grow in partial shade, although it does require a rich moist soil.

**Sowing:** hardy annual technique in summer for autumn to winter crops and spring to early summer for summer crops.

**Base fertilizer:** low.
**Spacing:** 15 x 10cm (6 x 4in).
**Care:** little needed.
**Problems:** none.
**Harvesting:** 6-10 weeks; cut whole plant or pick a few leaves at a time.
**Yield:** 8-10 plants per metre (yard) of row.
**Storing:** not satisfactory.
**Varieties:** no named varieties.

## Corn salad *Valerianella locusta* Valerianaceae

Corn salad or lamb's lettuce is a insignificant-looking plant but one that is surprisingly hardy and therefore a useful ingredient of winter salads. The small, indented leaves have a mild, slightly nutty flavour.

**Sowing:** hardy annual technique in growing position in summer for winter use, in spring for a summer crop.
**Base fertilizer:** low.
**Spacing:** 15 x 10cm (6 x 4in).
**Care:** little required but pull away browned leaves regularly.
**Problems:** none.
**Harvesting:** 8-9 weeks; cut whole plant or pick a few leaves at a time.
**Yield:** 10 plants per metre (yard) of row.
**Storing:** not satisfactory.
**Varieties:** no named varieties.

## Dandelion *Taraxacum officinale* Asteraceae

A common perennial garden weed that makes an unusual salad plant, especially in spring or autumn. The leaves are sharply flavoured, but are best blanched like endive.

**far left** Rocket will run to seed quickly in dry weather; and its hot and spicy taste may then become too strong.

**left** Land cress is one of the hardiest of the leafy salad crops for growing outdoors.

**above** Pick over purple sprouting broccoli selectively, taking only the ripe spears; it's a classic 'cut and come again' crop.

**Sowing:** hardy annual technique in growing position in late spring but confine by planting within large sunken plant pots.
**Base fertilizer:** low.
**Spacing:** 35 x 35cm (14 x 14in).
**Care:** little needed. Blanch a few plants at a time by placing a large pot (with the drainage hole blocked) over them. Check regularly and pull off small leaves. Pull off flowerheads before seeding.
**Problems:** none.
**Harvesting:** 15-45 weeks. Cut rosette when blanched, plant will re-grow from root.
**Yield:** 3 plants per 30cm (12in) diameter pot.
**Storing:** not satisfactory.
**Varieties:** no named varieties in Britain.

### Good King Henry *Chenopodium bonus-henricus* Chenopodiaceae

An old-fashioned perennial crop that makes an acceptable alternative to the annual spinaches, although inferior, I find, to perennial spinach (page 139). It grows best in a moist, rich soil and tolerates partial shade during the summer. Once established, it can be propagated by division.

**Sowing:** hardy annual technique in spring.
**Base fertilizer:** low; manure plot well before sowing.
**Spacing:** 30 x 30cm (12 x 12in).
**Care:** little required.
**Problems:** none.
**Harvesting:** 12 weeks; pull leaves as required.
**Yield:** 0.5-1kg per metre (1-2lb per yard) of row.
**Storing:** not satisfactory.
**Varieties:** no named varieties.

### Leafy Vegetables
### Broccoli *Brassica oleracea* Italica Group Brassicaceae

These brassicas are grown for their green or purple flowerheads (although white winter cauliflower [page 140] is also technically a broccoli). There are two main groups: first the winter and spring-maturing, biennial, purple-sprouting types which occupy the ground for a number of months, and second the summer and autumn-maturing, annual, calabrese types. There is also a perennial form that produces a very large plant but bears small green flowerheads every spring. All are valuable in a number of ways: they are 'cut-and-come-again' crops and so useful in a small garden; they freeze well; they have a mild flavour; and they look more attractive than most of their relatives.

**Sowing:** hardy annual technique into a seed bed or small pots in late spring.
**Planting:** after six weeks into growing positions.
**Base fertilizer:** medium.
**Spacing:** 30 x 30cm (12 x 12in); 1 x 1m (3 x 3ft) for perennial broccoli.
**Care:** water regularly as the flower shoots (spears) start to form.
**Problems:** birds, cabbage root fly, caterpillars, club-root.
**Harvesting:** 40-45 weeks (sprouting broccoli) or 12 weeks (calabrese). Pick individual spears of broccoli. When the large main head of calabrese has been cut, smaller side-shoots will develop over a period of weeks.
**Yield:** 0.7kg (1½lb) per plant.
**Storing:** freeze.
**Varieties:** 'Nine Star Perennial' (perennial); 'Corvet' F1 (calabrese); 'Purple Sprouting Early' (sprouting).

### Brussels sprouts *Brassica oleracea* Gemmifera Group Brassicaceae

The Brussels sprout is not one of the most attractive plants, but it is a traditional and very important winter vegetable. It is often said that sprouts require frosting in order to develop their best taste, but there is no real evidence that this makes any difference. They are tall plants that require firm soil and deep planting and, in most areas, must be staked too; but the Brussels sprout illustrates the differing requirements of commercial growers and gardeners. All the modern varieties are F1 hybrids on which the buttons mature simultaneously; ideal for mechanical harvesting, but less useful in the garden, where the old 'cut-and-come-again' open-pollinated varieties have much to commend them.

**Sowing:** hardy annual technique into a seed bed in spring.
**Planting:** into growing position after six weeks.
**Base fertilizer:** high.
**Spacing:** 1 x 1m (3 x 3ft) for normal picking or 50 x 50cm (20 x 20in) with an F1 variety for a crop of small buttons for freezing.
**Care:** firm the soil after planting and, in exposed gardens, earth up the base and stake the plants.
**Problems:** aphids, birds, cabbage root fly, caterpillars, club-root, whitefly.
**Harvesting:** 27-36 weeks when the buttons are firm.
**Yield:** 1kg (2lb) per plant.
**Storing:** freeze.
**Varieties:** 'Cambridge No.5', 'Fortress' F1; 'Peer Gynt' F1.

## Cabbage/savoy *Brassica oleracea* Capitata Group Brassicaceae

The 'humble cabbage', as it has often been described, is certainly an unsophisticated but a very useful plant and by using a combination of different types it is perfectly possible to have fresh green vegetable all year round. Cabbages are generally divided according to their maturing times into spring (including non-hearting spring greens), summer and autumn (including red cabbages) and winter types (including the mainly crinkle-leaved types known as savoys). Chinese cabbage is a completely different plant (page 159).

**Sowing:** hardy annual technique into a seed bed: in summer for spring cabbages, early spring to late spring for summer and autumn cabbages, late spring for winter cabbages. Cabbages for non-hearting spring greens are sown at close spacing into their growing positions.
**Planting:** into final positions after six weeks.
**Base fertilizer:** high.
**Spacing:** 30 x 30cm (12 x 12in) for spring cabbage, 35 x 35cm (14 x 14in) for summer, autumn and winter cabbage; 15 x 15cm (6 x 6in) for non-hearting greens.
**Care:** water as the heads start to swell.
**Problems:** aphids, cabbage root fly, caterpillars, clubroot, whitefly.
**Harvesting:** 20-35 weeks, once heads are hard.

**Yield:** 0.3-1.25kg (10oz-2½lb) per plant depending on variety.
**Storing:** not necessary, choose varieties with sequential maturing times.
**Varieties:** 'Hispi' F1 (spring); 'Golden Acre' (summer); 'Christmas Drumhead' (autumn); 'Ruby Ball' (red).

## Leaf beet (Perennial spinach), Seakale beet, Spinach beet, Swiss chard *Beta vulgaris* Cicla Group Chenopodiaceae

These are attractive-looking alternatives to spinach, which has the annoying habit of running to seed in dry weather. Unfortunately, the flavour of chards does tend to be stronger and the plump leaf stalks and midribs are best separated from the broad leaves and cooked separately. Spinach beet is the best of all the alternatives to spinach.

**Sowing:** hardy annual technique in spring.
**Base fertilizer:** high.
**Spacing:** 30 x 25cm (12 x 10in).
**Care:** maintain soil moisture.
**Problems:** none.
**Harvesting:** 12 weeks, pull leaves as required; cropping will continue through the winter, but cloche protection needed in colder areas.
**Yield:** 1kg per metre (2lb per yard) of row.
**Storing:** not satisfactory.
**Varieties:** no named varieties normally available.

## Sorrel *Rumex acetosa* Polygonaceae

Sorrel is an extremely hardy perennial but one

**below** Brussels sprouts mature from the bottom of the stem upwards; so be sure to pick them in the correct order.

that has rather passed from favour in the kitchen garden, although it is still popular in restaurants. It will thrive on most soils and even, usefully, in some shade. The young leaves have a sharp, lemony flavour, which can be added sparingly to mixed salads or made into soup.

**Sowing:** hardy annual technique in spring or autumn.
**Base fertilizer:** low.
**Spacing:** 20 x 20cm (8 x 8in).
**Care:** little needed.
**Problems:** none.
**Harvesting:** 6-10 weeks; pick outer leaves, allowing the heart to produce a supply of fresh new foliage.
**Yield:** five plants per metre (yard) row.
**Storing:** not satisfactory.
**Varieties:** no named varieties normally available.

### Cauliflower *Brassica oleracea* Botrytis Group Brassicaceae

It is by the quality of his or her cauliflowers that a good vegetable gardener is judged. The high score awarded to the cauliflower class at horticultural shows is a reliable indication that they are difficult to grow, easily the most taxing of the brassicas. They are also large plants that are unsuitable for the smaller kitchen garden. The two most important facts concerning their cultivation are that they resent both root disturbance and being allowed to become dry,

both of which may lead to 'blindness' (a failure to form a proper curd). Cauliflowers are divided into three main groups: summer, autumn and winter varieties. Botanically, winter cauliflowers aren't true cauliflowers but a form of broccoli; and nor are they harvested in the winter; they are winter hardy but mature in spring.

**Sowing:** hardy annual technique in spring, depending on variety, into 9cm (3½in) pots to minimise root disturbance when planting out. Start earliest sowings in a greenhouse or cold frame.
**Planting:** into final positions after six weeks.
**Base fertilizer:** high.
**Spacing:** 50 x 50cm (20 x 20in) for summer varieties, 60 x 60cm (24 x 24in) for autumn and winter varieties.
**Care:** maintain soil moisture at as constant a level as possible. In hot summers, protect the developing curds by pulling up some of the outer leaves and tying them over the top.
**Problems:** aphids, cabbage root fly, caterpillars, club-root.
**Harvesting:** 18-25 weeks (summer and autumn varieties); 40-50 weeks (winter varieties), when curds are full and white.
**Yield:** 0.5-1kg (1-2lb) per plant.
**Storing:** freeze.
**Varieties:** 'Dok Elgon' (summer/autumn); 'Walcheren Winter Armado April' (winter).

### Celery *Apium graveolens* Apiaceae

Good celery is superb but poor celery, like much of that for sale in supermarkets, is tasteless. There are two distinct types: traditional, fine-tasting stalks come from trenched celery, the useless pith from self-blanching types. While it is possible to grow reasonable-tasting self-blanching celery, to my mind it will always be second best and since it is not hardy it must be pulled before the autumn. Both types of celery require a very rich, very moist soil; remember that its natural habitat is marshland. For trenched celery you must prepare a trench in the spring, approximately 40cm (16in) wide and 30cm (12in) deep, with a layer of well-decayed compost or manure in the bottom.

**Sowing:** half-hardy annual technique at medium temperature into 9cm (3½in) pots.

**Planting:** with minimal root disturbance after the danger of frost has passed. Trenched varieties should planted in the bottom of the trench, which is then flooded with water.
**Base fertilizer:** medium.
**Spacing:** 20 x 20cm (8 x 8in) for self-blanching types, 20cm (8in) apart in the trench for trenched varieties.
**Care:** water thoroughly and don't allow soil to dry out. When trenched varieties are about 30cm (12in) tall, fill the trench with soil and continue to draw soil around the plants to create a ridge, so that only the tops of the plants show. You can wrap newspaper around the stalks to keep them clean of soil or use special celery collars, though these can attract slugs. I prefer not to protect the plants but simply to tie the stalks together, pile earth against them and discard the outer stalks before using.
**Problems:** leaf spot, splitting due to shortage of water, slugs.
**Harvesting:** 25 weeks for self-blanching types or 40 weeks for trenching types; cut once the stalks reach acceptable size.
**Yield:** 2kg per metre (4lb per yard) of row.
**Storing:** not satisfactory.
**Varieties:** 'Giant White' (trenched); 'Golden Self Blanching 3' (self-blanching).

### Kale *Brassica oleracea* Acephala Group
Brassicaceae

This very useful vegetable is too often dismissed as cattle fodder. Yet it is very hardy and provides appetising winter and early spring greens when there are few other fresh green crops around, although you must pick the shoots when young.

**Sowing:** half-hardy annual technique in a seed bed in late spring (earlier for curled varieties).
**Planting:** after six weeks into growing positions.
**Base fertilizer:** high.
**Spacing:** 45 x 45cm (18 x 18in).
**Care:** stake in exposed gardens.
**Problems:** aphids, birds, cabbage root fly, club-root.
**Harvesting:** 30-35 weeks.
**Yield:** 1kg (2lb) per plant.
**Storing:** freeze.
**Varieties:** 'Pentland Brig'.

### Spinach *Spinacia oleracea*
Chenopodiaceae

A delicious and much maligned vegetable, spinach is tastier than any of the substitutes. although leaf beet runs it closest. It is tricky to grow, however, because it readily runs to seed in warm summers, even in rich soil and when watered carefully. Full sun is essential to prevent leaves from becoming tough and bitter.

**Sowing:** hardy annual technique in growing position sequentially from early to late spring.
**Base fertilizer:** medium.
**Spacing:** 25 x 15cm (10 x 6in).
**Care:** water carefully and don't allow soil to dry out.
**Problems:** leaf spot.
**Harvesting:** 8-15 weeks, when leaves are large enough. Pull a few leaves from each plant to encourage more growth.
**Yield:** 0.5-1kg per metre (1-2lb per yard) of row.
**Storing:** freeze.
**Varieties:** 'Longstanding Round'.

### Perennial Vegetables
### Rhubarb *Rheum* x *cultorum*
Polygonaceae

Rhubarb is too often treated as the joke of the kitchen garden and, as a consequence, is probably the most neglected of all crop plants. Although it will crop year after year with little attention, just a little care will pay rich

**below** The cauliflower variety 'All the Year Round' belies its name but is a good old summer type.

**right** Trenched celery has immeasurably better flavour than self-blanching but although it starts life in a trench, it ends up surrounded by a ridge.

**below** The bane of every spinach grower; the crop runs to seed very readily in hot and dry conditions.

dividends. Choose your variety carefully, for the chances are that it will be the only one you buy in a gardening lifetime.

**Sowing:** although rhubarb can be grown from seed, this is never worthwhile as you won't obtain the best varieties.
**Planting:** as crowns on well manured ground in spring.
**Base fertilizer:** medium.
**Spacing:** 1m (3ft) each way; one plant is usually enough, although if you want to force an early crop, additional plants will be needed.
**Care:** mulch liberally with compost or well-rotted manure each spring.
**Problems:** none.
**Harvesting:** pull, rather than cut, stems from spring (in mild areas) to summer. Force plants by placing a large, upturned pot over them in late winter; allow the plant to rest for two years before forcing again.
**Yield:** 2kg (4lb) per plant.
**Storing:** freeze.
**Varieties:** 'Timperley Early'.

## Seakale *Crambe maritima* Brassicaceae

This large, attractive plant is a native of the British coast. It is grown for the young tender shoots produced in the spring and, when forced the shoots have a unique and delicate flavour and can be either cooked or eaten raw. The plants will crop for about six years, when they should be replaced by new plants raised from root cuttings. Seakale requires an open, sunny site and deep, rich, free-draining soil.

**Sowing:** hardy perennial technique; germination can be slow and erratic. Sow into 9cm (3½in) pots for transplanting.
**Planting:** thongs (prepared root cuttings) can be purchased as an alternative to seed. Plant in late autumn.
**Base fertilizer:** low; but prepare the planting position carefully, with plenty of manure.
**Spacing:** 45 x 45cm (18 x 18in).
**Care:** remove flowering shoot to preserve the plant's energy. Force by covering the crowns in mid-winter, first with dry leaves and then with a bucket, upturned pot (with blocked drainage hole) or a traditional clay forcing pot.
**Problems:** club-root.
**Harvesting:** cut young blanched shoots when they reach 15-20cm (6-8in). Stop in late spring to allow the plant to build up its reserves.
**Yield:** 0.5kg (1lb) per plant per year.
**Storing:** not satisfactory.
**Varieties:** no named varieties normally available.

## Asparagus *Asparagus officinale*
## Asparagaceae

The most delicious and prized of the perennial vegetables. Plants can crop for 10 years or more, but in any one year the yield is low in relation to the space required; it is not a crop for a small garden. Asparagus can be raised from seed but this is time-consuming and unreliable. For a crop that requires such a high investment of effort, it makes sense to buy plants of a good named variety; preferably a modern all-male strain. Buy one-year-old crowns, preferably frame rather than field-raised, from an asparagus specialist.

**Planting:** one-year-old crowns, in spring. Prepare a trench 20cm (8in) deep and 30cm (12in) wide, mound soil 7.5cm (3in) high in the centre and plant the crowns on this, then refill the trench. Asparagus was once invariably grown on raised beds but this is only necessary on very heavy soils.
**Base fertilizer:** medium.
**Spacing:** 30 x 30cm (12 x 12in).
**Care:** apply a liquid feed after the end of cutting. Cut the shoots down in autumn and apply a generous mulch of compost or well-rotted manure. Top dress with a general fertilizer in the spring. There is a mistaken belief that, as it is a coastal plant, salt is a beneficial feed. It isn't.
**Problems:** asparagus beetle, rust, slugs.
**Harvesting:** two years after planting (don't harvest until the plants are three years old). Cut young spears about 10cm (4in) long, about 8cm (3¼in) below soil level. From early summer onwards, stop cutting and allow the plants to produce foliage.
**Yield:** once established, 25 spears per plant per year.
**Storing:** freeze.
**Varieties:** 'Connover's Colossal'; 'Lucullus'.

## Globe artichoke *Cynara scolymus*
## Asteraceae

These plants, although impressive in flower, are just too big for their own good. A small garden simply doesn't offer the space for them and the yield from each plant, even over the three or four years of its productive life, is small. The amount that is edible on each head (in reality an unopened flower) is minute. Globe artichokes require plenty of sun and

a warm, light and well drained soil.
**Sowing:** seed-raised plants are never reliable.
**Planting:** off-sets in spring; every few years remove off-sets from established plants to start afresh and discard the old stock.
**Base fertilizer:** medium.
**Spacing:** 1 x 1m (3 x 3ft).
**Care:** treat the plant as you would a herbaceous perennial; cut the foliage down in autumn and mulch well in spring.
**Problems:** aphids.
**Harvesting:** 18 months; cut the terminal flower first, then cut the others as they swell, but before the flowers open.
**Yield:** about six heads per plant per year for three or four years.
**Storing:** not satisfactory.
**Varieties:** no named varieties normally available.

## Root Vegetables
### Beetroot *Beta vulgaris* Chenopodiaceae

This is the easiest of the root crops for its root is usually round and, as it forms at the surface of the soil, growth checks arising from trying to penetrate rough or stony ground are rare.

**above** Seakale is an old and much neglected vegetable but it must be forced by excluding the light to produce tender shoots.

**below** Asparagus is now grown on flat beds, not as it once was on ridges; but the crop must be fed and mulched after cutting.

right Each beetroot 'seed' is in reality a small cluster of individual seeds, so more than one plant emerges from each sowing position.

below Distorted or fanged carrots are an indication of a stony or very rich soil.

Germination and early stages of growth are frustratingly slow but by sowing sequentially and choosing several varieties, cropping can continue for nine months of the year.

**Sowing:** hardy annual technique directly into growing position sequentially from early spring to summer; each 'seed' is generally a cluster of individuals so thinning is necessary after emergence; use cloches in the early part of the season.
**Base fertilizer:** high.

**Spacing:** 18 x 10cm (7 x 4in).
**Care:** keep well watered to prevent woodiness and bolting in early varieties.
**Problems:** leaf spot.
**Harvesting:** 11-16 weeks before roots reach tennis-ball size.
**Yield:** 1.5-2.5kg per metre (3-5lb per yard) of row.
**Storing:** lift roots in autumn, twist off (don't cut) leaves and store in boxes of dry soil-less compost or sand; or cover with straw in early winter and leave in the ground. In most years, they will survive satisfactorily in the ground simply by being earthed up.
**Varieties:** 'Boltardy'; 'Cheltenham Green Top'.

## Carrot *Daucus carota* Apiaceae

I regard carrots as the most versatile and most attractive of all the root crops. They take up little space and their feathery foliage makes a useful contribution to the ornamental kitchen garden. Unfortunately, they have two drawbacks. Firstly, their roots will become irregular or fanged on soils that are hard or stony, recently amended with fresh manure or where an impervious pan has been allowed to develop below the surface. Secondly, they are prone to attack by the carrot fly, whose larvae tunnel into the roots.

**Sowing:** hardy annual technique in growing positions sequentially from spring to summer, using cloches for earliest sowings. Sow thinly to avoid thinning seedlings later, as this releases an aroma attractive to carrot fly.
**Base fertilizer:** low.
**Spacing:** 15 x·6cm (6 x 2¼in).
**Care:** disturb foliage as little as possible, water regularly when roots begin to swell; plants are liable to split if they are allowed to dry out.
**Problems:** aphids, carrot fly, fanging, splitting.

**Harvesting:** 12-16 weeks, when roots have reached desired size.

**Yield:** 1-1.5kg per metre (2-3lb per yard) of row.

**Storing:** lift roots in autumn, cut off foliage and store in boxes of dry soil less compost or sand; or cover with straw and leave in the ground; like beetroot, they will survive perfectly well outdoors in most areas.

**Varieties:** 'Fly Away' F1 (more or less all season, carrot fly resistant); 'Early French Frame' (early, spherical); 'Autumn King 2' (maincrop).

## Chicory *Cichorium intybus* Asteraceae

The chicories are leafy salad plants, superficially similar to cos lettuces. They are widely grown on the Continent but are increasing in popularity in Britain too. There are two types: radicchio or sugar loaf types which can be eaten freshly cut but are bitter; chicon or Witloof types, which must be forced in darkness to alleviate the bitterness. Confusingly, the French chicorée frisé is the plant we call endive; the plant called endive in France is chicory in English.

**Sowing:** hardy annual technique outdoors in spring.

**Base fertilizer:** low.

**Spacing:** 30 x 20cm (12 x 8in).

**Care:** maintain soil moisture. Lift the roots in autumn or early winter, cut the foliage about 2.5cm (1in) from the root and store in boxes of dry sand until required for forcing. Pot up into pots of compost from early winter through to spring; around six roots to a 23cm (9in) pot should suffice. Place the pot in a warm, dark place or cover with a similar-sized pot with the hole blocked.

**Problems:** none.

**Harvesting:** blanch for three weeks; cut chicons when 10-15cm (4-6in) high.

**Yield:** one chicon per plant.

**Storing:** not satisfactory.

**Varieties:** no named varieties normally available.

## Cardoon *Cynara cardunculus* Asteraceae

A relative of the globe artichoke, and similarly huge, but grown for its stems, which are blanched in their growing positions in the autumn like celery. Cardoons need a sunny but sheltered site on light, well drained soil.

**Sowing:** hardy annual technique in growing position in mid-spring; or sow individually into 9cm (3½in) pots.

**Planting:** pot grown plants after danger of frost has passed.

**Base fertilizer:** manure plot well before planting. Feed regularly with a general-purpose liquid feed.

**Spacing:** 50 x 50cm (20 x 20in).

**Care:** Water regularly. In autumn tie the stems together and blanch using a collar of newspaper, cardboard or black plastic, supported with a stake in exposed gardens.

**Problems:** slugs.

**Harvesting:** after three weeks; lift whole plant and trim off leaves and roots.

**Yield:** two plants per metre (yard) of row.

**Storing:** not satisfactory.

**Varieties:** no named varieties normally available.

## Florence Fennel, Finocchio
## *Foeniculum vulgare azoricum* Apiaceae

Fennel is well-known both in the herb garden and in the border for its beautiful feathery and aromatic foliage. To grow the distinct variety *F. v. azoricum* as a vegetable, the swollen stem base must be nurtured to form a bulb. It is a big plant that requires a warm, sunny position, light soil and plenty of water to succeed.

**Sowing:** hardy annual technique directly into the ground sequentially from late spring to summer.

**Base fertilizer:** medium.

**Spacing:** 35 x 35cm (14 x 14in).

**Care:** don't allow the soil to dry out; as soon as the bulb reaches 2-3cm (¾-1¼in) in diameter, draw soil over it and continue to earth up for the rest of the season.

**Problems:** no pests and diseases but prone to bolting if sown too early or when growth is checked. Difficult to grow in colder areas where growing season is shorter.

**below** Cardoons are very large plants and must be blanched in their growing positions in autumn.

**Harvesting:** 12-15 weeks, when the bulb is 8cm (3in) in diameter.
**Yield:** 3 bulbs per metre (yard) of row.
**Storing:** freeze.
**Varieties:** no named varieties normally available.

## Jerusalem artichoke
### *Helianthus tuberosus* Asteraceae

A relative of the sunflower, it can grow just as large, so in smaller gardens is best confined to one side and used as a windbreak. Jerusalem artichokes take a long time to mature, but have the advantage that they will grow in almost any soil and will tolerate shade. Any fragment of tuber missed during harvesting, however, will re-grow to produce a crop the following year. The tuberous roots are an acquired taste; my preference is to boil them and then serve them cold with a vinaigrette dressing.

**Planting:** tubers can be planted from early to late spring 10-15cm (4-6in) deep.
**Base fertilizer:** low.
**Spacing:** 1m x 50cm (3ft x 20in).
**Care:** earth up the base of the plants when they are 30cm (12in) high and stake if necessary. Pinch out flower buds as they form.
**Problems:** none.
**Harvesting:** 45-50 weeks, cut stems in early autumn and lift roots as required during winter.

**Yield:** 1.5-2.5kg (3-5lb) per plant.
**Storing:** leave in ground.
**Varieties:** 'Fuseau' (smooth tubers).

## Hamburg parsley *Petroselinum crispum tuberosum* Apiaceae

I have included this curious plant because I would like to see it grown more widely. It is more shade tolerant than any other vegetable, very hardy and combines the foliage of broad-leaved parsley with roots like a slender parsnip, but with a slight celery flavour. Any fairly well-manured soil is suitable.

**Sowing:** hardy annual technique into growing position in spring (under cloches if possible).
**Base fertilizer:** medium.
**Spacing:** 30 x 30cm (12 x 12in).
**Care:** maintain soil in moist condition.
**Problems:** none.
**Harvesting:** 30-35 weeks, which is when roots are about 20cm (8in) long.
**Yield:** three roots per metre (yard) of row.
**Storing:** as parsnip.
**Varieties:** no named varieties normally available.

## Kohl rabi *Brassica oleracea* Gongylodes Group Brassicaceae

This is one of the most prized of the brassicas in parts of central and eastern Europe, but has never become popular in Britain. It is more closely related to the cabbage and the cauli-

**right** It takes ingenuity to create an attractive feature of a Jerusalem artichoke.

flower than the turnip, which it superficially resembles. The edible part is the swollen stem base rather than the root and hence it suffers less from hard or stony soils than other more conventional root crops. Kohl rabi must be grown quickly and without a check to its growth; if deprived of water or allowed to grow too slowly it becomes tough and tasteless.

**Sowing:** hardy annual technique in growing position, sequentially from spring to summer. Later sowings should be of purple varieties only.
**Base fertilizer:** medium.
**Spacing:** 30 x 15cm (12 x 6in).
**Care:** water regularly.
**Problems:** cabbage root fly, club-root.
**Harvesting:** 8-12 weeks, when bulbs are about 6-7cm ( 2¼-2¾in) in diameter.
**Yield:** 6 bulbs per metre (yard) of row.
**Storing:** not satisfactory.
**Varieties:** 'Purple Vienna'; 'Superschmelz'.

## Salsify *Tragopogon porrifolius* Asteraceae

Seldom-grown, but nevertheless useful root crop that can be grown and used in much the same way as the parsnip. Salsify, like most root vegetables, will grow best on a light, free-draining soil, free from stones or clods of earth.

**Sowing:** hardy annual technique in growing position in late spring.
**Base fertilizer:** low.
**Spacing:** 30 x 15cm (12 x 6in).
**Care:** little, apart from watering in dry weather.
**Problems:** none.
**Harvesting:** 24 weeks; judge maturity by timing from sowing.
**Yield:** 0.5kg per metre (1lb per yard) of row.
**Storing:** lift roots in late autumn, cut off leaves and store in boxes of dry soil-less compost or sand.
**Varieties:** no named varieties normally available.

## Scorzonera *Scorzonera hispanica* Asteraceae

Another rarely-grown root crop, scorzonera is a perennial, has darker, slender roots and a milder flavour than salsify. It is grown in exactly the same way.

**Sowing:** hardy annual technique in growing position in late spring.
**Base fertilizer:** low.
**Spacing:** 30 x 15cm (12 x 6in).
**Care:** little, apart from watering in dry weather.
**Problems:** none.
**Harvesting:** 24 weeks, judge maturity by timing from sowing.
**Yield:** 0.5kg per metre (1lb per yard) of row.
**Storing:** lift roots in late autumn, cut off leaves and store in boxes of dry soil-less compost or sand.
**Varieties:** no named varieties normally available.

## Swede *Brassica napus* Napobrassica Group Brassicaceae

Superficially one of the easiest and most un-demanding of vegetables, in practice swedes are difficult to grow well in gardens. Unless you have plenty of space and can grow large numbers of plants in blocks, as farmers do, rather than rows my advice is to give over the space to something more rewarding.

**Sowing:** hardy annual technique in growing position during late spring or early summer.
**Base fertilizer:** low.
**Spacing:** 30 x 20cm (12 x 8in).
**Care:** little required.
**Problems:** aphids, cabbage root fly, clubroot, flea beetle, mildew.
**Harvesting:** 20 weeks when roots are approximately 10cm (4in) in diameter.
**Yield:** 4-5kg per metre (8-10lb per yard) of row.
**Storing:** lift roots in late autumn, cut off leaves and store in boxes of dry soil-less compost or sand.
**Varieties:** 'Marian'.

## Turnip *Brassica rapa* Rapifera Group Brassicaceae

Many people dismiss the turnip as boring to grow and eat. I feel, however, that it's one of the vegetables that is most unexpectedly reward-ing when it is home grown, closely spaced and eaten

**above** Hamburg parsley is one of the least known vegetables but is an interesting crop, combining some of the virtues of parsley, parsnip and celery.

**below** Salsify is one of the forgotten vegetables but makes an interesting change from parsnip.

right Turnips are conveniently divided into 'white top' (as here) and 'purple-top' varieties.

below Cankers of several types are the main disease problems on parsnips. This is orange brown canker but all can be avoided by selecting a resistant variety like 'Avonresister'.

small. It is easy to grow too, and much less demanding of good soil than carrots or other root crops.

**Sowing:** hardy annual technique directly in growing position, sow in succession from spring (for early varieties) or summer (maincrop varieties).

**Base fertilizer:** low.
**Spacing:** 20 x 10cm (8 x 4in) (early varieties) or 25 x 12cm (10 x 5in) (maincrop varieties).
**Care:** don't allow soil to dry out.
**Problems:** aphids, cabbage root fly, club-root, flea beetle.
**Harvesting:** 6-12 weeks, when 3-4cm (1¼-1½in) in diameter.
**Yield:** 1-1.5kg per metre (2-3lb per yard) of row.
**Storing:** lift maincrop varieties in late autumn, twist off leaves and store in boxes of dry soil-less compost or sand; or cover with 10cm (4in) of straw in early winter and leave in ground.
**Varieties:** 'Snowball'; 'Purple Top Milan'.

### Parsnip *Pastinaca sativa* Apiaceae

The parsnip is perhaps the easiest of the root vegetables to grow, but its strong flavour is not to everyone's taste. Nonetheless, those who have savoured home-grown roast parsnips will always find room in their garden for a row or two. Parsnips are as intolerant of fresh manure as carrots, though the shorter-rooted varieties are easier to grow than carrots in slightly rough or stony soil.

**Sowing:** hardy annual technique in growing position in spring.
**Base fertilizer:** low.

**Spacing:** 30 x 15cm (12 x 6in).
**Care:** little needed; water only if very dry.
**Problems:** aphids, canker.
**Harvesting:** 30-35 weeks, as leaves start to die down in autumn.
**Yield:** 1kg per metre (2lb per yard) of row.
**Storing:** leave in ground
**Varieties:** 'Avonresister'; 'Gladiator' F1.

### Potato *Solanum tuberosum* Solanaceae

The potato is the vegetable most taken for granted. It is only attractive for a brief period when in flower, and being both half-hardy and vegetatively propagated, is prone to an abnormal number of problems. Yet there really is no substitute for a home-grown new potato early in the summer, so do find space for two or three rows of an early variety.

Although potatoes grow best on fairly well manured ground, their soil requirements are undemanding and they are the first crop that should be grown on a new piece of land. Their extensive root system helps to break up the soil, their dense leaf canopy suppresses weeds and the earthing up needed also helps to eliminate weed populations.

**Planting:** Buy tubers of early varieties in late winter to early spring and spread them out in trays to sprout in a warm, light place. Plant early varieties in mid-spring, maincrops in late spring. Always buy certified 'seed' potato tubers and don't save your own tubers for replanting as they will have accumulated virus.
**Base fertilizer:** high.
**Spacing:** 60 x 30cm (24 x 12in) for early varieties, 75 x 35cm (30 x 14in) for maincrops; plant individually with a trowel 12cm (5in deep).
**Care:** draw soil around the emerging shoots to protect them from frost; then continue earthing up until ridges are about 30cm (12in) high to prevent tubers being exposed to light. Water regularly when in flower.
**Problems:** aphids, blight, slugs, tuber rots, viruses.
**Harvesting:** 13 weeks (early varieties), 22 weeks (maincrops); start to lift early varieties when they are in flower and tubers are 6-7cm (2½ -3in) in diameter. Harvest maincrops about two weeks after the tops have died down.

**Yield:** 2kg (4 lb) for earlies to 3kg (6 lb) for maincrops per metre (yard) of row.
**Storing:** store maincrop varieties in double paper sacks in a cool but frost-free place.
**Varieties:** Early: 'Charlotte'; 'Estima'; 'Rocket'; 'Sharpe's Express'. Main Crop: 'Desirée'; 'King Edward'; 'Pink Fir Apple'.

### Radish *Raphanus sativus* Brassicaceae

The easiest vegetable to grow, radish will succeed in almost any soil or situation, although they will be tough and tasteless if grown in shade and denied water. They are very quick, growing and ideal for filling spaces between longer-term crops. There are two main types of radish: the familiar spherical- or cylindrical-rooted summer salad types and the less widely-grown winter types. Winter radishes also include spherical and cylindrical types, of which the large but fast-growing Japanese mooli is the best known. A common mistake is to sow the summer varieties after early summer, when it is very difficult to prevent them from bolting. Winter radishes, on the other hand are best sown from mid-summer onwards, although some bolt-resistant mooli varieties can be sown earlier.

**Sowing:** hardy annual technique in growing position from early spring to early

**above** Potatoes are earthed up initially to protect the tender shoots from frost but later to ensure the tubers don't become green.

**below** Winter radishes are unexpected looking plants and in some ways are more like tiny turnips.

summer for summer types, summer sowings for winter radishes; protect earliest sowings with cloches.

**Base fertilizer:** low.

**Spacing:** 8 x 2-4cm (3 x 1-1½in) for summer varieties or 15 x 15cm (6 x 6in) winter varieties.

**Care:** water regularly to prevent soil drying out.

**Problems:** flea beetle.

**Harvesting:** 3-6 weeks (summer varieties) or 9-12 weeks (winter varieties), when summer types are approximately 2cm (¾in) in diameter and winter varieties are approximately 5cm (2in) in diameter.

**Yield:** 0.5kg per metre (1lb per yard) of row (summer varieties) or 1.5kg per metre (3lb per yard) of row (winter types).

**Storing:** lift roots of winter varieties in early winter, cut off leaves and store in boxes of dry soil-less compost or sand; or cover with straw and leave in the ground.

**Varieties:** 'French Breakfast'; 'Short Top Forcing' (salad). 'Black Spanish Round' (winter).

### Onion *Allium cepa*
### Shallot *Allium cepa* Aggregatum Group
### Alliaceae

As any cook knows, onions are absolutely essential in the kitchen. Those with large swollen bulbs are generally used for cooking, the young slender types are eaten raw as spring or salad onions, while those varieties that form small, spherical bulbs are used for pickling. All onions require similar growing conditions; a rich soil, well manured in the previous season. This is especially important for the longer-growing bulbing onions. Salad onions and pickling onions are always grown from seed. Bulb onions can be grown either from seed or from sets, small immature bulbs raised specially for planting. Starting from sets shortens the growing season and eliminates the uncertainty of growing from seed, especially in cold areas. Shallots are strongly flavoured onions that produce clusters of small bulbs. They were traditionally always grown from sets, though varieties to grow from seed are now available.

**Sowing:** hardy annual technique in growing positions, sequentially from spring to summer and again in late summer for winter hardy varieties for a spring crop. Alternatively sow seeds of bulbing varieties in small pots or modules in a greenhouse in mid-winter in 9cm (3½in) pots for transplanting. Sow groups of four or six seeds together; this will result in medium-sized bulbs more suitable for kitchen use.

**Planting:** pot sown seedlings or prepared onion sets in spring; plant sets with their tips just protruding from the soil. Plant sets of over-wintering varieties in autumn.

**Base fertilizer:** medium.

**Spacing:** 25 x 10cm (10 x 4in) for bulb onions; 15cm x 1cm (6 x ½in) for salad onions; 20 x 10cm (8 x 4in) for shallots.

**Care:** dust seed with approved systemic fungicide or dip sets in appropriate fungicide before planting to protect against neck rot; water and weed carefully, hoeing between the rows may damage the shallow roots.

**Problems:** downy mildew, eelworm, neck rot, white rot.

**Harvesting:** 18-22 weeks (spring sown or planted), up to 45 weeks (autumn sown or planted); about two weeks after the foliage has turned yellow, lift and dry in the sun (use cloches to protect the drying bulbs in wet weather or put them in trays on a greenhouse bench).

**Yield:** 1.5kg per metre (3lb per yard) of row.

**Storing:** hung up in nets, tied into strings or laid on slatted trays in a dry, frost-free place.

**Varieties:** 'White Lisbon Hardy' (salad onions); 'Ailsa Craig'; 'Bedfordshire Champion' (bulb onions); 'Brunswick' (red); 'Senshyu Semi-Globe Yellow' (overwintering). 'Barletta' (pickling onions); 'Golden Gourmet' (shallots).

### Garlic *Allium sativum* Alliaceae

This strongly flavoured relative of the onion is an essential ingredient in many Mediterranean and eastern dishes, yet it is hardy and very easy to grow; simply plant cloves and they will multiply to produce tight clumps or bulbs. Most

**below** All bulb onions should be allowed to dry on the soil surface for a few days before being stored.

strains require a cold period and a long growing season so are planted in autumn. Garlic grows best in a light, free-draining soil; on heavier soils planting can be delayed until early spring.

**Planting:** Plant individual cloves (buy certified, virus-free stock if available; if not, supermarket cloves, preferably of British origin) on free-draining soil in autumn.
**Base fertilizer:** medium.
**Spacing:** 25 x 15cm (10 x 6in).
**Care:** little needed.
**Problems:** none.
**Harvesting:** 30-35 weeks, when tops die down, lift and dry in the sun.
**Yield:** 6-8 bulbs per metre (yard) of row.
**Storing:** hung up as strings in a dry, frost-free place.
**Varieties:** no named varieties normally available.

## Leek *Allium ampeloprasum* Alliaceae

Leeks are delicious: pretty when small and tender, dreadful to look at and eat when large and tough. Unless the winter is very hard, their blue-green foliage can be rather attractive, although they are scarcely plants for the ornamental kitchen garden. They are very hardy and less demanding than onions as they don't require such a well-manured, moisture-retentive soil.

**Sowing:** hardy annual technique into a seed bed in spring or directly into growing positions, although this is less successful.
**Planting:** into growing positions in early summer when the plants are about 20cm (8in) tall. Trim the root and leaf tips before planting. Drop the transplants into holes 15cm (6in) deep and then fill the hole with water.
**Base fertilizer:** medium.
**Spacing:** 30 x 15cm (12 x 6in).
**Care:** when the plants have filled their holes, draw earth around the base to blanch them until late autumn.
**Problems:** *Botrytis* grey mould, rust, white tip disease.
**Harvesting:** 30-45 weeks
**Yield:** 1.5kg per metre (3lb per yard) of row.
**Storing:** leave in ground until required.
**Varieties:** 'King Richard' (early); 'Musselburgh' (winter).

**above** Leek transplants should be dropped into holes and then well watered.

## Celeriac/Turnip rooted celery
*Apium graveolens rapaceum* Apiaceae

Celeriac is a variant of celery in which the swollen crowns are eaten, but is only rarely grown in British gardens. It occupies a considerable amount of space and, like celery, requires a rich, moisture-retentive soil and copious watering if it is not to become hard and woody.

**Sowing:** half-hardy annual technique at medium temperature. Raise plants in 9cm (3½in) pots to minimise root disturbance.
**Planting:** in growing position after the danger of frost has passed.
**Base fertilizer:** medium.
**Spacing:** 30 x 30cm (12 x 12in).
**Care:** two to three weeks after transplanting, start to pull away the lower leaves to expose the crown as it swells. In autumn, gradually earth up the stem bases to cover them.
Problems: slugs on young plants.
**Harvesting:** 30 weeks, once swollen roots and stem bases are 10-15cm (4-6in) in diameter.
**Yield:** 1kg per metre (2lb per yard) of row.
**Storing:** cover with straw in the autumn and leave in the ground until required.
**Varieties:** 'Monarch'.

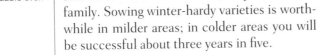

**above** Cloches provide protection for over-wintering broad beans like 'Aquadulce Claudia' and are valuable even in mild areas.

**below** Sweet peppers are best grown in greenhouses in most areas and although traditionally green or red, a much wider colour range is now available.

## Vegetable Fruits
### Broad bean *Vicia faba* Papilionaceae
Very hardy vegetable that offers the earliest, and therefore most welcome, crop of the bean family. Sowing winter-hardy varieties is worthwhile in milder areas; in colder areas you will be successful about three years in five.

**Sowing:** hardy annual technique in growing position from early spring onwards, using cloches for the earliest sowings. Winter-hardy varieties are sown in late autumn, preferably with cloche protection.
**Base fertilizer:** low.
**Spacing:** 23 x 23cm (9 x 9in) for shorter varieties or 45 x 30cm (18 x 12in) for taller varieties.
**Care:** support taller varieties with canes and string. Pinch out growing tip of stem as soon as the first pods start to form; this will limit aphid damage and encourage other flowers to set. The young shoot tips can be cooked and eaten.
**Problems:** aphids (blackfly), grey mould, leaf spots, bumble bees, rust and sparrows (remove flowers).
**Harvesting:** 15 weeks (spring sown), 25 weeks (autumn sown), when pods reach approximately 8cm (3in).
**Yield:** 3kg per metre (6lb per yard) of row.
**Storing:** freeze.
**Varieties:** 'Aquadulce Claudia' (early/overwintering); 'Imperial Green Longpod', 'Red Epicure'.

### Capsicum or Sweet pepper *Capsicum annuum* Solanaceae
These green, red, yellow or other coloured fruits are valuable ingredients of salads as well as being prepared as cooked dishes such as stuffed peppers. The hot chilli or cayenne peppers are of a quite different type. Capsicums are closely related to tomatoes and aubergines, but while they are comparably hardy, I recommend that they are grown in a greenhouse as they need a long growing season. Only in the very warmest areas are they successful outside.

**Sowing:** half-hardy annual technique at medium temperature in early spring. Sow in 9cm (3½in) pots, since they resent the disturbance caused by pricking-on.
**Planting:** in a greenhouse in mid-spring.
**Base fertilizer:** use growing bags or ring culture pots with John Innes No. 2 potting compost.
**Spacing:** three plants to a growing bag or 40cm (16in) between ring culture pots.
**Care:** feed as tomatoes.
**Problems:** red spider mite, white fly.
**Harvesting:** 18 weeks, when fruits are firm; there is no difference in ripeness between differently coloured fruits.
**Yield:** 6-8 fruits per plant.
**Storing:** freeze.
**Varieties:** 'Salad Festival'.

### Courgette *Cucurbita pepo* Cucurbitaceae
### Marrow *Cucurbita pepo* Cucurbitaceae
Old gardening books described the cultivation of marrows rather than courgettes, but this is a vegetable that has rather gone out of fashion as marrows, especially the trailing kinds, take up a great deal of space and produce large fruits that are mostly water. Nonetheless, the modern courgette is more than merely a marrow picked young. Many varieties are now available (including types with dark green, pale green, yellow and even round fruits) which continue to crop throughout the summer if they are

picked regularly. The large yellow flowers, picked before the fruit starts to swell are regarded as a luxury item by top restaurants. Some types of summer squash are also treated as courgettes, notably the 'patty pan' squashes, with flattened, wavy edged fruits in pale green or yellow. Courgette varieties are compact bush plants but, like the marrow, they require a rich soil and plenty of water; the best way to achieve this is to take considerable care in preparing the planting position.

**Sowing:** half-hardy annual technique at medium temperature in mid-spring. Sow seed in pairs, sideways into the compost, in 9cm (3½in) pots and remove the weaker seedling.
**Planting:** in final positions outdoors when danger of frost has passed.
**Base fertilizer:** low, but prepare the planting position by digging a hole 30-40cm (12-16in) deep and wide and refilling with a mixture of three parts of manure or compost to one part soil.
**Spacing:** 60cm (24in) each way, for courgettes and bush marrows; 1.2m (4ft) for trailing marrows.
**Care:** water copiously once the fruits start to set.
**Problems:** fruit rot (protect the fruits by laying straw beneath them), mildew, virus.
**Harvesting:** 8-15 weeks, cut courgettes when they are about 10cm (4in) long; marrows when 25cm (10in) long.
**Yield:** 15-20 courgettes or 2-3 marrows per plant.

**Storing:** freeze courgettes; marrows will keep for up to three months in a cool, frost-free place.
**Varieties:** 'Gold Rush' F1; 'Zucchini' F1; (courgette types): 'Long Green Trailing' (marrow types).

**above** A golden variety of courgette such as 'Gold Rush' adds interest and attractiveness to the garden and the kitchen.

### Aubergine *Solanum melongena* Solanaceae

A close relative of the potato and tomato, but more tender. The purple, usually elongated, fruits cannot be eaten raw, but are delicious roasted, fried or grilled. Aubergines can be

**far left and left** Although the aubergine is often imagined to have elongated purple fruit, oval white varieties exist also; it's not called the egg plant for nothing.

**right** Long experience has convinced me that the melon 'Sweetheart' really has no rivals for cool greenhouse and frame cultivation.

grown outside but are only likely to be successful under tall cloches and in mild areas; my advice is always to grow them in a greenhouse.

**Sowing:** half-hardy annual technique at medium temperature in early spring; a long growing season is needed. Sow into 9cm (3½in) pots to avoid the disturbance caused by pricking on.
**Planting:** into growing bags, ring culture pots or, less satisfactorily, into the greenhouse border.
**Base fertilizer:** growing bag compost or use John Innes No. 2 potting compost in ring-culture pots.
**Spacing:** three plants to a growing bag or 40cm (16in) between ring culture pots.
**Care:** feed as tomatoes.
**Problems:** aphids, red spider mite, white fly.
**Harvesting:** 20 weeks, when fruits are fully coloured and approximately 15cm (6in) long.
**Yield:** 5-6 fruits per plant.
**Storing:** not satisfactory.
**Varieties:** 'Ova' F1 (white, spherical); 'Slice Rite' (purple).

## Pumpkin *Cucurbita maxima* Cucurbitaceae

Pumpkins were, at one time, only of interest to those planning for Halloween or an entry for the local giant vegetable contest. However, in recent years the giant varieties have been joined by smaller and tastier pie pumpkins and by their relative the winter squash. These are available in a wide range of shapes and colours and are notable because, once fully ripe in the late autumn, they can be stored through the winter. Cultivation of both pumpkins and squashes is similar to that for courgettes and marrows, but do bear in mind that most are trailing plants that consume a large area of the vegetable plot.

**Sowing:** half-hardy annual technique at medium temperature in mid-spring. Sow seed in pairs, sideways into the compost, in 9cm (3½in) pots and remove the weaker seedling.
**Planting:** in final positions outdoors when danger of frost has passed.
**Base fertilizer:** low, but prepare the planting position by digging a hole 30-40cm (12-16in) deep and wide and refilling with a mixture of three parts of manure or compost to one part soil.
**Spacing:** 60cm (24in) for compact bush varieties, 1.2m (4ft) for trailing varieties.
**Care:** water copiously once the fruits start to set.
**Problems:** fruit rot (protect the fruits by laying straw beneath them), mildew, virus.

Harvesting: 10-15 weeks.
Yield: 2-3 per plant, harvest after the plant starts to die back, but before the first severe frost.
Storing: in a cool shed for up to three months.
Varieties: 'Atlantic Giant'.

## Melon *Cucumis melo* Cucurbitaceae

The melon is botanically a fruit, is sweet tasting and eaten uncooked, but is nonetheless normally listed with the vegetables in the seed catalogues, along with its close relatives the cucumbers and marrows. They share many features with cucumbers and their cultivation is much easier than in years gone by now that hardier varieties are available. Like cucumbers, they can be grown in an unheated greenhouse, and are excellent in a cold-frame but are never really successful outdoors in Britain.

Sowing: half-hardy annual technique at medium temperature in mid-spring. Sow seed in pairs, sideways into the compost, in 9cm (3½in) pots and remove the weaker seedling.
Planting: into growing bags or pots of John Innes No. 2 compost in a greenhouse. Directly into a well-manured planting position in a cold-frame.
Base fertilizer: low; in a frame, prepare planting positions as for courgettes or marrows.
Spacing: two plants per growing bag or 45cm (18in) apart in a frame.
Care: water regularly and feed with a tomato fertilizer once the fruits have started to form. When five or six female flowers are fully open, pick two or three male flowers and use them to pollinate the females, which can be recognised by the small swelling below the petals. Pinch off any further flowers that form and restrict overall growth by pinching out shoot tips. Train greenhouse melons up canes and along horizontal wires attached to the greenhouse roof. Support developing fruits with nets. In frames, pinch out shoot tips and train four shoots in a cross-pattern, outwards to the corners of the frame, pinching out their tips when they have filled the area. Support the fruit clear of the ground.
Problems: mildew, virus.
Harvesting: 12 weeks, when fruit are nearly ripe, press gently on the end opposite the stalk; if it is slightly soft, the fruit is ripe.
Yield: 4-6 fruits per plant (greenhouse), 3-4 fruits per plant (frames).
Storing: not satisfactory.
Varieties: 'Sweetheart' F1.

## Cucumber *Cucumis sativus* Cucurbitaceae

Cucumbers originate from the humid subtropics but plant breeding has produced varieties hardy enough to perform satisfactorily in British gardens. I have given details of greenhouse growing, though unless you want a very early crop, the greenhouse space can be better used for other things and I find that outdoor varieties are more worthwhile.

Sowing: half-hardy annual technique at medium temperature in mid-spring. Sow seed in pairs, sideways into the compost, in 9cm (3½in) pots and remove the weaker seedling.
Planting: after the danger of frost has passed. Outdoors prepare a planting position by digging a hole 30-40cm (12-16in) deep and wide and refilling with a mixture of three parts manure or compost to one part soil.
Base fertilizer: low (outdoor varieties). For greenhouse varieties use growing bag compost then liquid feed.
Spacing: two plants per growing bag or 45cm (18in) outdoors.
Care: water copiously and feed greenhouse plants every two weeks with tomato fertilizer when the first fruits have set. Allow the plants to trail or train them up canes.
Problems: mildew, virus.
Harvesting: 12 weeks, when fruit are of acceptable size. Note that most outdoor varieties have short, ridge-type fruit, unlike shop-bought cucumbers.
Yield: 20-25 fruit per plant (greenhouse types), 7-10 fruit per plant (outdoor types).
Storing: not satisfactory.
Varieties: 'Petita' F1 (greenhouse).

below Outdoor ridge cucumbers may be bristly and look less appetising but often have better flavour than their smooth-skinned greenhouse counterparts.

**above** Ever keen to ensure that the vegetable garden looks attractive, I grow purple, yellow and green podded varieties of French bean.

**below** Gentle pressure with a (clean) finger-nail will cause milky juice to flow if sweet corn is ripe enough to pick.

## French bean *Phaseolus vulgaris* Leguminosae

Despite what some other nationalities might think, I regard the French bean as serving primarily to tempt the palate until the runner bean crop is ready. That said, it is easy to grow and offers a wide range of types including climbing varieties which give a much higher yield from a given area than the 60cm (24in) tall dwarf or bush varieties.

**Sowing:** half-hardy annual technique in growing positions in mid- and late spring, using cloches for the earliest sowings until all danger of frost has passed.
**Base fertilizer:** medium.
**Spacing:** 45 x 8cm (18 x 3in).
**Care:** use twigs or pea and bean netting to support the plants as they grow.
**Problems:** aphids.
**Harvesting:** 8-13 weeks, when pods are full and snap cleanly.
**Yield:** 1kg per metre (2lb per yard) of row for bush varieties, 1.5kg (3lb) for climbing varieties.

**Storing:** freeze.
**Varieties:** 'The Prince' (dwarf green pod); 'Purple Tepee' (dwarf purple pod); 'Corona d'Oro' (climbing yellow pod); 'Hunter' (climbing green pod).

## Sweet corn *Zea mays* Poaceae

This is the only grass crop grown as a garden vegetable. Ripe cobs picked straight from the garden are deliciously sweet, but the yield is often disappointing given the size of the plants. Sweet corn takes up a large amount of space because, being wind-pollinated, plants must be grown in large blocks rather than rows to ensure success. It is a crop for larger gardens and warm, sunny areas.

**Sowing:** half-hardy annual technique at medium temperature, raising plants individually in 9cm (3½in) pots.
**Planting:** in growing positions outside when danger of frost has passed.
**Base fertilizer:** low.
**Spacing:** 45 x 45cm (18 x 18in).
**Care:** water carefully to prevent the soil drying out; earth up around the stem bases when roots start to grow above soil level. Shake the plants when the male flowers (tassels) are fully open to aid pollination.
**Problems:** fruit fly.
**Harvesting:** 13 weeks, when the tassels turn brown, carefully peel back the sheath surrounding the cobs and press a few seeds with a thumbnail; when a runny but creamy liquid oozes out they are ready.
**Yield:** 2 cobs per plant.
**Storing:** freeze.
**Varieties:** numerous very similar varieties.

## Tomato *Lycopersicon esculentum* Solanaceae

The tomato must be the most important summer vegetable in most gardens. Certainly more people have greenhouses to enable them to grow tomatoes than for any other reason. Despite the general improvement in flavour of commercial varieties in recent years, there's no doubt that the taste of the varieties available to gardeners offers a compelling argument in favour of the home-grown crop. There are two main ways of growing tomatoes: in a greenhouse or, in milder, more sheltered areas, outside in the garden. Some varieties can be grown in both situations but the unstaked bush tomato is only for outdoor growing. In the greenhouse, tomatoes may be grown in the soil of the greenhouse border, in pots or growing bags or, best of all, in ring culture beds.

**Sowing:** half-hardy technique at medium temperature. Sow into 9cm (3½in) diameter pots approximately nine weeks before the plants are to be planted into their growing conditions.

**Planting:** outdoors, when the danger of the last frost has passed. In a greenhouse maintained at a minimum of 7°C (45°F), mid-spring.

**Base fertilizer:** in greenhouse, use growing bag compost or, in ring culture beds, John Innes No. 2 soil-based compost. Outdoors, medium.

**Spacing:** indoors two plants per standard sized growing bag, or 45cm (18in) apart in ring culture pots or border soil. Outdoors, 75 x 45cm (30 x 18in).

**Care:** greenhouse and staked (cordon) outdoor varieties must be tied in regularly to their supports and the side-shoots removed. Outdoor bush varieties should have straw placed beneath them to keep the fruit out of contact with the soil. Water constantly; the soil or compost must not be allowed to dry out. Feed with a proprietary liquid tomato fertilizer from the time that the first fruit truss sets; twice a week for indoor and once a week for outdoor plants.

**Problems:** aphids, blight (outdoors), blossom end rot, white fly, virus.

**Harvesting:** 16 weeks (greenhouse), 20 weeks (outdoors); when fruit are fully coloured. Green fruit may be collected at the end of the season and either used to make pickles or preserves or ripened in warmth; it is warmth, not light that brings about ripening.

**Yield:** 3.5kg (7lb) per plant (greenhouse); 1.75kg (3½lb) per plant (outdoors).

**Storing:** not satisfactory.

**Varieties:** Greenhouse and outdoors: 'Alicante', 'Gardener's Delight' (small fruit, very sweet taste), 'Sungold' F1 (small fruit, very like 'Gardener's Delight' but yellow), 'Yellow Perfection' (yellow fruit). Greenhouse only: 'Buffalo' (large fruited beefsteak type), 'Sweet 100' F1 (small fruit, almost as good a flavour as 'Gardener's Delight'). Outdoors

only: 'Incas' (plum tomato); 'The Amateur', 'Red Alert', 'Sleaford Abundance' F1.

### Pea *Pisum sativum* Papilionaceae

It's unfortunate that the fresh garden pea has declined in popularity in favour of the frozen article, because the range of types for home-growing has never been more interesting. In some years and on poor soils, however, yields can be disappointingly low, so it is important to improve the fertility of the soil (preferably by trenching in the autumn) and to ensure that the plants are weaned carefully over their vulnerable seedling stage. There are several types of pea: round-seeded varieties for autumn or early spring sowing, these give the earliest crops; wrinkle-seeded types for later sowing (divided into early, second early and maincrop varieties, by maturity); mangetout varieties, in which the young pod is eaten whole; and petit pois types, which produce very small peas even when mature. Within each group, tall and dwarf varieties are available; for most gardens, I strongly recommend the latter.

**Sowing:** hardy annual technique in autumn or early spring under cloches (round-seeded varieties); sequentially from spring to summer (wrinkled-seeded varieties); mid- to late spring (mangetout and petit pois varieties).

**above** Ring culture offers a clean, efficient, disease-free method of growing greenhouse tomatoes and other crops.

**below** Pea moth renders the crop unpleasant and useless and is best avoided by delaying the sowing of the main crop in areas where it is troublesome.

right The runner bean was first grown in European gardens as an ornamental; by selecting varieties with different flower colours, their attractiveness can be appreciated.

below The Chinese cabbage is the easiest of the Oriental vegetables for European gardens although the older varieties were very prone to bolt if sown early.

**Base fertilizer:** none.
**Spacing:** in bands of three rows, 10cm (4in) apart, with 60cm (24in) between the central row of adjoining triple rows; plants 10cm (4in) apart within the rows.
**Care:** support plants using twiggy sticks or pea and bean netting; net to protect plants from birds; mulch around young plants to retain soil moisture.
**Problems:** birds, mice, mildew, pea moth, root rot.
**Harvesting:** 12-16 weeks, when pods are full; pick regularly from the bottom of the plants. Mangetout varieties should be picked when still flat and about 8cm (3in) long.
**Yield:** 1.5kg per metre (3lb per yard) of row.
**Storing:** freeze.

**Varieties:** 'Feltham First' (early); 'Kelvedon Wonder' (second early); 'Hurst Greenshaft' (maincrop); 'Sugar Ann' (sugar pod); 'Waverex' (petit pois).

**Runner bean** *Phaseolus coccineus* Papilionaceae
The runner bean is the archetypal English summer vegetable. It has the enormous advantage of taking up very little space for the huge crop it produces. The plants are attractive too; it's worth remembering that they were originally introduced from South America as ornamental climbers. A very appealing effect can be achieved by alternating varieties with different coloured flowers. Runner beans can happily be grown on the same site for several years, though root problems may eventually force a move. The soil must be deep and well manured; a 45 or 60cm (18 or 24in) deep trench, liberally dressed with manure when it is refilled in autumn, is ideal.

There are several ways to support the plants but a wigwam of canes or tall sticks, at least 2m (6ft 7in) tall or a ridge-tent-style arrangement with canes laid horizontally across the tops to support the ridge are the simplest. Alternatively, to save on the cost of canes in the ridge-tent system, one cane may be fixed horizontally close to soil level along each row of upright canes and some of the uprights replaced with strings tied to the lower and upper horizontal canes.

There are two main types of runner bean: the traditional string beans, with a fibrous 'string' along the edge of the pod which must be removed before cooking, and the newer stringless varieties, easier to prepare but not as tasty. There are also a few low-growing, dwarf varieties, though in limited space dwarf French beans are a better proposition.

**Sowing:** half-hardy annual technique in 10cm (4in) pots in a greenhouse or, better, in growing positions in late spring.
**Planting:** pot-raised plants after the danger of frost has passed.
**Base fertilizer:** medium.
**Spacing:** 60cm (24in) between two rows of canes and 15cm (6in) between adjacent canes (or strings) in the rows, with one plant at the base of each cane.
**Care:** water frequently to prevent the soil drying out; if difficulty is experienced in inducing the lowest flowers to set, mulch heavily when the plants are about 1m (3ft) tall.
**Problems:** bees and birds removing or damaging the flowers, leaf spot, root rot.
**Harvesting:** 12 weeks when pods are 15-20cm (6-8in) long (depending on variety); pick regularly to ensure a continuing set of new pods.
**Yield:** 8-9kg per metre (16-20lb per yard) or row.
**Storing:** freeze.
**Varieties:** 'Polestar' (stringless, red flowers); 'White Emergo' (string, white flowers); 'Painted Lady' (string, bicoloured); 'Hammonds Dwarf Scarlet' (dwarf).

## Oriental Vegetables
### Chinese cabbage *Brassica rapa* Pekinensis Group Brassicaceae

This is perhaps the exotic vegetable that has been taken most successfully to the British palate. Although it is called a cabbage and looks like a cos lettuce, it is closely related to the turnip. It is cooked and eaten differently from all of them; the secret is to cook it very lightly by flash steaming. Chinese cabbage tends to bolt when grown under British conditions because of the combination of long days and cool temperatures. The trick, therefore, is to wait until after midsummer, choose a very fast growing variety, sow direct and never allow the soil to dry out.

**Sowing:** hardy annual technique in growing position in midsummer (although it is claimed some varieties are reliable when sown as early as mid-spring, I am sceptical).

**Base fertilizer:** medium.
**Spacing:** 25 x 25cm (10 x 10in).
**Care:** water carefully but regularly.
**Problems:** cabbage root fly, club-root, slugs.
**Harvesting:** 9-10 weeks, when the heads are firm.
**Yield:** 0.6-1kg (1-2lb) per plant.
**Storing:** not satisfactory.
**Varieties:** 'Green Rocket' F1.

## Edible Flowers

Many garden flowers make attractive and interesting additions to salads. Some, like borage, *Calendula*, chicory, chives, marjoram, marrows and courgettes, sage, scorzonera and thyme are normal residents of the kitchen or herb garden, others grow in ornamental beds and borders. Among those worth adding to dishes for their decorative and edible value are *Bellis* daisies, meadow cranesbill, roses, sweet violets, viper's bugloss and white clover.

But it's never wise to experiment with eating unusual parts of plants unless you are sure of their safety and you should always avoid eating the flowers of laburnum, yew, monkshood (*Aconitum*), anemones, aquilegias, clematis, daphne, hellebores, poppies (even though the ripe seeds are edible), pinks and carnations, foxgloves, euphorbias and most bulbous plants. Among native flowers that look attractive but should be avoided are self-heal (*Prunella*), buttercups, celandines, deadly nightshade, many of the umbellifers, bryony and henbane. And remember that the tomato-like fruits of the potato are extremely poisonous.

**below** Nasturtiums are perhaps the most familiar and easiest to grow of all edible flowers and are now obtainable in a wide range of delightful colours.

# Herbs

Although to a horticulturist or botanist, the term herb is used for any plant lacking a woody structure, it has a quite different but not very strict meaning in the garden; and in this book. A herb is simply any plant, woody or not, that is strongly aromatic and is used either for medicinal purposes or for culinary flavouring rather than as a food in its own right. Although herbs are a big group and include types of plant with very different habits (annuals such as basil, perennials such as mint and shrubby plants like rosemary and bay), their growing requirements are remarkably similar.

### Site and soil

Most herbs grow best in full sun in a light, free-draining soil with a pH of about 7. A few will tolerate shade although flavour is seldom as strong as in full sun, so if your garden is very shaded or your soil very heavy, remember that many herbs are highly successful when grown in containers, such as large tubs or even window boxes. And this is worthwhile, even if you are also able to grow them in beds in the garden, as they can then be grown in the house or greenhouse over winter.

Plenty of water and a free-draining compost are essential; I use a soil-based John Innes No. 2 potting compost in terracotta pots. It's important, however, to select a pot of size appropriate to the vigour of each type of plant and grow them as single subjects. Pots and hanging baskets planted with a mixture of herbs are often seen for sale, but as growth rates vary so much, these are never as successful as single-subject containers. Position containers in warm, sunny places and remember that, although most herbs are plants of relatively dry places (many originate in the Mediterranean), extra watering will be needed in the summer months. A balanced liquid feed once or twice during the growing season is also beneficial for vigorous herbs.

An alternative to containers, where soil is heavy and becomes waterlogged over winter or is otherwise unsuitable, is to create a small raised bed for herbs and improve the soil in the bed by adding garden compost.

### Types of herb garden

To grow a basic range of herbs for the kitchen, you will need an area of 4-9m² (4.5-10 sq yds) although if you plan to specialise and incorporate many of the medicinal species also, then a very much greater area will of course be needed. The arrangement of the plants can be informal (simply placing the taller types at the back and the smaller to the front)

**below** The herb garden is the classic example of the way that the functional and attractive can be so easily combined.

although many gardeners find a formal style more attractive, mimicking the regimented herb gardens that have been used since mediaeval times.

One popular version of the formal planting is to arrange the plants in a cartwheel pattern, using either a real cartwheel and planting the herbs between the spokes, or constructing a facsimile wheel, from bricks for instance. But whatever scheme is used, do bear in mind the need easily to reach all parts of the bed for picking the plants; stepping stones are very useful in a large area.

If you have room and want to add a mediaeval or Tudor feel to the planting, an edging of box (*Buxus sempervirens* 'Suffruticosa') will be effective but it will need regular trimming. An alternative is to use weather-resistant bricks to divide up the herb garden.

Always bear in mind that herbs vary greatly in their vigour, so not all will remain neatly within their allotted planting space. Some, such as the mints, are best kept in pots sunk into the ground to prevent them from spreading too far. Within a few years, moreover, most herbs become woody and are then best replaced with fresh stock; with the exception of the shrubs, they shouldn't be considered long-term plants.

### Sowing and planting

Herb plants are sold widely, not only in garden centres but in supermarkets, markets and particularly by herb specialists who often supply by mail order and offer a far greater range of varieties than more general outlets. Many medicinal herbs and annual and biennial kitchen herbs, can be raised from seed. However, most of the best varieties of culinary herb don't come true from seed and so must be propagated by division or by cuttings (see page 70).

As herbs are sold as small plants, and as most are not notably hardy, I prefer to plant them in the spring after the bed has been double dug in the previous autumn. A light dressing of bone meal (wear gloves to apply) is the only fertilizer treatment needed at planting time but the plants should be watered in well. No culinary herbs require staking although some of the more ornamental medicinal types produce tall flower spikes that will need some form of support.

### Aftercare

A herb garden in a sunny position with a well-drained soil will be prone to drying out in summer; a light mulch of well-rotted leaf mould applied in spring can help reduce the need for summer watering. Feeding should be minimal, a light dressing of a balanced general feed, such as fish, blood and bone as growth starts in the spring is all that is needed. Herbs do suffer from a small range of pests and diseases but you should be prepared to tolerate some damage, as disfigured foliage can be cut out and fresh young leaves should begin to appear within a few weeks. I don't encourage gardeners to use chemical controls in the herb garden; with the few problems such as mint rust that are serious and debilitating, it makes sense to begin again with new plants.

### Harvesting and preserving

Herbs are best used fresh, so extending the season by bringing some indoors in

**above** The herb garden lends itself to many different styles and the formal approach, dating back to Ancient times, is still popular.

**below** Drying herbs requires no special equipment and the traditional way in a well ventilated shed is still the best although many gardeners now use a microwave oven.

**above** The many varieties of basil now available are among the numerous herbs that thrive well in containers.

pots or putting cloches over them is worthwhile. Even so, for a year-round supply of herbs some will have to be preserved. Only keep the best quality young leaves, pick them in the early morning before the heat of the day causes the volatile oils to evaporate and preserve them as soon after picking as possible. Freezing works well; simply place freshly picked herbs in small freezer bags or chop them up and drop them into ice cube trays of water. Drying herbs does reduce the flavour considerably, but when it is necessary, try using a microwave oven, if hanging them up in a warm, airy room is impracticable. Once dried, the leaves can be rubbed off the stalks and kept in screw-topped jars. Inserting sprigs of herbs into bottles of wine vinegar or good quality oil is an alternative method of preservation.

Important annual (and tender) herbs that are best raised from seed:

[A] = annual
[B]= biennial

*Alliaria petiolata* Jack-by-the hedge, Garlic mustard [B]
*Anethum graveolens* Dill [B]
*Angelica archangelica* Garden angelica (best grown as a [B])
*Anthriscus cerefolium* Chervil [A]
*Apium graveolens* Wild celery, Smallage [B]
*Atriplex hortensis* Orache [A]
*Borago officinalis* Borage [A]
*Brassica spp.* Mustards [A]
*Calendula officinalis* Pot marigold [A]
*Carthamus tinctorius* Safflower, False saffron [A]
*Carum carvi* Caraway [B]
*Claytonia perfoliata* Winter purslane, Miner's lettuce [A]
*Coriandrum sativum* Coriander [A]
*Echium vulgare* Viper's bugloss [B]
*Eruca vesicaria* Salad rocket [A]
*Euphrasia officinalis* [A]
*Helianthus annuus* Sunflower [A]
*Hesperis matronalis* Sweet rocket (best grown as [B])
*Linum usitatissimum* Flax [A]
*Melilotus officinalis* Meliot [B]
*Myosotis spp.* Forget-me-not [A] (some)
*Ocimum basilicum* Basil [A]
*Oenothera biennis* Evening primrose [B]
*Onopordon acanthium* Cotton thistle [B]
*Papaver spp.* Poppy [A]
*Petroselinum crispum* Parsley [B]
*Pimpinella anisum* Aniseed [A]
*Portulaca oleracea* Summer purslane [A]
*Reseda luteola* Weld [B]
*Satureja spp.* Savory [B] (Summer savory is grown as an [A])
*Sesamum indicum* Sesame [A]
*Stellaria media* Chickweed [A]
*Tagetes patula* French marigold [A]
*Trigonella foenum-graecum* Fenugreek [A]
*Tropaeolum majus* Nasturtium [A]
*Verbascum thapsus* Mullein [B]

### Herbs for shade

While the best site for a herb bed is without a doubt in full sun, some herbs can tolerate light shade. Those that need moist shade have been denoted by [Moist]:

*Ajuga reptans* Bugle
*Alchemilla mollis* Lady's mantle
*Alliaria petiolata* Jack-by-the-hedge, Garlic
    mustard
*Allium schoenoprasum* Chives
*Angelica archangelica* Angelica [Moist]
*Anthriscus cerefolium* Chervil
*Apium graveolens* Wild celery, Smallage
*Armoracia rusticana* Horseradish
*Calamintha grandiflora* Calamint
*Cardamine pratensis* Lady's smock,
    Cuckoo flower
*Dictamnus albus* White dittany, Burning bush
*Eruca vesicaria* Salad rocket
*Eupatorium purpureum* Trumpet weed
    [Moist]
*Filipendula ulmaria* Meadowsweet [Moist]
*Foeniculum vulgare* Fennel
*Fragaria vesca* Wild strawberry
*Hesperis matronalis* Sweet rocket [Moist]
*Hydrastis canadensis* Yellow root, Golden
    seal [Moist]
*Hypericum perforatum* St John's wort
*Lamium* spp. Dead-nettles
*Levisticum officinale* Lovage
*Lonicera caprifolium* Perfoliate Honeysuckle
*Mentha* spp. Mint
*Myosotis* spp. Forget-me-not
*Myrrhis odorata* Sweet Cicely
*Petroselinum crispum* Parsley

*Persicaria bistorta* Bistort [Moist]
*Primula* spp. Primrose, Cowslip
    ([Moist] for primroses)
*Pulmonaria* spp. Lungwort [Moist]
*Rubia tinctoria* Madder
*Rumex acetosa* Sorrel
*Scutellaria lateriflora* Skullcap
*Sium sisarum* Skirret
*Smyrnium olusatrum* Alexanders [Moist]
*Stachys officinalis* Betony [Moist]

**above** Some herbs, notably mint and horse-radish, are invasive and must be confined in some way.

Although the tightly curled moss parsley varieties (**left**) are the prettiest, the broader leaved Italian parsley (**far left**) has the better flavour.

# The Lawn

Once it's mown, and preferably edged too, a lawn can almost instantly bring to a garden a neatness and tidiness that nothing else can emulate. And despite the work involved in the mowing, there is no easier way of keeping an area of garden under control. Grass is the easiest of all plants to grow and it's the most efficient at suppressing weeds. A lawn need not only be thought of as a permanent part of the garden for, in the early stages on a new site, it makes a great deal of sense to grow grass over the majority of it, beds and borders then being cut out as time and other practicalities allow.

**below** There is still no substitute for a neatly mown and edged lawn in enhancing the attractiveness of the whole garden.

The special feature of grass that makes it such a useful plant is its ability to tolerate mowing. It achieves this by having the cells responsible for growth at the base, not the top of the stem. So while if you cut off most types of plant at ground level, they will die through an inability to regenerate, grass will thrive on this treatment and not only grow again but also be stimulated into producing further shoots. The only other way that a plant can survive being mown is if its growing point is at the shoot tip and the shoot itself is telescoped such that the whole thing is sunk below mowing level; and this is the mechanism by which common lawn weeds such as dandelions and daisies survive.

Although lawns can and do grow on all types of soil, they are generally least successful on very heavy clays and very light sands; although to some extent, the difficulties on light soils can be overcome if additional feeding and watering is given. Lawns will also grow in most aspects but you will never have a successful lawn if the area is heavily shaded. The reason for this will be evident if you walk through a woodland; there are very few grasses growing there and those that do are species that don't respond satisfactorily to mowing.

## Site preparation

Having selected the area where your lawn will be laid, it's important to begin the site preparation as far in advance as is practicable. The area should be dug thoroughly, much as you would for the preparation of a vegetable garden (page 55). If it can be double dug, so much the better, but because of the likely size of the area concerned, this isn't an operation to be undertaken lightly. It's nonetheless important to remove all perennial weed growth, especially couch grass.

While broad-leaved weeds can be controlled fairly satisfactorily by selective weedkillers after the lawn is established, weed grasses will be extremely difficult to eradicate. If the area is infested with couch, my advice would be to begin your preparation in late spring and to use the systemic weedkiller glyphosate throughout the summer. Then dig the area in the autumn with a view to laying the new lawn in the following spring. This may seem a long time over which to be patient but the effort will be more than repaid in the years to come.

If the site is markedly irregular, you will need to level it. This is done simply with wooden pegs and string. Hammer in the pegs

2m (6½ft) apart and a few centimetres deep in a grid pattern. Lay a plank across adjacent pairs of pegs in turn, place a spirit level on top and then hammer in the pegs until all are level. Then tie string between the pegs at the level required; if you tie the string at the same distance below the top of each peg, you will have a level grid pattern. Fill up to the strings with top soil; you will probably have to buy some specially for the purpose if you don't want to excavate a large hole elsewhere in the garden. Firm the soil as you fill; I find there is nothing better for this than the back of a garden rake, but always finish with a surface about 1cm (½in) higher than you really require to allow for the soil settling. On a very irregularly sloping site you may need to grade the area but don't imagine that the surface of a good lawn must always be flat. A gentle, fairly uniform slope can be most attractive.

## Laying the lawn

The best times of year for laying a new lawn are mid-spring and early autumn although in favourable seasons, turf can be laid at any time when there are no hard frosts and when rain can be expected with some confidence; artificial watering is never as effective at helping a lawn to establish. About one month before you

intend to lay the lawn, rake the surface with a spring tined lawn rake, carefully removing any large clods and stones. Rake alternately in directions at right angles to each other in order not to produce or accentuate any humps and hollows. Having prepared the site for your new

**above** A patchy appearance and sparse grass very often means poor drainage or that the lawn is shaded for much of the day.

**left** If a lawn is to be grown from seed, it is worth spending much time and effort in the soil preparation; you won't have another chance.

**above** Be sure that you sow seed in marked out small areas at a time; this way you will find it much easier to obtain uniformity.

way over the surface. Tamping down the soil with the back of a garden rake may also help.

### Turf or seed?

Up to this stage, the operation is the same whether you intend to lay turf or sow seed and so let's now consider their relative merits. Having put down more of both in my time than I care to remember, my choice now is firmly on the side of turf. It's quicker, easier and more sure of success although it is also certainly more expensive. Seedling lawns are at the mercy of the weather and the local bird population. They are also at the mercy of being swamped by weed seedlings too, especially as there is no longer a suitable weedkiller available to gardeners for newly sown lawns. Nonetheless, in saying this, I realise that there will be many gardeners who do still prefer seeding and who may simply have an area of potential lawn that would be prohibitively costly to turf. For them, there is now an extensive range of lawn seed mixtures although I advise you not to become too enthusiastic about those that are offered for sowing in shade or partial shade. For the reasons that I have already indicated, the results may be marginally better than with a normal lawn seed mixture but nothing will permit you to grow a lawn satisfactorily in a woodland glade.

### Seed

The principal choice to be made in seed mixtures is between those sold for fine lawns and those for lawns that will have to bear considerable wear and tear. In essence, a fine lawn seed mixture, comprising various fescues and bent grasses, is only worth using for a lawn that is seldom walked on. For the normal domestic lawn it's essential to choose a blend containing hard-wearing rye grasses; among which the modern hybrid varieties can give a very attractive appearance, possessing little of the coarseness of the older types. Spread the seed as uniformly as you can at the rate of about 175g/4m$^2$ (1½oz/sq yd). This is easier than it might sound if you mark off the area into squares with string or canes for you will find that most seed companies supply a small measure or shaker with the seed; or sometimes rather imaginatively provide a picture showing the density of seed to aim for. Although it's sometimes suggested that the seed should be

lawn, you will need to apply a pre-sowing or turfing fertiliser and this should be done about three weeks later; or about one week before the start. It's simplest to use an autumn lawn feed with a relatively low nitrogen content and you should use this even if you are starting your lawn in the spring. Apply it at the manufacturer's recommended rate and rake it carefully into the top few centimetres (inch) of the soil.

The surface should then be firmed but this must not be done with a roller. Unless you have a very wide, lightweight roller and are skilled in using it, you will undo all of your hard work and finish up with a surface like a roller-coaster track. There is no better tool for firming the surface than a pair of feet (preferably many feet), shod in boots. Tread steadily and evenly (not with a 'heeling in' action), working your

**left** Turves should be laid off-set, like bricks in a wall, but be careful not to use small pieces at the edges as they will become ragged.

left uncovered, I much prefer to spread finely sieved soil over the surface to a depth such that the seed is just rendered invisible. It's then essential to provide protection from birds; the simplest way to do this is to spread lightweight fruit cage netting over the area, supporting it on upturned plastic plant pots on the tops of canes. Use a lawn sprinkler with a very fine spray to ensure that the surface neither dries out nor is washed into ridges. The seed should germinate in 14 to 21 days.

## Turf

Lawn turf too has improved beyond recognition and I hope that the days of 'meadow turf', bought through the small ad columns of the local newspaper are gone forever. Meadow turf is for grazing cattle not for lawns. For relatively little extra cost you can now buy specially grown turf, available in three or four different grades of fine or hard wearing components comparable with the seed mixtures. It's worth remembering several important things when planning to turf a lawn. The turf will be delivered in rolls and they are extremely heavy so have them dropped as close as possible to the area where they are to be laid. If you can't lay them within about seven days, the grass will turn yellow and so they must be unrolled and stored flat; but of course you will need an area at least as large as your new lawn on which to do this. Lay the turves overlapping, rather like the bricks in a wall and use a lawn edging iron to cut them to shape. Always stand on a plank when cutting and laying the turf to avoid damaging it. And never lay a

**below** A cylinder mower will always give the closest finish but the height of the blades should be adjusted to suit the conditions.

above Broad-leaved weeds in lawns soon begin to curl and distort after treatment with a selective weedkiller.

small piece of turf at the end of a row as it will dry and shrink. Pull a full-sized piece to the edge and use a small cut-off piece to fill in the gap that this leaves. Firmly tamp down the turves with the back of a strong garden rake and brush fine soil in between them. Don't worry if you spill soil on the surface; the rain will soon wash it in. Use a sprinkler on the new lawn if rain doesn't fall within a few hours and do not allow it to dry out fully for about 10 days; after this time it should have taken root and can be walked on. It can be cut with a rotary mower (preferably a hover model) after about a further fortnight if the mower blades are set high.

## Lawn care

Once established, your lawn must be given some care and attention if it's to be elevated from being merely a patch of green to a garden feature of which you can be proud. The most important routine lawn task is mowing and on page 51 I have given some guidance on the type of mower to choose. Try to mow at least once a week during the main growing season; from mid-spring to early autumn in what used to be called an average year. Outside these months, the amount of mowing needed will depend on the prevailing temperature and the degree to which the grass has grown; there's no reason why it shouldn't be cut in mild periods during the winter. But set the cutter blades to their highest at these times; cutting the grass short when frosts are still likely is asking for trouble. During the summer, however, the blades can be lowered appreciably although it's unwise, other than on bowling greens, to cut grass at the lowest blade setting for this merely encourages moss growth. If your mower has a grass collector, you should always use it for I find that unless you are cutting almost daily, the mowings will block the surface of the grass and prevent the free penetration of air and water.

In my comments on lawn tools, I have already referred to the other important lawn-care tasks; edging, raking and scarifying. But lawns must also be fed and two lawn fertilizers are needed, one for spring and one for autumn. I only use liquid, high nitrogen 'green-up' feeds in the summer in years when very prolonged rain falls after the spring feed has been applied and a great deal of it has, in consequence, been washed away. I find it best to delay applying the spring feed until mid- to late spring when the soil is really warm and moist; not so much for the benefit of the fertilizer itself but to ensure that the weedkiller that is combined with it is applied in conditions in which it's likely to be

right Fairy rings of toadstools often cause concern to gardeners but they can't effectively be eradicated and the best solution is to give the lawn additional fertiliser.

effective. Any weeds that do escape this treatment are dealt with later by localised application of a selective weedkiller in liquid form either with a watering can (kept specially for the purpose) or with a weedkiller sprayer (although not with a hose-end dilutor).

One lawn problem causes gardeners more concern than any other: moss. There are gardeners who are obsessed with trying to rid their lawns of moss; generally my advice is to expend their emotional and physical energies elsewhere. To kill moss is not difficult. Any of the modern selective moss killers will do it, although none better than lawn sand. But the moss will always return unless it's possible to correct the underlying causes. Moss will thrive when the grass is closely mown, when the lawn is shaded, poorly drained and the grass not fed. On many lawns, the site characteristics are all but impossible to alter or correct and all I can do is to ask that you keep the problem in perspective. Don't mow too closely, and try to aerate and scarify the lawn as frequently as possible, feed the grass twice a year and use lawn sand once a year.

Apart from weeds, lawns suffer relatively little from other problems; there are few pests and diseases likely to cause concern. Perhaps the commonest of the symptoms that you are likely to see are brown patches although their causes are numerous. Fungal diseases are one possibility, leatherjackets or wireworms are others; but urine from bitches and spilled lawn mower petrol are at least as frequent. The more or less circular rings of toadstools called fairy rings also cause concern although I happen to find them attractive. Without wholesale excavation, you will be unlikely to be able to do anything to control them so you may as well persuade yourself that they are fascinating.

## Non-grass lawns

The idea of having a lawn using plants other than grass obviously appeals to many gardeners as I'm asked about it frequently. These plants must have the same characteristic of being able to create flat areas of greenery that can be walked on and tolerate mowing or at least trimming. The most important among them are some of the carpeting species of thyme and *Dianthus* and the non-flowering variety of camomile called 'Treneague', but they should not be considered as real alternatives to grass.

None of them tolerate the amount of wear and tear that grass turf can absorb. All of them look dismal in winter and will, in any event, only thrive in the sunniest situation and on light free-draining soil. And all of them must be hand-weeded because, being broad-leaved plants, selective weedkillers can't be used on them. In the right position, they can be very pretty but I feel that you should consider them as curiosity features for large gardens rather than substitutes for genuine lawns.

**above** Small areas can be planted rather effectively with plants like camomile but they aren't easy to care for and are no real substitute for grass.

# Bedding Plants

So much more can be achieved with bedding plants than their name suggests that I can envisage the time when seed companies will inflict on us some name such as 'patio plants' or 'summer specials' that, hideous as it may be, reflects their increasingly important role away from beds and in containers. But despite their different uses, these are all essentially short-term plants giving colour for a season, the season usually being summer, although let's not forget that spring and even winter bedding plants are available too. Under the overall umbrella title, we can find both hardy and half-hardy annuals, with others that are treated as annuals for practical purposes but are in reality tender perennials, together with a few biennials. These differences can be confusing but only become really relevant if you want to raise your own plants from seed or are puzzled over which plants to retain and which to dispose of at the end of the season.

**above** Bedding plants are now obtainable in every colour you can imagine (and a few that you can't) and can be grown in a remarkable variety of ways.

## Site

When planting an entire bed with bedding plants, the soil should be prepared as for vegetables because, like them, these plants only have a short time to establish their roots, grow and yield a product so they must be given the best possible conditions. A sunny site with a soil that has been improved with well rotted organic matter is ideal but some bedding plants can tolerate a certain degree of shade, especially if the ground is maintained in a moist condition, while some hardy annuals can tolerate a dry, poor soil but need the sun. Winter bedding must always have the best conditions

Even apparently unpromising sites can be used for bedding plants, therefore, if appropriate types are chosen. Indeed, almost any problem corner in the garden, with the exception of dry shade, could be completely transformed with the right choice of species. As these are relatively small plants with a great deal of impact, narrow beds close to a house wall and alongside lawns can easily be brightened up. Being low-growing too, many are wind tolerant although in such sites, you should avoid those with highly-bred large flowers and brittle stems.

## Space required

Correct spacing between plants is important as it affects not only the size that each individual can attain but also the overall effect of the bed. The aim is to allow each plant to grow to its full potential but to plant it close enough to its neighbours so that the amount of bare soil visible once the plants are in flower is minimal. Seed packets and plant labels give a guide to suggested spacings and most offer distances of between 15 and 30cm (6 and 12in) but do remember that dwarf varieties will need closer spacing than this.

In containers, moreover, these normal planting distances aren't really relevant and plants can be placed much closer together, provided you are prepared to supply them with extra water and fertilizer. As a guide, a 30cm (12in) diameter hanging basket will need at least eight small plants. When sowing hardy annuals *in situ* in spring, you can sow thinly in rows, usually 10-15cm (4-6in) apart, depending on the type of plant, and then thin out to the recommended spacings later, or, and I think much better, broadcast sow by simply scattering the seed from your hand or packet and lightly raking it in. The boundaries of the

**left** Mark out with sand the areas for each type or colour of annual to help you with the sowing.

areas for broadcast sowing each type of plant can usefully be marked out with sand, adjacent areas being indented into one another, jig-saw fashion.

## Containers

As I have hinted, the most popular use of bedding plants in the modern garden is for containers, where a good compost is the key to success. A multi-purpose soil-less brand is suitable although I prefer soil-based John Innes No. 2 potting compost, provided the extra weight is not a drawback. Be sure to choose plants with the appropriate habit for each type of container (remember that bedding plants are available in all forms, from upright, compact and bushy to slender, lax and trailing), but if hanging baskets or window boxes are to be sited in exposed positions, it makes sense to avoid cascading plants with brittle stems, like ivy-leaved pelargoniums.

## Buying bedding plants

Raising your own bedding plants from seed is very satisfying, gives you the greatest choice of varieties and, for large bedding schemes, is the cheapest option. If you don't have a greenhouse or don't have time or inclination to raise your own plants, there is another very satisfactory alternative: young plants, sometimes called 'plugs', which may be purchased from garden centres or nurseries or by mail order. To be accurate, the plug itself is the compost in which the plant is grown and there are various forms of 'baby plants' of which the plug, in the strict sense, is only one. A genuine plug is a small, often wedge- shaped 'cell' in a larger tray or con-

**below** If you can't or don't want to raise your own plants from seed, it's now possible to buy bedding plants at all stages of growth.

**above** Great satisfaction does come from raising your own plants from seed.

**below** Although bedding plants are ideal for containers, the watering and feeding necessary are in inverse proportion to the size of pot.

begonias, petunias, busy lizzies and pelargoniums, especially 'Century' and 'Multibloom' varieties, although you will find a much wider range among baby seedlings, including 20 or more of the most popular bedding plants, such as African marigolds and alyssum. The widest range, as with seeds, is available by mail order but do check first in your catalogues the last date by which the orders must be placed. Understandably, the producers need to know well in advance how many plants will be needed to fulfil the requirements; unlike seeds, it isn't simply a matter of dipping into the bag for a few more.

When buying plants and pondering the relatively high cost, it's worth bearing in mind that some of the interesting tender perennials that have become more widely available in recent years can't be raised from seed and are propagated by cuttings. Once you have purchased a plant you can maintain your stock by taking cuttings at the end of the season, but you will need a greenhouse to do this successfully.

### Sowing and planting

There are two main ways of raising bedding plants from seed: the hardy annual technique and the half-hardy annual technique (page 71). Biennials are treated slightly differently and I describe the method below.

If you have purchased plantlets, these must be kept somewhere light and frost-free and, as they dry out easily, they should be kept moist and transferred as soon as possible either to their growing positions or to a small pot because the nutrients in the small plug of compost are soon exhausted. Plantlets in small mesh pots or Jiffy 7 modules can be left in their containers when transplanted, as the roots will grow through the mesh into the fresh compost. Bedding plants sold in strips of modules must be separated into individual plants; do this carefully to keep root damage to a minimum but work quickly so the roots themselves don't dry out.

It makes sense to consider all bedding plants, whether they are strictly hardy, half-hardy or tender, as in need of hardening-off; even hardy plants, taken straight from the warmth of a propagating house, will not be robust enough to survive outdoors without the benefit of a spell in a cold-frame. A double layer of garden fleece is also handy for giving

tainer, filled with compost and containing one small plant. Depending on the size and manufacturer, more or less similar versions may be called 'Miniplants', 'Easiplants', 'Supaplants', 'Starter Plants', 'Easi Plugs', 'Maxi Plugs' or by other comparable names. And depending on the garden centre that you visit and depending, in turn, on their suppliers, you may well also see small square 7cm (2¾in) pots containing groups of seedlings ready for planting out, as well as individual seed or cutting-raised plants, such as fuchsias, in tiny mesh pots. The name 'plantlets' is also sometimes used for some of these plant categories. The range of plants that are available as plugs varies, again depending on the seed company or supplier from which they originated. Among those that you will find most frequently are fibrous-rooted

plants protection from unexpected late frosts. Bedding plants do vary in their tolerance of frost, but those that I find among the most susceptible are ageratums, begonias, gazanias, impatiens, marigolds, salvia, verbenas and zinnias, so if you have a large number of bedding plants to handle, it makes sense to plant these out last.

Water the plants while they are still in their pots (this is very important and minimises root damage)and then position them to obtain the correct spacings and patterns. Dig a planting hole with a trowel and tip the plant out of its pot, position it in the hole and firm in well with your fingers. After planting, water in with a dilute general liquid feed to help the plants to become established. It may be sensible to place slug pellets close to the plants as a precaution against slug and snail damage, provided you can do this without exposing them to interference by pets or birds.

## Feeding and watering

Bedding plants in containers need regular watering and feeding. A number of recent developments help make both operations easier. Controlled-release fertilizers in the form of granules, tablets or plugs may be inserted in the compost when planting the container but, valuable as these are, they only postpone the point at which supplementary liquid feeding must begin. Without these additions, you should begin liquid feeding about six weeks after planting and continue weekly until the end of the season. The type of fertilizer isn't critical, but one that contains a high ratio of potash to nitrogen and phosphate is ideal; many gardeners use a tomato feed.

Bedding plants that can draw on the moisture and nutrients in the soil do not need to be watered and fed as often as container plants, but extra watering after planting and during dry spells will be necessary. A general balanced

**below** By careful choice of varieties, you can use annuals to produce scaled down versions of the different plant heights that are such a feature of herbaceous borders.

**above** It isn't always recognised that bedding plants mix well with perennials and are invaluable in filling gaps in borders.

fertilizer can be forked in just before planting; thereafter little feeding should be necessary although if the foliage appears pale, as it may do after heavy rain has washed fertilizer from the soil, give a supplementary liquid feed.

### Other care

Regular dead-heading of faded flowers will help to maintain the display during the summer, as it will encourage more buds to be produced. Concentrate particularly on containers where dead flowers are more noticeable and remove any dead or diseased foliage at the same time. You may not have the time to dead-head bedding plants in the open garden, so when planning your displays, include plenty of plants with colourful foliage and also look out for plants that may be described as self-cleaning. These have petals that drop off naturally and so lessen the need for dead-heading.

### Problems

The main problem with bedding plants is that they are sold, bought and planted too early in the year, before the danger of frost has passed. If you can resist this temptation, then you will find they are fairly trouble-free if watered and fed. Bedding plants can become stressed if kept in small pots for a long time before they are planted out, and yellowing leaves are a sign that they are short of nutrients. Among common pest and disease problems are *Botrytis* grey mould, aphids and mildew (page 98).

### Using bedding plants

So many bedding plants are now used in containers that it's becoming easy to forget how they can quickly brighten up other parts of the garden. As they only last for one season, a small border or bed devoted to bedding plants is ideal for those who like to try different displays each year. Each season, you will begin with the equivalent of a blank sheet of paper (although it's worth adding that many hardy annuals and biennials will self-seed so you might have the odd surprise), and plants can be used for informal as well as formal displays. For a formal pattern, choose modern, highly-bred varieties (many are F1 hybrids) as these will give you uniformity of height and flowering, and choose single colours rather than mixtures or you will lose the strong impact of the design. Include plenty of foliage plants to reduce the amount of dead-heading required and as an insurance against bad summer weather; unseasonal wind and rain can spoil many flower displays, particularly where the blooms are of the large, double type.

By using bedding plants informally, you can create the effect of a herbaceous border in small beds whereas the real thing requires very much more space in order to be effective. In these situations, choose bedding plants with interesting shapes and more subtle flowers; dwarfness, uniformity and strong colours are not essential so explore among the less highly-bred plants with more open habits. Plant in drifts rather than rows and use cascading plants like 'Surfinia' petunias to grow along the ground and intermingle with other types.

Bedding plants are invaluable for filling in the gaps between longer term plants in a mixed or shrub border. Choose a bedding plant that is in scale with the rest of the border; short, uniform bedding plants may be suitable for edging at the front but will do nothing for gaps further back. Remember also that if you want some of the taller bedding plant varieties, you may have to raise your own from seed as many of the varieties sold as plantlets or plugs in packs are shorter growing. And when choosing a plant to fill gaps, you should decide whether you want it just for one year or if you want it to seed itself and become a more permanent feature.

## Carpet bedding

Carpet bedding was once the most popular way of growing bedding plants. It reached its peak during the 19th century but its last main refuge today is in municipal parks. It attempts to re-create the patterns on Oriental carpets by using bedding plants grown principally for their foliage, and carefully clipped to remove the flowers and maintain a bushy habit. For carpet bedding to work well, a very high standard of planting and after-care is required.

Having prepared a weed-free, stone-free bed, mark out the plan using a stick then highlight these markings with sand trickled from an empty bottle. Lay the plants out (still in their pots and trays) in their final positions. You will

need to have sufficient of each type plus spares to make the pattern; you don't have the flexibility of numbers that exists when simply filling gaps in the border. Work from the centre of the display outwards but avoid compacting the soil with your feet, using planks on which to stand if necessary. Do one colour section at a time before moving on to another colour. After planting each section, trim off any long shoots with single-handed shears and water thoroughly. After the pattern has been planted it will need regular watering and trimming while any plants that die or look unhealthy must be removed and replaced with spares.

**above** The old idea of carpet bedding can be brought up to date to produce the effect of carpet tiles.

**below** By selecting from the huge colour range now available, some stunning blends can be created very easily.

## Bedding plants by colour

Many bedding plants are sold as mixtures of colours but you can create more impact in the garden if you seek out single colours and then combine them in bold drifts or blocks. This is always easier to do if you raise your own plants from seed using pure, individual varieties.

Below I've given some suggestions of bedding plant genera within which you will find each of the main colours, but this list is certainly not intended to be exhaustive. Each year more new varieties appear and many individual types of bedding plant are available in all of the colours that you might want.

### Blues/purples/mauves

*Ageratum, Alyssum, Anchusa, Aster, Brachyscome, Browallia, Campanula, Centaurea, Convolvulus, Cornflower, Felicia, Heliotrope, Lobelia, Nemesia, Nemophila, Nierembergia, Nigella, Nolana, Petunia, Salvia, Scabious, Scaevola, Verbena, Viola.*

### Oranges/yellows

*Argyranthemum, Bidens, Calceolaria, Calendula, Canna, Chrysanthemum, Coreopsis, Erysimum, Eschscholzia, Gaillardia, Gazania, Gerbera, Helianthus, Impatiens, Lanata, Limnanthes, Mimulus, Petunia, Rudbeckia, Tagetes, Tropaeolum, Viola, Zinnia.*

### Pinks

*Antirrhinum, Argyranthemum, Begonia, Bellis, Callistephus, Dianthus, Diascia, Gazania, Godetia, Impatiens, Lavatera, Nicotiana, Osteospermum, Pelargonium, Petunia, Verbena, Viola, Zinnia.*

**above** The only truly effective bedding plants for shady places are busy lizzies (*Impatiens*) and, as here, *Begonia semperflorens*.

**right** Because biennials such as wallflowers occupy the ground for a long time, they are grown in beds for transplanting.

### Reds

*Antirrhinum, Begonia, Callistephus, Canna, Coleus* (foliage), *Dianthus, Fuchsia, Impatiens, Nemesia, Nicotiana, Papaver, Pelargonium, Petunia, Salvia, Verbena, Viola.*

*Note:* most bedding plants exist in white-flowered forms so I haven't listed these separately

## Bedding plants for shade

A carpet of bedding plants under shrubs or beside walls can help to lighten a shady spot, but do try to improve the soil if it is dry. Containers in light shade often work well, as the amount of watering is reduced and they can quickly be replaced; no matter how much care you take, the flowering life of almost all bedding plants will be shorter in a shaded spot. [Moist] indicates the need for moist soil or compost

*Begonia semperflorens,Coleus, Fuchsia* [Moist], *Hedera, Impatiens* (a wide range of habits, flower types, flower colours and foliage colours available; [Moist] (in reality, a high humidity so benefit from misting rather than wet compost), *Lobelia, Mimulus* [Moist], *Viola* (not winter-flowering pansies), *Nemophila* [Moist], *Nicotiana*

## Bedding plants suitable for taking indoors as house plants in autumn

Well-grown bedding plants are often still in flower when the first frosts strike. A few favourite, good-quality specimens can be lifted and potted up to continue indoors.

*Cuphea, Fuchsia, Lantana, Pelargonium, Scaevola, Tradescantia.*

## Biennials

A biennial is a plant that flowers in its second year. Many are used as spring bedding plants: sown close together in summer in a nursery bed, then transplanted at wider spacing in the final positions in autumn to flower in the spring. It may be difficult to keep the seedlings and young plants watered over the summer but plants are often for sale at garden centres in the autumn.

*Bellis, Dianthus, Erysimum, Matthiola, Myosotis, Primula, Viola.*

## Plants for carpet bedding
### Massed foliage plants

*Alternanthera, Echeveria, Iresine, Perilla, Sagina boydii, Saxifraga moschata, Sedum lydium, Sempervivum.*

## Dot plants

*Agave, Abutilon, Canna, Cordyline, Yucca.*

## Some hardy annual bedding plants

*Alyssum, Anchusa* (best as an annual but can also be treated as a biennial), *Calendula, Centaurea, Clarkia, Consolida, Convolvulus, Coreopsis, Dianthus, Eschscholzia, Godetia, Gypsophila elegans, Helianthus, Iberis, Lavatera, Limnanthes douglasii, Linaria, Malope, Matthiola, Nemophila, Nigella damascena, Papaver, Scabiosa, Viola.*

**above** I don't think there are many more lovely sights in the world of bedding plants than a drift of Californian poppies (*Eschscholzia*).

# Herbaceous Perennials

I think that the herbaceous perennial is, at the same time, one of the most useful yet one of the most troublesome of plants in the modern garden. The name perennial suggests that such plants may be left undisturbed for many years, as indeed they can, although I must stress that being perennial is not the same as being immortal. After four or five years, almost all types of herbaceous perennial will require some rejuvenation, as I shall explain shortly. However, being not only perennial but also herbaceous brings with it certain special problems.

**above** Herbaceous perennials provide long-term summer interest.

**below** Although in many ways impractical because it is so labour-intensive, there's no denying the beauty of a well planted herbaceous border.

A tree or a shrub maintains its perennial nature through a permanent above-ground woody framework, and a bulbous plant survives discreetly below ground, its leafy parts generally having shrivelled to nothing. However, a herbaceous perennial has an inconvenient in-between life style. It dies down to a rootstock, in effect a clump of roots with a crown at or just below the soil surface although the expression 'dies down' does not accurately describe the fact that we are left with an above-ground mass of dead stems. The herbaceous rather than woody nature of the above-ground structure is, I think, the cause of the most labour-intensive aspect of herbaceous perennial gardening as in many instances, the stems are inadequate fully to support the flowerheads. Most herbaceous perennials will therefore, require support of some form.

## Ways of using herbaceous perennials in the garden

Summer bedding plants offer nothing in the winter. Herbaceous perennials do not offer very much, although the appearance of the dead remains of flower stems and foliage can be attractive under snow and frost, while a small number of species are evergreen and so have some foliage appeal. But at the end of the day, it must be admitted that herbaceous perennials are primarily plants for the summer and as they are larger than bedding plants, this is a disadvantage in small gardens and means that careful consideration must be given to the way they are used. The traditional herbaceous border looks stunning in summer but must be a reasonable size to work well.

Where year-round interest is important, as it is in almost all modern gardens, you will be wise instead to consider a mixed border where shrubs, trees, bulbs and bedding are used along with perennials. A permanent framework of evergreen and deciduous shrubs provides winter colour, leaving the perennials to add seasonal highlights. Bulbs and bedding plants can be included to fill gaps between the more permanent occupants. And an often unappreciated advantage of using perennials is that the vast majority can be moved around in the dormant season until you obtain the effect you want.

Both herbaceous and mixed borders work best when planted in a minimum of three layers according to plant height and some suggestions are given in my plant lists below. But don't stick to the three layers too rigidly; a few taller plants with interesting shapes or an airy feel near the front can add interest and attractiveness. Larger clumps of fewer plants will create more impact from a distance than a huge mass of different individuals.

## Beds

Island beds offer a popular way of growing perennials in a circular or oval bed that is viewed from all sides. In such beds, the taller plants are in the centre and the middle and frontal plants encircle them. More air and light reaches each plant, resulting in sturdier, healthy growth, less likely to need staking or to succumb to mildew. This is the theory. Island beds do, however, require considerable space to work well and I readily admit that, in small gardens, I dislike them.

## Specimens

One of the most exciting features of perennials is the way they rise up from what appears to be nothing to create an impressive mass of vegetation, and then disappear again. It's for this reason that I always have prime specimens growing through gravel and in comparable positions, away from conventional bed or border plantings. Large but interesting plants like *Anemone* x *hybrida*, acanthus, *Euphorbia characias,* alceas, and verbascums can be used as single specimens in this way, even in small gardens.

## Containers

In general, herbaceous plants are too tall for most containers and don't flower for long enough. However, as you might expect with such a diverse group there are exceptions. Many of the foliage perennials, when grown as single subjects in large pots, provide a foil for other flowering plants and can offer a contrast of texture. Try using plants such as artemisias, bergenias, heucheras, hostas, yuccas or many of the ornamental grasses and ferns. Smaller foliage plants like ajugas, hederas, lamiums, *Lysimachia nummularia* 'Aurea' and vincas can be used as fillers in mixed containers; and remember that by taking small divisions from existing plants in your garden, the cost is nil. Plants that may be grown as flowering specimens in containers include chrysanthemums, dicentras, geraniums, hellebores, hemerocallis and sedums. Hostas in particular are usually thought of as foliage plants yet they make good flowering specimens in containers, so seek out those varieties with especially good flowers from specialist nurseries.

The smaller perennials are suitable for pots at least 25cm (10in) in diameter and at least 23cm (9in) deep. Most large specimen plants will need 30-40cm (12-16in) diameter containers. Permanent plants, like hostas, that will be left for many years to develop impressive clumps are best in 45cm (18in) diameter tubs. For long-term plantings left outdoors for several years, I strongly advise using John Innes No 3 compost which will keep its structure for longer, but you should add extra nutrients either by means of a liquid feed twice a month during the growing season or by replacing the top 5cm (2in) of compost with fresh each spring.

## Natural plantings

Garden designers are at last beginning to realise the importance of looking at natural plantings when creating gardens; something I have advocated for many years. This approach has been quicker to take hold in Germany and

**below** In the modern garden, the herbaceous border has tended to give way to the mixed border with its permanent framework of shrubs.

**above** The island bed
surrounded by lawn is a much
misused device for growing
herbaceous perennials.
I believe that to work well,
it must be big, big enough
not to see round it.

the United States than in Britain where we have tended to be traditional and conservative and planned our herbaceous borders on principles of colour and size alone. In the United States, for example, inspiration has been taken from the way that herbaceous plants grow in the prairies while in Germany, natural communities of herbaceous plants have been mimicked as low-maintenance plantings in parks for many years. The plants are chosen and spaced according to ecological principles, offering schemes that are a cross between wild gardens and border plantings, as we have come to accept them.

### Site and soil

Most perennials prefer sunny or partially-shaded positions but some can tolerate or even need rather deeper shade. A few perennials must have a sheltered site either because their stems, flowers or leaves are prone to wind damage or because they need enhanced warmth.

The majority of the plants considered here are hardy in most parts of Britain, but in cold areas or if exposed to a waterlogged soil or strong winds they can fail over winter unless protected. There are perennials suitable for all soil types, but to grow the widest range, the soil should be neither waterlogged in winter nor baked hard in summer. Less than ideal soils can, of course, be improved by the addition of well rotted organic matter.

### Where to obtain perennials

Seed catalogues have large sections devoted to herbaceous perennials and it may be thought, therefore, that raising them from seed is the best way to obtain them. In general, I find that it is not; largely because the best (in the sense of most attractive or functionally useful) varieties can't usually be raised in this manner. They must be propagated vegetatively and thus must be purchased from nurseries or garden centres as plants, although I must add one rather important group of exceptions. Many people, me included, enjoy growing plants in their wild form and there are many species that have never been subjected to hybridisation and selection and which exist, therefore, only in their natural, unaltered state. A great many, indeed the majority amongst them, do not have the mass appeal that attracts those nurserymen who cater for the mass market.

Inevitably, therefore, plants of these species should be sought from specialist suppliers or, to return to my main point, you may raise them yourself from seed (which may in turn have to be obtained from a specialist rather than a mass-market company). By and large, you will succeed best if you use the hardy annual technique (page 71), but always grow on the young plants in pots for at least a season before planting them out in the garden. This will ensure that they are robust and have a strong enough root and crown system to enable them to survive.

For established plants, division is a straight-forward method of vegetative propagation and an important method of renewal, although those perennials that are slightly less hardy should be divided in spring rather than autumn. Some plants don't respond well to lifting and dividing at any time so cuttings may be taken from them instead (see page 76).

When buying perennials you will find they are sold in various ways. A few are still available as bare-rooted plants and if you want a large number of plants for ground cover, this is an economical way of buying them but they must be planted soon after lifting. In garden centres and nurseries, a selection of perennials in small pots should be on display from spring onwards. These offer an economical way to buy a range of different plants but do be sure to obtain named varieties or you could find yourself buying inferior seed-raised plants.

Because most herbaceous plants aren't amenable to being confined in small containers for long periods, plants should be purchased while they are fresh. When buying in late spring or summer, moreover, you will probably fare better by buying larger plants in larger pots which will be more expensive but offer you a sizeable plant that may even be large enough to be divided before planting. Large pots of perennials are often reduced in price at the end of the summer simply because they are no

longer flowering. These are well worth buying if they have a healthy root system and undamaged crown; autumn is a good time for planting perennials and the plants will flower in the following year.

Garden shows are excellent sources of unusual perennials raised by specialist nurseries. Not only can you see the plants and avoid any carriage charges, but many small, specialist suppliers find it uneconomical to offer mail order, so short of a personal visit to the nursery itself, a show may offer your only opportunity of adding to your collection. I would, nonetheless, add from personal experience that you may find the plants, although hardy, are sometimes very young and have been grown under cover, so will need growing-on and hardening-off before they are ready to be planted out.

**above** Although grown less commonly in containers, carefully chosen subjects, like these hostas and variegated ground elder, will be very effective.

**below** *Gunnera* is one of the perennials that benefits from a protective covering around the crown in winter.

## Planting

A new border will benefit from careful planning to ensure that you really do stand a chance of obtaining the desired effects through all the seasons. If you have room, try and incorporate some stepping stones or at least provide some access to the back of the border so the plants can be maintained easily. For the greatest impact in a bed or border, aim to have fewer

but larger clumps of perennials. To achieve this, plant between three or five plants of the same variety in a group. Isolated individuals will be slower to provide the desired effect and, in the early stages, will look distinctly lonely.

Within a season or two the plants in a group will join up to form an impressive clump. Many types of perennial grow very quickly, once established, so ensure you have allowed an adequate planting distance between them. Most labels and catalogues give a recommendation for the plant that usually ranges between about 30 and 90cm (1-3ft). The recommendations can be adapted, however: closer spacing will give you quicker cover, wider spacing will save you money. When using perennials as ground cover, the correct planting distances can make a great deal of

difference to the effectiveness of the weed suppression and subsequent maintenance.

When putting a few plants into an existing border, dig a planting hole with a volume twice that of the root ball. Where an entire border is being planted, dig as thoroughly as possible as far in advance as possible. In particular, take care, either by digging or chemical control, to eradicate all perennial weeds and then double dig the ground as you would for a vegetable plot (page 00). Spring and autumn are the usual times for planting, although container-grown subjects can be planted at any convenient time if watered thoroughly during dry spells. Be guided by your soil; plant when it is easy to work and not wet and sticky. Anything perennial that is prone to winter wet or is of doubtful hardiness is best planted, as it is best divided, in spring or early summer.

When planting up a whole bed, lay out the plants (while still in their pots) in their final positions so that you can check planting distances. Groups or drifts of infilling and ground-cover plants are more effective than single plantings. Water the plants well while they are still in their pots, dig a hole large

**right** Garden Shows often offer as good a way as any of seeing a wide range of plants; usually with the opportunity to buy or place orders on the spot.

**182**

enough to take the whole root ball, tip the plant from its pot and plant. Fill in the hole and firm the soil gently. Water in a dilute liquid feed to help the plants establish.

When planting an area of new ground, it's sometimes recommended that woven plastic or paper sheet should be laid down over cleared ground. A cross is then cut at each planting position and the plants inserted and planted. While it's true that such a sheet mulch keep down weeds and helps retain moisture, this system only really works for a single-subject covering of ground cover. In a mixed or herbaceous border where you will need to be lifting and dividing plants, filling in gaps and generally adjusting the planting plan, this sort of sheeting is simply not of any practical use.

To keep down weeds and help prevent water evaporating from the surface of the soil, apply a generous loose mulch to weed-free beds in spring. A 5cm (2in) layer of well-rotted manure, chipped bark, cocoa shells or similar material is effective and attractive. Any organic loose mulch will, in time, be incorporated into the soil by earthworms and general cultivation to improve the soil.

### Watering and feeding

Newly-planted perennials must be watered during dry spells; over a large area use a sprinkler or a seeping hose for this purpose. Once established, perennials should not need regular watering if they have been well mulched in spring. Any that indicate that they do require additional watering, by evidence of wilting or other poor performance, are probably unsuitable for the particular site or have sustained root damage. Large-leaved perennials, especially those with thin leaves, inevitably require a good deal of water and particular care should be taken in ensuring that they are placed in an appropriate site. Feeding should take the form of a twice-yearly dressing with a balanced general fertilizer such as fish, blood and bone or Growmore. Apply it first as growth begins in the spring (before mulching) and then again around midsummer but not during periods of drought. On each occasion a rate of 100-125g/m$^2$ (3-4oz/sq yd) is adequate. If growth seems poor during the growing season, for example if the leaves appear an unnatural pale green or yellow, liquid fertilizer should be applied as a supplementary foliar feed.

### Problems

The commonest cause of failure with hardy perennials is that the chosen species is inappropriate for the soil or site conditions. Sometimes the problem is not a failure of the plant itself but rather that it is too successful and invades the space of neighbouring plants. Perennial plants are prone to pests and diseases, as they are often planted close together with every opportunity for them to be stressed and, more importantly, for pests and diseases to travel easily from one to the other. Among diseases, powdery mildew is especially troublesome. Among pests, aphids are common in most years while in wet seasons, slug and snail damage can be extensive.

**above** Planting perennials in groups of three or five plants rather than singly means that clumps become established and attractive more swiftly.

**above** All herbaceous perennials will benefit from a moisture-retaining mulch applied in the early part of the season.

## Other care

The value of an annual spring mulch has been discussed elsewhere in this book but I make no excuse for mentioning it again here, as it saves much time that would otherwise be spent on weeding and watering later in the season.

Staking may be necessary and, although it is possible to grow a wide range of perennials that require no support (the dwarf varieties so beloved of nurserymen are generally the most reliable), taller varieties and many wild species will need some assistance if they are to be visually effective. There are many ingenious metal staking systems that can be tailored to the size and type of plant. A cheaper and more attractive alternative is to use brushwood twigs or to make your own supports, by pushing four or more bamboo canes around a clump and then wrapping string around to enclose the plant. Stakes should be in place by late spring if they are to be unobtrusive. Any pointed canes or wires tops should, of course, be covered to prevent eye injuries.

Dead-head plants regularly to extend the flowering season. During the summer herbaceous foliage can become very untidy; even a plant as appealing as *Alchemilla mollis* can take on a brown and dry appearance, while the attractive mound shape of hardy geraniums can flop suddenly after heavy rain or, con-

versely, during drought. Damaged foliage in a prominent position should be cut back with shears. Fresh mounds of foliage will soon begin to appear.

Perennials that become unsightly after flowering may be cut back in late autumn, once the top growth has been cleared, and any plants of borderline hardiness can be protected with a 15cm (6in) layer of chipped bark, dead leaves or straw held in place. An alternative approach that I favour is to leave the cutting-back until spring, allowing the dead shoot growth to act as nature's insulation. Any seed-heads remaining provide natural food for the birds and encourage them away from the kitchen garden. In all except the most mild areas, evergreen perennials, such as kniphofias, should have the foliage lightly /tied together in late autumn to protect the crown. All insulating coverings must be removed in spring however or the plants will grow soft and rot.

After four or five years, the vigour and flowering of perennials start to deteriorate as their roots become congested and, although the productive period can be extended by careful attention to feeding, all will eventually need rejuvenating. By lifting the plant out of the ground, dividing it and replanting younger, healthy sections into enriched soil your stock can be given a fresh lease of life. Division is best done in spring or autumn when the plants are dormant and on a day when the soil is easy to work. For further details on division see page 75.

## Herbaceous perennials by flower colour
### Blues/purples/mauves

*Aconitum, Aster, Campanula, Delphinium, Echinops, Eryngium, Erysimum, Geranium, Limonium, Liriope, Meconopsis, Nepeta, Omphalodes, Penstemon, Phlox, Platycodon, Salvia, Thalictrum, Veronica.*

### Oranges/yellows

*Achillea, Alchemilla, Anthemis, Coreopsis, Crocosmia, Doronicum, Euphorbia, Geum, Helenium, Hemerocallis, Kniphofia, Ligularia, Oenothera, Ranunculus, Rudbeckia, Verbascum.*

**Pinks**

*Anemone* x *hybrida, Aster, Astilbe,
Bergenia, Centranthus, Dicentra, Echinacea,
Geranium, Helleborus, Hemerocallis,
Heuchera, Paeonia, Papaver, Penstemon,
Persicaria, Phlox, Sedum.*

**Reds**

*Astilbe, Crocosmia, Helenium,
Hemerocallis, Lobelia, Lychnis, Paeonia,
Papaver, Penstemon, Phlox.*

**White**

*Anemone* x *hybrida, Astilbe, Astrantia,
Dicentra, Geranium, Gypsophila, Paeonia,
Papaver, Penstemon, Phlox, Polygonatum,
Ranunculus, Tellima, Tiarella.*

**Green**

*Euphorbia, Helleborus, Sedum.*

## Herbaceous perennials by size

For borders to be truly effective, plants must be
arranged at least approximately in layers: the
tallest at the back, grading through to the low-
growing types at the front. Here are some
suggestions for the three different layers, but
you should adapt these to the dimensions of

your particular bed. For
instance, in a shallow border two layers of some of
the plants listed below as
being suitable for mid-bor-
der and front of the border
might be more practical.
Bear in mind also that many
perennials, for example del-
phiniums and campanulas,
that are normally thought
of as tall, also exist in dwarf
varieties.

### Front of the border

*Ajuga, Alchemilla,
Bergenia, Coreopsis,
Dicentra, Doronicum,
Epimedium, Geranium,
Geum, Helleborus, Heuchera, Hosta,
Lamium, Liriope, Nepeta, Oenothera,
Omphalodes, Persicaria, Platycodon,
Pulmonaria, Ranunculus, Stachys,
Veronica, Viola*

### Mid-border

*Achillea, Anthemis, Aquilegia, Artemisia,
Aster, Astilbe, Astrantia, Centranthus,*

**above** Mildew is probably
the commonest disease
problem, encouraged, as
here on lupins, by close
spacing and hot dry weather.

**left** Staking early is the secret
to producing neat clumps of
perennials and I find these
adaptable interlocking wire
stakes are particularly good
and versatile.

*Eryngium, Erysimum, Helenium, Hemerocallis, Kniphofia, Limonium, Lobelia, Lychnis, Paeonia, Papaver, Penstemon, Phlox, Polygonatum, Rudbeckia, Salvia, Sedum.*

### Back of the border
*Acanthus, Aconitum, Alcea, Anemone* x *hybrida, Campanula, Echinacea, Echinops, Euphorbia, Ligularia, Lupinus, Thalictrum, Verbascum.*

## Herbaceous perennials by season
Most herbaceous perennials, whether grown for their foliage or flower, will be at their best over the summer months. Those that come into leaf or flower earlier or later are particularly noteworthy, therefore, and worth incorporating into borders and beds for the extra interest they provide.

### Early flowers (late spring or earlier)
*Aquilegia, Bergenia, Corydalis, Dicentra, Doronicum, Epimedium, Erysimum, Euphorbia, Geum, Helleborus, Omphalodes, Paeonia, Papaver, Pulmonaria, Ranunculus, Veronica, Viola.*

### Late flowers
*Anemone* x *hybrida, Aster, Helenium, Kniphofia, Liriope, Rudbeckia, Sedum,* 'Herbstfreude'.

## Evergreen foliage
All these perennials retain at least some foliage for most of the year even if some look distinctly untidy in mid-winter. Remember not to cut back evergreen perennials in autumn; simply remove any dead foliage by hand and tie them up as I have described.

*Ajuga, Astrantia* (foliage not evergreen but variegated form attractive in spring), *Bergenia, Epimedium* (some), *Euphorbia*(some), *Geranium* (some), *Helleborus, Heuchera, Lamium, Liriope, Pulmonaria, Stachys, Tellima, Tiarella.*

## Herbaceous perennials for shade
Many plants will grow in shade if the soil is moist, for this will mimic the floor of many woodlands, habitats in which a large number of garden perennials have evolved. However, few plants will thrive in the combination of shade

**above** The colour range in perennials is enormous and even within a single group of similarly-sized plants, like these Michaelmas daisies, a wide variety of colours is available.

**right** Euphorbias have become one of the most popular groups of perennials in recent years; and yet, by contrast with Michaelmas daisies, the colour range is limited. It is size and shape that varies.

and a dry soil; those that do have been marked with *, but even so, help in the form of soil improvement will make the difference between the merely satisfactory and the very attractive.

*Aconitum, Actaea, *Ajuga, Alchemilla mollis, Anemone x hybrida, Aquilegia, Aruncus, Astilbe, Astrantia, Bergenia, Brunnera, Campanula, Cimicifuga, Dicentra, Digitalis, Epimedium, *Euphorbia, *Geranium, Haberlea, Hacquetia, Helleborus, Hepatica, x Heucherella, Hosta, *Lamium, Linnaea, *Liriope, *Lunaria, Lysimachia, Mimulus, Mitella, *Omphalodes, *Pachysandra, Phlox, Podophyllum, Polygonatum, Pulmonaria, Rodgersia, Sanguinaria, *Symphytum, *Tanacetum parthenium, Tellima grandiflora, Thalictrum, *Tiarella, Tolmeia, Trachystemon,* Uvularia, Vancouveria, Veratrum, Veronica, Viola, Waldsteinia.

## Herbaceous perennials for ground cover

All these plants have weed-suppressing foliage if spaced correctly, but it is important to ascertain whether the site is sunny or shaded before choosing. Many of these plants are deciduous but this doesn't affect their weed smothering ability (weeds don't grow in winter). When covering large areas, costs can be kept down by ordering bare-rooted plants in bulk or by regular division of your own stock plants.

*Ajuga, Alchemilla, Astilbe, Bergenia, Epimedium, Geranium, Hemerocallis, Heuchera, Hosta, Lamium, Liriope, Nepeta, Omphalodes, Persicaria, Polygonatum, Pulmonaria, Stachys.*

**below** Shaded borders need be no bar to the growing of herbaceous perennials; a great many lovely varieties positively revel in these conditions.

# Native Plants

Most people will recognise the plants in this section as 'wild flowers' although I prefer the term 'native plants' as it embraces not only the familiar herbaceous flowering species but any perennial, shrub or annual that is a natural part of the British Flora. Different people have different reasons for wanting to grow them in their gardens. Some native plants are quite simply very attractive, others remind us of childhood associations with the countryside and many provide valuable food for butterfly caterpillars, birds and other appealing types of wildlife.

**above** One of the consequences of growing native plants is the food supply that it offers to butterflies, moths and other insects.

**below** Native plants provide splendid ground cover in wild areas, provided you weed out the less attractive ones.

### Site and soil
One huge advantage of growing native plants is that, wherever you live and whatever type of soil you have, you will always be able to find species that will thrive. Woodland natives can grow in shaded areas, plants from meadows can utilise sunny sites and plants from waterside or marshy areas can tolerate the wet, boggy soils that defeat conventional garden plants.

### Ways of using native plants
Unless you already have a very obvious semi-wild habitat such as a woodland, hedge or stream in your garden, or have space for a wild flower meadow, I suggest that you grow a selection of garden-worthy natives alongside other plants in borders and beds. In a small garden, native plants need careful management; most either have a short flowering season or are invasive, sometimes both. Nonetheless, their common propensity to spread can be utilised, and native plants (bugle, geraniums, ivy and dead-nettle among others) can make easy ground-cover subjects for difficult sites, especially under trees.

### Space required
How long is a piece of string? Simply adding a few native plants to existing garden features can take up as much or as little room as you choose. To create a wild flower meadow, however, a minimum area of about 100m² (120sq yds) is needed, although by leaving areas along the edges of large lawns or among established fruit trees, some semblance of the same thing can be produced in much less space.

### Sowing and planting
You should of course never collect plants from their native habitats. It is both undesirable and illegal. Many, however, can fairly easily be raised from seed using the hardy annual technique, although some require treatment to break the dormancy (page 72). Wild-flower seed is commonly sold as mixtures but with the possible exception of those blends produced specially to create wild flower meadows, my advice is to avoid them, as germination times and conditions vary and at best you will obtain a random mixture of seedlings. You will then lose control over the choice of plants and, commonly, one species takes over. It's far better to choose a range of individual species. These can be sown directly into separate areas within the habitat, or raised in pots and then planted out so they can establish well and then spread naturally. Increasingly it's possible to buy a selection of native plants from specialist nurseries and some garden centres where they are sold rather like bedding plants. To prepare an area for sowing or for planting up a native plant meadow, use the same methods as you would for a lawn (page 164) but use no fertilizer.

### Problems
Where a soil has been used previously as a conventional garden, the overall fertiliser and especially the nitrogen content will be rela-

tively high. In these conditions, plants with a high demand for nitrogen, such as the more vigorous grasses, clover and vetches, will proliferate at the expense of others. There are two ways around this: the seed mixture can be augmented with plants such as yellow rattle (*Rhinanthus*) which are semi-parasitic and will depress the vigour of some of the more aggressive species; or you can first grow a nitrogen-demanding vegetable crop such as a brassica to use up the surplus nutrient.

Many gardeners achieve a good display of meadow flowers in the first season but flowering then declines and, almost invariably, this is because they have cut the meadow before the plants have had time to set their seed. It is important to leave the cutting until late in the summer and to use a scythe, not a mower. Wait until most of the plants have flowered and set seed and then leave the cut sward to dry, exactly as in traditional hay-making. Turn the cuttings several times to allow the seed to fall and be dispersed and then remove the 'hay' for composting.

## Watering and feeding

Once established, no watering or feeding should be necessary and most of the after-care in native plant gardening involves managing the competition between the species.

## Natives plants for walls and other wild places

Biting stonecrop (*Sedum acre*), Common fumitory (*Fumaria officinalis*), Herb Robert (*Geranium robertianum*), Ivy (*Hedera helix*), Ivy-leaved toadflax (*Cymbalaria muralis*), Red valerian (*Centranthus ruber*), Toadflax (*Linaria vulgaris*), Wallflower (*Erysimum cheiri*), Wild strawberry (*Fragaria vesca*).

## Natives plants by season

Most spring-flowering natives are associated with woodland habitats and the summer-flowering natives with meadows:

### Spring flowers

Bugle (*Ajuga reptans*), Cheddar pink (*Dianthus gratianopolitanus*), Common dog violet (*Viola riviniana*), Cowslip (*Primula veris*), Green hellebore (*Helleborus viridis*), winter to early spring; Herb Robert (*Geranium robertianum*), spring through summer; Marsh marigold (*Caltha palustris*), Primrose (*Primula vulgaris*), Stinking hellebore (*Helleborus foetidus*), late winter to early spring, Wallflower (*Erysimum cheiri*), White campion (*Silene dioica*), Wood anemone (*Anemone nemorosa*) late spring to summer.

### Summer flowers

Bloody crane's bill (*Geranium sanguineum*), Common toadflax (*Linaria vulgaris*), Corncockle (*Agrostemma githago*), Cornflower (*Centaurea cyanus*), Corn marigold (*Chrysanthemum segetum*), Dusky crane's bill (*Geranium phaeum*), Field scabious (*Knautia arvensis*), Foxglove (*Digitalis purpurea*), Great bellflower (*Campanula latifolia*), Greater knapweed (*Centaurea scabiosa*), Hemp agrimony (*Eupatorium cannabinum*), Lady's mantle (*Alchemilla mollis*), Masterwort (*Astrantia major*), Meadow crane's bill (*Geranium pratense*), Ox-eye daisy (*Leucanthemum vulgare*), Pheasant's eye (*Adonis annua*), Purple loosestrife (*Lythrum salicaria*), Red valerian (*Centranthus ruber*), Sea campion (*Silene maritima*), Small scabious (*Scabiosa columbaria*), Sneezewort (*Achillea ptarmica*), Teasel (*Dipsacus fullonum*), Thrift (*Armeria maritima*), Wild thyme (*Thymus vulgaris*), Wood crane's bill (*Geranium sylvaticum*), Yellow loosestrife (*Lysimachia vulgaris*).

## Natives plants for a shady border

Bugle (*Ajuga reptans*), Common dog violet (*Viola riviniana*), Dusky cranesbill (*Geranium phaeum*), Foxglove (*Digitalis purpurea*), Green hellebore (*Helleborus viridis*), Lady's mantle (*Alchemilla mollis*), Lords and ladies (*Arum maculatum*), Primrose (*Primula vulgaris*), Snowdrop (*Galanthus nivalis*), Stinking hellebore (*Helleborus foetidus*), White dead nettle (*Lamium album*), Wood cranesbill (*Geranium sylvaticum*).

**above** The yellow rattle (*Rhinanthus*) is a partial parasite and is an invaluable plant in reducing the aggressiveness of grasses.

**below** The wild flower meadow is perhaps the most beautiful of all native plant features, but it isn't easy to manage.

# Bulbous Plants

I am using the term 'bulbous plants' here in its broadest sense to include all of those species that produce swollen storage organs that technically may be bulbs, corms, tubers or rhizomes. Most of these are generally sold in a dry, dormant state but I have also, for convenience, stretched the definition to embrace a number of herbaceous perennials that have a swollen stem or root, many of which are sold as growing plants. What all these plants possess, however, is a head start: the storage organ with its flowering potential means that flowers can come very reliably and predictably in the first growing season.

### Site and soil

Most bulbs require a well drained soil but are able to tolerate moderate acidity or alkalinity. This need for good drainage is particularly important from early summer onwards: although many spring-flowering bulbs grow in rather wet woodland conditions in the wild, it is when the bulb is wet throughout the year that there is the risk of fungal decay. This is why, when planting bulbs, they should be placed on a shallow bed of sharp sand (horticultural sand) mixed with a little bone meal (wear gloves to apply) to aid rooting. Obvious exceptions to this generalization, of course, are waterside plants such as bog irises and *Zantedeschia* that do require permanently wet conditions. In general, most spring-flowering bulbs are hardy and will happily tolerate varying degrees of shade as they originate from woodland habitats. However, summer flowering bulbs are commonly slightly more tender and require a warmer, sunny spot.

### Space required

Bulbous plants vary enormously in size from tiny

**below** Almost all bulbs will establish more readily if they are planted on a bed of sand which will minimize rotting around the base.

species suitable for an alpine trough to substantial plants like *Crocosmia* that are at home in large borders. But they are versatile and the tiny snowdrop that can be grown in a window box by a flat dweller with no garden will be equally successful when allowed to naturalise under the canopy of a natural woodland. Very few bulbs are invasive, notable exceptions among common and popular types being the bluebell (*Hyacinthoides*) the grape hyacinth (*Muscari*) and lily of the valley (*Convallaria*), all which should be planted with care in most gardens.

### Buying bulbous plants

It is most important to obtain good-quality bulbs. Buy the largest size available and check that they are firm and plump, and free from any obvious lesions which would suggest decay and damage within. Popular types such as many daffodils, narcissi, tulips and hyacinths are now commonly sold loose, so you have the chance to handle the produce before purchase. When choosing daffodils, if possible select those with two 'noses' which will give at least two flower stems. Be particularly wary of very cheap bulbs with minimal labelling and, above all, avoid any that could have been (illegally) collected from the wild. Wild populations of cyclamen and species crocus have been seriously depleted in their natural habitats, so with these and other small species bulbs, be sure that the packaging bears a written guarantee that they have been raised in cultivation.

I always advise buying individual varieties rather than mixtures. Although the cost saving may be considerable, a mixed planting will never give as attractive a display. Perhaps the biggest drawback is that no two varieties will flower at identical times and you will soon discover that the flowers of the later-flowering types are pushing their way through the deadheads of the earlier varieties to create a most unsatisfactory jumble. Nonetheless, don't be surprised to obtain a few 'rogue' plants in your packets of supposedly pure varieties. Large Dutch crocus especially are notorious at throwing up strangers and I find it almost impossible to obtain a packet of a purple-flowered type that doesn't contain one or two orange-flowered individuals.

Snowdrops are now commonly sold 'in the green', a short-hand way of referring to plants in full leaf shortly after flowering has finished, as they establish and flower much more reliably when planted in this way rather than as dry dormant bulbs in autumn. An alternative and increasingly popular way for bulbs to be sold in supermarkets and garden centres is as pots of growing plants in bud. Here at least, you have the opportunity to ensure that you have pure colours and that the plants are of uniform quality.

## Planting

Conventional wisdom is that most bulbs should be planted as soon as possible after purchase and before shoot growth begins but there are a few exceptions and my own experience adds a few more each year, so I suspect that there is scope for gardeners to experiment here. Tulips are perhaps the best-known exceptions. They are available for purchase in early autumn but should be stored somewhere cool until early winter. If tulips are planted in Britain before late autumn, for example, they are very likely to produce shoots that will be damaged by frost.

As I have mentioned, snowdrops are now often sold 'in the green' and I find that snowflakes (*Leucojum*) and winter aconites (*Eranthis*) are most successful when treated in a similar way and, more recently, have discovered that species of *Fritillaria* will flower much more reliably in their first season (they are notorious at being slow to establish or re-establish) if the bulbs are stored until they

begin to produce shoots and are then planted in early spring.

Most bulbs should be planted in groups of between six and 12 if their flowers are to have maximum impact; in large areas groups of up to 20 should be considered. I would guess that more disappointments with bulbs, however, come from planting them too shallowly than from anything else. In general, bulbs should be planted with their bases at a depth equal to about two and a half to three times their maximum diameter, but do take your soil conditions into account. On a light soil, planting could be up to 25 per cent deeper to prevent drying out, but on heavy soil, planting slightly more shallowly should reduce the risk of rotting. Exceptions to the size rule are *Lilium candidum* and cyclamen which should be planted just below the surface, nerines, which should be planted like shallots with the tip of the bulb appearing just above the soil, and crown imperial (*Fritillaria imperialis*) which has a hollow where the stem emerges, so is best planted on its side to prevent water from accumulating there

**above** The variety now available of bulbs, both pre-packed and loose is huge; obtain the best results from single varieties not mixtures.

**below** The large-flowered Dutch crocus look stunning in spring. Keep the orange coloured varieties away from the mauves and whites for the best effect.

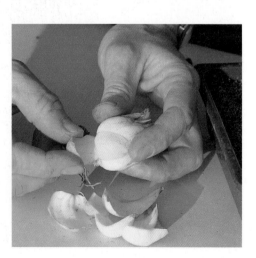

**above** Always plant bulbs with a trowel; I find this much easier than a bulb planter.

**below** Lily bulbs can readily be multiplied by removing a few of the fleshy scales and growing them on.

and leading to rotting. The distance between bulbs in the open garden should usually be equivalent to approximately three times their diameter. They are, therefore, relatively closely spaced compared with other plants and, in containers, can be almost touching.

A trowel or spade is perfectly adequate for planting bulbs in bare soil, although when planting beneath grass, an area of turf should be lifted with a fork and spade, the soil excavated to the required planting depth and the bulbs planted as a group before replacing soil and turf. Special bulb planters are available which take out a core of soil but I have never found them easy or worthwhile. As with other plants raised for use as cut flowers, bulbs grown solely for this purpose are best planted in the vegetable garden, ideally in rows using a draw hoe to produce a drill.

## Propagation

After a few years (generally between two and seven), most bulbs will produce smaller, so-called 'daughter' bulbs which can be detached and grown on to flowering size (which may also take between two and seven years). Established clumps of many types of bulb need lifting and splitting every four to five years because they have multiplied in this way, although naturalised daffodils, snowdrops, crocuses and similar types used for large-scale, extensive plantings should be left quite undisturbed.

Two particularly useful methods of propagation may be used with what are generally among the most expensive of bulbs, lilies. If you look closely at a lily bulb, you will see that it comprises a group of thick, overlapping scales, rather like a bloated onion. These are really separate leaves and can be used to produce new plants. Autumn is the best time for this, during the short period while the bulbs are dormant.

Pull two or three scales from each bulb (not more or you may weaken the bulb itself) and put them into a plastic bag with some moist soil-less compost. Tie the bag and leave it in the airing cupboard for about five weeks, when each scale should have formed tiny roots and can be potted up on its own. As an alternative to scales, try bulbils, small, dark coloured bulb-like objects that form on the stems of some lily varieties. When the stem is dying at the end of the season, cut it from the plant before the bulbils are shed. Carefully remove the individual bulbils and 'sow' them, simply by pressing them into the surface of a soil-less compost in a propagator. Lilies raised in either of these two ways should flower in two years.

## Problems

Having a swollen, fleshy underground storage organ makes bulbous plants especially liable to attack by pests and diseases. When buying or storing bulbs, therefore, check for signs of softness or rotting by fungi, poor handling which can lead to the loss of the protective fibrous tunic in bulbs such as tulips, and physical damage particularly to the base of the plant and growing point. Shrivelled bulbs or tulips with gum oozing from them should also be avoided but surface mould is not generally harmful provided the bulbs are sound and will be correctly stored. Dry, light or corky bulbs should also be avoided. On larger bulbs, such as tulips and daffodils, you can check the basal plate to ensure that it is intact as, being a reduced stem, this is the point from which the roots develop.

Shallowly-planted bulbs or corms such as crocus are sometimes forced to the surface after heavy frosts: they should survive if replanted more deeply. In some areas mice, voles and squirrels dig up and eat bulbs; they seem irresistibly drawn to crocuses. Slightly deeper planting and burying a covering of fine mesh chicken wire over them when planting will help dissuade potential trouble-makers. Flowers are sometimes pecked by birds for no very apparent reason but little can be done to protect them from this. Lilies can be attacked by the bright red lily beetle which is extremely difficult to control and some lilies especially suffer from the build up of viruses after several years. Affected plants should be destroyed and replaced with new stock.

Established clumps of bulbs that stop flowering (they are said to have become 'blind') may be lifted and divided, then replanted in enriched ground, although I must say that to induce them to flower again is very difficult and, unless the plants are extremely valuable, you will be better advised to start afresh with new bulbs.

### Feeding and watering

In the first season, a bulbous plant has its own food reserves to produce a flower but still needs feeding in the early stages to help the roots establish. Feeding in subsequent years is very important to build up the reserves for future flowering. Apart from the small amount of bone meal (wear gloves to apply) that I add to the planting sand (see above), I also apply a top dressing of bone meal or a proprietary bulb fertilizer in spring. Thereafter a second top dressing is applied in midsummer or the plants can be liquid fed during the six week period after flowering each year. Bulbous plants seldom require any additional watering unless they are in containers and/or in leaf during

**below** Removing the dead flowers of daffodils may be a chore but it encourages the plant to channel all of its resources in to the bulb.

**above** Bluebells are the classic examples of bulbs that will naturalise beneath trees; but must never of course be removed from the wild. Always be sure that bulbs you buy were raised in cultivation.

particularly dry periods. They will, however, respond to mulching and this is especially true of lilies which benefit enormously from a leaf mould mulch just as growth is beginning in spring, and of established plantings of cyclamen, which should be mulched as soon as the foliage dies down to encourage germination of seeds and further spread of daughter corms.

### Other care

Taller bulbs, such as some types of lily, may need staking while non-hardy bulbs, such as dahlias and gladioli, must be lifted at the end of the growing season and stored in a frost-free place. Once the first frosts have blackened dahlia foliage, cut down the stems to leave about 10cm (4in) above ground level and then use a fork to lift the tubers carefully. A small cane makes a convenient tool to poke away the soil between each but the whole mass should then be stored upside down somewhere airy and frost-free for a week or so to dry. I then dust the tubers with flowers of sulphur and wrap each clump individually in an envelope made from a whole copy of a quality newspaper. I leave the envelope open at the top and pack them, open end uppermost, in a cardboard box kept in a frost-free place.

Gladiolus foliage is unlikely to blacken quite as dramatically as that of dahlias but by late autumn, they too should be cut down and the corms cleaned of excess fibrous matter. Packed in paper bags, they can be kept in conditions similar to the dahlia tubers.

### Ways of using bulbous plants in the garden

Bulbous plants are so versatile and so diverse that even a small garden can accommodate a wide variety in many different locations. But don't skimp on your purchases; to be truly effective, most bulbous plants should be used in large numbers.

Most of the low-growing, spring-flowering bulbs are woodland plants that make use of the light that penetrates to the woodland floor before the leaves of deciduous trees form a shade canopy. So it makes perfect ecological sense to use these plants under and between deciduous shrubs in our gardens. Here they can be left to spread and need little attention. For autumn and winter interest in the same site, cyclamen or colchicums work with comparable effectiveness.

Growing bulbs in grass is popular and works well if care is taken to choose varieties that can compete with the grass. Snowdrops and daffodils are familiar favourites, but among others that are good are large-flowered Crocus Dutch hybrids, dog's tooth violet (*Erythronium*), *Narcissus cyclamineus*, snake's head fritillary (*Fritillaria meleagris*) in damp sites, and squills (*Scilla*). Remember that the grass must be left for six weeks after the bulb flowers have faded before cutting. This isn't, of course, practical on a normal lawn but where the lawn merges into a wildlife garden or where there is rough grass between trees, it offers an attractive low-maintenance option.

There is great scope for experimenting with bulbous plants in containers, either as temporary displays or permanent plantings. Smaller spring-flowering bulbs can be planted alongside evergreens for added interest and, for an impressive but temporary spring display, plant bulbs with different flowering times in layers in a large container. Place the latest flowering at the bottom and the earliest at the top; they can be crammed in so they are almost touching and then, after the first season, they may be lifted and replanted around the garden. As single subjects, I find growing the large-flowered hybrid tulips in containers more successful than planting them in open beds; partly because, once flowering has finished, the container can be moved out of view while the old foliage dies back fully.

*Agapanthus* can be left in containers for year after year but, like all permanent plantings, they need a soil-based compost such as John Innes No. 2 and should be fed each year after flowering. Lilies are the most wonderful of summer container bulbs, not only for their elegance and fragrance but for the practical reason that they are less susceptible to soil pests when grown in pots. They too can be moved discreetly out of the way once faded.

Bulbous plants can also be grown on their own as single varieties in dedicated beds and bearded irises, dahlias, gladioli and tulips are often planted very effectively this way. A sheltered warm spot, perhaps at the base of a fence or house wall is ideal for bulbs such as *Amaryllis*, *Crinum*, *Gladiolus*, *Nerine* and *Sternbergia* that are of borderline tenderness.

The taller types of bulbous plant make valuable additions to mixed or herbaceous borders, but it's important to plan how to disguise the bulb foliage once flowering is over. Growing tulips towards the back of the border with a perennial, like *Hemerocallis*, that quickly comes into leaf further forward is one solution. Another idea is to grow alliums rising up though a carpeting plant such as hardy geraniums. And of course such plants as lilies or dahlias in pots can be plunged in the border to fill summer gaps.

Many of the more choice smaller bulbs would be lost in a border yet are charming in a rockery or alpine trough. The small irises like *Iris danfordiae* and *I. reticulata* grow well in a spot that is baked in summer and a rock garden is also an ideal position for many of the delightful small tulip species.

## Bulbous plants by season

Everyone is familiar with spring-flowering bulbs like bluebells, crocus, daffodils, snowdrops, tulips and hyacinths. Yet there are many, unjustifiably neglected bulbs that can be grown for colour in the other three seasons and I have listed some ideas, although this selection is far from exhaustive.

### Spring

*Anemone nemorosa*, *Arisarum*, *Arum* (with added interest later from foliage and fruits), *Bulbocodium*, *Chionodoxa*, *Convallaria*, *Corydalis*, *Crocus* (apart from the well-known Dutch hybrids there are many others such as the *Crocus sieberi* hybrids and *Crocus tommasinianus*), *Erythronium*, *Fritillaria*, *Hyacinthoides*, *Ipheion*, *Gagea*, *Leucojum*, *Muscari*, *Narcissus*, *Ornithogalum*, *Puschkinia*, *Scilla*, *Trillium*, *Tulipa*.

### Summer

*Agapanthus*, *Allium*, *Alstroemeria*, *Amaryllis*, *Camassia*, *Cardiocrinum*, *Crinum*, *Crocosmia*, *Dahlia*, *Eremurus*, *Gladiolus*, *Galtonia*, *Iris*, *Lily*, *Schizostylis*, *Zantedeschia*.

### Autumn

*Colchicum*, *Crocus sativus*, *Crocus speciosus*, *Cyclamen hederifolium*, *Nerine*, *Sternbergia*.

### Winter

*Anemone blanda*, *Crocus ancyrensis*, *Crocus laevigatus fontenayi*, *Cyclamen coum*, *Eranthis*, *Galanthus*.

## Some bulbous plants for shade

*Anemone*, *Arisarum*, *Arum*, *Asarum*, *Cardiocrinum*, *Chionodoxa*, *Colchicum*, *Convallaria*, *Cyclamen*, *Eranthis*, *Erythronium*, *Fritillaria*, *Galanthus*, *Hyacinthoides*, *Iris foetidissima*, *Leucojum*, *Lilium*, *Ornithogalum*, *Scilla*, *Trillium*.

**above** I grow all of the large flowered tulips in pots; they are less prone to slug damage and can be removed from view when the flowers fade.

**below** *Agapanthus* are the most wonderful of large summer flowering bulbs for mild and coastal gardens.

# Alpines

There is no more diverse group of plants than those embraced by the name 'Alpines'. They are also popularly called rock-garden plants or rock plants; the names are interchangeable although all are slightly misleading. Rock-garden plants implies they can only be grown in a rock garden or among rocks; this is untrue. Alpines implies that they all originate in the Alps. This is equally untrue. What they do have in common is an origin in mountains and other high places; but there are representatives from far beyond the European Alps and species are now available from every mountain range in the world. They embrace a huge number of plant families, many with closely related 'lowland' members too; there are alpine equivalents of numerous familiar border perennials and a few shrubs, although in addition there are many groups that are uniquely plants of high places.

The important features that alpine plants share are that they are small plants originating in habitats that are not merely cold but experience other climatic extremes. In full exposure to the midday sun there is little shade, so the rocks of a mountain top or exposed Arctic landscape become very hot; yet once night falls, the temperature plummets. Rainfall is often very high, but the rainwater drains away rapidly. Despite the toughness required to survive such conditions, alpines are often difficult to grow in gardens as most need both a very free-draining soil and absence of the cold, clinging damp that is feature of temperate, lowland winter. So it is very important to know which are the more demanding plants and which are more tolerant and to match these to suitable sites in your garden. Here, my emphasis is on the easier types that will tolerate garden conditions; none of them require the additional shelter of an alpine greenhouse.

## Ways of using alpines in the garden

Most people think first of growing alpines in a rock garden but unless you are prepared to give some thought and planning to fitting such a difficult feature into the rest of the garden, I would advise the far simpler options of troughs, walls, tufa or raised beds.

If your heart is set on a rock garden, however, do bear in mind certain important considerations as no other garden feature is more difficult to create with an authentic appearance, and more gardens are spoiled by ridiculously inappropriate rock gardens than anything else. A rock garden is not a random

**below** The alpine meadow may not be easy to recreate in a garden but the individual plants may be grown very readily on a smaller scale.

pile of stones with plants scattered among them. It must appear as if it is a natural outcrop of rock. This means a simple understanding of geology. Most sedimentary rocks, like sandstone, lie in bedding planes while massive rocks, whether sedimentary ones like limestone or igneous ones like granite, don't. The rocks you use must blend with those that occur naturally in the area where you live; a limestone rock garden in the middle of a sandstone landscape will look frankly stupid. But, and this is the biggest consideration of all, the rock must either be obtained from an approved quarry source or be a very good artificial substitute. Far too much stone has been taken without thought or permission from the countryside at large and gardeners must not support this unlawful and reprehensible trade.

Design your rock garden as a feature that fits in with the rest of the garden; slopes often lend themselves to rock gardens where a position in the middle of a level lawn will not. Take any opportunity you have to see an expert at work and observe how much thought they give to placing each stone. I am often tempted to suggest that gardeners visit great public gardens to obtain an idea of how best to create a garden feature but, with some notable exceptions, most of them are no better in terms of the authenticity of their rock gardens than many an amateur's would be. Your best bet is to look long and hard at natural rock outcrops.

I hope, however, that you will at least begin your alpine gardening experiences with a small raised bed, trough or similar restricted area. Design considerations aside, most soils will need the addition of grit to improve drainage and this is much easier to achieve on a smaller scale. A small amount of leaf mould should be added to improve soil structure but, for once in gardening, the addition of large amounts of organic matter isn't recommended as it can render the soil too moisture retentive. Position your chosen feature so the plants can be enjoyed at close quarters; remember that their diminutive features are the primary attraction. A sunny spot is preferable, light shade can be tolerated but no alpines will thrive in deep shade. Shelter is not needed, they are very tolerant of wind and an open, very well ventilated situation is desirable.

## Space required

A rock garden of course can be as large as you choose to make it but seldom looks right if less than about 10m² (11sq yds). Alpines will, however, grow in the smallest space so a single little trough or piece of tufa could accommodate from six to 12 specimens and, of course,

Pack as much soil as you can into the crevice while holding the plants and then trickle in water. If you use alpine plants for rather larger scale plantings in walls, you will find it easier to use seed, although the time before you will have well sized plants will, of course, be longer and your choice of varieties will be smaller.

### Problems

Alpines are fairly free from pests and diseases, probably because they are in active growth at a time of year before many pests and disease organisms are themselves active. Aphids can be troublesome on some species, nonetheless, although the biggest problem is allied to their intolerance of clinging damp. *Botrytis* grey mould can then be troublesome and is especially prevalent if dead leaves have been allowed to accumulate around the plants.

### Feeding/watering

A top dressing of bone meal (wear gloves to apply) applied in autumn will slowly release phosphate and so encourage root development. This should be followed by a further light application of bone meal (wear gloves to apply) or a very light dressing with fish, blood, and bone in spring. Watering is only needed for newly-planted alpines and in dry periods in summer, although those in containers will need watering more frequently.

### Other care

Alpines with hairy leaves or that are shaped so that water collects in the crown should be protected by placing an open-ended cloche over them during the winter. Remove any dead leaves that accumulate around the plants, especially in autumn, to reduce the likelihood of rotting. Displays can be improved by the removal of dead flowerheads although this is not essential. Grit should be used as a mulch (never use organic mulches); it not only enhances the appearance and helps prevent water from collecting around the neck of the plants but prevents soil, which contains contaminating spores, from being splashed onto the plants.

### Alpines for interest outside the spring

Most alpines flower in spring but to provide continuing interest, it is important to select later-flowering species and also to appreciate

**above** Care and ingenuity, and an understanding of the way the plants grow naturally, is needed to achieve the best results with alpines.

alpines can be squeezed into cracks in walls or paving. A raised bed should ideally be at least 2 x 1m (6½ft x 3ft). But bear in mind that not all alpines are minute so plant choice is an important consideration too; some plants described as rock plants spread rapidly to 60cm (1ft) or more.

### Propagation/sowing/planting

Many alpines can be grown successfully from seed; there is no need for a greenhouse as the seed should be sown in the autumn in seed trays or pots, then left outside over the winter so the low temperature will break the dormancy of the seed. However, a very wide range of plants, usually in small pots, is available from garden centres and specialists from early spring onwards and many of them can be readily propagated from semi-ripe cuttings during the summer. Plants may also be divided every few years, in much the same way as border perennials (page 75).

Alpines are easy to plant; use a trowel and make a planting hole twice the volume of the root-ball. Mix in a handful of garden compost and grit with a light dusting of bone meal (wear gloves to apply). Water in after planting and continue to water during dry weather, at least for the first season. Planting in rocks, tufa or in walls is more time-consuming and tricky. Use a sharp tool to clear away any debris and push in some soil before easing in the plants (young plants are easiest to insert) with a metal dibber.

those, such as many species of *Saxifraga* and *Sempervivum*, that have foliage appeal. The following lists include many genera that, of course, contain non-alpine species too.

### Summer flowers
*Aster alpinus* (begins in spring, continues into summer), *Campanula, Chiastophyllum oppositifolium, Dianthus, Diascia, Dodecatheon, Erinus alpinus* (begins in spring, continues into summer), *Erodium reichardii, Gentiana septemfida, Geranium, Hebe, Parahebe, Penstemon pinifolius, Saponaria* (begins in spring, continues into summer), *Saxifraga* (some, such as *Saxifraga ewersii*), *Silene alpestris, Thymus* (begins in spring, continues into summer), *Veronica prostrata* (begins in spring, continues into summer).

### Autumn flowers
*Cotoneaster* (dwarf forms for fruits), *Gentiana sino-ornata, Saxifraga cortusifolia, Saxifraga fortunei, Silene schafta*.

## Alpines for shade
There are rather few shade-tolerant alpines but I have found the following to be fairly successful and valuable for those who have more shaded gardens and also for planting on the shaded side of large rocks in an otherwise sunny rock garden.

*Campanula cochleariifolia, Campanula thyrsoides, Chiastophyllum, Gentiana* (North American, Himalayan and eastern Asian types), *Oxalis* (especially *O. acetosella, O. denophylla* and *O. laciniata*), *Phlox adsurgens, Primula, Saxifraga* (most are suitable but not the mat-forming encrusted types).

## Invasive alpines
These are plants that can swamp the slower-growing alpines in a trough or small rock garden, although they can be considered for covering larger areas.

*Alyssum saxatile* (named varieties are generally not invasive), *Arabis* (some), *Campanula, portenschlagiana, Campanula poscharskyana, Cerastium tomentosum, Helianthemum* (some), *Iberis sempervirens, Oxalis latifolia, Oxalis pes-caprae, Sedum acre, Viola odorata*.

## Commonly grown Alpines requiring special conditions
### Should be planted laterally into the sides of wall or rocks
*Haberlea* (needs shade), *Lewisia, Ramonda myconi* (needs shade).

### Moist, more organic, acidic conditions
*Cassiope, Gentiana* (some, including *Gentiana asclepiadea* and *Gentiana sino-ornata*), *Primula* (some; see companion volume).

**above** A mulch of grit will enhance the appearance of your plants, maintain moisture, suppress weeds and slugs, and prevent soil from being splashed onto delicate flowers.

**left** Lewisias are particularly intolerant of moisture on the flowers and so planting them in vertical faces often gives the best results.

# Trees

Trees, like shrubs and many climbers, have a woody framework that remains above ground all the time. This framework gives a maturity and added dimension to our gardens: it encloses spaces and adds vertical interest to what could otherwise be very flat, open areas. There is no strict rule governing the difference between trees and shrubs, but a useful practical distinction, and one that I have tried to follow here, is that a mature tree is generally above 6m (20ft) in height on a single stem.

I am sure that more problems are caused through gardeners using trees incorrectly or inappropriately than arise in any other aspect of gardening. Quite simply, the reason is that trees are so big and any mistakes made in choice of species or variety and in planting position are therefore magnified. Leaving aside the small minority of gardeners who have space to plant woods or even copses, for the remainder, a tree is a specimen feature. And in most modern gardens, the overall space available dictates that it must be a solitary feature. This being so, the tree for the modern gardener has an exacting list of attributes to satisfy.

It must be of a size appropriate to the scale of the garden so that, visually, it is correct. It must also be of a size that will not dominate the space around it to the extent of adversely affecting the growth of other plants. And its size must not be such that it poses a physical threat to the structure of the house or other buildings.

But having a tree of the correct size is only part of the story. It must not possess other anti-social features such as large quantities of huge leaves that obstruct drains and paths when they fall; nor give rise to sticky honeydew that cascades over people, cars and other vegetation. And on the positive side, it must have all-year-round appeal; for after all, when it is alone or at best, one of a very small number, a tree really must earn its keep.

The most obviously attractive parts of a tree are its leaves but you should bear in mind the length of time that they are present to be admired. Deciduous trees generally have more attractive leaves than evergreens but, whereas the latter bear them all year round, a deciduous species that comes into leaf late and sheds its foliage early is scarcely offering very much value. Moreover, the foliage of many deciduous trees changes colour (and in a few instances, shape) as the season progresses. One that offers changing leaf interest, therefore, is especially to be cherished. Once the leaves have fallen from a deciduous tree in autumn, much of interest and attractiveness may still remain in the shape of the twigs, bark and buds, although there are rather few trees worth growing for these attributes alone.

Almost all trees also bear flowers, collectively generally called blossom when they are present in large numbers, and many trees are

**below** Positioning of trees is very important. Many are subject to aphid infestation and consequent sticky honeydew which will drip onto garden benches or other objects placed beneath.

chosen for their blossom alone. Nonetheless, many trees selected for a stunning floral display offer a fairly depressing spectacle for the months after the blossom has fallen. Flowers may be followed by fruit which can also be attractive, in colour and/or shape. But the period over which fruit can contribute to the appeal of a garden tree is generally limited by the local birds who will view it, quite understandably, as a free and convenient food supply.

Of course, the overall shape of a tree is an important feature and there can be wide variation within species from the markedly upright or fastigiate to the wide-spreading, drooping, weeping or pendulous.

## Ways of using trees in the garden

As I have suggested, in most gardens, trees will be grown as isolated specimens although a group of two or three chosen for their appropriate size and other features will be effective in many modern gardens. In larger gardens, several trees might be grown together as a woodland or as part of a very large mixed border or shrubbery but no matter how big an area you have available, do select a blend of deciduous and evergreen species and types with contrasting and complementary features, just as if you were choosing herbaceous perennials.

I must add one, perhaps unexpected, word of caution. On small-scale plantings with perennials or shrubs, I frequently advise gardeners to plant more individuals than they will ultimately need and to plant them fairly close together with a view to removing some later. I would recommend this with trees too, except that in many places (in designated Conservation Areas in Britain) trees automatically acquire legal protection once they attain a certain (rather small) size and may not then be removed with permission from the statutory local authority.

Even very small gardens can still have their quota of trees because dwarf or extremely slow-growing forms may be selected for planting in large containers. Among those that I have found especially successful are: some of the oriental forms of *Acer, Amelanchier, Caragana, Eucalyptus, Ilex, Magnolia, Prunus* and also *Malus*, the ornamental crab-apples which have the inestimable merit of being obtainable on the dwarfing rootstocks bred for apple growing

(page 128). Dwarf conifers can also be grown very successfully in containers and here the choice is legion.

## Site and soil

Some trees will grow almost anywhere but most have their own preferences so find out about your site and choose a tree that will thrive there. Trees can be moved during the dormant season if you make a mistake with the siting but it is time consuming and could check growth. Chalky soil will restrict your choice as will waterlogged soil. A large or medium-sized tree that is not hardy for your area will be

**above** Careful choice of trees can give appeal from bark, flowers, fruit and foliage.

**above** Provided you choose relatively small varieties, trees can be used within mixed borders.

**below** Ornamental crab apples have the considerable advantage of being obtainable grafted onto growth limiting apple rootstocks so trees of individual size can be selected.

difficult to look after so check the hardiness of the more unusual varieties. And, when planting trees as part of a windbreak, pay attention to local conditions such as cold winds or salt spray when making your selection.

## Space required

A small tree grown in a container will fit in a tiny courtyard but all other trees must be chosen in relation to their growth rates, their ultimate height and the proximity of buildings or other large features. There is much debate between arboriculturists and insurance companies over what constitutes a 'safe' planting distance from buildings. Soil type plays an important role; the effects of tree roots on the foundations of a building will be much greater in a clay soil prone to shrinkage than in a free-draining sand. My own rule is never to plant the large weeping willow (*Salix* x *sepulcralis chrysocoma*) or any of the large poplars in a garden, and never to plant any tree closer to a house than a distance equal to one and a half times its ultimate height.

## Planting

The traditional time for planting trees is during the dormant season from late autumn until early spring but this is only crucially relevant for bare-rooted plants. Most trees are now supplied through garden centres in containers and these can be planted at all times of the year; although it is still generally easier to establish them during the dormant period.

I can't over-emphasise the importance of giving thorough and careful preparation to the planting position. Dig a hole of volume approximately twice that of the root-ball of the tree and pile the soil at the side. Then mix with this a similar volume of well rotted manure or garden compost and several handfuls of bone meal (wear gloves to apply). Break up the soil in the base of the hole with a fork then gradually refill, pressing it down gently with your boot until the remaining hole is deep enough for the tree's roots to be spread out in it while leaving the original soil mark on the trunk base level with the soil surface.

With a container-grown plant, water the compost thoroughly and tease away some of the roots around the sides and bottom of the compost ball as you place it in the hole. Then insert a stout stake on the leeward side of the tree (to ensure that it is blown away from, and not on to it). Although very short stakes have become rather popular and are effective, I prefer a purpose-cut one of approximately 1.5m (5ft), made of treated timber, and driven at least 60cm (2ft) into the ground. The tree's trunk should be secured to the stake with two adjustable belt-style tree ties, one close to the top and one close to ground level. Then gradually fill in around the roots with the soil and organic matter mixture, pressing down gently with your boot. Water the area around the plant very thoroughly, then finally, make a small mound of manure or compost around the base of the trunk.

## Propagation

Most people require only one tree and will purchase it from a garden or nursery. However, trees can be propagated by seed, cuttings or by layering (page 00). But tree propagation of any sort is a long, slow business and seed-raised plants may well differ from their parents.

## Problems

The commonest problem is that trees become too large for a particular site or they fail to establish when young. Mature trees do not suffer unduly from pests or diseases; mildew may appear but can be tolerated, coral spot can cause die-back so should be cut out promptly as soon as it is seen. The spectre of honey fungus haunts many tree owners but this is an overestimated threat. Undoubtedly, where an old diseased tree stump is present, honey fungus may spread from it to affect living plants but some attention can prevent its affecting an entire garden; and with care and commonsense, honey fungus can be permanently kept out of existing sites.

## Feeding and watering

Because trees will ultimately grow tall, and appear well able to take care of themselves, it is easy to forget that, in their early years, they are vulnerable and need watering, mulching and feeding to establish a root system strong enough to support the top growth. Once the roots are functioning and supporting the tree, no watering or feeding should be required. Trees planted in lawns or other grassed areas should have an area of approximately 1m (3ft) in diameter around their base kept free from grass for at least six years after planting. And this or any other area of soil around a young tree must also be kept free from weed growth. Apply a general purpose fertilizer such as fish, blood and bone around the base in late spring and then re-apply a thick organic matter mulch.

Old trees may become undernourished and in order to rejuvenate such trees the nutrients should be targeted at the youngest roots which are to be found at the perimeter of the rootball. Mark out a circle a little beyond the outside of the leaf canopy. At 60cm (2ft) intervals around this circle, dig holes roughly 60cm (2ft) deep, taking care to damage the tree's roots as little as possible. Incorporate well-rotted organic matter and a balanced general fertilizer such as fish, blood and bone or Growmore into the soil, then replace the soil dug out and firm gently. Water thoroughly if conditions are dry.

## Other care

Few ornamental trees require routine pruning but damaged or diseased branches must be removed using a saw. Make sloping cuts close to but not flush with the trunk, taking especial care not to damage the collar at the branch base from which the healing tissues will develop. And always clean up jagged ends from broken branches to limit the risk of decay organisms entering the tree. Small shoots arising on the trunk of trees should be rubbed out as they form in order to maintain an attractive clean bole; the longer they are left, the greater will be the scar when they are removed.

Very large specimens that are casting shade on the garden can have the crown thinned but this is a task for an expert and you should engage a professional qualified tree surgeon. A few types of ornamental trees produce suckers (small shoots arising from the roots); pull rather than cut these out using strong gloves, as cutting may simply encourage more suckers to arise. Tree ties should be checked regularly so they can be adjusted as the girth of the trunk increases or retied if they have come adrift in windy weather.

Commonly-grown trees that should only be planted as specimens in very large gardens (other than as dwarf or other selected forms):

*Acer pesudoplatanus, Cedrus, Fagus, Fraxinus, Juglans, Pseudotsuga, Quercus, Salix x sepulcralis chrysocoma.*

## Trees with attractive bark

*Abies, Acer capillipes, Acer griseum, Acer, grosseri hersii* and other 'snake-barked' maples, *Prunus* (some, especially *P. serrula*), *Salix, Sorbus, Stewartia, Taxodium, Thuja.*

## Tree fruits

Tree fruits can take a huge range of forms and this is a very limited selection. It's perhaps worth adding that

**above** Care to provide a stout stake and a proper belt-style tree tie is essential for the assured establishment of young trees.

**below** Never leave old pruning stubs as these will attract decay fungi which can then spread into the living tissues.

volume, 'Stefan Buczacki's Plant Dictionary'. *Abies* (cones), *Acer capillipes*, *Ailanthus altissima*, *Arbutus*, *Carpinus*, *Catalpa*, *Cedrus* (cones), *Cercis*, *Cornus*, *Cotoneaster*, *Crataegus*, *Gleditsia*, *Idesia*, *Ilex*, *Koelreuteria*, *Magnolia*, *Malus*, *Morus*, *Ostrya*, *Phellodendron*, *Picea* (cones), *Pinus* (cones), *Prunus*, *Pterocarya*, *Rhus*, *Sorbus*, *Taxus*, *Tetradium*.

## Trees for autumn colour

I have limited my selection here to those that in my experience give the strongest autumn colour in European gardens; many others give some attractive colour change for a short time:

*Acer griseum*, *Acer rubrum*, *Amelanchier*, *Crataegus*, *Ginkgo*, *Liquidambar*, *Nyssa*, *Parrotia*, *Pyrus*.

## Fastigiate trees

These are commonly-grown trees that have attractive varieties with an upright growth or narrow habit and are especially valuable in limited space. These varieties are often called 'Fastigiata', 'Erecta' or, sometimes 'Columnaris'

**above** Sycamores (*Acer pseudoplatanus*) are not good choices as garden trees for their seedlings will appear everywhere.

varieties with fruit differently coloured from the norm will always arouse interest and attention. Most cotoneasters and most hollies, for instance, have red fruits; so yellow ones are especially to be cherished (see the companion

**right** *Acer pennsylvanicum* is just one of several attractive *Acer* species grown for their beautiful bark.

although this is used for broader forms also.

*Acer platanoides, Acer pseudoplatanus, Acer rubrum, Acer saccharinum, Betula, Carpinus, Cedrus, Chamaecyparis lawsoniana, Crataegus, Cupressus, Fagus, Fraxinus, Gingko, Ilex, Juniperus, Liriodendron, Picea, Pinus, Populus, Prunus, Quercus, Robinia, Sorbus, Taxus, Thuja, Tilia, Tsuga.*

## Pendulous trees

These are commonly-grown trees that have attractive varieties with a weeping or pendulous habit. These varieties are often called 'Pendula'.

*Abies, Alnus, Betula, Caragana, Cedrus, Cercidiphyllum, Chamaecyparis, Cotoneaster, Crataegus, Cupressus, Fagus, Fraxinus, Gleditsia, Ilex, Juniperus, Laburnum, Ligustrum, Malus, Morus, Picea, Pinus, Populus, Prunus, Pyrus, Quercus, Salix, Sophora, Tilia.*

## Trees for the coastal gardens

These are trees tolerant both of strong winds and salt spray, although those than are tolerant of the colder conditions associated with exposed inland sites are denoted [inland].

*Acer platanoides* [inland], *Acer pseudoplatanus* [inland], *Alnus, Arbutus, Castanea, Cotoneaster, Crataegus* [inland], x *Cupressocyparis* [inland], *Cupressus, Eucalyptus, Fraxinus* [inland], *Ilex, Juniperus* [inland], *Phillyrea, Pinus* [inland], *Populus* [inland], *Quercus* [inland], *Salix, Sorbus* [inland], *Trachycarpus.*

## Trees with variegated foliage

*Acer campestre, Acer negundo, Acer platanoides, Acer pseudoplatanus, Castanea, Catalpa, Cedrus, Chamaecyparis lawsoniana, Cornus, Crataegus, Fagus, Gingko, Ilex, Ligustrum, Liquidambar, Liriodendron, Platanus, Populus, Quercus.*

## Non-coniferous evergreens

Too frequently, gardeners are directed only towards conifers when seeking evergreen trees. Admittedly, that is where the greatest selection lies and it is true that many other evergreen trees are either too tender or too dull to merit planting in gardens. Below is a selection of some I think particularly worthy of attention. [F] denotes those plants with excellent flowering appeal, in addition to foliage.

*Acacia* [F], *Arbutus* [F], *Cotoneaster* (semi-evergreen) [F], *Embothrium* [F], *Eucalyptus, Eucryphia* [F], *Ilex, Ligustrum* [F], *Magnolia* [F], *Nothofagus, Phillyrea* [F], *Prunus* [F], *Quercus, Sophora, Trachycarpus* [F].

## Blossom trees by season
### Spring
*Acer platanoides, Alnus, Amelanchier, Magnolia* (some), *Malus, Prunus* (many), *Pyrus, Salix.*

### Late spring/early summer
*Aesculus, Caragana, Cercis, Cornus, Cotoneaster, Crataegus, Davidia, Embothrium, Fraxinus, Halesia, Idesia, Laburnum, Paulownia, Phillyrea, Sorbus.*

### Summer
*Castanea, Catalpa, Cladrastis, Eucryphia, Koelreuteria, Ligustrum, Liriodendron, Magnolia* (some), *Pterocarya, Robinia, Stewartia, Styrax, Tilia, Toona, Trachycarpus.*

### Autumn
*Arbutus*

### Winter
*Acacia, Magnolia* (some), *Prunus* (few; some in late winter).

## Trees for shallow soils
*Acer campestre, Acer platanoides, Acer pseudoplatanus, Acer saccharinum, Aesculus, Ailanthus, Alnus, Betula, Crataegus, Fraxinus, Platanus, Populus, Prunus avium, Robinia, Salix, Sorbus, Tilia.*

**above** By choosing a fastigiate or upright variety, it may be possible to grow examples of quite large trees in limited space.

# Shrubs

Shrubs, like trees, are long-term plants with a woody framework that remains above ground. While trees have a single central woody stem, shrubs have several smaller stems that arise in various ways and subsequently branch in various ways, resulting in an overall appearance that is very different and distinct. This growth habit gives rise to a wide range of different forms with widely varying appeal. Nonetheless, there are a number of genera and even a number of species that span the boundary between trees and shrubs and several plants appear in both my tree and shrub lists. Just as with trees, there are evergreen and deciduous shrubs, each with slightly different but complementary roles to play in the garden.

**above** There's no hard and fast line between a large shrub and a small tree, but trees are reckoned to be more than 6m (20ft) tall on a single stem.

**below** The traditional old garden shrubbery could be attractive but was often a rather sombre affair.

In this section of the book, I have excluded two groups of important shrubs as they are considered in separate chapters: roses, which have become so distinct and so varied a group within themselves, and hedges, which are simply shrubs or trees planted in a line and pruned rather severely.

### Ways of obtaining the best from shrubs in the garden

I've long believed that the shrub is the most important type of plant in the modern garden. In this respect, the modern garden is very different from that of a century or more ago. Then, the shrubbery was often a monotonous and rather sombre place, dominated by tough evergreens that assumed their value in the 19th century urban environment because of their tolerance of the atmospheric pollution that accompanied the years following the Industrial Revolution. Colour in those gardens was provided by herbaceous plants or by roses. Today, the shortcomings of this kind of planting have been widely recognised and the dedicated shrubbery is now a rarity, found only in larger gardens.

The modern shrub has other roles. It is at its most valuable when used to provide the permanent framework for the mixed border, where it supplies interest and attractiveness all year round, most importantly in the winter, when the herbaceous perennials, bulbs and annuals have died down. But shrubs can also be used most valuably as individual specimens or small groups amongst other types of plant or in grass. The interest and appeal they supply can take many forms: massed blossom or striking individual flowers, perfume, attractive bark colour or texture, leaf colour and shape or simply the overall form and shape of the plant.

The appeal of shrubs has increased greatly as more species and varieties have become available and this is true especially of the greater number of relatively low-growing vari-

eties which are so useful in smaller, modern gardens. Much of this choice arises from the vast numbers of new introductions brought back by plant collectors from the Far East, China especially, and the careful work of selection and hybridisation that ensued in the West.

When planning a mixed border, decide on the shrubs (and trees if they are also to be included) before selecting the herbaceous perennials and use a mixture of evergreen and deciduous types. As it is hardest to obtain reliable colour and interest in the border in late autumn to early winter, begin by choosing shrubs with variegated evergreen foliage or attractive fruits. Place these at the back of the border, or in the centre of an island bed. In the middle of the border, choose shrubs for flowering or foliage interest in spring and summer or perhaps a variegated holly or other evergreen trained in a standard or column shape. Shrubs for the front of the border must be neat, particularly where the edge of the border meets the lawn, and evergreen types such as small hebes

or lavenders are invaluable here. In a shallow border, growing a shrub such as a pyracantha trained two-dimensionally against the back wall will economise on space, but remember to allow access for pruning.

A border dedicated solely to shrubs, at one time called a shrubbery, tends to be less interesting year-round than a mixed border but it has a place in large gardens where maintenance is a problem. To increase its appeal, consider incorporating scented, winter-flowering shrubs that can be used for cutting like *Chimonanthus praecox*, *Sarcococca* or a *Viburnum*. When creating a shrub border, adherence to the correct planting distance will leave large gaps in the early years but don't be tempted to plant closer than recommended or your plants will soon suffer through increased competition. It is much better to mulch well between the plants and use inexpensive short-term perennials or even annuals to fill the gaps, gradually taking them out, or planting fewer each year, until the shrubs reach maturity.

**above** In the modern garden, shrubs are more likely to be interplanted with other types of plant than grown in a dedicated shrubbery.

**above** Containers allow you to grow shrubs that, like this camellia, have requirements for a particular type of soil even if your garden soil is different.

and heavy rain for summer flowers. The alternative is to rely on the more weather-tolerant and generally longer-lasting appeal that derives from particularly fine foliage or overall shape. For this, the oriental species of *Acer*, *Cornus kousa* and its relatives, *Cotinus coggygria*, *Fothergilla*, *Liquidambar* and *Sambucus*, among others, are definitely worth considering. Although foliage is generally more tolerant than flowers of adverse weather, do be aware that very cold winds and exposed sites will often cause damage to some golden and variegated-leaved forms especially.

Even the smallest garden has room for a few shrubs in containers. To be suitable for container growing, a shrub must be able to tolerate both the restriction of its roots and periodic drying out. Container growing always offers you the opportunity to grow plants that are intolerant of the natural soil conditions in your garden, but it confers special benefits with shrubs as there are just so many fine species and varieties that require acidic conditions, and a few that similarly need an alkaline environment. Simply by selecting an appropriate compost, you can have the best of both worlds.

Among particularly attractive acid-loving shrubs are heathers, for small containers, while compact varieties of *Camellia*, *Pieris*, *Rhododendron* (and azalea) would make excellent single subjects for larger pots. Other, less-demanding shrubs that adapt well to containers are *Daphne*, among which some varieties, together with *Hamamelis* have appealing early-season flowers and fragrance. Evergreen shrubs are particularly valuable, as in the winter they may provide perhaps the main colour on a terrace while in the summer they are an excellent foil for flowering plants. Among those I have found most amenable to containers are *Aucuba*, which is both attractive and tolerant of difficult conditions, and *Buxus* which, of course, is a fine topiary subject, readily clipped into appealing shapes. Containers that are light or mobile enough to be transported under cover over the winter allow you to grow shrubs like *Abutilon* and *Callistemon* that are of borderline hardiness.

## Site and soil

You will find shrubs that are appropriate for almost every type of garden and every position in a garden. Full sun is certainly no prerequi-

Small, tough evergreen shrubs with good leaf cover can be used as ground cover. This may not be the most exciting way of planting and I'm the first to admit that the invention of the 'ground cover' has been one of the saddest facets of 20th century gardening. No plant that is 'used' rather than 'chosen' is ever likely to be enhancing the appeal of your garden very much, but it does offer a way of dealing with a problem area such as a shady slope.

There is no compulsion about growing shrubs in borders and those with outstanding beauty or form make fine isolated specimens. If it is impact from flowers that you are seeking, then look no further than *Camellia*, *Magnolia*, *Philadelphus*, *Syringa* or tree paeony (*Paeonia*), but always be aware that the drawback with relying on spectacular flowers for the appeal of a specimen shrub is that they are vulnerable to weather damage: late frosts with spring flowers

site, for the natural habitat of a very large number of shrubs is the relative shade of woodland. Shrubs vary widely in their tolerance of exposure. Understandably, many of the woodland species do require some shelter but, conversely, there are shrubs that grow naturally in the most exposed of cliff-top or mountainside locations and will survive in exposed gardens even without the need for a windbreak. With such a wide rage in tolerance, however, it is important to check the site requirements carefully before purchase.

A soil-based John Innes No. 3 potting compost is best for most long-term container-grown shrubs but those requiring acidic conditions should be grown in specially formulated ericaceous compost; normally these are peat-based, although plenty of other options are now available.

### Space required

With such a wide diversity in size and shape, there will be a shrub appropriate for every planting position. Nonetheless, I repeat a maxim that I have always followed: if you find it necessary to restrict the size of a shrub by pruning in order that it doesn't exceed the allotted position, then you have the wrong plant. Once again, therefore, before making your purchase, ascertain the size and, most importantly, the potential growth rate of your chosen shrub.

### Planting

Shrubs are planted in much the same way as trees (page 00) but staking is generally unnecessary because, having a multiple number of stems, they will be physically more balanced. Evergreens will benefit greatly from a protective screen of hessian or other windbreak material during the first winter after planting. Protection from competing weeds and other plants when the shrub is young is now considered more important than soil improvement. When planted in lawns or long grass, an area of bare soil about 1m (3ft) in diameter around the base should be left and mulch material and fertilizer applied in this area to help the new plant to establish.

### Propagation

Most shrubs today are bought as container-grown plants from garden centres or nurseries and this is the ideal way to increase your stock. Nonetheless, purchasing significant numbers for a new or large garden can be an expensive undertaking. Often, friends and neighbours with mature shrubs are often willing to allow you to take cuttings and, if you are patient, they will grow to an acceptable size. And if you have individual shrubs of borderline hardiness or plants, like *Fremontodendron*, that are actually known to be relatively short-lived, it is also worth taking some cuttings every year as an insurance policy.

Softwood, hardwood or semi-ripe cuttings may be appropriate for different types of shrub and I have given information on the techniques to follow on page 00. As with some trees, certain types of shrubs are stubbornly difficult to strike from cuttings; quite commonly because they have extremely hard, fine-grained wood or because they exude copious latex when cut that inhibits rooting. It's largely for this reason that many shrubs are commercially grafted in order to obtain strong planting stock in quantity and this, in turn, explains why plants like *Hamamelis* are always relatively expensive.

Layering offers an easy, if rather slow, propagation technique for those shrubs with branches low to the ground and is a popular way of rejuvenating heathers (*Calluna* and *Erica*). Some shrubs can be raised from seed

**above** By selecting appropriately-sized varieties, a shrub planting can be made in the most improbable of places.

**below** When planting large shrubs in lawns or among grass, it's important to leave a circle of bare soil around the base to minimise competition.

mous rewards for very little effort and, certainly, if you hard prune shrubs to encourage the growth of young foliage you should feed the plants routinely immediately afterwards. I feed shrubs in the early part of the season with a general purpose fertilizer (fish, blood and bone or Growmore) where foliage is the main feature. Those grown for their flowers can be fed with rose fertilizer instead and I give a second application in the summer, although it is important to water this in thoroughly if the weather is dry.

Shrubs in containers need more watering and feeding than the equivalent plants grown in the open ground but only when they are in active growth. The compost should not be allowed to dry out, but with rather few exceptions, of which rhododendrons are the most important, it should not be allowed to remain constantly wet. I give container shrubs the same fertilizers as I give to those in open ground but give an additional application during the summer.

**above** Coral spot is one of the commonest shrub diseases, often spreading from old prunings.

**below** It's all too easy to allow shrubs to become congested and unattractive. A little regular pruning would have prevented this.

and this can be a very satisfying procedure, although named varieties of most species do not come true. Nonetheless, among those that are generally easy and successful are *Callistemon*, *Colutea*, *Gaultheria*, *Leycesteria* and *Spartium junceum*.

### Problems

Most shrubs are relatively free from serious pests and diseases, although they can succumb to root disease or pests if stressed, as a result of being crowded too closely together or underfed, for example. Mature shrubs that exhibit leaf-spotting on foliage or aphids on shoots will generally suffer little long-term harm and the problems can be tolerated. Coral spot is common on dead and weak stems and should be cut out promptly before it spreads to affect healthier tissues. Honey fungus will attack many types of shrub as it will many trees, but this disease isn't the wholesale threat to gardening that is sometimes imagined.

### Feeding and watering

Shrubs need mulching and watering for the first few years after planting but, once established, they should need little attention. Feeding is not essential but it will bring enor-

### Other care

Part of the attraction of shrubs is that they need little further attention once established. Shrubs in containers, however, even if hardy, can suffer overwinter because the root-ball may freeze in the small volume of compost or, in a very wet winter, the compost may become sodden and the roots waterlogged and so predisposed to decay. In cold winters, plants in small containers especially should be moved to a cold greenhouse or a sheltered part of the garden and the container wrapped in bubble plastic or similar insulating material.

It's possible to a grow a wide variety of shrubs in a garden for many years and not to prune any of them; clear evidence that it isn't essential. And I've already pointed out that needing to prune a shrub to limit its size is nothing more than evidence that you have chosen the wrong plant for the position. Nonetheless, this doesn't mean that shrubs never need pruning. Many do need regular attention to give of their best, usually when a particular feature, such as young foliage, flowers or winter stems, is to be encouraged. And it is sound gardening practice to remove any diseased or damaged shoots regularly so problems aren't allowed to spread to the entire plant. I have covered the general principles of pruning on page 00 and detailed requirements of individual shrubs will be found in the descriptions given in the companion volume.

## Choosing shrubs for particular attributes

In the accompanying lists, I've selected the particular attributes and the specific garden situations that experience has indicated are those that gardeners most often seek. The selections are inevitably limited and I have chosen those that I find particularly appealing. Details of each will be found in the individual descriptions given in the companion volume. Always bear in mind, moreover, my comment that whatever type and size and wherever your garden is situated, there will be a shrub that can offer the features you need.

## Shrubs with attractive fruit

The appeal of ornamental fruit may lie in their shape or colour or the sheer quantity in which they are produced. The majority of shrubs produce seed (even if it isn't always viable and named varieties don't necessarily come true) and these may be borne in single-seeded fruits or large, multiple structures. They may be large, brightly coloured and fleshy to attract birds or be dull coloured yet fantastically shaped to facilitate dispersal by the wind.

*Acer japonicum, Acer palmatum, Arbutus, Arctostaphylos, Aronia, Aucuba, Berberis, Callicarpa, Cercis, Chaenomeles, Chionanthus, Clerodendrum, Colutea, Cornus, Corokia, Cotoneaster, Daphne, Decaisnea, Dipteronia, Dorycnium, Elaeagnus, Euonymus, x Gaulnettya, Gaultheria, Hippophaë, Ilex, Leycesteria, Ligustrum, Lonicera, Mahonia, Myrica, Myrtus, Pernettya, Photinia, Poncirus, Prunus, Ptelea, Pterostyrax, Pyracantha, Rhamnus, Rhodotypos, Ruscus, Sambucus, Skimmia, Staphylea, Symphoricarpos, Vaccinium, Viburnum.*

## Shrubs for autumn colour

Most deciduous shrubs exhibit some change in leaf colour in the autumn but I have limited my selection here to those that tend to give the best displays in European gardens. In individual places (especially on more acidic soils) and in particular years, others may be equally effective. In North America, the colours tend generally to be more intense, probably because

the combination of warm days and cold nights in autumn enhances the effects. In Europe, and especially in British gardens, as the nights cool, the days become cooler too.

*Acer japonicum, Acer palmatum, Cotinus, Disanthus, Enkianthus, Fothergilla, Hamamelis, Lindera, Prunus, Rhus.*

## Shrubs for coastal or other exposed sites

These are shrubs tolerant both of strong winds and salt spray, although those that are tolerant of the colder conditions associated with exposed inland sites are denoted [inland]:

*Arbutus, Arundinaria, Atriplex [inland], Brachyglottis, Bupleurum, Callistemon,*

**below** Although *Aucuba* is usually grown for its foliage, attractive fruits are produced also on female clones.

*Calluna* [inland], *Cassinia, Ceanothus, Choisya, Cistus, Colutea, Corokia, Cotoneaster* [inland], *Cytisus, Elaeagnus* [inland], *Erica* (some) [inland], *Escallonia, Euonymus* [inland], *Fatsia, Fuchsia, Grindelia, Griselinia,* x *Halimiocistus, Halimium, Hebe, Helianthemum, Helichrysum, Hippophaë* [inland], *Hydrangea, Ilex* [inland], *Laurus, Lavatera, Leycesteria, Magnolia, Myrtus, Olearia, Perovskia, Phlomis, Phormium, Piptanthus, Potentilla* [inland], *Pyracantha* [inland], *Rhamnus* [inland], *Romneya, Rosmarinus, Rubus* [inland], *Santolina, Skimmia, Sorbaria* [inland], *Spartium, Spiraea, Symphoricarpos* [inland], *Tamarix* [inland], *Ulex* [inland], *Yucca.*

### Shrubs with variegated foliage

The appeal of variegated foliage is universal, although it is a feature that few shrubs exhibit naturally. Largely this is because the variegated condition almost always confers physiological weakness. Lacking at least some chlorophyll present in its all-green counterparts, the variegated leaf is less efficient at food production. It is also at a competitive disadvantage so when, as commonly happens, variegated shrubs undergo partial 'reversion' to produce some shoots with all-green foliage, these should be cut out promptly or they will gradually take over at the expense of the variegated ones.

*Abutilon, Aralia, Arundinaria, Aucuba, Buddleja, Buxus, Cornus, Coronilla, Daphne, Elaeagnus, Euonymus,* x *Fatshedera, Forsythia, Fothergilla, Griselinia, Hebe, Hydrangea, Hypericum, Ilex, Kerria, Leucothoë, Ligustrum, Myrtus, Osmanthus, Pachysandra, Philadelphus, Phormium, Pieris, Pittosporum, Prunus, Pseudowintera, Rhamnus, Rubus, Salvia, Sambucus, Sasa, Symphoricarpos, Vinca, Weigela, Yucca.*

**below** *Fothergilla* is one of the most reliable of shrubs for autumn foliage colour.

## Winter-flowering shrubs

Although shrubs can offer the appeal of attractive bark, buds or simply overall shape in winter, there's no denying that winter flowers are of special merit. Those in the following list all include some representatives that will flower reliably in the coldest months, although in extremely hard frosts or very cold winds, the flowers may be at least temporarily damaged.

*Abeliophyllum, Camellia* (some), *Chimonanthus, Cornus mas, Cornus officinalis, Corylus, Daphne, Garrya, Hamamelis, Jasminum, Lonicera, Luculia, Mahonia, Pachysandra, Rhododendron, Ribes, Salix, Sarcococca, Sophora, Sycopsis, Viburnum.*

## Shrubs for alkaline soils

It's commonly said that gardeners with acidic soil have a particular advantage in the large numbers of very attractive shrubs that either tolerate or require such conditions. By contrast, gardeners with alkaline soil are believed to have a much more limited selection. In offering this list, I hope to indicate that this view is mistaken. I have singled out some particularly appealing shrubs that thrive markedly well on alkaline soils; many more will tolerate it, and will tolerate it even better if they are given a once or twice-a-year application of a fertilizer containing sequestered iron.

*Aucuba, Berberis, Brachyglottis, Buddleja, Cercis, Cistus, Colutea, Deutzia, Euonymus, Forsythia, x Halimiocistus, Hebe, Helianthemum, Hibiscus, Hippophë, Holodiscus, Hypericum, Indigofera, Kerria, Kolkwitzia, Laurus, Lavandula, Ligustrum, Lonicera, Mahonia, Neillia, Olearia, Ononis, Paeonia, Philadelphus, Potentilla, Prunus, Pyracantha, Rhamnus, Rhodotypos, Rhus, Ribes, Rosmarinus, Sambucus, Sarcococca, Sorbaria, Spartium, Spiraea, Symphoricarpos, Syringa, Weigela.*

# Hedges

A hedge is simple to define: a number of shrubs (or sometimes trees) planted in a row and treated as a single entity. It is, however, one of the most under-valued of garden features, far too often being considered as almost entirely functional with little aesthetic merit. And although most commonly used as garden boundaries, hedges can be positioned anywhere in a garden and are as valuable for dividing up a large area as they are at delimiting it from a neighbouring property. For boundaries, I believe hedges should generally be the first choice; even if in some instances they must be used alongside fences or walls. Hedges extend the life of the garden up to its very limits and have a softness that no physical barrier ever will.

Good hedges are not created overnight and, as long-term features, they must be accorded some planning and forethought. To create a successful hedge requires an appropriate plant species (to be suitable for hedging, a shrub must be able to withstand clipping and to produce new shoots from fairly old wood), a very well prepared site (you will never have the chance again), appropriate plant spacing (plants must be placed close enough together to produce a continuous barrier with no gaps within five or six years), and a good deal of care in the early training and pruning. Thereafter, a modest amount of attention (more, in truth, than most hedges ever receive) will be richly rewarded.

**below** Hedges can be both utilitarian boundaries as well as attractive features within a garden.

## The pros and cons of hedges

I believe the advantages of hedges far outweigh their drawbacks but you will need to make your own assessment for your location and circumstances. What is suitable for a rural location may not be practical for a small town or suburban garden.

Hedges offer a much-needed refuge for a great deal of wildlife, providing nesting and roosting places for birds and shelter for small mammals and insects. Many kilometres of hedges have been lost from our countryside through intensive farming, so having even a short run of hedge (depending on the species chosen) in your garden will be a small contribution to redressing the balance. Of course, among the wildlife residing in your hedge will be a number of pest species and disease-causing organisms but that is true of many other wildlife garden features and is a small price to pay for helping the survival of one of

the most important and fascinating of semi-natural habitats.

As living entities, hedges blend far better with the remainder of the garden than any fence ever can. Once established, they are also more efficient as windbreaks, being pliable and offering close to the 50 per cent permeability to wind that is so desirable. A fence, even a very robust one, can readily be broken in a gale, but a hedge, being rooted in the ground, is immeasurably more durable. When did you last see a hedge damaged by a storm?

Like other young plants, however, a young hedge will require some protection in its early years and this can be provided by temporary windbreak netting or hurdles that can be re-used elsewhere in the garden later on. Simply planting a hedge alongside a fence makes a very sensible option. By the time the hedge is maturing, the fence will be coming to the end of its life.

## Choosing the right hedge

Hedges are long-term features and mistakes made in plant choice will be very visible and soon regretted; I know, I have done it. So choose your species carefully. Probably the two most important criteria are first, rapidity of growth, and second, the choice between a year-round screen and a hedge that reflects the changing seasons.

Quick-growing hedges are usually preferred for boundaries, windbreaks and screens but never forget that rapid growth won't stop when the hedge reaches your desired height. Any fast-growing hedge will always need more trimming. Where privacy is your main concern, evergreens must be your favoured choice; and quick privacy unavoidably limits your choice to conifers. No other evergreen tree or shrub hardy enough to be used as a hedge can match a conifer for rapidity of growth combined with density. If the purpose of the hedge is less for privacy and more as a windbreak, however, this function can be satisfied at least as well by a deciduous species.

Perhaps this is the place to discuss Leyland cypress (x *Cupressocyparis leylandii*), the garden plant that generates more emotion than any other. Leyland cypress can increase in height by over 1m (3ft) in a year, and for rapidly producing a screen there is nothing comparable. I know of gardens in exposed, upland areas

that simply could not exist without the protection of a Leyland hedge. Yet there is hardly a single garden in a lowland and, especially an urban area, for which I would recommend it and I would never advise it for hedges less than 2m (6½ft) in height. The best fast-growing dense conifers for normal use are western red cedar (*Thuja plicata*), tsuga (*Tsuga heterophylla*), one of the most under-valued of all conifers, is in fact one of the many forms of Lawson cypress (*Chamaecyparis lawsoniana*), of which there are more varieties of this one species than of any other cultivated tree. However, they vary enormously in their colour and growth form (some tend to become bare at the base after a few years) and a specialist nursery will advise you on the best hedging variety currently available.

**above** Always check carefully before beginning hedge cutting each season; it's important to wait until nesting birds have completed the raising of their young.

**below** Leyland cypress has achieved a notoriety for its size and speed of growth; but only when it is planted in an inappropriate place or neglected.

## Ways of using hedges in the garden

Most hedges mark the boundary between one garden and another, or between a garden and a public place such as a pavement. However much you value your privacy, always remember that hedges taller than 1.8m (5ft 9in) are difficult to keep neatly trimmed on top; you will need a platform to cut them safely and this, in turn, requires access and a level site. The importance of hedges to deter intruders should also be considered and in urban areas where casual intrusion may be a regular problem and you have only a relatively short run of hedge to provide, consider using dense prickly but also ornamental species, such as *Berberis*.

Hedges can also be very effectively used to subdivide a garden into 'rooms' or simply to screen less attractive features. Robustness

**above** The most attractive and neat low or dwarf hedging is achieved with *Buxus sempervirens* 'Suffruticosa'.

**below** For the densest and thickest hedge, it's advisable to plant in a double row, with the plants offset.

and density are less important. Ornamental species that will grow on most sites, such as flowering current (*Ribes sanguineum*) or *Forsythia* merit consideration.

Low hedging, especially the very slow-growing form of box (*Buxus sempervirens* 'Suffruticosa') or lavender that has been used for many years to provide the boundary around the formal beds, knot gardens and parterres, is again becoming popular as a way of adding an attractive and easily maintained formal touch to a garden. Although the cost of large numbers of plants may be considerable, both are easy to propagate yourself providing you are willing to wait the additional year or two for cuttings to attain planting size. Space the box plants at between 10cm (4in) and 20cm (8in) and lavender at between 20cm (8in) and 30cm (12in), depending on the numbers available. Low box hedging of this type can be trimmed carefully to give the very attractive impression of the 'under and over' effect of ropes draped across each other. This type of hedge is best cut with flat sides and top and none of the taper that is desirable with taller hedges. You will find that single-handed sheep shears are best for maintaining these low hedges.

In larger gardens, or where part of the area has been given over to native plants, there is nothing better than a hedge of native shrubs, although as many are rather slow to establish and rather slow growing thereafter, you may need a temporary boundary while the hedge becomes established (see list below).

### Site and soil

With suitable ground preparation and appropriate species, hedges can be established on most soils and on most sites, even those in fairly deep shade where holly (*Ilex*) and, to some extent, yew (*Taxus*) are valuable. Even a very windy, exposed site will cause no problems, particularly if suitable native species are chosen, at least in the long term; although a screen of Leyland cypress may be needed to aid initial establishment. Coastal areas offer perhaps the greatest restriction, for plants tolerant of both wind (albeit generally rather mild wind) and salt spray are required. These sites do, however, open up the possibility of using some of the more attractive hedging plants; *Escallonia* and *Fuchsia* are excellent in mild coastal areas being both evergreen and flowering, but useless elsewhere as they are killed back in hard winters. In colder coastal districts, try *Cotoneaster*, hawthorn (Crataegus), sea buckthorn (*Hippophaë rhamnoïdes*) or, if density is not important, *Tamarix*.

### Space required

The width taken up by a single row hedge of normal height is in the order of 60-90cm (2-3ft), although a staggered double row will take up at least 50 per cent more. By contrast, a low edging of box may be little more than 10cm (4in) wide. When estimating the area that your hedge will occupy, however, remember to allow access to the hedge for cutting. Moreover, the hedge roots will extend beyond the width of the hedge itself and you will find it very difficult to establish new plants near any mature hedge as the soil will be dry and low in nutrients. Privet (*Ligustrum*) is notorious for draining the nearby soil but in all such cases you must be prepared to dig a trench, sever some of the roots and incorporate very considerable quantities of organic matter. Even then, additional feeding and watering of the nearby plants will be needed more or less permanently.

**left** Even a well-maintained hedge such as this one can develop bare patches at the base.

## Planting

Thorough soil preparation is needed before planting a hedge; and thorough preparation means double digging and adding generous quantities of well rotted manure or garden compost, plus a liberal dressing of bone meal (wear gloves to apply). Spring is the best time to plant and, when the plants are in position, water, mulch and continue to water well during the first summer. Buy the best hedging plants you can afford, as a hedge is a long-term feature and, believe me, you will long regret any economies. For a short length of hedge, container-grown specimens can be used but for hedging of serious length, the cost will probably be prohibitive and it is more realistic to buy bare-rooted plants in bulk from a specialist hedging or forest nursery.

Correct spacing between plants is important for uniform growth, the planting distance varies with each species (see page 219) and you will need to know it before you can estimate how many plants you require. Tall plants will benefit from staking in the early years; if this is neglected, the plants will rock in strong wind and can develop in a crooked fashion that will affect the overall line of your mature hedge.

Where a particularly thick hedge is needed for screening or perhaps protection from livestock, consider planting a staggered double row. The distance between the two rows should be equal to three-quarters of the distance that is recommended between individual plants.

## Problems

Bareness at the base of individual hedging plants is a common problem and it points to lack of care and training in the early years. Very commonly, gardeners allow their hedge to reach its allotted height before they begin to trim back. This is understandable; we are all impatient for our hedge to reach its height as soon as possible, but this is a misguided course of action. Every year after planting, you should cut off between one-third and one-half of the previous season's growth from the leading shoots. This encourages bushiness as a result of the development of well-branched side-shoots. And once the lateral growth has begun to exceed the desired width, lightly trim the side-shoots.

To try to correct an established hedge that has become bare and leggy, leave plenty of shoots low down on the hedge untrimmed.

above **above** The garden vacuum cleaner has revolutionised the collection of hedge trimmings.

**below** Holly is undervalued as a boundary hedge because it is slow growing but it certainly produces an impenetrable barrier.

one side of the main stem. Feed, mulch and water well. In the following year, if the hedge is growing strongly cut back the other side. If recovery is sluggish, put off the cutting back of the second half for another year. With very seriously misshapen and overgrown hedges, especially of native plants such as hawthorn and blackthorn (*Prunus spinosa*), the whole may very effectively be rejuvenated by laying, but this is really a task for an expert.

## Feeding and watering

Hedges are usually neglected after planting, partly out of idleness, partly out of lack of appreciation of the benefits, or possibly because of a belief that feeding will result in the need for more trimming. In reality, applying a general purpose fertilizer such as fish, blood and bone or Growmore in spring, followed by a mulch will help produce a thick, bushy hedge rather than a tall straggly one but the fact remains that not one gardener in a hundred ever does it.

## Other care

It is stating the obvious to say that hedges need trimming but this is the only main care they need once they are established. The task is much easier if you have good equipment: top-quality, stainless steel hand shears that are oiled and sharp or a well-maintained power trimmer with the necessary safety equipment. Further information on the choice of appropriate tools is on page 51.

When they are long enough, pull them down and fix them securely by pegging them into the ground. Trim these shoots with secateurs until dense growth has been restored. A similar technique can be used for covering gaps within the body of the hedge.

A gap in the hedge, caused by death of an individual plant or by too wide a spacing can be filled in with new plants. The neighbouring plants must be cut back to create a gap in which you can work. A sharp-edged spade will be needed to slice down through the existing roots to make a planting hole. It is essential to prepare the planting hole well with organic matter, and plant good quality, container-grown specimens, and water and mulch well in the following season.

Complete rejuvenation of hedges is possible if the species respond to cutting back hard, as is the case with yew, hawthorn, beech and, to a lesser extent, box and tsuga. Cut back hard on

Lay out old sheeting or polythene to collect the clippings and/or use a garden vacuum cleaner. All types of hedge trimmings may be shredded and then composted. With practice it is possible to cut a straight hedge by eye but, for the best results, use lightweight stakes, garden string and a spirit level. Large-leaved species such as laurel will look better if finished off with secateurs to ensure the leaves are not sliced through although clearly this is impracticable with long hedges.

While informal hedges are left to grow irregularly, a more defined outline is needed for conifer and other formal hedges. An outline that tapers from the top gently down to the base (called a batter) will allow more light to reach the lower leaves, and keeping the top almost pointed or at least narrow means that snow is less likely to settle and open up the structure of the hedge. A timber frame can be made to put over the hedge while trimming to help achieve the desired taper.

Note: in the following lists, the distances are my recommended plant-to-plant spacings.

### Evergreen hedges other than conifers

These are all slower growing than conifers but offer a less uniform and more varied textural appearance.

Box (*Buxus sempervirens*) 25cm (10in), or 10cm (4in) for dwarf hedging; *Cotoneaster* 60cm (24in) for *C. lacteus* and other vigorous species and 30-45cm (12-18in) for *C. simonsii*; *Escallonia* 45cm (18in); Holly (*Ilex aquifolium*) 60cm (24in); Laurel (*Prunus laurocerasus*) 60cm (24in); Lavender (*Lavandula*) 30cm (12in) for low hedges; *Lonicera nitida* 30cm (12in); Privet (*Ligustrum ovalifolium*) 35cm (14in).

### Conifer hedges

All of these provide rapid, sometimes very rapid cover. The slowest growing is yew but it is nonetheless far faster than is generally appreciated and results in the most beautiful and the densest of all hedges.

Lawson cypress (*Chamaecyparis lawsoniana*) 45cm (18in); Leyland cypress (x *Cupressocyparis leylandii*) 1m (3ft); *Thuja plicata* 45cm (18in); *Tsuga heterophylla* 45cm (18in); Yew (*Taxus baccata*) 45cm (18in).

### Deciduous foliage hedges

The merit of these as screening and protection lies either in their dense habit (hawthorn and sea buckthorn) or the fact that they retain the dead foliage (beech and, to a lesser degree, hornbeam)

Beech (*Fagus sylvatica*) 30cm (12in); Hawthorn (*Crataegus monogyna*) 30cm (12in); Hornbeam (*Carpinus betulus*) 30cm (12in); Sea buckthorn (*Hippophaë rhamnoïdes*) 60cm (24in).

### Ornamental (flowering and fruiting) hedges

Although many flowering shrubs can be used as hedging plants, either as single species or in mixtures, the following have proved particu-

larly successful and are amenable to being lightly trimmed to shape.

*Berberis* 45-60cm (18-24in); Buckthorn, plums, sloe (*Prunus*) 60cm (24in); *Escallonia* 45cm (18in); Flowering currant (*Ribes sanguineum*) 60cm (24in); *Forsythia* 60cm (24in); *Pyracantha* 45cm (18in); Roses 45cm (18in); Rosemary (*Rosmarinus*) 30cm (12in); Snowberry (*Symphoricarpos* x *doorenbosii*) 60cm (24in), *Spiraea* 45cm (18in).

### Native species for hedging

These should be planted in mixtures; but look at the composition of existing local hedges first to decide on the frequency for each species. The main 'framework' plants should be spaced at 60cm-1m (2-3ft).

Alder buckthorn (*Rhamnus frangula*), Beech (*Fagus sylvatica*), Bird cherry (*Prunus avium*), Blackthorn (*Prunus spinosa*), Crab apple (*Malus sylvestris*), Dog rose (*Rosa canina*), Field maple (*Acer campestre*), Guelder rose (*Viburnum opulus*), Hawthorn (*Crataegus monogyna*), Hazel (*Corylus avellana*), Holly (*Ilex aquifolium*), Hornbeam (*Carpinus betulus*), Myrobalan plum (*Prunus cerasifera*), Privet (*Ligustrum vulgare*), Spindle (*Euonymus europaeus*), Yew (*Taxus baccata*).

**above** Flowering hedges are especially effective within gardens as they don't generally have sufficient robustness to form a good boundary.

# Roses

Roses are such familiar and well loved plants that, as a group, they need neither defining nor describing although I'm sure that few gardeners are fully aware of the multiplicity of subdivisions and their characteristics. There is no universally accepted classification of them but the groupings I have used here are those I have found most useful, being based mostly on ancestry and breeding history which dictate the flowering characteristics. Rose varieties are often referred to as 'old' or 'modern', old being those discovered or bred before around 1920, although there's no real dividing line.

**above** The range of size, flowering period, colour and form among roses is quite astonishing.

All roses are flowering shrubs, although breeding and selection have given us a huge range in size and overall form, and probably the really important sub-divisions are into the old rose varieties and most modern shrub roses, which really are treated in much the same way as any other flowering shrub, on the one hand, and modern bush roses on the other. The modern roses are popularly divided into hybrid teas (or large-flowered roses) and floribundas (or cluster-flowered roses) and these do need rather careful attention, especially with regard to pruning. There are climbing variants in almost all of the groups.

The small, tree-like standard roses popular as focal points in gardens are not distinct varieties but are simply produced by budding (a miniaturised from of grafting) a flowering variety atop a tall-stemmed rootstock. Strictly, they are called standards if the flowering variety is budded at a height of around 1m (3ft), half standards if at 80cm (2½ft) and quarter standards if at 45cm (18in).

### Site and soil

There are species or varieties of roses appropriate to almost every type of garden, large or small. It is perhaps easiest to begin, therefore, by mentioning the two unusual situations where they are least likely to succeed.

Strongly acidic soils and very cold, windy and exposed sites will not suit them although improving the soil with organic matter and lime or the provision of some robust shelter should enable a few representative types to be grown. Almost all roses will perform better in a sunny position, although the colour of some of the modern varieties does fade in very strong sunlight. No rose will tolerate deep shade but a few will be successful in partial or dappled shade. Those with large double flowers are easily damaged by rain and wind but most roses are hardy although among those groups that I describe here, the tea roses are the most tender and generally fare best with some shelter.

The ideal conditions for most types of rose are met essentially by a moisture-retentive soil. Conventional gardening wisdom tells us that a clay soil is a prerequisite for successful rose cultivation, but while this type of soil probably gives the best results most easily, any soil, even a light sand, can be rendered suitable for rose growing if large quantities of organic matter, in the form of well rotted manure or garden compost, are dug in prior to planting and a thick organic mulch is applied routinely to the soil surface both in spring and autumn.

### Ways of using roses in the garden

A bed where roses are grown to the exclusion of most other plants is a traditional garden feature but is undeniably bleak in winter and spring and can only be really successful in large gardens where there is room for other features to offer winter interest. Even then, despite such incidental advantages as having all the roses in the same place for pruning and spraying, the addition of other plants such as an edging of evergreens or an underplanting of spring bulbs is almost essential.

In today's garden, it makes far more sense to use roses as variants in your repertoire of flowering shrubs. Pursuing this concept, the modern mixed border provides an ideal location, with carefully selected roses placed in the middle or towards the front where very effective and charming combinations can be made with herbaceous perennials such as hardy geraniums or campanulas. Specimen roses can also be trained up posts or tripods to add height in the centre and towards the back of the border.

Many of the larger shrub, pillar or climbing roses can also make wonderful individual focal points in summer away from the border. In a small garden, an arch, trellis panel or post can be used as support; given the space, few sights are more uplifting in the height of summer than a rose-bedecked pergola. And remember that roses, especially the older varieties, mix well with the kitchen garden or the herb bed where their textures blend particularly well with the more artisan vegetation.

Miniature, patio and ground-cover roses all have their self-explanatory places in the garden but they also work particularly well in containers. I consider a 20cm (8in) diameter container to be the minimum practical size for them, and terracotta pots work particularly well. I use a soil-based John Innes No. 3 potting compost and mulch the compost surface in spring. Additional watering and feeding, of course, are essential.

## Space required

For the most restricted space, use miniature and patio roses, which range from around 20cm/20cm (8in/8in) up to about 45cm/30cm (18in/12in). Most modern bush roses are around 1m/50cm (3ft/20in) but shrub roses, both ancient and modern, range from about 1m/1m (3ft/3ft) up to 3m (10ft) or more, while some are appropriate for smaller gardens, some are most definitely not. Climbing roses range upwards from about 2.5m (8ft) in height – there is no real boundary between tall, lax shrubs and short climbers; all can be used as pillar roses – and at the other extreme, can be 10m (33ft) or more. Ground-cover roses are about 60-90cm (2-3ft) in height but can spread to 2m (6½ft) or more.

## Choosing and planting

Roses were once invariably sold in the autumn as bare-rooted plants, often by mail order from a rose specialist. The widest choice of rose varieties can still be obtained in this way but increasing numbers are now being sold as container-grown plants in bud or flower at garden centres or rose nurseries.

A good-quality, bare-rooted plant should have between three and five stems each neatly pruned back to between 25cm (10in) and 45cm (18in) in length. Almost all roses are grafted on to a rootstock, so check that the graft union is sound and that the roots are well covered with compost. The plants should be placed in the centre of the container and not seem lop-sided; the compost should appear fresh and free from moss and weeds and there should be little or no root growth emerging from the drainage holes in the container.

For a dedicated rose bed, the area should be double dug six months in advance of planting. Roses within an established border should be planted as you would any flowering shrub: in a hole at least twice the volume of the root-ball. The planting hole for climbers and ramblers should be about 20cm (8in) from their support. Bare-rooted plants should have their roots lightly pruned to encourage new fibrous roots to develop; container-grown plants should have their roots teased gently away from the root-ball. Fork well rotted manure into the base of the planting hole with a handful of bone meal (wear gloves to apply). Place the plant in position with the graft union 2-3 cm (¾-1¼in) below soil level and fill in. Finally cut back the shoots to 15cm (6in) above soil level, or with standards, to 15cm (6in) above the graft union at the top of the stem. Standard and half-standard roses should be staked.

If new roses are planted directly into soil from which old roses have been removed, they can suffer from a condition known as 'rose sickness' or 'rose replant disease'. The cause is not fully understood but it is thought that there is a

**above** No one can deny that a rose bed in winter is no great beauty.

**below** It's important to choose a variety appropriate to the space you have available. A vigorous climber like this 'Chaplin's Pink Climber' will take up much more space than a small compact shrub.

above There is no substitute for manure in preparing the ground for planting roses.

below Blackspot, mildew, rust and aphids are the scourges of the rose garden; and when they all appear together, the result can be devastating.

build up in the soil of a microscopic fungus that attacks the roots. The new roots of young roses are vulnerable. There are three solutions: rest the area from roses for at least two years; replace the soil in each planting hole with soil from an area elsewhere in the garden; or use container-grown roses as new stock.

## Propagation

Very few gardeners actually propagate their own roses although it isn't difficult. Roses can be grown from seed, although only the species will normally come true. Hips should collected when they are fully ripe and the seed separated and washed from the flesh. The dry seeds should be stored in an airtight container in a refrigerator and sown shallowly in early spring in a gritty, soil-based compost in a cold-frame. Germination should occur over a period of weeks and the seedlings potted on. They should flower within two years.

Hardwood cuttings (page 77) can successfully be taken in late autumn of most rose species and also most of the older varieties, although modern varieties are trickier to strike. Most roses can also be layered.

## Problems

Roses are affected by a range of pests and diseases but mildew, blackspot, aphids and, to a lesser degree, rust, are almost ubiquitous. In most years, particularly if you want to grow old varieties, some spraying will be necessary (page 00) but almost all modern varieties have, at least initially, a degree of resistance to the diseases. Resistance to aphids is more haphazard.

## Feeding and watering

Use a proprietary rose fertilizer twice a year; first immediately after the spring pruning and then again as the first flush of flowers begins to fade in early summer. Roses growing on an alkaline soil will benefit from an application of a fertilizer containing sequestered iron once a year in early spring. Newly-planted roses need regular watering during their first season but, subsequently, little extra watering should be

needed if the plants are mulched twice a year (spring and autumn). The exceptions are roses in containers and climbers in dry situations near to walls which will benefit from additional water in most seasons.

## Pruning

Rose pruning remains far too much of a mystery to many gardeners; although undeniably there are almost as many approaches to it as there are rose growers. Over the years, I have settled on eight different categories:

### Method 1
Use with: species roses and most of the groups of shrub roses including albas, bourbons, centifolias, some china roses, damasks, gallicas, hybrid musks, hybrid perpetuals, modern shrubs, moss roses, noisettes, polyanthas, rugosas, tea roses and ground-cover roses.
• Very little pruning needed. Cut out damaged, dying or diseased shoots. Every other year, cut out one or two of the oldest shoots.

### Method 2
Use with: English roses, floribundas, and larger patio roses.
• Cut out damaged, dying or diseased shoots. Also cut out the oldest one-third of shoots and shorten the remaining shoots by one-third of their length.

### Method 3
Use with: hybrid teas.
• Cut out damaged, dying or diseased shoots. Cut back all remaining shoots by half their length.

### Method 4
Use with: miniature roses and smaller patio roses.
• Cut out damaged, dying or diseased shoots. Also thin out shoots to avoid congestion; then cut back long, flowered shoots to 10cm (4in) above the base of the plant. Cut back all remaining shoots by one-third of their length.

### Method 5
Use with: wichuraiana ramblers.
• Train young plants to form a framework. Each year cut back up to one third of the old

stems and cut back the old flowered side-shoots on the remainder to within 10cm (4in) of their junction with the main stems.

### Method 6
Use with: multiflora ramblers.
● Train young plants to form a framework then, for the next two or three years, cut back old flowered side-shoots after flowering to within about 10cm (4in) of their junction with the main stems. On older plants cut back old flowered stems to soil level.

### Method 7
Use with: bourbon climbers, hybrid musk climbers, modern climbers, species climbers.
● Very little pruning is needed. Train young plants to form a framework. Then, each year, cut out any dead, dying or diseased wood, tie in any vigorous new shoots, bending them as close as possible to the horizontal and cut out one or two old shoots each year, if sufficient new shoots are able to replace them. If there are insufficient new shoots, leave the main framework unpruned. After tying in, cut back any very long shoots to contain them within the available space.

### Method 8
Use with: climbing floribundas, climbing hybrid teas, climbing tea roses, hybrid perpetual climbers, noisette climbers.
● Train young plants to form a framework. Then each year, cut back the old flowered side-shoots to within 10-15cm (4-6in) of their junction with the remaining framework. Every few years, replace one or two old shoots with new shoots if available. If not, leave the main framework untouched.

Dead-head all roses by cutting back the dead flowerhead to a bud just above the first leaf that has five, rather than three leaflets. Don't, however, dead-head species and shrub roses that are grown for their hips.

## Recommended hybrid tea roses by colour
Originally these popular modern roses were hybrids of which one parent was a tea rose and the other a hybrid perpetual. Their large flower form and fragrance came from the first parent and the long flowering period from the second. Today, most are bred from crosses between other hybrid tea varieties.

### White
'Pascali', 'Polar Star', 'White Wings'.

### Yellows (including some bicolored varieties)
'Grandpa Dickson', 'Peace' (pale yellow with pink flush), 'Piccadilly' (scarlet and yellow), 'Sutter's Gold' (yellow with hint of pink and reddish veins).

### Oranges
'Dawn Chorus', 'Just Joey', 'Mrs Oakley Fisher' (apricot), 'Remember Me', 'Whisky Mac'.

### Pinks
'Betty Uprichard', 'Dainty Bess', 'Double Delight' (pinkish-red edges around a white centre), 'Fragrant Cloud', 'Ophelia', 'Picture', 'Prima Ballerina', 'Silver Jubilee', 'Super Star'.

### Reds
'Alec's Red', 'Crimson Glory', 'Deep Secret', 'Ena Harkness', 'Ernest H Morse', 'Harry Wheatcroft' (orange-scarlet with yellow stripes), 'Josephine Bruce', 'Royal William'.

### Blue
'Blue Moon' (in reality a silver-mauve).

## Recommended floribundas by colour
These are popular modern roses valued for their clusters of small flowers and more-or-less continuous flowering. Most were originally the result of crosses between hybrid teas and polyanthas but today, most are the result of crosses between existing floribunda varieties or between floribundas and hybrid teas.

### White
'Iceberg' (also available as a climbing form), 'Margaret Merrill' (white with slight pink flush).

### Yellows
'Allgold' (also available as a climbing form), 'Amber Queen', 'Ards Beauty', 'Arthur Bell', 'Champagne Cocktail' (yellow with pink flecks), 'Golden Wedding', 'Masquerade' (petals are yellow at first then pink then red but all colours occur at the same time; also available as a climbing form), 'Mountbatten', 'Tango' (yellow and orange).

**above** Floribunda roses are pruned by removing about one third of the old growth.

**above** Hybrid tea roses are pruned by removing about half of the old growth.

**Orange**
'Beautiful Britain', 'City of Belfast' (orange-scarlet), 'Glenfiddich', 'Harvest Fayre', 'Matangi' (orange-red with silver white), 'Melody Maker', 'Southampton', 'The Queen Elizabeth'.

**Pinks**
'City of Leeds', 'Dame Wendy', 'Dearest', 'Elizabeth of Glamis', 'English Miss', 'Many Happy Returns'.

**Reds**
'Evelyn Fison', 'Festival', 'Glad Tidings', 'Piccolo' (red-orange), 'The Times Rose'.

## Some recommended miniature and patio roses

These are dwarf versions of floribunda or hybrid tea roses and are ideal for small gardens and for containers.

'Angela Rippon' (deep pink, miniature), 'Easter Morning' (white, miniature), 'Sweet Dream' (peach, patio), 'Top Marks' (vermillion, patio), 'Yellow Doll' (yellow, miniature).

## Recommended shrub roses (excluding modern shrubs)

**Gallicas:** no more than 1.2m (4ft) high, early-summer flowering, fragrant.
*Rosa gallica officinalis* (crimson, pre-13th century), 'Cardinal de Richelieu' (rich purple, 1840), 'Complicata' (mid-pink, origin unknown), 'Tuscany Superb' (dark velvety red, 1848).

**Centifolias:** thorny, medium-sized, very fragrant.
'Blanchfleur' (white, slightly pink, 1835), 'De Meaux' (rich pink, 1789), 'Fantin-Latour' (shell pink, origin unknown).

**Moss roses:** glands on the sepals have elongated to give a moss-like growth.
*'Alfred de Dalmas'* (pale pink, 1855), *'Gloire des Mousseux'* (shell pink, 1852), *'William Lobb'* (purplish-pink, 1855).

**Damasks:** most are pink, heavy perfume, thorny, medium-tall.
*Rosa* x *damascena semperflorens* (pink, origin unknown but very old), 'Ispahan' (shell pink, pre-1832), 'Madame Hardy' (white with green eye, 1832).

**Albas:** fairly tall, good shade tolerance, disease prone.
*Rosa* x *alba* (white, pre-16th century), 'Céleste' (pink, origin unknown), 'Königin von Danemark' (pink, 1826).

**Rugosas:** mainly 20th century varieties derived from the Japanese *Rosa rugosa*, a coarse-leaved very tough and disease-free plant.
'F J Grootendoorst' (red), 'Fru Dagmar Hastrup' (pink), 'Sarah van Fleet' (pink).

**Hybrid musks:** small, neat shrubs including some lovely peach colours, some fragrance.
'Ballerina' (pink and white), 'Buff Beauty' (yellow-peach), 'Francesca' (apricot-yellow).

**China roses:** light, airy open habit, repeat-flowering.
'Cramoisi Supérieur' (red, 1832), 'Pompon de Paris' (rose-pink, 1839).

**Bourbons:** characteristics intermediate between chinas and damasks, beautiful but many are disease-prone.
'Boule de Neige' (white, 1867), 'Souvenir de la Malmaison' (salmon-pink, 1843), 'La Reine Victoria' (lilac-pink, 1872), 'Madame Isaac Pereire' (dark pink-purple, 1881).

**Hybrid perpetuals:** long-flowering season but often upright.
'Baronne Adolphe de Rothschild' (soft pink, 1868), 'Souvenir du Docteur Jamain' (rich red, 1865), 'Reines des Violettes' (deep pink, 1860).

**Polyanthas:** small, continuous-flowering shrubs with masses of small flowers.
'Ceile Brunner' (pale pink), 'The Fairy' (pink), 'Perle d'Or' (apricot-pink).

## Some recommended modern shrubs
Flowering shrub rose, bred or discovered relatively recently (generally since 1945).

'Bonica' (soft pink, 1982), 'Fred Loads' (salmon-orange, 1968), 'Fritz Nobis' (soft pink, 1940), 'Frühlingsgold' (golden-yellow, 1937), 'Golden Chersonese' (golden-yellow, 1963), 'Jacqueline du Pré' (white, 1989), 'Nevada' (cream-white, 1927), 'Nymphenberg' (pink with hints of yellow, 1954).

## Some recommended climbers and ramblers by colour

### White
'Albéric Barbier' (wichuraiana rambler), 'Bobbie James' (multiflora rambler), 'Climbing Mrs Herbert Stevens' (climbing hybrid tea), 'Rambling Rector' (multiflora rambler), 'Sombreuil' (climbing tea).

### Yellow
*'Golden Showers'* (modern climber), *'Goldfinch'* (multiflora rambler), *'Maigold'* (modern climber), *'Meg'* (climbing hybrid tea, yellow-pink).

### Orange
'Gloire de Dijon' (climbing tea, peach), 'Schoolgirl' (modern climber).

### Pinks
'Albertine' (wichuraiana rambler), 'Aloha' (modern climber), 'Climbing Madame Caroline Testout' (climbing hybrid tea), 'Climbing Eden Rose' (climbing hybrid tea), 'Compassion' (modern climber), 'Dorothy Perkins' (wichuraiana rambler), 'Handel' (modern climber, pink with cream-white), 'Madame Gérgoire Staechelin' (climbing hybrid tea), 'New Dawn' (wichuraiana rambler), 'Pink Perpétu' (modern climber), 'Zéphirine Drouhin' (bourbon climber, thornless).

### Reds
'American Pillar' (wichuraiana rambler), 'Climbing Ena Harkness' (climbing hybrid tea), 'Crimson Shower' (wichuraiana rambler), 'Danse du Feu' (modern climber), 'Dream Girl' (modern climber), 'Dublin Bay' (modern climber), 'Guinée' (climbing hybrid tea), 'Parkdirektor Riggers' (modern climber), 'Paul's Scarlet Climber' (multiflora rambler), 'Violette' (multiflora rambler).

## Some recommended species roses
Species roses tend to have smaller, single flowers but are worth growing if you have a large garden and for their historical importance. A few of the plants listed are, strictly speaking, near-species.

*R. canina, R. eglanteria, R. elegantula persetosa, R. foetida bicolor* 'Austrian Copper', *R. glauca, R. moyesii, R. primula, R. sericea omeiensis pteracantha, R. virginiana, R. xanthina.*

## Some recommended ground-cover roses
These are mainly modern varieties and, although not strictly speaking effective ground cover in the weed-suppressing sense, they have a procumbent habit that lends itself to growing in raised beds or in large hanging baskets.

'Avon' (pale pink), 'Ferdy' (salmon-pink), 'Flower Carpet' (bright rose-pink), 'Macrantha Raubritter' (silver-pink), 'Max Graf' (rose-pink), 'Norfolk' (yellow), 'Nozomi' (silver-pink), 'Paulii' (white), 'Pink Bells' (vivid pink), 'Red Blanket' (deep pink), 'Rosy Cushion' (pink), 'Snow Carpet' (white), 'Suffolk' (red), 'Surrey' (light pink), 'Sussex' (apricot-pink), 'Swany' (white).

## Some roses for attractive fruit
Roses with single flowers are the most reliable producers of good hips.

Most species roses (see species list but also *R. macrophylla* 'Master Hugh', *R. x richardii* 'Holy Rose', *R. x alba*), *R. rugosa* and Rugosa varieties such as 'Fru Dagmar Hastrup' and 'Scabrosa', Some ramblers such as 'Bobbie James' and 'Rambling Rector', Some hybrid musks such as 'Penelope' and 'Wilhelm'.

## Roses for autumn colour
Rugosa varieties have effective and reliable autumn foliage colours.

## Roses for coastal gardens or other exposed sites
*R. pimpinellifolia* and varieties derived from it. Most species roses. 'Dunwich Rose', Rugosa varieties.

**above** Miniature roses in pots bring rose growing within every gardener's reach.

**below** Roses make wonderful companions for clematis. Here *Rosa* 'Francis E. Lester' complements *Clematis* 'Comtesse de Bouchaud'.

# Ornamental Grasses

One of the biggest mistakes that a gardener creating an ornamental garden can make is to believe that grasses must be confined to the lawn. Anyone doing so will miss the beauty of a large number of quite distinct plants that complement perfectly the flowers of more conventional ornamentals.

**above** Ornamental grasses make fine companions for herbaceous perennials; here *Pennisetum alopecuroïdes* and *Cortaderia selloana* 'Pumila' are planted with *Phormium* and *Sedum* 'Herbstfreude'.

Botanically, true grasses belong to the plant family Poaceae (formerly called the Gramineae) and have hollow round stems with solid nodes. The more-or-less flat, narrowly-elongated leaf blades extend from a leaf sheath that can be split or peeled back. Grass flowers are wind- rather than insect-pollinated so have no reason to be brightly coloured or fragrant but are, nonetheless, often attractive in a subtle way. In practice, true grasses and their woody counterparts, the bamboos, are often grouped together with the sedges and rushes from other, distinct families, and sold simply as 'ornamental grasses'. The group embraces both annuals, readily raised from seed, and perennials, with a range in size, colour, inflorescence form and overall shape. The variations on what seems a rather restricted habit are remarkable.

Most ornamental grasses thrive best in full sun in an open position on well-drained soil. A few require rather more moist conditions (some are marginal aquatics), while several are naturally plants of woodland and can tolerate some shade. Several aren't fully hardy and need a warm, sheltered position.

## Using ornamental grasses in the garden

Incorporating a few grasses into a mixed or herbaceous border is a simple way of adding autumn and winter interest, particularly where there is not space to grow winter-flowering shrubs. They are particularly effective when combined with late-flowering perennials such as Michaelmas daisies and herbaceous *Sedum* varieties, like 'Herbstfreude'. The increasing popularity in the use of perennials in more natural plantings is likely to extend further the role of ornamental grasses in this type of mixed association. They are also, by contrast, most appropriate for some of the modern minimalist plantings and are especially good when growing through gravel. Use them too as dot plants between low-growing ground covers such as heathers or bergenias where they add height without casting much shade. Their light, airy shape also contrasts well with the solid form of conifers while some of the smaller-growing grasses such as *Festuca glauca* are valuable in mixed plantings with bedding plants.

The pampas grasses (*Cortaderia*) have long been popular as isolated specimens (often rather inappropriately) in lawns but there are many others of almost comparable size, such as *Stipa gigantea* with its nodding, silvery flowerheads, that can play a similar and often more attractive role.

Growing grasses in containers offers many advantages: grasses need little maintenance and are tolerant of drying out or lack of fertilizer, while the container offers an easy way to control the more vigorous types like the popular *Holcus mollis* 'Albovariegatus', and those like *Hakonechloa macra* 'Alboaurea' that are not reliably hardy in all areas but can easily be taken into a cold greenhouse over winter. The clump-forming types make the most interesting single subjects for containers and can often be left untouched for many years to produce impressive fountains of foliage.

## Space required

It is self-evident that the size range is huge and so a plant for most situations can easily be found but be aware that some grasses are invasive or may self-seed vigorously, so do check their characteristics carefully.

## Sowing and planting

Most annual grasses are easy to raise from seed either in the spring or the autumn. Use the hardy annual method but raise them initially in pots. Perennial grasses are usually best bought as plants because most of the best named forms don't come true; *Festuca glauca*, for instance, is grown for its blue-green foliage but the colours are much more marked and intense in named varieties than in the wild species. In other instances, of which the pampas grasses are important examples, seed-raised plants are notorious at failing to flower satisfactorily.

## Problems

Pests and diseases are seldom important and choosing a species that is too vigorous for the available space is the commonest problem. Not all grasses are hardy and they can suffer over winter if not sited carefully; pampas grasses and *Helictotrichon sempervirens* commonly fail through lack of shelter.

## Feeding and watering

Feeding is rarely needed, although a spring application of sulphate of potash will help encourage good flowering. Watering will be needed after planting but once established, most grasses will tolerate dry spells. The few that need a moist soil should be mulched and, if necessary, watered during dry periods.

## Other care

Although annual grasses may be dead-headed to prevent self-seeding, the persisting flower-heads are among the most important attributes of many ornamental grasses and should be retained until the weather eventually causes them to become unsightly. Untidy or damaged foliage should be trimmed off specimen plants and the growth cut back to ground level with shears in early spring to encourage new foliage. The old foliage of pampas grasses should be pulled away using very strong gloves; advice to set fire to the clump is bad advice as it is likely to damage the crown.

## Some attractive perennial grasses, sedges and rushes by size
### Low-growing varieties
*Elymus magellanicus, Festuca glauca, Hakonechloa macra* 'Alboaurea', *Holcus mollis* 'Albovariegatus', *Stipa arundinacea*.

### Medium varieties
*Deschampsia cespitosa, Glyceria maxima* 'Variegata', *Milium effusum* 'Aureum', *Molinia caerulea* 'Variegata', *Panicum virgatum*.

### Tall varieties
*Calamagrostis* x *acutiflora, Cortaderia selloana, Helictotrichon sempervirens, Miscanthus sacchariflorus, Phalaris arundinacea, Stipa gigantea*.

## Some annual grasses
*Briza media, Hordeum jubatum, Lagurus ovatus, Pennisetum villosum, Zea mays*.

## Some perennial grasses for (moist) shade
*Carex hachijoensis* 'Evergold', *Hakonechloa macra* 'Alboaurea'.

## Some variegated perennial grasses
Variegation of the linear leaves is one of the most appealing features of ornamental features and can take many forms with vertical marginal or central (or, in a few cases, horizontal) stripes in gold-yellow or cream-silver-white.

*Alopecurus pratensis* 'Aureomarginatus' (green and yellow), *Carex hachijoensis* 'Evergold' (green and yellow), *Glyceria maxima variegata* (green and cream, tinged pink), *Hakonechloa macra* 'Alboaurea' (green, yellow and white), *Holcus mollis* 'Albovariegatus' (green and white), *Molinia caerulea caerulea* 'Variegata' (green and cream), *Phalaris arundinacea picta* 'Picta' (green and white).

## Some attractive hardy bamboos for European gardens
Creating a Japanese style in a European garden is hampered more than anything because many of the bamboos so characteristic of the real thing are insufficiently hardy.

*Chimonobambusa marmorea* 'Variegata', *Chusquea culeou, Fargesia murieliae,* x *Hibanobambusa tranquillans* 'Shiroshima', *Himalayacalamus falconeri* 'Damarapa', *Indocalamus latifolius, Indocalamus tessellatus, Phyllostachys aurea, Phyllostachys nigra, Phyllostachys viridiglaucesens, Pleioblastus auricomus, Pleioblastus humilis pumilus, Pleioblastus pygmaeus, Pleioblastus variegatus, Pseudosasa japonica, Sasaella masamuneana albostriata, Semiarundinaria fastuosa, Shibataea kumasasa, Yushania anceps*.

**above** *Stipa gigantea* makes a fine large specimen; and is a welcome change from Pampas grass.

**below** Few groups of plants offer such a wide range of attractively variegated foliage as the ornamental grasses.

# Climbers

A climber is simply a plant with rather pliable stems that requires support; something that it can lean against or cling to. A climber can be tender or hardy, woody or herbaceous, perennial or annual, evergreen or deciduous and almost every major group of plants, with the significant exception of conifers, includes some climbing forms. Here I shall deal with the main perennial climbers; annual types are described on page 252 while the important group that comprises climbing roses is considered in the preceding chapter. Although there is no strict division, I have also excluded from here those many lax shrubs that are best grown against a wall or other support although many can be effective free standing. They will be found among other shrubs on page 206.

In their natural habitats, climbers use other, generally larger plants, such as trees and shrubs as supports, although cliffs and other rock faces are also used. Sometimes, climbers simply scramble along the ground, their own stems intertwining to form a knotted mound of growth. The appeal of climbers for gardeners is very self-evident: they give the garden another dimension by increasing the growing area vertically.

**below** It always helps to bear in mind the way that plants grow naturally; here you can see that honeysuckle is a wild unkempt plant, not appropriate therefore for a neat house wall.

## Site and soil

Many types of climber are naturally plants of woodland and many, therefore, are fairly shade tolerant, although some have a requirement for shade at the roots but will only flower satisfactorily if their upper parts are in full sun. As with other types of garden ornamental, there are climbers adapted to most types of soil but almost all will benefit from careful attention being given to soil preparation before planting. The base of a wall, hedge, fence, tree or other support is almost inevitably dry and often impoverished too. Thorough incorporation of organic matter, regular feeding (using liquid fertilizers during the growing season) and watering are most important.

The hardiness of climbers, as with other types of plant, varies widely but remember that a sunny wall or fence will create a more sheltered, warm micro-climate than elsewhere in the garden, so slightly tender subjects need not be ruled out. Conversely, some evergreen climbers, even if hardy, have foliage that can be damaged by cold or salt-laden winds.

The formally-trained climbers require regular attention to pruning and training and in tying to their supports. Care must be taken to ensure that the support ties are checked annually; a vigorous climber like a wisteria grows considerably in girth; a wire that was loose one autumn can be almost a garrotte by the next.

**left** The planting position for climbers is often dry and impoverished and in need therefore of special care in its preparation.

## Ways of using climbers in the garden

Any house or garden wall can be enhanced by climbers and you need have no fear that their roots will damage the foundations as they are all plants with low water demands, the feature that above all dictates how their presence is mediated through heavy soils.

Self-clinging climbers can disfigure plaster work and paint and will damage old, crumbling bricks and mortar. The majority of climbers, however, are not self-clinging and will need support in the form of horizontal wires or trellis (page 27). Robust trellis can also be used within the garden as a free-standing screen or form part of a larger feature such as an arbour.

Archways offer wonderful scope for growing climbers and are invaluable structural features, helping to divide a garden into discrete and contrasting areas. In large gardens, pergolas provide an unrivalled opportunity to display large climbers such as roses (or a combination of roses and clematis) in a most dramatic and stunningly beautiful fashion. For smaller areas, perhaps as a centrepiece to a bed or to add height to a border, pillars, tripods or obelisks, either rustic or else painted and elaborately formal, can be extremely effective.

Using another plant as a host to support a climber mimics the way they grow naturally but, for both to thrive and to keep your maintenance simple, choose plants that are of complementary vigour. Robust climbers such as some of the species Clematis require a large and equally robust tree; more slender, less vigorous plants like Tropaeolum can be allowed to thread their way through smaller subjects such as heathers.

Almost any plant can be grown in a container of appropriate size, and climbers are no exception but in general I don't recommend growing them in this way. Larger climbers have extensive root systems, so large containers are

**above** When planting a large climber such as wisteria, remember how far it will protrude from the wall when mature.

**below** Aphids are the commonest pests of climbers.

needed. The top growth can soon become unkempt and out of control if not regularly trained and it is all too easy to create a rather unsightly feature with a long length of bare stem and all the flowers and foliage at the top. As an alternative to a container, always remember that a climber can be grown on a paved area by lifting up a paving slab or chiselling out a planting hole.

Where your only option is a container, however, try using a tub at least 40cm (16in) high and 30cm (12in) in diameter with a wooden support tripod designed to fit over the top of the container. For a climber grown against a wall, a semi-circular pot with a trellis fan will save space while small-flowered varieties of clematis or other climber may also be allowed to tumble over the edge of a tall pot; never forget that without support, climbers become trailers.

### Space required

The space taken up by a climber depends not only on the species but also on how it is trained and pruned and where it is grown. The same clematis may be confined to an area 2m (6½ft) in height and 1m (3ft) in width if it is pruned 'by the book'. But if allowed freer rein, the same plant could easily occupy 2.5 x 2.5m (8 x 8ft). It is important, therefore, to assess first the space that you have available and then decide which plant would be most appropriate to occupy it. And remember that large woody climbers, such as wisteria, will always take up addi-tional space because they protrude from their supports by 1-1.2m (3-4ft); this in addition to a basic height and spread of 6-11m (20-38ft).

### Planting

Most climbers are sold as container-grown plants, although the less common types which will, of necessity, be obtained from specialist nurseries may be sent bare-rooted.

Never dig a planting hole immediately adjacent to a wall or other support; the soil will be prone to drying out and the root spread will be lop-sided. Plant instead with the stem of a small climber about 15cm (6in) away from the wall and a large one 20-25cm (8-10in). Dig a hole that is twice the volume of the root-ball and mix the soil removed with equal volume of well-rotted organic matter and a handful of bone meal (wear gloves to apply). With most types of climber, branching from low down is desirable and can be encouraged by cutting off at least a quarter of the above-ground growth after planting. Water well after planting, and apply an organic mulch. You should also keep the area around the climber free of weeds and other plants, at least until the plant is well established.

### Propagation

Perennial climbers can generally be propagated by cuttings in the usual way (page 00), with the exception of clematis. They have the greatest concentration of natural root-producing hormone between, rather than at the nodes, so cuttings should be taken internodally and then pushed into the growing medium up to the level of the node. Evergreen climbers, like all evergreen plants, are harder to strike from cuttings as, no matter when they are taken, leaves are still present so moisture is lost. For this reason, evergreen climbers, like evergreen shrubs, are often propagated most readily by layering; anchoring a stem in the soil while it is still attached to the parent (page 00). Some perennial climbers may be raised from seed but the offspring are often variable and in general, buying named forms as plants offers the most rewarding results.

### Problems

Climbers are rather more prone than free-standing plants to certain problems because of the sheltered, warm, dry environment in which they grow. Among diseases, powdery mildew is especially prevalent while, among pests, aphids generally appear earlier and in larger numbers each year on climbers than elsewhere in the garden. To help minimise these problems, try to ensure that supports are constructed so as to permit some air movement around the plants.

When climbers are grown on walls, the trellis should be raised on battens at least a few centimetres from the wall surface for this reason. Mulching and supplementary watering can help overcome dryness at the roots thus reducing the stress on the plants but, as a last resort, chemical treatments are available for most pest and disease problems (page 98).

### Feeding and watering

As climbers are so often planted in relatively impoverished and dry conditions, close to a wall or other support, they respond particularly well to supplementary feeding and watering. For foliage climbers, a balanced general fertilizer such as blood, fish and bone or Growmore is suitable. Apply at a rate of around $70g/m^2$ (2oz/sq yd); in practice a handful around each plant (wear gloves), annually in spring and again in midsummer. Flowering climbers may be given a rose fertilizer at the rates recommended for roses but all fertilizers should be watered in if the soil is dry.

### Pruning

Formative pruning plays an important role during the initial training of climbers; maintenance pruning may or may not be needed thereafter. Remember that a climber is simply a long thin shrub, and its pruning will make much more sense (page 64).

### Some self-clinging climbers

Climbers that require no support additional to that of the wall against which they are planted have many advantages. Remember, nonetheless, that the wall itself must be of sound construction and that the plants may obstinately refuse to climb for several years; no amount of coaxing will induce them to do so until they are ready. Pruning requirements of these plants are minimal but they should always, like other climbers, be kept clear of window frames, gutters and roofing materials.

*Hedera, Hydrangea anomala petiolaris, Hydrangea serratifolia, Parthenocissus, Schizophragma hydrangeoides, Schizophragma integrifolium*

### Some climbers with attractive flowers

*Akebia quinata, Aristolochia durior* (unusual rather than attractive), *Asteranthera ovata, Berberidopsis corallina, Bignonia capreolata, Billardiera longiflora, Campsis radicans, Clematis, Decumaria barbara, Dregea sinensis, Fallopia baldschuanica, Hydrangea anomala petiolaris, Hydrangea serratifolia, Jasminum, Lapageria rosea, Lonicera, Mutisia oligodon, Passiflora, Periploca graeca, Schizophragma hydrangeoides, Schizophragma integrifolium, Senecio scandens, Solanum crispum, Trachelospermum jasminoïdes, Wisteria.*

### Some climbers for autumn colour

*Ampelopsis glandulosa brevipedunculata, Berchemia racemosa, Celastrus orbiculatus, Parthenocissus, Vitis vinifera, Vitis coignetiae, Wisteria.*

### Some climbers with attractive fruit

*Ampelopsis glandulosa brevipedunculata, Billardiera longiflora, Celastrus orbiculatus, Schisandra rubriflora, Vitis vinifera.*

**above** Self-clinging climbers especially need regular attention if they are not to damage window frames and roofs.

**below** Some climbers, like this passion flower, are almost worth growing just for the appeal of their fruits.

# Annual and Herbaceous Climbers

Apart from sweet peas, annual climbers are among the most neglected groups of garden plants and I believe that far too few gardeners appreciate the scope that they offer. They put on all of their growth in one short spell and by autumn are gone, but for the summer, they provide rapid cover and generally very attractive and brightly-coloured flowers. They can therefore quickly brighten up fences or large perennial plants that would otherwise be dull in summer and yet do so without taking up much space, without requiring pruning and without any long-term problems of invasiveness. The less vigorous types can be grown very effectively in containers and some offer either flowers or fruits that can be harvested for indoor decoration.

**below** No annual climber has seen such a resurgence in recent years as the nasturtium, now obtainable in some lovely colours.

### Site and soil

Because most annual climbers are only half-hardy, the length of the growing season is a limiting factor and they all require a sunny, warm site. Among the few worth trying in light shade are hops, nasturtiums, *Rhodochiton* and *Thunbergia alata*. Soil requirements vary with the species but those that are likely to succeed in well-drained but impoverished soil include *Caiophora*, *Cobaea* and nasturtiums. Those that require a richer, more moisture-retentive soil include *Codonopsis*, gourds, *Eccremocarpus* and sweet peas.

### Ways of using annual and herbaceous climbers in the garden

Annual climbers may be used in much the same way as perennial types but any screening effect will, of course, be temporary. They are particularly effective at brightening up permanent climbers that have become bare at the base and at adding interest to conifer or other evergreen hedges. And if you have moved to a new garden and require quick colour and interest for the first season, use annual climbers to add height alongside bedding plants for a very striking effect.

Two of the less vigorous annuals that I find particularly successful and attractive as single-subject container plants are *Rhodochiton atrosanguineum* and *Thunbergia alata*. Both can be easily trained up a small wigwam of canes and the latter is also an interesting plant for hanging baskets where it threads its way up the support chains.

### Space required

Most are vigorous in habit and will spread but only for one season. A wigwam of canes will take up a circular space of about 1m (3ft) and will support about 20 plants. Such a structure can be used very effectively and conventionally for sweet peas but can equally be used for climbing nasturtiums. By contrast, those same nasturtiums, allowed to scramble over the ground (in a manner very familiar to visitors to Monet's garden at Giverny) will occupy many square metres of space.

## Sowing and planting

Annual climbers are raised each year from seed, and as only a few plants are needed, use the half-hardy annual technique (page 71) in pots. Sweet peas and nasturtiums can be sown directly into their flowering positions using the hardy annual technique although I always think sweet peas are best when raised in pots in early spring before being transplanted outside. Half-hardy climbers should be hardened-off and planted out after the last frosts. Pinching out the stem tips will encourage more branching and better coverage of the support.

The few herbaceous climbers like hop (*Humulus lupulus*) are best propagated by leaf bud or semi-ripe cuttings in summer as plants raised from seed are of inferior quality and very variable.

## Problems

The main problem with annual climbers is that, like other annuals, they have only one season in which to grow and flower and so are very much at the mercy of the weather. Cold or dry springs can check growth, lack of sun or early frosts can mean they might not reach flowering potential.

They are subject to the same pest and diseases as other climbers but slugs and snails can be extremely destructive, large white butterfly caterpillars can devastate nasturtiums while root rots can be a problem with sweet peas if the soil is cold and wet at planting time.

## Feeding and watering

A small amount of a general balanced fertilizer should be raked into the soil around the plants in spring. Then every week or fortnight, apply a high potash liquid feed, such as a tomato fertilizer; at least part of which may be applied to the foliage with a sprayer for the quickest results.

A notable exception to the need for feeding is the nasturtium (*Tropaeolum majus*) which must always be grown in poor soil in order to encourage flower production at the expense of foliage.

## Other care

Cut down hops and the perennial species of *Tropaeolum* in late autumn, mulch and feed in early spring. The perennial tropaeolums will also benefit from some protection over the crown in colder areas.

## Annual/herbaceous climbers with attractive flowers

*Asarina antirrhinifolia, Caiophora lateritia, Cobaea scandens, Codonopsis, Eccremocarpus scaber, Ipomoea, Lathyrus, Rhodochiton, Thunbergia alata, Tropaeolum.*

## Annual/herbaceous climbers for foliage appeal

*Humulus lupulus* 'Aureus', *Tropaeolum majus* 'Alaska', *Tropaeolum majus* 'Jewel of Africa'.

## Annual/herbaceous climbers with attractive fruit

*Caiophora lateritia, Cucurbita* (gourds), *Humulus lupulus* 'Aureus'.

**above** The neat and attractive *Thunbergia alata* is a climber that I use to climb the chains of hanging baskets.

**below** The sweet pea is unquestionably the finest and most fragrant of all annual climbers.

# Ferns

Ferns are the modern representatives of a very ancient group of plants, one that has changed little for several million years. They are much less advanced, in an evolutionary sense than most of the other plants in our gardens; they have no flowers and produce no seeds, they are also more-or-less all green although some of the deciduous species do display some autumn colour changes. They are rarely sold with any enthusiasm in garden centres and you will obtain much the best range from specialist suppliers. I find them among the most fascinating, beautiful and rewarding plants in my garden. The foliage is both striking and remarkably variable. They are easy to care for by comparison with most other perennials and they will thrive in those deeply shady areas that so many gardeners find problematic.

**above** The small, damp and shaded bed is ideal for a collection of ferns.

### Site and soil
Most ferns require shady, damp sites although a few can tolerate drier and more exposed situations. Most ferns also prefer neutral to acidic soil but a few, like *Polypodium*, require alkaline conditions.

### Ways of using ferns in the garden
In common with many gardeners, I have found a damp, shaded corner of my own garden in which little else would grow and have very successfully given it over to a collection of ferns, popularly called a fernery. But I also use individual ferns dotted amongst other plants, in woodland, at the back of shrubberies and in the shadier parts of mixed borders; they are especially wonderful in acidic soils where they can be used to break up the strident colours of rhododendrons and azaleas.

Small species like maidenhair ferns fill crevices in damp walls and ferns also combine well with other large-leaved foliage plants such as hostas in moist, shaded borders or near water. Some species such as *Dryopteris wallichianum* make impressive isolated specimens as their fronds erupt in a shuttlecock shape, while in mild gardens, few plants are as arresting or unusual as the enormous, so-called tree ferns, *Dicksonia*.

Ferns aren't the most obvious choices as container plants and yet I have used hanging baskets of ferns very effectively to provide interest in shady corners. Any fern that reaches no more than 45cm (18in) makes a suitable hanging basket subject but those that I have found most reliable are *Asplenium scolopendrium* (the wavy and crested-leaved forms), small species of *Blechnum*, *Polypodium vulgare* 'Cornubiense' (which are able to tolerate both sun and dryness), *Polystichum setiferum* 'Divisilobum Densum' and small neat varieties of maidenhair fern.

### Space required
The smallest ferns like some of the *Adiantum* species will squeeze into wall crevices and grow to no bigger than the palm of a hand. Apart from the tree ferns, the biggest hardy species is the royal fern (*Osmunda regalis*) which requires an individual space of 2 x 1m (6½ft x 3ft) or more but be aware that some medium-sized ferns, most notably *Matteuccia*, spread invasively by underground runners.

### Planting
Ferns can be propagated very rewardingly by sowing the spores found on the undersides of their fronds but this is a slow process that can take up to two years. Moreover, not all ferns produce spores, so most will be obtained as

container-grown plants. Buy from an outlet where the plants are not left to scorch and dry out on the display bench, or order from a fern specialist. Ferns can be planted at any time of year when the soil isn't frozen, but avoid dry periods.

## Problems
Ferns must be kept moist but as long as you can satisfy that requirement you'll find them remarkably trouble-free. Pests and diseases are very seldom troublesome.

## Feeding and watering
Mulch in autumn and spring with compost or leaf-mould; in my experience, they respond less well to animal manures. A light dressing of bone meal (wear gloves to apply) or a balanced general fertilizer in early spring is all the feed required.

## Other care
Deciduous ferns die down with the first frosts but I like to leave the old fronds in place over winter to provide protection for the crown. They must then be cut off in the spring, taking care not to damage the unfolding young shoots or crooks. Evergreen or wintergreen types may be left to their own devices, although they tend after some years to form a rather untidy mound and I now prefer to cut down all of the old

fronds in spring, again choosing a time when the worst of the frosts are over but before the brittle new shoots have begun to unfurl. Fern fronds should always be cut and not pulled as the crowns on small species can be damaged, while on larger types the tough sharp stems can easily cut the fingers.

## Ferns for winter appeal
*Adiantum, Asplenium, Blechnum (B. tabulare* only hardy in mild areas), *Dryopteris* (only evergreen in mild areas or mild winters), *Matteuccia, Polypodium, Polystichum*

## Ferns for drier sites
*Asplenium, Cystopteris, Polypodium* (will grow on the dry tops of walls), *Polystichum, Woodsia*

## Ferns for larger gardens
*Blechnum tabulare, Dicksonia antarctica, Dryopteris filix-mas, Dryopteris dilatata, Matteuccia, Onoclea, Osmunda regalis, Polystichum setiferum*

# Water Garden

My own experience tells me that the gardener who has once had a pool or other water feature in their garden is unlikely ever to be without one again. The value of water in the garden is easy to define. Visually, it has a very special quality that catches the light and catches the eye. Aurally, it is uplifting too, the merest, gentlest sound of water movement being sufficient to bring life to any garden landscape. And it has the indefinable appeal that can only be summarised crudely by that bland word 'interest'. Time seems to fly by when you sit by a pool and half an hour can pass as if in an instant, for a well planned pool contains not only plants, fish and snails but also a myriad other creatures, attracted as magnetically to the water as we are. Insect life abounds below, on and above the water surface and can range from beetles, pond skaters and caddis larvae to dragonflies. Amphibians will almost inevitably arrive as if by magic; frogs, toads and newts will lay their spawn and bird life too will seek out the water of your pool, especially if you can keep a small area free from ice in the winter; although one always hopes that the local heron population will not discover your stock of fresh fish.

**below** Not the least of the attractions of a garden pool is the wealth of wonderful insect life it attracts.

But before describing anything further on the subject of water gardening, one point must be made. Garden pools and young children should not co-exist. A child can drown in only a very few centimetres of water and simply to stay your impatience for aquatic horticulture for a few years is a small price to pay to avert possible tragedy. If your garden already has a pool, you have two main options: either to cover the whole with a robust net which will be functionally effective although aesthetically fairly dreadful, or to fill in the pool and convert the area to some other purpose, a bog garden perhaps.

The plants to be grown in and around water are usually grouped according to how wet are their preferred conditions. At one extreme are the submerged plants that help to oxygenate the pool (although I must add that some means of agitating the water, such as a fountain, will do this too). Floating plants have no roots or have roots that simply dangle into the water but are not anchored. Water plants grow within the pool and are anchored in the mud; water lilies are the classic examples. Plants that grow in the water at the edge of a pool are called marginals and this category merges into that of bog plants which grow in the more or less permanently wet soil close by.

## Types of water garden

A formal pool, such as might be found in a courtyard, is unashamedly artificial with the hard landscape dominating. It always looks wrong to blur the edges of such a pool with dense planting whereas an informal pool does have soft, irregular edges and is best merged into plantings of marginal and bog plants.

Self-contained water features such as wall fountains are growing in popularity and allow even the smallest garden to have a water feature, although they are often too small to accommodate aquatic plants and the plant life here should consist of other garden plants in containers or nearby beds. A circulating pump for such a feature may be housed in a hidden reservoir, either sunken below soil level or held above ground in a bowl or barrel.

## Site

Given that a water feature should be sited so it fits into the overall design of the garden, the principal requirement is that it should have maximum exposure to sunlight as almost no water plants will thrive in shade. Bog gardens, however, can be placed very effectively in at least partial shade. But avoid siting a pool near large overhanging trees as fallen leaves will decompose and cause noxious gases to accumulate in the water.

## Space required

Self-contained water features will fit into the smallest of spaces. Very small pools can be constructed but the larger the pool, the easier it is to maintain a viable balance between water, plants and animal life. My experience has been that the minimum effective size for a garden pool is about 1.5x 1.2m (5 x 4ft) with a depth of at least 30cm (12in), but the deeper the better.

## Construction

Constructing a pool is no longer the major piece of civil engineering that once it was. The modern pool is lined with plastic, but while it is

possible to purchase ready-shaped (or 'preformed') rigid liners, much the most versatile method is with butyl rubber sheet.

Excavate the hole for your pool, ensuring that you leave rounded corners and sloping sides; and leave some shelves or ledges for shallower planting. Remove any stones from the base and then carefully line the hole with about 2cm (¾in) of fine sand on which the rubber will be bedded. Drape the sheeting over the hole, taking care to fill in with sand around the sides. Leave a generous overlap at the edges, of twice as much width as the pool is deep, and anchor this with stones. Then carefully fill the pool with water; the weight of the water will stretch the rubber, and cover the edges with your chosen edging material such as slabs, rocks or soil.

Allow a minimum of two weeks for the pool to settle down before you introduce first plants and then, about three weeks later, fish and snails. The time intervals between setting up the pool and planting will inevitably be longer if you build it in autumn, for it is unwise to introduce plants to any pool before mid-spring.

While a natural bog garden by a natural pool or stream will have a good depth of waterlogged soil, an artificial pool, created using a liner, will isolate the water and the nearby soil will not necessarily be wet. Bog gardens are best created next to pools by extending the liner to

**above** Frogs are welcome visitors to garden pools and play a part in keeping garden pests under control.

**below** The use of butyl rubber sheet has made garden pool construction a much simpler matter.

**above** Water plants are almost always most satisfactorily planted in purpose made containers.

lined (hessian was used formerly but a double layer of garden fleece is very effective) but those with a fine mesh and the newer fabric baskets require no liner. Use a soil low in fertilizer (specially prepared sachets of slow release aquatic plant fertilizer are, however, perfectly safe) or buy an aquatic compost for planting. If you have fish in the pool, place a layer of clean grit over the top of the compost to prevent them from uprooting the plants. Be sure to position the planted basket at the appropriate depth for each plant species, using bricks on which to stand them if there are no suitable ledges. When planting bog plants in already waterlogged soil, be sure to work from planks.

### Problems

The biggest problems are green slime or blanket weed and 'pea soup' in the water. Both problems are algal. Blanket weed is a filamentous green algae while pea soup is caused by myriads of single-celled algae. Blanket weed can be introduced on new plant purchases so check new plants carefully (and similarly check them for the presence of tiny floating fronds of duck-weed). Try to avoid allowing nitrogenous fertilizer into the water; top up pools with rain water when possible and prevent fertilizer run-off from pot plants. Pull out excessive growths of blanket weed by hand in the summer, and resist the temptation to use chemical algicides, for these merely result in masses of dead blanket weed that then begins to decompose. Adding barley or lavender straw to the water is also a very effective control measure and having a fountain or other means of moving the water will also minimise these problems.

Pests and diseases do not normally cause problems in pools although water lilies and water irises especially can become infested with aphids and water lilies with a small brown beetle. These should merely be hosed away and no chemical pesticides used near any pool or water garden. Dead leaves and dead flowerheads should be cut away as necessary and feasible.

### Feeding

Once established, most water plants are vigorous and feeding should not be necessary. Plants in the bog garden should be fed as any other border perennials but at a reduced rate

create an impervious area that can be filled with soil. But this must be at least 30-45cm (12-18in) deep and it is sensible to install a perforated hose between the liner and the soil so the ground can be topped up with water during dry spells.

### Planting

Most submerged and floating plants can simply be dropped into the water; attach a small weight to those that will root in the mud at the pool bottom. Water plants and marginals may be planted directly into the mud or into planting baskets.

Planting baskets, usually made of plastic, are invaluable as they make maintenance easier and a wide range of sizes of basket is available. Those with a wide mesh should be

with a light dressing of a general fertilizer such as blood, fish and bone in the spring. A spring and autumn mulch with compost rather than animal manure helps prevent bog gardens drying out in summer.

## Other care

Plants will in time become congested and flowering can deteriorate but aquatic plants should only be divided in spring.

## Water-lilies by colour and vigour

Water-lilies are the most important of all pool plants but exist in a wide range of vigour and also of preferred water depth, so varieties must be selected with considerable care.

## Large, water depth 30-90cm (12in-2ft 11in), surface spread up to 1.5m (5ft)
### Reds
'Attraction', 'Charles de Meurville'

### Pinks
'Colossea', 'Gloire du Temple-sur-Lot'

(pale pink fades to white), 'Mrs Richmond' (pale pink darkens to red), *N. tuberosa* 'Rosea'

### Yellows
'Colonel A J Welch'.

### White
'Gladstoniana', *N. alba*, *N. tuberosa*.

## Moderately large, water depth 20-60cm (8-24in), surface spread up to 1m (3ft)
### Reds
'Atropurpurea', 'Conqueror', 'Escarboucle', 'William Falconer'.

### Pinks
'Amabilis', 'Madame Wilfron Gonnére', 'Marliacea Carnea', 'Marliacea Rosea', 'Masaniello', 'Odorata William B Shaw'.

### Yellows
'Marliacea Chromatella', 'Moorei', 'Sunrise', 'Caroliniana Nivea', 'Gonnére', 'Marliacea Albida', *N. odorata*.

**below** Water-lilies are prone to aphid attack but these should be washed off with a hose and chemical sprays never used near water.

### Small, water depth 15-45cm (6-18in), surface spread up to 60cm (24in)

**Reds**
'Gloriosa', 'James Brydon', 'Robinsoniana' (orange-red).

**Pinks**
'Brakeleyi Rosea', 'Firecrest', 'Indiana' (pink turning orange-red), 'Rose Arey'.

**Yellows**
'Commanche' (orange-yellow slowly turning red), 'Odorata Sulphurea Grandiflora', 'Sioux' (yellow then orange then red).

**White**
'Albatross'.

### Very small water depth 10-30cm (4-12in), surface spread up to 30cm (12in)

**Reds**
'Ellisiana', 'Froebelii', 'Graziella', 'Laydekeri Fulgens', 'Laydekeri Purpurata'.

**Pinks**
'Laydekeri Lilacea'.

**Yellows**
'Aurora' (yellow then orange then red), *N. x helvola*, 'Paul Hariot', 'Solfatare' (yellow then orange-yellow then red).

**White**
*N. tetragona* (syn. 'Pygmaea Alba') (the only water lily that is tiny enough for an aquarium).

### Floating plants
*Azolla caroliniana, Eichornia crassipes, Hottonia palustris, Hydrocharis morsus-ranae, Stratiotes aloides, Trapa natans, Utricularia vulgaris.*

### Submerged plants
*Callitriche, Ceratophyllum demersum, Crassula helmsii, Eleocharis acicularis, Elodea canadensis, Fontinalis antipyretica, Lobelia,* dortmanna, *Myriophyllum, Potamogeton, Ranunculus aquatilis.*

### True water plants
*Aponogeton distachyos, Hippuris vulgaris, Nuphar, Nymphoïdes peltata, Orontium aquaticum, Persicaria amphibia, Pontederia cordata, Sparganium erectum.*

### Marginal plants
*Acorus calamus, Alisma plantago-aquatica, Butomus umbellatus, Calla palustris, Caltha palustris, Cotula coronopifolia, Equisetum hyemale, Houttuynia cordata, Hypericum eloïdes, Iris ensata, Iris laevigata, Iris pseudacorus, Iris versicolor, Lobelia cardinalis, Mentha aquatica, Menyanthes trifoliata, Mimulus, Myosotis scorpioïdes, Peltandra undulata, Ranunculus, Sagittaria sagittifolia, Typha, Veronica beccabunga, Zantedeschia.*

### Bog plants by size and colour
#### Small under 45 cm (18 in)
*Alchemilla mollis* (yellow flowers), *Anaphalis margaritacea* (white flowers, greyish foliage), *Ajuga reptans* (blue or white flowers, coloured foliage forms available), *Arum italicum* 'Pictum' (red fruits, marbled foliage), *Astilbe* (pinks, reds and white available, also taller forms up to 1.5m/5ft), *Bergenia* (pink or white flowers, foliage is green or purple), *Brunnera macrophylla* (blue flowers, some forms have cream or white variegation to their foliage), *Dicentra formosa* hybrids (pink or white flowers), *Dodecatheon meadia* (purple flowers), *Fritillaria meleagris* (shades of purple and white chequered flowers), *Gentiana pneumonanthe* (deep blue flowers), *Geum rivale* (purple flowers but selected forms with pinkish orange or yellowish orange flowers available), *Heloniopsis orientalis* (pinkish mauve flowers), *Iris chrysographes* (red-purple), Iris innominata (flower colour varies), *Leucojum* (white flowers), *Lysimachia nummularia* 'Aurea' (golden-yellow foliage), *Parochetus communis* (blue flowers), *Persicaria millettii* (red flowers), *Phormium* dwarf hybrids (foliage plants available in many coloured forms), *Potentilla palustris* (dark purple flowers), *Primula alpicola, Primula denticulata, Primula rosea, Primula cockburniana* (various colours available), *Pulmonaria* (blue, white, deep purple or red

**below** Numerous water lily varieties are now available but it's essential to use one of appropriate vigour for the size of your pool.

depending on the species, some have white leaf markings), *Saururus cernuus* (creamy flowers), *Saxifraga fortunei* (white flowers but some forms have reddish leaves), *Stylophorum diphyllum* (yellow flowers), *Symplocarpus foetidus* (yellow-green spathe with red spots), *Tiarella cordifolia* (white flowers), *Tradescantia virginiana* (white, blue or purple flowers depending on the form, some have golden-yellow foliage).

### Medium 45-90cm (18in-2ft 11in)
*Campanula lactiflora* (white or blue flowers), *Eupatorium maculatum* 'Atropurpureum' (purplish flowers), *Euphorbia palustris* (yellow/lime-green bracts), *Filipendula palmata*, *F. purpurea* (pink or red flowers), *Gentiana asclepiadea* (blue flowers, white form available), *Geranium phaeum* (deep purple, almost black flowers), *Hemerocallis* (wide range of flower colours available), *Hosta* (white or lilac flowers but mainly grown for foliage in a variety of shades and markings, hostas also available as small and large bog plants), *Iris sibirica*, *I. orientalis* (purple), *Lysichiton* (yellow or white spathe depending on species), *Physostegia virginiana* (white or various shades of pink depending on the form), *Primula florindae* (yellow flowers), *P. pulverulenta* (pale pink to mauve flowers), *P. beesiana* (red with yellow flowers), *P. x bulleesiana* (various colours), *P. bulleyana* (deep orange), *P. burmanica* (red-purple flowers), *P. helodoxa* (yellow flowers), *P. Inshriach* hybrids (orange-pink flowers), *Schizostylis coccinea* (white, pink or red flowers depending on the form), *Tricyrtis hirta* (white or yellow flowers with purple or red spots), *Trollius europaeus* (yellow flowers, some forms have orange flowers), *Uvularia grandiflora* (yellow flowers).

### Large over 90cm (2ft 11in)
*Artemisia lactiflora* (cream-white flowers), *Aruncus dioicus* (white flowers), *Cimicifuga* (white flowers, some forms have purple foliage), *Darmera peltata* (white or mauve flowers), *Eupatorium cannabinum* (purplish flowers), *Filipendula ulmaria*, *F. rubra* (cream-white or pink flowers, some forms have golden foliage), *Gunnera manicata* (giant green leaves, brownish flower spike), *Lychnis chalcedonica* (red flowers), *Lysimachia* *punctata* (yellow flowers), *Lythrum salicaria* (purple flowers), *Persicaria amplexicaulis* (red, pink or white flowers, depending on form), *Phormium tenax* (dark green leaves with red edges), *Rheum* (reddish purple leaves, white or pink flowers depending on the species), *Rodgersia* (bronzed foliage, white or pink flowers depending on species), *Thalictrum flavum* (blue-green foliage, yellow flowers), *Veratrum nigrum* (very dark purple, almost black, flowers).

Note: Many ferns and grasses also make good bog plants, see page 234 and page 226.

**above** The garden pool offers huge scope for a wide range of plants, from those that grow within the water, through the marginals to the bog plants that will thrive in wet soil nearby.

**Achene**: a dry fruit with one seed, formed from a single carpel and with no special method of opening for seed liberation.

**Adelgid**: sap-sucking insect, related to aphids but only on conifers, may cause characteristic galls. Difficult to control.

**Aerosol**: a colloidal suspension of solid or liquid particles in a gas; used to formulate some garden pesticides. Aerosols produce the smallest droplets and most effective coverage but are also the most expensive way to apply pesticides.

**Alga (pl. algae)**: primitive uni- or multi-cellular plants producing a thallus but differing from other thalloid organisms such as fungi in possessing chlorophyll. Blanket weed and seaweed are common multi-cellular algae; other algae occur as green jelly-like matter on lawns or a green powdery covering to trees and fences.

**Alpine**: vague term for plants growing naturally in mountainous areas (not necessarily the Alps). In gardens, they generally require very good drainage and although tolerant of very cold conditions, are prone to damage from clinging damp.

**Alternate host**: either of the two unlike host-plants of a pest or pathogen that requires both to complete its life-cycle.

**Alternative host**: host-plant other than the main host for a pest or disease organism. Weeds and wild plants are often alternative hosts of pests and diseases.

**Aluminium ammonium sulphate**: inorganic chemical used in gardens as a mammal repellent.

**Aminotriazole**: old name for Amitrole.

**Amitrole**: persistent herbicide sold in mixture with other herbicidal compounds for treating paths and other unplanted areas.

**Ammonia**: pungent colourless gas containing nitrogen and used to manufacture fertilisers. Ammonia gas is liberated when many nitrogen containing chemicals break down in the soil and if allowed to accumulate may be damaging to plants.

**Ammonium carbonate**: see Cheshunt Compound.

**Ammonium hydroxide**: contact action fungicide used in combination with copper sulphate as Bordeaux Mixture.

**Ammonium nitrate**: nitrogen containing fertiliser, usually granulated with calcium carbonate as Nitro-Chalk and particularly useful for supplying nitrogen to plants in acidic soils.

**Ammonium sulphate**: the most widely used artificial fast-acting nitrogen fertiliser. Contains 21 per cent nitrogen and is most common as a component of the artificial fertiliser mixture Growmore.

**Ammonium thiocyanate**: persistent herbicide sold in mixture with other herbicidal compounds for treating paths and other unplanted areas.

**Angiosperm**: flowering plant. All flowering plants belong to the group Angiospermae which differ from the Gymnosperms (conifers and their relatives) by having the ovules borne within an enclosed ovary which, after fertilisation, becomes a fruit.

**Annual**: a plant that completes the cycle from seed to seed within a single season. Commonly divided in gardening into Hardy and Half-hardy Annuals.

**Ant**: small, social insects related to bees and wasps. No ants cause direct damage to plants but their mining activities can disturb roots.

**Antennae**: paired sensory structures on the heads of insects and other invertebrates. They are often long, thread-like and conspicuous (as in cockroaches, grasshoppers and aphids) but may be small and relatively inconspicuous.

**Anther**: swollen terminal part of a stamen, producing pollen grains.

**Anthocyanin**: blue-red pigments causing those colours in flowers and leaves.

**Anthracnose**: literally 'charcoal-like'; a type of plant disease characterised by black sunken lesions, as in weeping willow anthracnose.

**Aphid**: small sap-sucking insects existing as winged and wingless individuals; probably the most important plant pests in temperate climates. Damage is caused directly and also by encouraging sooty moulds which feed on honeydew secreted by the insects. Aphids are the major means by which plant viruses are transmitted in temperate regions. May be controlled relatively easily with contact and systemic insecticides.

**Arachnid**: sub-division of Arthropods including mites, spiders, scorpions, harvestmen and ticks

**Arthropod**: the largest group of Animals. Have exoskeletons, and includes Arachnids, Crustaceans, Insects and Myriapods.

**Ascomycete**: one of the major groups of fungi containing the largest number of species. Includes familiar large 'cup fungi' as well as a huge number of plant pathogens including powdery mildews.

**Atrazine**: persistent herbicide sold in mixture with other herbicidal compounds for treating paths and other unplanted areas.

**Auxin**: plant hormone essential in regulating plant growth. Chemically similar substances are used in rooting powders and other artificial growth regulators.

**Axil**: the angle between the upper side of a leaf stalk or branch and the stem from which it emerges.

**Bacterium (pl. bacteria)**: simple uni- or multi-cellular organisms lacking chlorophyll. Bacteria are ubiquitous and vital in the breakdown of organic matter. Some cause important diseases of man and animals but are less important than fungi as plant pathogens.

**Balance of nature**: popular term to describe the relatively stable state in which populations of organisms and their environments exist.

**Bark**: a protective corky layer of dead cells on the outside of older stems and roots of woody plants. Shredded bark is used in gardens as a mulch and path material but has very little fertiliser value.

**Basic slag**: phosphate containing fertiliser, a by-product of steel manufacture and of vari-able composition. Used mainly to encourage clover and related plants.

**Basidiomycete**: one of the major groups of fungi, considered the most advanced and embracing mushrooms and toadstools and important plant pathogens like rusts.

**Bed**: vague term for a planted area; often used to describe an area of annual plants as distinct from a border which contains perennials. See also Raised bed.

**Benazolin**: selective herbicide used with others in lawn weedkillers.

**Bendiocarb**: contact and systemic insecticide used to control ants and other crawling pests.

**Berry**: a succulent, many-seed fruit such as a tomato or gooseberry. Many fruits popularly called berries are botanically something quite different, often a drupe.

**Berry**: type of fruit, fleshy, usually several seeded and without a stony layer around the seeds.

**Biennial**: a plant that requires two seasons to complete the cycle from seed to seed. Generally, they flower in the first year and set seed in the next. Relatively few are important garden ornamentals (wallflowers, Sweet William) but many vegetables grown as annuals are biennial.

**Bifenthrin**: widely used contact insecticide for edible and ornamental plants.

**Big bud**: condition of blackcurrants in which some buds swell to abnormal size as a result of infestation by a species of mite that transmits a virus-like organism which causes reversion disease.

**Bill hook**: cutting tool with wooden handle and curved blade, used for heavy-duty pruning and lopping.

**Bioallethrin**: contact insecticide available to gardeners in mixture with permethrin.

**Biological control**: the control of plant pests and, to a much lesser extent, diseases by using an organism that is a natural parasite or predator. The use of wasp like *Encarsia* to control greenhouse whitefly is one of the best known.

**Biotroph**: an organism that feeds on living cells; a parasite.

**Bitter pit**: small dark spots on and within the flesh of apples, brought about by calcium deficiency, enhanced by drought.

**Bitumen**: impure mixture of hydrocarbons found in asphalt and tar. Formerly used to paint wounds on trees but the practice is now discouraged as it may be counter-productive to the healing process.

**Black leg**: a plant disease in which the stem turns soft and black; as on pelargoniums and potatoes.

**Black spot**: a disease of roses caused by the fungus *Diplocarpon rosae*. Many other fungi causes black spotting on other types of plant.

**Blight**: imprecise term for a plant disease, usually one with rapid death of shoots and leaves; as in fireblight, potato blight. Also occasionally for insect infestations.

**Blossom end rot**: condition on tomatoes and related plants in which a black lesion arises on the fruit at the blossom (distal) end. Caused by calcium deficiency exacerbated by water shortage.

**Bone meal**: fertiliser derived from ground animal bones. A valuable source of phosphate and a small amount of nitrogen. The phosphate is slowly released so bone meal is used when planting perennials and also in fertiliser mixture fish, blood and bone. Steamed bone flour is more finely ground with little nitrogen.

**Borax**: insecticide used in gardens as an ant killer and also to count-eract a soil deficiency of boron.

**Bordeaux Mixture**: an old contact action fungicide containing copper sulphate and ammonium hydroxide, still valuable in the control of potato blight and some other diseases.

**Border, herbaceous**: a type of planting popular in the nineteenth century in which only herbaceous perennial plants were used. They were labour intensive and offered little interest in the winter.

**Border, mixed**: a type of planting that has taken the place of the herbaceous border. A permanent framework of shrubs is used, between which herbaceous peren-nials, annuals and bulbs are planted.

**Boron**: chemical element and plant nutrient, particularly important in the growing points of plants. Rarely deficient in soils and may be corrected by applying borax.

**Botrytis**: a genus of fungi, especially used to mean the species *Botrytis cinerea*, the cause of grey mould diseases on an enormous range of plants. *Botrytis cinerea* is both saprotrophic and biotrophic.

**Brodifacoum**: rodenticide, used in gardens as a mouse poison.

**Brown rot**: a plant disease in which the tissue turns brown. Used especially of fungal diseases of apples and other fruit caused by species of *Sclerotinia* and also of decay diseases of trees in which the casual fungus degrades cellulose to leave the brown lignin. See also White Rot.

**Bryophyte**: a green plant in the group including mosses and liverworts, which possess true conducting tissues but no real roots.

**Budding**: an abbreviated form of grafting where the scion is a single bud which is inserted into a slit in the bark. Used especially with roses and enables many plants to be produced from limited material.

**Bulb**: a vegetative reproduction and storage organ comprising a very short stem (the basal plate) from which the roots arise, with a mass of swollen, overlapping immature leaves. Onions and hyacinths are common examples.

**Bulbil**: a miniature bulb, commonly produced above ground in leaf axils (as in lilies) or in place of flowers (perennial onions).

**Bumble bee**: large bees that are important plant pollinators and occasionally cause damage by eating into the corolla tubes of flowers to obtain nectar.

**Bupirimate**: systemic fungicide available in

mixture with triforine, especially for treating rose diseases.

**Burrowing bee**: small species of bee that sometimes cause concern on lawns by throwing up small piles of soil as they excavate their nests.

**Bush cricket**: long-horned plant-eating grasshoppers, causing serious damage in warm climates but rare in Britain.

**Butoxycarboxim**: systemic insecticide available as impregnated cardboard 'pins' for use in pots.

**Cabbage white**: popular name for the large white butterfly, *Pieris brassicae*, whose caterpillars are important pests.

**Calcicole**: a plant that is able to grow satisfactorily on strongly alkaline, calcium rich soils.

**Calcifuge**: a plant that is unable to grow satisfactorily on strongly alkaline, calcium rich soils and displays leaf chlorosis.

**Calcium**: an abundant and important mineral, occurring most significantly as calcium carbonate. It is an essential plant nutrient, especially critical in the structure of cell walls and the development of growing points. It may be deficient on acidic soils when the problem can be corrected by the addition of lime.

**Calcium carbonate**: the most widespread natural form of calcium, occurring as limestone or, in a purer state, as chalk. Ground limestone is the most widely used form of lime.

**Calcium chloride**: a solution of the salt calcium chloride is sometimes used to correct symptoms of calcium deficiency such as bitter pit.

**Calcium phosphate**: the principle mineral in bone meal and an important source of phosphorus.

**Calcium sulphate**: gypsum, a mineral that offers a useful source of calcium for soils when it is important not to raise the pH.

**Calyx**: collectively, the sepals of a flower.

**Cambium**: a layer of actively dividing cells in plants that lies between the xylem and the phloem tissues.

**Canker**: a disease of woody plants with localised and gradually extending death of the cambium beneath the bark resulting in a characteristic target-like lesion. Occasionally used for other types of disease, as in parsnip canker.

**Capillary watering system**: watering system for use in greenhouses and elsewhere that entails water slowly but constantly dripping from very narrow bore capillary tubes.

**Capitulum**: type of inflorescence; a disc like structure comprising many individual small flowers in a single head as in the daisy.

**Capsid bug**: sap feeding insects that are common but elusive pests of plants causing ragged holed in leaves and sometimes, as with apples, distortion of the fruit. Difficult to control and damage must usually be tolerated.

**Capsule**: a dry type of fruit formed from a compound ovary and which liberates its seeds by splitting longitudinally. Irises are common garden examples.

**Captan**: contact fungicide now available to gardeners only in rooting powders where it is added to minimise rotting of cuttings.

**Carbendazim**: systemic fungicide chemically related to thiophanate-methyl and benomyl (now withdrawn). Widely used for the control of many diseases but less effective against downy mildews and related diseases and rusts.

**Carbohydrate**: type of organic compound containing carbon, nitrogen and oxygen and including cellulose, starch and sugars. Carbohydrates are essential nutrients in plants and are formed during photosynthesis by the combination of carbon dioxide and water from the air.

**Carbon**: the most important chemical element in living organisms and a component of all organic chemical compounds.

**Carbon dioxide**: colourless, odourless gas present in the air and essential for plant life as it is one of the raw materials for photosynthesis.

**Carotene**: yellow and orange pigments that impart these colours to flowers, leaves and, sometimes roots, as in carrots.

**Carpel**: the female reproductive parts of a flowering plant, comprising an ovary and ovules, a stigma and a style.

**Catch crop**: a quick growing crop such as radish, grown between the rows of a slower growing crop or grown in a short period of time between harvesting one and sowing or planting another.

**Caterpillar**-the larva of a butterfly or moth; superficially similar larvae occur in other insect groups, especially sawflies.

**Catkin**: type of inflorescence; a hanging spike, as in hazel.

**Cell**: the basic structural unit of plants, animals and other organisms, cells of similar type and function forming a tissue. In plants, each cell comprises a watery mass of protoplasm, a controlling nucleus and other structures, bounded by a cellulose cell wall. Depending on their function in the plant, cells vary widely in size, shape and the extent to which their walls are impregnated with other materials. Heavy impregnation with lignin for instance, produces woody tissue.

**Cellulose**: a chemically complex carbohydrate that is the major constituent of plant cell walls.

**Centipede**: myriapod arthropod, related to millipedes but with fewer legs; important in feeding on insects and other plant pests.

**Certified stock**: plant material guaranteed to be of a defined quality, especially free from virus.

**Chafer**: large species of beetle with voracious larvae, common in old grassland and sometimes causing serious damage to plant roots.

**Chalk**: pure form of calcium carbonate.

**Cheshunt compound**: old but still available contact fungicide containing copper sulphate and ammonium carbonate.

**Chlamydospore**: a type of asexually produced fungal spore that is resistant to desiccation or other adverse environmental conditions.

**Chlorophyll**: green pigment in plants that traps energy from sunlight to facilitate the process of photosynthesis.

**Chloroplast**: microscopic structure in plant cells containing chlorophyll.

**Chlorosis**: condition in which plant leaves and other green parts turn pale and yellow. It arises typically in conditions where plants are unable to absorb iron from the soil, to make chlorophyll.

**Chlorpyrifos**: contact insecticide used in gardens to control ants and other crawling insects.

**Chocolate spot**: leaf disease of broad beans, causing small brown spots.

**Chrysalis**: pupa of a butterfly or, less commonly, a moth.

**Classification of plants**: there is a basic division of the Plant Kingdom into flowering plants, conifers and their relatives on the one hand and flowerless plants on the other. Flowerless plants include ferns, horsetails, mosses, liverworts and algae. The flowering plants in turn have a major subdivision into Monocotyledons and Dicotyledons but the principle criterion by which they are grouped into Families is flower structure. Unlike leaves and other vegetative features, flowers are affected very little by environmental factors. Below the level of the Family, plants are grouped into smaller units, most notably genera and species although for gardeners, the further subdivision into varieties and cultivars is also important.

**Clay**: one of the three major particle size based divisions of the mineral components of soil; silt and sand being the other two. Clay particles are less than 0.002 millimetres in diameter and are especially important because they attract and hold plant nutrients. A clay soil therefore is a very nutrient rich.

**Click beetle**: beetles able to flip themselves into the air when lying on their backs. They are important in gardens for their larvae are wire-worms which normally feed on grass roots and cause serious problems in potatoes and other root crops.

**Climax community**: an ecological term for the type of vegetation that will ultimately develop in any particular area. The most important plants in the community will be the physically largest species that local soil, climatic and other influences allow. Over much of southern Britain, the climax community is deciduous woodland.

**Climbing plant**: climbing plants are important in gardens as the group includes many very attractive ornamentals. The climbing habit has arisen in many different and quite unrelated plant groups however and a climbing plant is no more than a tall, slender shrub that requires the support of another plant or some physical structure. Among the many ways that have arisen to help climbers to support themselves are thorns (roses), tendrils (clematis), twining stems (runner bean) and adhesive aerial roots (ivy).

**Cloche**: a under-appreciated appliance, its name derived from the French for a bell. Glass or plastic cloches placed over plants will provide protection and added warmth, so allowing extensions of growing time at the beginning and end of the season.

**Clone**: a group of genetically identical individuals produced by asexual rather than sexual reprod-uction. The many varieties of plants such as apples and potatoes that are routinely produced vegetatively instead of by seeds are clones.

**Clubroot**: a disease of the family Brassicaceae caused by a soil-inhabiting, fungus-like organism called *Plasmodiophora*. It is the most serious disease of the vegetable garden for once present in the soil, the spores can persist for at least twenty years. Avoidance is very important therefore and it should be remembered that the disease is brought into unaffected gardens either in soil or on plant roots.

**Cocoon**: a silken case constructed by an insect larva such as a caterpillar to protect the pupal stage.

**Codling moth**: one of the most common pests of apple trees, the larvae tunnelling into the fruit unseen close to the eye. This pest is a good instance of the value of pesticide-free control using pheromone traps.

**Coir**: waste product from coconut, forming the mainly fibrous husk around the edible nut. The fibrous component is used to make matting and rope but the more granular material has also found moderate success as a peat substitute in potting composts. Nutrient regulation is difficult however.

**Cold frame**: a glazed frame used for hardening off plants before they are put outdoors and for growing such crops as melons and cucumbers.

**Compost**: a word that confusingly has two quite different gardening meanings. Garden compost is the part decomposed remains of garden waste and is a valuable soil amendment and low level source of nutrients. Seedling and potting composts are either home-made or, more usually, proprietary mixtures for growing plants in containers. There is a basic division of potting composts into soil-based mixtures, most typically the John Innes range, and soil-less composts, still made predominantly with peat although with other, sustainable materials such as coir also. All such composts have carefully calculated amounts of fertiliser added to enable plants to be grown for some time before additional feeding is needed.

**Conidium (pl. conidia)**: an asexually produced fungal spore.

**Contact chemical**: a pesticide (fungicide or insecticide) that, by contrast with a systemic product, works by coming into contact with the target organism.

**Copper**: a nutrient trace element of largely unknown importance in plants. Occasionally deficient on highly organic soils.

**Copper oxychloride**: contact action fungicide used as an alternative to Bordeaux Mixture.

**Copper sulphate**: contact action fungicide used with ammonium hydroxide to form Bordeaux Mixture and with ammonium carbonate to form Cheshunt Compound.

**Coral spot**: a very common disease of woody plants, caused by the fungus *Nectria cinnabarina* and characterised by small pink pustules. It is common on dead twigs but is able to spread from there to cause dying back of live stems. It offers a classic illustration of the importance of clearing away old prunings and similar debris in the cause of garden hygiene.

**Corm**: a vegetative reproduction and storage organ comprising a swollen stem base with buds in the axils of the scale-like leaf remains.

**Corolla**: collectively, the petals of a flower.

**Corona**: the trumpet-shaped part of the corolla in a daffodil.

**Corymb**: type of inflorescence with individual flower stalks becoming shorter towards the top so that all flowers appear at the same level.

**Cotyledon**: also called a seed leaf; leaves that form part of the embryo of a plant within the seed. They are simpler than the later, true leaves and often contain nutrient for the emerging seedling. The two big divisions of flowering plants, the Monocotyledons and the Dicotyledons have one and two cotyledons respectively. Gymnosperms have varying numbers.

**Coumatetryl**: rodenticide, used in gardens as a mouse and rat poison.

**Crane Fly**: the harmless adult, also called a daddy-long-legs or, more correctly a tipulid, into which a leatherjacket larva develops.

**Cricket**: insects related to grasshoppers but seldom causing damage to plants outdoors in cool climates although some species may be troublesome in greenhouses.

**Crustacean**: group of Arthropods that includes such familiar creatures as crabs and shrimps but, in gardens, most importantly, woodlice.

**Cucumber mosaic virus**: commonly referred to as CMV, one of the really ubiquitous plant viruses, affecting a huge number of different types of plant and causing a wide range of symptoms. Almost invariably aphid-transmitted.

**Culm**: a hollow jointed stem, as of a grass.

**Cultivar**: a variety of a plant that has arisen, either deliberately or by accident, in cultivation. Cultivars (abbreviated to cvs.) can occur within species (*Calluna vulgaris* 'H. E. Beale'), within sub-species (*Euphorbia characias* ssp. *wulfenii* 'Lambrook Gold)' or within natural varieties (*Brassica oleracea* var. *capitata* 'Hispi'). Popularly in gardening, and in this book, they are called varieties.

**Cultivation**: general term used popularly in two ways: either to mean gardening in its entirety (the growing of plants under the gardener's influence) or, more specifically, the various techniques such as hoeing and digging that are used in the soil.

**Cultivator**: someone who cultivates but also a machine to till the soil; usually one with rotating blades or tines and called a rotary cultivator ('rotavator' is a brand name).

**Cuttings**: short pieces of stem or root cut from a parent plant and induced to form roots. The commonest method of vegetative multiplication.

**Cutworm**: larva (caterpillar) of noctuid moths that live in the upper layers of the soil and attack young plants by eating through stems. Controlled by regular hoeing or by applying insecticide to the soil.

**Cyme**: type of inflorescence in which,

unlike a raceme, terminal flowers form and so the continued growth of the inflorescence depends on the production of new growing points, as in *Lamium*.

**Cypermethrin**: contact insecticide used in gardens to control ants and other crawling insects.

**Daddy-long-legs**: see Crane fly

**Damping off**: disease of seedlings and young plants, divided into pre-emergence damping off, where death of the seed occurs before germination or of the seedling as it emerges; and post-emergence damping off where the seedling appears above soil level and then dies. Several different fungi may be responsible. The problem is best avoided by using healthy seed, new compost and clean pots and trays.

**DDT**: dichlorodiphenyltrichlor-oethane; once a widely used and very effective insecticide but now withdrawn because of persistence in the environment.

**Dead heading**: the removal of the faded flower heads of ornamental plants; an important task because it stimulates new flower buds to develop and also removes potential infection points for diseases.

**Deciduous plant**: one that loses and replaces all of its leaves annually.

**Deep bed system**: also called raised bed system. System for growing vegetables in which a defined area (the bed) is dug and manured to a depth of about 45cm (18in) and then not dug again for several years. The use of the system depends on making the bed small enough for cultivation and other operations to be done without walking on the soil and compacting it.

**Deltamethrin**: contact insecticide used in gardens to control ants and other crawling insects.

**Derris**: see Rotenone.

**Diazinon**: contact action organophosphorus insecticide available to gardeners in mixtures with other insecticides.

**Dicamba**: herbicide, selective for broad-leaved weeds and very widely used as a component of lawn weedkiller mixtures.

**Dichlobenil**: granular pre-emergence herbicide of unique type in being applied in cold weather among established shrubs to control annual and perennial weeds.

**Dichlorophen**: an organic protectant fungicide only now available as a constituent of rooting powders to prevent basal rotting of cuttings, but also widely used as a moss killer.

**Dichlorprop**: herbicide, selective for broad-leaved weeds and widely used in lawn weedkiller mixtures.

**Dicotyledon**: one of the two main groups of flowering plants, characterised by having two cotyledons emerge from the germinating seed. Dicotyledons generally have relatively small, more or less rounded leaves by contrast with the long, typically grass-like leaves of Monocotyledons.

**Dieback**: a disease, especially of woody plants, in which there is progressive death of the shoots from the tips downwards. Causes are varied and may result from airborne infection or root damage.

**Difenacoum**: rodenticide, used in gardens as a rat poison.

**Dikegulac**: artificial plant growth regulator available in products to limit the growth of some hedges.

**Dilutor delivery system**: a system in which a reservoir of concentrated chemical solution (usually a soluble fertiliser) is attached to the delivery end of a hose-pipe. Water passed through the reservoir, draws out predetermined volumes of concentrate and so enables large volumes of liquid fertiliser to be delivered easily to plants.

**Dimethoate**: systemic insecticide for the control of sap-sucking pests; one of the last systemic insecticides still to be available for garden use.

**Diploid**: plant having two sets of chromosomes in its cell nuclei.

**Diquat**: contact herbicide, available to gardeners in mixture with paraquat and/or other chemicals. The mixture of diquat and paraquat is valuable for the rapid killing of weeds on soil that is to be replanted or sown immediately afterwards.

**Diuron**: residual herbicide available to gardeners in mixture with other chemicals for the control of weeds on paths and other unplanted areas.

**DNA**: deoxyribonucleic acid, the main constituent of chromosomes in living organisms and self-replicating; responsible for transmitting char-acteristics from parent to offspring.

**Dolomite**: mineral containing magnesium and present in dolomitic limestone which should be used instead of normal limestone when magnesium is known to be deficient.

**Dormancy**: a resting state in which organisms remain alive but with little active growth. In temperate gardens, most plants exhibit winter dormancy but many bulbous types are dormant in the summer. The hibernation of animals (including many garden pests) is a form of dormancy. Living organisms tend to be vulnerable to damage whilst dormant as their healing processes too are in a resting state; this fact is the principle behind the control of many pests and diseases.

**Dot plant**: plant of striking individual appearance used to create a focal point in a larger planting.

**Downy mildew**: plant diseases caused by certain fungi in the group Oomycetes. Less important overall than the unrelated powdery mildews and controlled by a different range of fungicides, those based on copper still being effective. The symptoms are usually discrete areas of white or grey-purple mould in damp conditions.

**Dried blood**: organic fertiliser used as fairly quick acting source of nitrogen but dependent for its value on its breakdown by bacteria in the soil rather than simply by chemical changes in liquid solution.

**Drought**: period without rain. Until the 1960s a drought in Britain was defined as a period of fifteen days without measurable rain but recognition that this can have greatly differing impact at different times of the year means that 'official' droughts are no longer designated. Plants suffer from water shortage during drought periods but this can be ameliorated if the soil has previously been mulched whilst in a moist

condition. Physiological drought is a condition in which water may be present in the soil but plants are unable to make use of it; as for example when it is frozen.

**Drupe**: a type of fruit in which an outer skin and inner fleshy layer enclose a single hard seed.

**Dwarfing agent**: artificial chemical used to limited shoot elongation in plants and used commercially to produce dwarf plants such as pot chrysanthemums. Dwarfing agents are not available for garden use.

**Ecology**: the science of the study of the interrelationships of organisms with each other and with their environment. A much mis-used and misunderstood term.

**Eelworm**: microscopic eel-like animals, usually 1-2mm (1/16in) in length and known more correctly as Nematodes. Many species live in water, soil and as parasites in plants and animals. A small number cause important garden plant diseases and are also significant in transmitting plant viruses. No plant-attacking species cause harm to humans.

**Enchytraeid worm**: also known as pot worms. Small white worms, related to earthworms which help breakdown of organic matter. None cause harm to plants.

**Epidermis**: outermost tissues of plants, often impregnated with chemicals such as waxes to prevent desiccation through water loss.

**Ethylene**: organic chemical produced by ripening plant tissues and itself hastens the ripening process. Placing a ripe fruit such as a banana (which produce large quantities of ethylene) among tomatoes will hasten their ripening. Commercially, ethylene is applied artificially to ripen fruit.

**Evergreen plant**: one that loses its leaves piecemeal over a long period; the individual leaves do not however last forever.

**F1 hybrid**: the offspring from the crossing of two inbred parents. F1 hybrids have become very important in commercial horticulture because of their uniformity and generally larger size and greater vigour. It should be remembered however that uniform maturity of crops is more valuable in commerce than in gardens where having a crop mature over a long period can be very useful. F1 hybrid seed is expensive because the crosses are labour intensive and must be made anew each year. Seed saved from an F1 hybrid will result in mixed offspring, generally unlike the parent.

**F2 hybrid**: the offspring from allowing the members of an F1 pop-ulation to cross among themselves. Less vigorous and uniform but cheaper than F1 hybrids.

**Fairy ring**: more or less circular concentric rings on a lawn. An outer ring of darker more lush grass surrounds an inner ring of brown, dying or stunted grass. A ring of toadstools, generally of *Marasmius oreades*, may be present between the two. Fairy rings are almost impossible to eradicate and are best treated by giving additional aeration and fertiliser to the brown area.

**Family**: a classificatory grouping of plants containing similar genera. The name of a plant family ends in -aceae and similar families are grouped in an Order.

**Family fruit tree**: tree in which more than one variety has been grafted onto the same rootstock.

**Fanging and forking**: bifurcation and other distortion of the roots of carrots and sometimes other root crops; usually caused by the presence of unrotted manure, large stones or clods or an impervious pan layer in the soil.

**Fatty acid**: a type of organic acid, present in many soaps; some types are used to produce 'natural' or organic insecticides

**Fenitrothion**: a broad spectrum organophosphorus contact insecticide, used especially to control the raspberry beetle.

**Fern**: non-flowering green plant, reproducing by spores but having fairly advanced conducting and other tissues. Many are widely used for their ability to grow in damp moist places and for the attractiveness of their leaves or fronds.

**Ferrous sulphate**: inorganic iron compound, widely used as a moss killer and the active ingredient of lawn sand.

**Fertilisation**: the union of male and female cells to produce offspring; the essence of sexual reproduction and in plants, follows pollination. Also used in gardening to mean the application of fertiliser to soil or plants.

**Fertiliser**: plant nutrient applied artificially by gardeners. Often divided into artificial fertilisers, produced in a chemical factory, and organic fertilisers, derived from a naturally occurring source.

**Filament**: stalk of a stamen, surmounted by the anther.

**Fireblight**: serious bacterial disease of woody plants in the rose family. Particularly damaging on pears.

**Fish meal**: organic fertiliser containing 6-10 per cent nitrogen; generally used as a component of fish, blood and bone.

**Fish, blood and bone**: general purpose fertiliser containing bone meal, fish meal and dried blood. Almost invariably however, as this mixture is deficient in potash, potassium sulphate is added to give a product containing N:P:K approximately 5.1:5:6.5; to the purist, this is therefore no longer organic but organically based.

**Flame gun**: paraffin or gas fuelled flame producing apparatus for killing weeds and weed seeds. Of limited value because of its inability to penetrate the soil, and the likelihood of damaging plants or paving.

**Flatworm**: organisms belonging to the group Platyhelminthes, also including flukes and tapeworms. Not plant pests but Southern Hemisphere species (including the New Zealand Flatworm) have become established in Britain and cause serious impact through feeding on earthworms. Harmless to humans but at present, no control measures are available.

**Flea beetle**: small beetles, characterised by active jumping behaviour when disturbed. Several are important plant pests, feeding especially on leaves of vegetables.

**Floret**: reduced form of flower, typical of the family Asteraceae where the mass of apparent petals in each 'flower' is in reality a collection of many individual florets. The petal-like outer ones are termed ray-florets,

the tubular ones making up the central area, the disc florets.

**Flowers**: the reproductive structure of most important garden plants, except ferns. Flowers are evolved, modified leafy shoots and display an enormous variety of form, colour and/or scent, almost all adaptations to facilitate pollination by either wind or animals, often insects.

**Fly**: insects belonging to the group Diptera which includes the house fly and a number of important garden pests such as carrot fly, cabbage root fly and many midges. Other flying insects with the suffix fly (whiteflies, greenflies, blackflies, craneflies, sawflies for instance) belong to other insect groups.

**Food chain**: a series of organisms living in a natural community, each member feeding on another and itself eaten in turn by another.

**Foot (of plant)**: the base of the stem.

**Fork**: traditional garden forks usually have fine tines but versions exist with more and also with curved tines for such purposes as lifting manure and compost. The fork is one garden tool where stainless may not be the best option because the tines can bend very easily. Carbon steel is generally better.

**Frit**: the basic materials in a more or less fused state used for making glass; plant micro-nutrients are often produced in a frit form for mixing into plant composts.

**Froghopper**: small sap feeding insects capable of making huge leaps; familiar species produce harmless cuckoo spit on plants.

**Frost**: temperature at or below 0°C (32°F) causing damage to plant tissues. An air frost arises when the temperature is at freezing at a height of 1.2m/4ft (above soil level; a ground frost when it is freezing at or just above soil level.

**Fruit**: the ripened, fertilised ovary of plant, containing one or more seeds.

**Fungus (pl. fungi)**: an organism lacking chlorophyll, reproducing by spores and composed of a mass of microscopic filamentous threads called hyphae. Mushrooms and toadstools are the familiar reproductive bodies of some fungi but huge numbers of others are wholly microscopic. Many cause important plant diseases but are also vital in the decay of organic matter in compost and soil.

**Fungus gnat**: popular name for sciarid flies which live in organic matter in soil and whose larvae may attack plant roots.

**Gall**: excrescence on plants brought about through disturbance of plant growth regulating mechanism, usually as a result of attack by pest or disease organism.

**Gall wasp**: small wasp-like insect that stimulates gall development in plant tissues as a result of its egg-laying activities.

**Gamete**: sex cell.

**Genetic engineering**: the artificial alteration of the DNA of cells with, among others, the objective of making improvements that would otherwise be impossible or achievable only after many generations of conventional breeding.

**Genus (pl. genera)**: a classificatory group containing closely related species; similar

genera are themselves grouped into a Family.

**Germination**: the process by which seeds or spores produce new growth and develop into new individuals. Commonly, a period of dormancy takes place after the formation of the seed or spore and certain conditions are then needed to break this dormancy; the reason why gardeners find some seeds difficult to germinate.

**Ghost spot**: pale circular spotting on tomato fruit as result of mild infection by the grey mould fungus.

**Gibberellin**: plant growth substance responsible for stem elongation.

**Glufosinate-ammonium**: persistent herbicide for use on paths and other unplanted areas.

**Glyphosate**: translocated total herbicide and the most important garden weedkiller for the control of deep rooted perennial weeds. Inactivated on contact with soil.

**Grafting**: technique in which two different plants, often of different variety or even species are artificially induced to grow as one. A length of stem (the scion) of one plant is inserted in the rooted part (stock) of another. An invaluable method of propagating plants that have some horticulturally desirable feature but inefficient rooting.

**Grass**: any member of the family Poaceae; those forms popularly called bamboos that produce a wood-like toughened stem and may reach tree size are separated in a sub-family Bambusoideae.

**Grass trimmer**: electric or petrol powered appliance with circular metal or whirling nylon cord for cutting long grass. They are valuable for rough grass but do not even approximate to the finish that can be obtained with a lawn mower. 'Strimmer' is a brand name for one type of grass trimmer.

**Green manuring**: the growing of a crop of plants solely to dig them into the soil to enrich the humus content. A useful technique but its value is often over-stated as the amount of both humus and nutrient that are supplied is very limited.

**Greenhouse**: also called a glasshouse; any building employing a translucent surface (glass or plastic) to trap warmth and so enhance plant growth. Popularly, an unheated greenhouse relies entirely on sun heat; a heated greenhouse contains an artificial heater also.

**Grey mould**: plant disease, generally involving some tissue decay, caused by the fungus *Botrytis cinerea* and with a grey mould growth.

**Ground cover plant**: low growing plant, either of more or less prostrate habit or one spreading readily by runners or other means. They are popular because they enable a large area of soil to be covered quickly and, theoretically, weed growth to be suppressed.

**Growing bag**: a plastic bag containing a (usually soil-less) growing medium, placed horizontally and with plants planted through slots cut in the plastic. Popularly used for tomatoes in a greenhouse. 'Grow-Bag' is a brand name for one type of growing bag.

**Growmore**: balanced general purpose artificial fertiliser containing N:P:K in the ratio 7:7:7. Derived from the National Growmore blend introduced in Britain during World War 2.

**Growth hormone**: chemical that controls the way in which plant cells and tissues grow and become differentiated; also called auxins.

**Grub**: vague term for an insect larva.

**Guano**: dried seabird droppings, mainly South American, used as a phosphate fertiliser.

**Gymnosperm**: conifers and related plants in the group Gymnospermae. Most produce seeds exposed in cones and the group includes many very important garden trees.

**Gypsum**: mineral containing calcium sulphate; sometimes used in horticulture as a source of calcium fertiliser when it is undesirable to raise the pH.

**Half-hardy**: term to describe a plant that is sufficiently hardy to grow outdoors in a temperate climate summer but will not withstand frost.

**Halo blight**: disease of plants characterised by circular spots with an outer, pale halo; bacterial halo blight of beans is the most important in gardens.

**Hanging basket**: hanging plant container, typically of basket form and characterised by very free drainage and a need for constant watering and liquid feeding.

**Hardening off**: process by which plants are accustomed gradually to outdoor conditions after being raised in warmth. Even very hardy plants may require hardening off.

**Hardy**: able to tolerate frost; in this book and its companion volume, I have used a table of increasing frost tolerance.

**Harvestman**: common garden arachnids, related to spiders and mites and with eight very long, thin legs. Harmless to plants.

**Hedge**: line of trees or shrubs, trimmed to form a boundary but also valuable as an ornamental feature within a garden.

**Heptenophos**: an organophosphorus insecticide with contact and systemic action, widely used in gardens for the control of pests on edible and ornamental crops.

**Herb**: popularly used to mean a plant with medicinal or culinary flavouring properties but also used, especially by botanists, to mean any non-woody flowering plant.

**Herbaceous perennial**: perennial plant with no woody structure, unlike a shrub. Contrary to popular belief, not all are deciduous and die down in the autumn; many are evergreen and may therefore need some winter protection.

**Herbicide**: weedkiller, a chemical to kill weeds.

**Hoe**: tool of which there are various types, used for breaking up compacted soil surface, drawing soil into heaps or ridges (draw-hoe) or cutting down weeds (Dutch hoe).

**Honey fungus**: species of toadstool, principally *Armillaria mellea*, causing death and decay on a huge range of mainly woody plants.

**Honeydew**: sweet excretion produced by aphids, scale insects and other insects that feed on sap. Contains sugars derived from sap and makes infested plants sticky, encouraging sooty moulds.

**Hoof and horn**: organic fertiliser derived from ground up animal remains, valuable as a slow-release form of nitrogen.

**Horsetail**: species of *Equisetum*; evolutionarily ancient group of non-flowering, spore forming plants. Some are very attractive but a few are invasive and ineradicable weeds.

**Horticultural soap**: organic contact insecticide derived from naturally occurring fatty acids.

**Hose pipe**: means of delivering water where it is needed in the garden; modern variants include perforated hose for delivering a fine spray among established plants and seeping hose which is laid on or below the surface and oozes water slowly and constantly.

**Host or host-plant**: a plant on which a pathogen or pest develops. Most pathogens and pests are restricted to a few host-plants on which they can develop successfully.

**Host range**: the complete range of host-plants on which a pathogen or pest can develop.

**Hoverfly**: popular name for Syrphid, wasp-like fly whose larvae feed on aphids and are important natural biological control agents.

**Humus**: part decomposed organic matter, especially when integrated within the soil.

**Hybrid**: offspring from genetically unlike parents.

**Hydrogen**: the most abundant element in the universe and an essential component of water and of many organic chemical compounds.

**Hypha**: microscopic colourless thread-like filament forming the basic structural unit of fungi.

**IAA**: indoleacetic acid, a plant hormone that can be synthesised artificially and is used as a component of rooting powders.

**Ichneumon fly**: a fly-like relative of wasps whose larvae are parasitic on caterpillars and are important in regulating pest numbers.

**Identification of plants**: plant identification is achieved most readily by using the characteristics of the flowers, the features by which plants are classified. These are less likely than leaves and other vegetative parts to vary under differing environmental conditions.

**Imidacloprid** froan insecticide for the control of aphids, vine weevil and some other pests in ready mixed potting composts.

**Immune**: free from infection or infestation; having qualities that prevent the development of a disease or pest.

**Inbred**: of an organism bred from closely related parents; a feature of the development of F1 hybrids.

**Indicator plant**: a plant that by its presence gives information about the underlying soil conditions; rhododendron for instance is an indicator of acidity, creeping buttercup, *Ranunculus repens* an indicator of a heavy soil.

**Infection**: entry of a parasitic organism into a host. A plant may be infected but is not diseased if no damaging symptoms develop.

**Infestation**: establishment of pest populations on or inside plants.

**Inflorescence**: a flowering shoot, a collection of flowers together forming a head. Among the commonest types are raceme, panicle, corymb, spike, spadix, catkin, umbel and capitulum.

**Infra-red radiation**: radiation of longer wave-length than visible light but shorter than radio waves; gives the warming effect of sunlight.

**Insect**: member of the Arthropod group Insecta, the most numerous group of all animals, comprising over 80 per cent of known species. Characterised by six legs, commonly two pairs of wings; numerous species, beneficial and pest, are important in gardens.

**Insecticide**: chemical to kill insects; some are also effective against mites, woodlice and other pests.

**Ioxynil**: post-emergence contact herbicide, formerly used extensively in newly sown lawns but withdrawn from garden use several years and should not now be used.

**Iron**: widespread chemical element, the cause of the brown colour of soils. Important plant nutrient, significantly in the manufacture of chlorophyll and often unavailable to plants in alkaline conditions.

**Japanese Knotweed**: *Reynoutria japonica*, arguably the most troublesome of all garden weeds and all but ineradicable by both chemical and physical means. It has been known to travel beneath a multi-lane road to the other side.

**John Innes base**: balanced fertiliser mixture containing all important plant nutrients and used in the John Innes soil-based composts.

**John Innes compost**: soil-based composts formulated at the John Innes Horticultural Institution in the 1930s (John Innes is not a brand name but a type of compost) and still the standard. There are four commonly available: Seed and Potting Nos. 1, 2, and 3 with increasing amounts of fertiliser for increasingly long-term plant growth.

**Lace bug**: small sap-feeding insects; the *Rhododendron* bug is the only important garden pest.

**Ladybird**: small brightly coloured beetles; both adults and larvae feed on aphids and are important in natural biological pest control.

**Larva (pl. larvae)**: immature form of an animal which develops into a physically very different adult by metamorphosis.

**Latent infection**: infection that does not produce obvious symptoms.

**Lawn**: area of mown grass; mimicked by areas of other low growing plants such as camomile.

**Lawn fertiliser**: fertiliser specifically formulated for use on lawns; different blends are produced for spring, summer and autumn use and it is important to choose correctly.

**Lawn sand**: a blend of ferrous sulphate (moss and weedkiller), ammonium sulphate (fertiliser) and sand (inert bulk).

**Layering**: method of propagating plants by pegging a horizontal shoot into the soil and leaving it undisturbed until it forms roots. It is then severed from the parent.

**Laying**: technique by which hedges are rejuvenated through cutting away some shoots and bending down and half breaking main branches. It is a highly skilled task but beautiful when done well and is particularly effective with hawthorn.

**Leaching**: the loss of minerals and other matter from soil by the downward movement of water, especially rain water.

**Leaf**: plant organ in which most photosynthesis takes place. In Dicotyledons, the leaf is typically more or less rounded and divided into a flattened blade and stalk. In Monocotyledons, it tends to be elongated and strap-like with parallel veins. Leaves may be modified to form hooks, tendrils and other structures for secondary roles.

**Leaf hopper**: sap-feeding insects related to froghoppers, cause mottling on leaf surface of roses and other plants; control is difficult but rarely necessary.

**Leaf miner**: larvae of flies and other insects that tunnel in the tissues between upper and lower leaf surfaces causes sinuous or blotch-like lesions. Disfiguring but rarely causing significant harm to plants.

**Leaf mould**: any mould growth on a leaf but specifically a disease of tomatoes causing yellowish mould, especially in greenhouses.

**Leaf spot**: small lesion on a leaf, usually more or less circular and commonly caused by fungal or bacterial infection.

**Leaf-cutter bee**: solitary species of bee, related to honey bee; cut semi-circular pieces from edge of rose and other leaves to build nests. No control necessary or practicable.

**Leaf-rolling sawfly**: species of sawfly causing rose leaves to roll, cigar fashion, in response to probing activities of egg-laying females. No treatment necessary or practicable.

**Leatherjacket**: larva of crane-fly, living in soil and feeding on stems and roots; cause typical yellow patches on lawns.

**Legume**: type of fruit, also called a pod, characteristic of the family Papilionaceae, formed from a single carpel and splitting along the mid-rib to expose the seeds.

**Lenticel**: one of many pores in the bark of woody plants through which gaseous exchange takes place.

**Lichen**: dual organism, comprising a fungus and an alga living symbiotically. Common on rocks, tree branches and lawns, especially in wetter areas. Non-parasitic but may harm plants when extensive growth smothers them.

**Life cycle**: series of changes that an organism undergoes from fertilisation to death.

**Life span of plants**: flowering plants are usefully grouped into annuals, which pass from seed to the seed of the next generation within a single season, biennials, which take two seasons and perennials, which live for longer but are certainly not immortal. The longest lived true plants are some bristlecone pines (*Pinus aristata*) which are over 5,000 years old.

**Life span of seeds**: in general, the larger the seed, the shorter the shelf life; peas and beans are best not kept (even if cool and dry) for more than two years although most brassicas will be viable after six or seven. In garden soil, most weed seeds decline fairly sharply after about the same time although some, such as poppies, remain viable for thirty or more years.

**Light**: the visible light component of solar radiation is crucially important as it includes the wavelengths needed for photosynthesis but light is also important in controlling flower initiation and other plant growth features.

**Lignin**: complex chemical polymer formed in plant cell walls to give strength. Lignified cells usually die but impart great structural stability by collectively forming wood.

**Lime**: shorthand name for calcium containing alkaline mineral; garden lime is finely ground calcium carbonate.

**Limestone**: sedimentary rock composed mainly of calcium carbonate.

**Liverwort**: primitive green bryophyte plant related to moss; occasionally cause problems on lawns.

**Loam**: soil containing approximately equal amounts of clay, sand and silt; an ideal all-round growing medium.

**Maggot**: vague term for insect larvae, especially leg-less forms such as fly larvae.

**Magnesian limestone**: limestone containing significant amounts of magnesium in addition to calcium.

**Magnesite**: mineral containing magnesium carbonate, the main magnesium source for plants.

**Magnesium**: chemical element and major plant nutrient, most important as a constituent of the green photosynthesis pigment chlorophyll.

**Magnesium carbonate**: see magnesite.

**Magpie moth**: small black and white moth whose black, white and yellow cat-erpillars are important leaf eating pests, especially of currants and gooseberries.

**Malathion**: non-persistent organophosphorus insecticide to control a wide range of garden pests although it has an unpleasant odour.

**Mancozeb**: contact fungicide of especial value against rusts and foliage blights.

**Mandibles**: horny jaw-like mouth-parts of insects; used to bite and to chew food.

**Manganese**: chemical element and minor plant nutrient, important in the formation of chlorophyll.

**Manganese sulphate**: inorganic compound that may be applied directly to plants to correct manganese deficiency.

**Manure**: imprecise term for animal excrement especially used as soil amendment and plant nutrient; as distinct from the term compost which is generally used for decomposed plant remains.

**Marl**: a calcareous clay; applying marl to soil (marling) was once common for the improvement of light, especially acidic soils.

**Mayweed**: species of *Matricaria* or *Tripleurospermum* (Asteraceae); common wild flowers and some, especially *Matricaria discoidea*, may be important weeds.

**MCPA**: translocated selective herbicide for control of broad-leaved weeds, either on lawns or non-cropped areas such as paths.

**Mealybug**: small sap-feeding insects

related to scales. Usually most troublesome on indoor plants.

**Mecoprop**: selective herbicide for control of broad-leaved weeds and one of the most important ingredients of lawn weedkillers.

**Meristem**: limited area of active cell division in plants in which differentiation into other tissues takes place. Cambium, which occurs beneath the outer bark of plant stems is an important example.

**Metaldehyde**: chemical molluscicide, the most important ingredient of garden slug killers.

**Methiocarb**: chemical molluscicide used as an alternative to metaldehyde and more reliable in wet weather.

**Microclimate**: small scale features of climate that operate within a restricted area. A garden has its own microclimate, comprising relatively warm and cool, wet and dry areas. Knowledge of microclimates is of great benefit in selecting appropriate plants for particular sites.

**Micropropagation**: the multiplication of plants by the precise excision of small pieces of tissues and the use of artificial culture to encourage them to differentiate and grow to maturity. An invaluable technique for the mass production of identical plants and also for the freeing of plants from virus contamination.

**Mildew**: one of two distinct and superficially similar but quite unrelated types of plant disease-causing fungi, known as downy mildews and powdery mildews.

**Millepede**: segmented arthropods of which some species are important plant pests, feeding on bulbs and other fleshy material. None have more than about two hundred legs.

**Mite**: small or tiny arthropods with eight legs, unlike the six of insects. Most are general scavengers but a few species, such as the web-forming red spider mites, are important garden plant pests.

**Mole cricket**: *Gryllotalpa*, a large subterranean insect related to grasshoppers. Serious pests in many countries but protected in Britain.

**Mollusc**: large group of soft-bodied unsegmented animals, including slugs and snails but also many marine shells and octopuses.

**Molybdate**: salt of the element molybdenum.

**Molybdenum**: chemical element and minor plant nutrient, used by plants to convert nitrate to ammonium and important therefore in nitrogen uptake.

**Monocalcium phosphate**: a major ingredient of superphosphate and bone meal, the two main types of phosphate fertiliser for plants.

**Monocarpic**: dying after flowering.

**Monocotyledons**: one of the two main groups of flowering plants, characterised by having one cotyledon emerge from the germinating seed. Monocotyledons generally have long, typically grass-like leaves by contrast with the relatively small, more or less rounded leaves of Dicotyledons.

**Monoculture**: the growing of one type of plant only on a given area of land. If this is continued every year, it is called intensive mono-culture and is a feature of much

modern arable farming. It is to be discouraged in gardens as it leads to the build up of pests and diseases and may result in nutrient imbalance in the soil.

**Moss**: evolutionarily primitive green bryophyte plant reproducing by spores and related to liverwort; cause major problems on lawns, especially where grass is stressed and unable to compete effectively.

**Mould**: imprecise term for a fungal growth.

**Mouth-parts**: the structures that surround the mouth in insects and mites. They are adapted for various functions, especially for biting and chewing solid food or for piercing plant tissues to extract sap.

**Mulch**: material laid over the soil surface in order to conserve moisture and suppress weeds. Most commonly compost or other organic matter is used but plastic sheet is employed also, especially as larger scale 'blanket mulch'.

**Mushroom compost**: residue of organic matter from artificial mushroom culture beds; useful as source of organic soil amendment but care is needed as it may contain insecticide residues and also pieces of limestone used as casing material in mushroom production.

**Mycelium**: a mass of fungal hyphae.

**Myclobutanil**: organic systemic fungicide with protectant and eradicant properties, particularly effective against rose diseases and apple scab.

**Mycoplasma**: see Phytoplasma

**Mycorrhiza**: fungal mycelium growing symbiotically on and sometimes within plant roots and aiding the uptake by the plant of nutrients from the soil. Long known to be important on trees but now recognised as significant for many other types of plant also.

**Myriapod**: many legged, segmented arthropods; millepedes and centipedes.

**NAA1-**: naphthylacetic acid, an organic acid used as an artificial plant growth regulator (hormone) because of its similarity to the naturally occurring IAA..

**Naming of plants**: plants are named by the Latin binomial system devised by the Swedish naturalist Carl von Linné (Linnaeus) (1707-1778). The binomial comprises a genus name and a specific or trivial name. For example, the plant known to the colloquial English speaker as the dog rose is given the binomial *Rosa canina*. This unique combination of the generic name *Rosa* with the specific name *canina* conveys immediate meaning to any botanist no matter what their native language. It also indicates that this plant is very similar to such other plants as *Rosa lutea*, *Rosa virginiana* or *Rosa watsoniana*. Often, the specific name attempts to give some brief diagnostic information about the plant; *lutea* suggests a rose with yellow flowers or *virginiana* one originating in Virginia, although, as in *watsoniana*, it may commemorate someone who played some part in its study. Sometimes, as in *canina*, the name is quite fanciful.

**Naphthalene**: strong smelling organic compound formerly used as an insecticide and now included in some animal repellents.

**Neck rot**: disease of onions caused by the fungus *Botrytis allii* and manifest by decay of the top of the bulb; carried on the seed but not evident until the crop is stored.

**Necrotic**: dead and usually dark-coloured plant tissues.

**Nectar**: sugary fluid secreted in nectaries, often but not always on flowers, and important in attracting pollinating insects.

**Needle cast**: conifer disease caused by fungi, generally in the Class Ascomycetes, in which there is wholesale shedding of the needles.

**Nematode**: see Eelworm

**Nitrate**: salt of nitric acid and the form in which many nitrogen containing fertilisers are applied to soil or plants.

**Nitro-chalk**: see Ammonium nitrate

**Nitrogen**: chemical element and the single most important plant nutrient, being a major constituent of protein. Nitrogen is readily washed from the soil and regular applications may be needed in gardens therefore.

**Noctuid moth**: one of a large family of moths, of which some caterpillars are important soil-inhabiting pests known as cutworms.

**Notifiable (pest or disease)**: required by law to be reported to the Ministry of Agriculture.

**NPK fertiliser**: fertiliser containing the three major plant nutrients nitrogen (N), phosphorus (P) and potassium (K).

**Nutritional disorder**: malfunction of a plant through imbalance or deficiency in one or more nutrients.

**Nymph**: the immature stage of those insects that develop directly to adult without an intermediate pupal stage such as aphids.

**Oedema**: a rough and warty outgrowth on the underside of leaves produced as a result of an excess of water in the plant.

**Oomycete**: one of the major groups of fungi, considered evolutionarily fairly primitive and including some important plant pathogens such as potato blight and downy mildews.

**Open-pollinated**: of a plant that is the result of chance fertilisation between non-selected parents.

**Organic**: a confusing term. Chemically, an organic substance is one containing carbon but it tends to be used in gardening to mean a substance of natural, as opposed to artificial origin.

**Organic gardening**: like, organic, a confusing term. It tends to be used to refer to gardening practices that have (or are believed to have) no adverse effect on the environment (are 'environmentally friendly'). Whilst the underlying principles are highly laudable, some of the logic behind what is and is not acceptable defies clear understanding.

**Osmosis**: the passage of water from a zone containing a chemical solution of high concentration, across a semi-permeable membrane into one of lower concentration. It is a physical process but takes place in many living organisms and is the principle means by which water passes between cells.

**Ovary**: the hollow basal part of a carpel of a

flower, containing one or more ovaries. After fertilisation and maturity, forms a fruit.

**Ovipositor**: the special structure that many female insects have to facilitate egg-laying. This may be relatively simple if eggs are just deposited on plants but in some groups such as sawflies it consists of a pair of saw-like blades that are used to cut slits in plant tissue before eggs are inserted.

**Ovule**: structure in seed plants that, after fertilisation, forms a seed.

**Oxygen**: chemical element; the most abundant element on earth and essential in plants for aerobic respiration and release of energy from food materials.

**Palm**: a tree like member of the plant family Arecaceae with a tough stem that resembles, but is structurally different from wood. Very few palms are hardy in Temperate climates.

**Pan**: a hard, fairly impervious layer that develops below the soil surface in response to various factors and results in impeded drainage and poor plant growth.

**Panicle**: type of large inflorescence, a branched raceme.

**Paraquat**: a non-selective, foliar-acting contact weedkiller with no residual activity; available most significantly to gardeners in combination with diquat for the rapid killing of annual weeds.

**Parasite**: an organism living on or in another organism and from which it obtains nutrient and to which it gives no benefit in return.

**Parthenogenesis**: a type of asexual reproduction in which unfertilised eggs develop normally to produce adults. Common in aphids, gall wasps and other groups of insects.

**Path weedkillers**: total herbicides, generally with a combination of chemical ingredients, with fairly long persistence for use on unplanted areas. They must never be used on land that is to grow ornamental or crop plants.

**Pathogen**: a parasitic organism that causes a disease.

**Peat**: dead plant material, often many thousands of years old, that has only partially decomposed through lying in water-logged conditions (commonly called bogs). There are two main types of peat, moss or *Sphagnum* peat, which is brown and highly acidic, and fen peat which is black and less acidic, and may even be alkaline. Because of the despoiling of valuable natural habitats by peat extraction, there has been a concerted campaign to find alternative, sustainable materials for the preparation of horticultural potting composts. Nonetheless, no other material completely replicates the moisture and nutrient retaining and physical properties of peat.

**Pedicel**: a flower stalk.

**Penconazole**: contact fungicide of especial value for the control of rust diseases on ornamental plants.

**Pepper**: domestic, kitchen pepper is used with moderate effectiveness as a cat and dog repellent.

**Perennial**: a plant that lives for more than two seasons. Many plants grown as half-hardy annuals in temperate climates are perennial in their native habitats.

**Perennial weed**: these weeds present different problems in control from annuals for many persist by very deep seated or far-reaching root or rhizome systems. Merely cutting off or killing the top will not eradicate them.

**Perlite**: a variety of a volcanic mineral called obsidian, formed by the solidification of lava globules and used as a substitute for sand when mixed with peat or other growing medium to open up the structure and provide freer drainage and air flow. Also used alone to support plant growth or to provide a base for striking cuttings; provided that all of the plants' nutrients can be applied in liquid form.

**Permethrin**: a synthetic pyrethroid insecticide, used for the control of a wide range of garden plant pests.

**Persistent (of a pesticide)**: persisting on plants or in soil for weeks or months after application, during which time it retains some of its pesticidal activity.

**Petal**: one of the parts forming the corolla of a flower, often conspicuous and brightly coloured. Evolutionarily, a modified leaf.

**pH**: potential of hydrogen, a measure of the concentration of hydrogen ions (charged atoms) in a solution. In practice, a measure of relative acidity or alkalinity on a logarithmic scale from 0 (extremely acidic) to 14 (extremely alkaline); the mid-point 7 is called neutral. Most garden soils lie between pH 5 and 7.5.

**Pheromone**: chemical insect sex attractant. Synthetic pheromone analogues are used in some insect traps such as the codling moth trap available to gardeners.

**Phloem**: tissue in plants that conducts proteins, sugars and other nutrients.

**Phosphate**: salt of phosphoric acid and the form in which the element phosphate is taken up by plants.

**Phosphorus**: chemical element and a major plant nutrient, involved in many important processes in plant tissues. Valuable in garden for its role in encouraging root development

**Photoperiod**: the length of daylight that produces optimum growth and flower and fruit development in any particular plant. The plant's response is called its photoperiodism or photoperiodic response. The artificial alteration of daylength is used to induce flowering and fruiting at unnatural seasons.

**Photosynthesis**: the formation of organic chemical compounds by green plants from carbon dioxide and water using the green pigment chlorophyll.

**Phyllode**: a flattened leaf stalk that looks and functions like a leaf.

**Phylloxerid**: small sap-sucking insects, superficially similar to aphids and with complex life cycles. Few are important garden pests but one species historically devastated European vineyards.

**Phytochrome**: a chemical in plants that is sensitive to light and is involved in plant growth response to the stimulus of light.

**Phytophthora**: a genus of fungi in the group Oomycetes; contains many important plant pathogens, including *Phytophthora infestans*, the cause of potato blight.

**Phytoplasma**: current name for organisms previously called mycoplasmas or mycoplasma-like organisms (MLOs). Superficially resemble bacteria but lack a cell wall and are responsible for some important plant diseases, although few in gardens. Sometimes (as in strawberries) can cause a strange symptom in which the flowers are entirely green.

**Phytotoxic (of a chemical)**: injurious to plants. Many pesticides are phytotoxic to some plants.

**Pigment**: coloured substance. In plants, the most important is the green photosynthesis catalyst chlorophyll but other important pigments are the yellow carotenes and red anthocyanins.

**Pillar plant**: tall, lax shrub or short climber, especially a rose, trained around a single vertical pillar.

**Pinnate**: of a leaf composed of more than three leaflets arranged in two rows along a common stalk, as in ash. Bipinnate and tripinnate leaves are those in which the leaflets are themselves pinnate.

**Piperonyl butoxide**: contact insecticide with a wide spectrum of activity and the ingredient of several garden insecticide products.

**Pirimicarb**: contact insecticide, valued for its high selectivity in the control of aphids without harming other insects.

**Pirimiphos-methyl**: organophosphorus contact insecticide used for the control of a wide range of garden pests although one week must elapse between spraying and harvesting edible crops.

**Pistil**: the female reproductive parts of a flower, comprising one or more fused or separate carpels.

**Plant breeding**: the artificial selection and hybridising of plants to develop new cultivars. Although practised for many centuries using processes that in effect speed up what could occur naturally, modern plant breeding is rather different. First because it brings together as potential parents plants that grow in geographically distinct regions and could never inter-breed naturally; and, more importantly, because it may now entail highly sophisticated techniques such as genetic engineering. Whatever the means, the goals remain the same: the 'improvement' of what occurs naturally to give plants with enhanced yield, better appearance, higher pest resistance or other attributes that we find advantageous.

**Plastic in the garden**: plastics of many kinds have taken the place of many more traditional materials in the garden like earthenware for plant pots and string for netting. However, many gardeners feel that whilst a cheaper and often more practical substitute, it is seldom as pleasing aesthetically. And it remains a curious anomaly that so much plastic is used by many organic gardeners (as mulch for instance) who seem oblivious to the huge amounts of energy and resources that are involved in its manufacture.

**Pod**: see Legume.

**Pollen**: fine powdery material produced in anthers and containing male cells (gametes).

**Pollination**: transfer of pollen from a male anther to a female stigma on either the same or different flowers as a prelude to fertilisation.

**Pollutant**: any substance that pollutes; in gardening, plants may be damaged especially by air-borne pollutants, as for example from road traffic or industrial processes. Different pollutants cause characteristic symptoms of injury but these are difficult to identify.

**Pome**: type of fruit in which the seeds are surrounded by a tough layer as in apple.

**Pool**: garden pools are of two main types: those that mimic natural or semi-natural ones and those that are unashamedly artificial. It is essential to decide which is more appropriate for each situation. Neither should be in gardens where small children are playing.

**Pot**: plant pots are manufactured in a wide range of sizes, usually expressed as the diameter of the top, the ratio of diameter to height being standard. For general garden use, 9cm (3 1/2in) and 12.5cm (5in) are the most useful sizes.

**Pot worm**: see Enchytraeid worm.

**Potash**: everyday term for potassium salt, especially potassium oxide, an important fertiliser.

**Potassium**: chemical element and major plant nutrient, especially important for flower and fruit production and a significant ingredient therefore of such mixtures as tomato fertilisers.

**Potassium chloride**: one of the two most widely used potassic fertilisers, formerly called muriate of potash, commonly containing 60 per cent potassium oxide.

**Potassium sulphate**: one of the two important potassic fertilisers, also called sulphate of potash, containing 48 per cent potassium oxide.

**Potato blight**: devastating disease of potatoes caused by *Phytophthora infestans* which renders the tubers rotten and valueless. A succession of outbreaks in Ireland in the 1840s led to the Irish Potato famine.

**Powdery mildew**: plant disease caused by fungi of the group Ascomycetes, characterised by velvety, generally off-white growth over leaves and other plant parts. Seriously debilitating, especially troublesome in hot, dry conditions but fairly effectively controlled with systemic fungicides or sulphur.

**Predator**: organism that preys on other organism; some such as ladybirds that feed on aphids are important biological control agents.

**Pricking out**: the transfer of seedlings from a seed tray to their growing positions.

**Propagation**: the multiplication of plants artificially, using either vegetative means (cuttings, division or layering for example) or natural reproductive processes (seeds).

**Propagator**: someone who propagates or a piece of equipment to facilitate propagation. In general, a device to maintain a moist environment is essential, whatever the method of propagation, and basic propagators are seed trays with a ventilated cover. As enhanced warmth is important for most types of propagation, many propagators incorporate a heating element.

**Propiconazole**: systemic fungicide for the control of rust diseases on ornamental plants, now superseded by penconazole.

**Pruner**: someone who prunes or a pruning implement, also called secateur.

**Pruning**: the artificial removal of parts of plants to improve their shape or productivity.

**Psyllid**: small sap-feeding insects including several garden pests; the immature forms are called suckers.

**Pteridophyte**: ancient plant group including ferns, horse-tails and clubmosses. Green plants with fairly advanced conducting tissues but reproducing by spores, not seeds. Important constituents of prehistoric coal swamps.

**Pupa (pl. pupae)**: also called chrysalis. The stage between the larva and the adult of certain insects such as butterflies, moths and flies.

**Pyrethrin**: synthetic insecticide with similar properties to pyrethrum.

**Pyrethrum**: naturally occurring chemical widely used as an insecticide and extracted from the flower heads of *Chrysanthemum cinerariaefolium*.

**Quassia**: a naturally occurring compound with insecticidal properties, extracted from the bark of certain tropical trees and used in garden insecticides.

**Quicklime**: popular name for calcium oxide, a calcium salt with a higher neutralising value than limestone (calcium carbonate) but unpleasant to handle and little used in gardening therefore.

**Race (of a pathogen or pest)**: strain of a species that can only attack some of the host-plants that are susceptible to the whole species.

**Raceme**: type of unbranched inflorescence with the flowers arranged in sequence on central stem and no terminal flower; as in foxglove.

**Rain**: the source of all water on earth but its relative unpredictability makes it a constant talking point for gardeners. It is unarguable that gardeners should conserve as much rain-water as possible, especially in areas where the tap-water is hard and unsuitable for calcifuge plants.

**Raised bed**: plant bed in which the soil is higher than the surrounding area. This gives improved drainage. The raised bed may be confined by walls or planks or simply mounded but the term raised bed has a special connotation in vegetable growing where it refers to a bed that is double dug initially but then not deeply dug again for several years, a situation made possible by its narrow width which obviates any need for walking on the soil and so compacting it.

**Rake**: a garden tool comprising a row of teeth set in a cross-piece attached to a long handle. Two types are important: the short-toothed garden rake and the longer-toothed or sprung-tined lawn rake.

**Rambler**: type of climbing rose derived either from *Rosa wichuraiana* or *Rosa multi-*

*flora*. Differ from most other climbers in flowering only on recently produced wood and require different pruning.

**Red spider mite**: probably the most common and important pest species of mite in gardens and greenhouses, causing characteristic bronzing of the leaves, fine webbing and leading to general debilitation of the plant.

**Repellents**: chemicals used to repel pests from plants, usually by their unpleasant taste or smell. Mostly used against birds and mammals.

**Resistant pest**: one able to withstand exposure to certain pesticides. Some pests have become highly resistant to pesticides, usually because frequent treatment of large populations with chemicals selects individuals that have inheritable characters conferring some degree of resistance.

**Resistant variety**: a variety (or cultivar) of plant that is resistant to a pest or disease and therefore little harmed by it. Resistance may take many forms ranging from the presence of a chemical toxic to an insect pest to the ability to produce cells that prevent the spread of fungal hyphae through the tissues.

**Resmethrin**: a synthetic pyrethroid insecticide, used for the control of a wide range of garden plant pests.

**Respiration**: in plants, the chemical reactions by which energy and carbon dioxide are released through the breakdown of carbohydrates and other complex organic substances.

**Resting (of a spore)**: able to become dormant to survive a period of adverse environmental conditions.

**Rhizome**: a thick, usually horizontal underground stem that facilitates the spread of plants through the soil and which may also form a food storage and perennating body.

**Ring culture**: greenhouse system of growing tomatoes and other plants in compost in bottom-less pots placed on a gravel bed and fed with liquid fertiliser. It offers a relatively pest and disease-free system.

**Rock garden**: area where alpine plants are grown. Has rather fallen from favour with the increased difficulty and cost of obtaining real or artificial stone and relative ease of growing alpines in other ways.

**Rock phosphate**: mineral that is the source of phosphorus for plant fertilisers. It may be treated with sulphuric acid to produce superphosphate or finely ground and used as fertiliser in its own right, containing 25-35 per cent phosphate.

**Rock plant**: see Alpine

**Rogueing**: removal and destruction of diseased or infested plants.

**Root**: serve two main functions in plants: to provide physical stability and, through the root hairs, to provide the medium for the uptake of water and mineral nutrients from the soil. In modified form (carrots, parsnips and other root crops for instance) roots also provide storage for food reserves. In a few plants, roots may be aerial and extract moisture and nutrients from the air and provide support for climbers.

**Root nodule**: small swellings on the roots of plants in the family Papilionaceae containing bacteria of the genus *Rhizobium*. These are uniquely able to convert (or 'fix') atmospheric nitrogen gas into a form that plants are able to utilise as fertiliser. These plants play an invaluable role therefore in soil nutrition, in garden rotations and themselves require little or no additional nitrogen fertiliser.

**Root rot**: decay of the roots is commonly caused by many fungi and some bacteria and tends to be serious in wet, anaerobic conditions. The effects are often manifest first by die-back to the shoot tips as water uptake is impaired.

**Root vegetable**: any vegetable in which a swollen root is the object of cultivation. Sometimes, vegetables such as potatoes (swollen stem tubers) or onions (swollen stem bases or bulbs) are for convenience considered as root vegetables.

**Rooting hormone**: substance used artificially to enhance rooting in cuttings. The active principle (usually IAA) is mixed with an inert filler and fungicide and sold as a powder or liquid formulation. Used to excess, they have growth inhibiting features.

**Rootstock**: a plant that is grown specifically for some attribute of its roots and onto which another variety is grafted. Rootstocks are commonly used with garden plants that have good flowering or fruiting ability but weak root systems. Roses are familiar examples. With some fruit trees, especially apples, rootstocks assume special importance because selected forms are available that exert a growth inhibiting effect on any variety grafted onto them. They are commonly called dwarfing rootstocks and offer the means of growing trees of defined size.

**Rotation**: the changing of the places where particular crops are grown in successive years. It is used especially with vegetables which in gardens are generally grown on a three-course rotation (any one crop on the same site once every three years). The principle is to minimise the build-up of pests and diseases and utilise the full range of soil nutrients but in gardens, unlike commercial horticulture, the small distance between plots means that the benefits are fairly limited.

**Rotenone**: correct term for insecticide often called derris. A contact, broad-spectrum insecticide extracted from the ground roots of the tropical plant genus *Derris*. Although in many ways safe, it is very toxic to bees and fish.

**Row crop**: a plant that is traditionally, like most vegetables, grown in rows. In reality, almost all crops will yield more per unit area if they are grown, not in rows, but spaced equidistantly in beds.

**Rust**: a plant disease caused by Basidiomycete fungi of the order Uredinales or the causal fungus itself. The name derives from the superficially brown and rust-like appearance of the lesions in many cases. Rusts diseases are of immense significance in world crop production and several are important in gardens.

**Safety in the garden**: much garden safety is a matter of common-sense but a great deal of official attention has been given to the subject in recent years so it is a folly to ignore advice and instruction given on product labels. It is based on sound fact. The two areas where care should be directed especially are in relation to garden chemicals and garden power tools. Used as directed, they are all safe but used thoughtlessly, or in the case of power tools, when the operator is likely to be distracted, accidents may occur. Older garden power tools which may not have as many in-built safety features should be checked by a professional.

**Sand**: an important component of soils (sand particles comprise mineral matter in the size range 0.006-2mm diameter). Also added to potting composts to 'open up' a heavy soils and improve drainage. For gardening use however, it is important to use horticultural sharp sand (finely crushed artificially), rather than river sand which has rounded particles, or sea sand which is contaminated with salt.

**Sand bench**: device in which sand is contained in a box-like structure within which thermostatically controlled heating cables are buried. Propagator or seed trays are placed on the heated surface to facilitate seed germination. Usually installed in a greenhouse but care must be take to ensure that the staging is strong enough to support the weight.

**Saprotroph**: organism that feeds on dead organic matter.

**Sawdust**: of limited value in the garden. Like all organic matter, should be composted before being added to soil or temporary depletion of nitrogen may ensue. Some conifer sawdusts also contain materials toxic to plants although these will be removed after composting. One use of sawdust is in mulching certain plants that require acidic conditions, blueberries especially.

**Sawfly**: small insects, related to wasps and bees. Larvae resemble caterpillars and many species are significant plant pests.

**Scab**: form of plant disease in which a rough and corky lesion forms on affected parts. Caused by a range of different organisms, especially Ascomycete fungi.

**Scale insect**: small sap-feeding insects that produce characteristic dull coloured scales, relatively immobile in the adult stage. Many are serious plant pests, causing general debilitation and also fouling foliage by honeydew secretions.

**Scion**: part of plant (usually stem or bud) inserted into the rooted part of another plant (the stock or rootstock) to form a union or graft.

**Scythe**: long handled tool with curved blade, used for cutting grass with a broad sweeping motion; used for cutting lawns before the invention of the lawn mower.

**Seaweed**: marine algae, especially large forms, some of which produce fronds many metres in length. Seaweed has long been collected in coastal regions and use as manure and fertiliser. Contains high concentrations of many trace elements but best composted or allowed to weather before use in order for salt to be washed out. Fresh seaweed attracts flies.

**Secateur**: also called pruner, a small cutting tool for pruning, embodying two slicing blades (by-pass or scissor action) or a single blade cutting against a blunt surface (anvil pattern).

**Seed**: the characteristic reproductive body of seed plants, the product of a fertilised ovule; commonly contained in a fruit.

**Seed and fruit dispersal**: methods of dispersing the seeds so that seedlings grow away from parents plants are many and varied. Common adaptations to facilitate dispersal include the development of feathery plumes (dandelions) or wings (ash, sycamore) for wind dispersal, prickles to adhere to animals (burdock) or, commonly, bright colours and a fleshy coast (hawthorn) to encourage birds to feed and so disperse seeds within their digestive tract.

**Seedling**: plant newly emerged from a seed.

**Sepal**: one of the parts that forms the calyx of a flower, usually positioned outside the petals and green and leaf like although some important groups of plants (the Ranunculaceae for example) have brightly coloured sepals that take the place of petals in bestowing the colour to the flowers.

**Sequestered iron**: iron in an organic form that can be taken up readily by plants, even in alkaline soils in which inorganic iron becomes unavailable.

**Shelter**: essential in exposed gardens in order for plants to become established. Commonly a shelter belt or screen of fast growing trees may be removed once slower growing species have become established to in the lee of them.

**Shot-hole**: a symptom of disease in which discrete more or less circular areas of leaf tissue dry and drop out, or a symptom of attack by certain wood-boring beetles on tree trunks.

**Shrubbery**: the dedicated shrubbery is seen less in modern gardens than the mixed planting of shrubs and herbaceous perennials. The days of the sombre nineteenth shrubbery of evergreen foliage have largely been replaced by mixed plantings of deciduous and evergreen, flowering and foliage types.

**Sickle**: short handled tool with sharply curved blade for cutting or slashing grass. A dangerous tool in inexperienced hands.

**Silt**: an important component of soils; silt particles comprise mineral matter in the size range 0.002-0.006mm diameter.

**Silver leaf**: disease of plants, mainly in the family Rosaceae and especially plums of which it is the most important disease. Leaves develop a silvery sheen because the upper and lower cell layers separate and air is admitted.

**Simazine**: a residual soil-acting herbicide available to gardeners in combination with other herbicides for use as a total weed-killer, especially on non-planted areas.

**Skin spot**: disease of potatoes causing small brown pimples on the tubers. Mainly a disfiguring condition but can cause loss in some varieties, especially 'King Edward'.

**Slaked lime**: popular name for calcium

hydroxide, a calcium salt with a higher neutralising value than limestone (calcium carbonate) but unpleasant to handle and little used in gardening therefore.

**Slime mould**: common name for Myxomycetes, non-parasitic organisms probably vaguely related to fungi and sometimes causing alarm in gardens when they are found in the form of large, sometimes brightly coloured protoplasmic masses. Cause no harm although severe infestations may smother small plants.

**Slow release**: of fertilisers formed or formulated in such a way that they break down chemically at a slow rate and so release their nutrient content into soil or compost over a long period of time. Bone meal is a common example but many artificial fertilisers are now formulated in resins that act similarly.

**Slug**: soft-bodied, non-segmented gastropod molluscs, closely related to snails but lacking a large hard shell. Some species cause much damage in gardens by feeding on soft plant parts; subterranean species are especially troublesome.

**Smut**: Basidiomycete fungi, related to rusts, and causing serious plant disease, although few are significant in gardens. Named for the characteristic black, sooty mass of spores produced.

**Snail**: soft-bodied, non-segmented gastropod molluscs, closely related to snails but possessing a large hard shell, although species exist that span the boundary between the two. Usually cause less damage to garden plants although some types such as hostas are seriously affected.

**Snow**: although of little importance in contributing moisture to the soil, snow is important first in providing a protective blanket against penetrating frost and second in causing damage, especially to evergreen trees' by its weight.

**Sodium**: minor plant nutrient but almost never deficient in British soils; shortage of sodium is not a problem in gardens. In high concentrations may damage plants.

**Sodium chlorate**: non-selective herbicide for total control of plant life. Only ever to be used on non-planted areas such as paths and drives because of its persistence but, unlike more modern products, will 'creep' through the soil to affect planted areas nearby. There are better modern alternatives.

**Sodium chloride**: common salt, sea salt. May be a problem when wind-borne onto plants in coastal gardens or in coastal soils, Has been used as a substitute for potassium chloride in times of shortage but contrary to popular belief, no garden plants, not even asparagus, require it.

**Sodium nitrate**: also called nitrate of soda, once widely used as a nitrogen fertiliser, containing 16 per cent of immediately available nitrogen but now largely replaced by ammonium nitrate.

**Soft rot**: decay of plant tissues in which there is breakdown of the cell wall, resulting in a soft and slimy mass. Commonly cased by bacterial action and a feature of much decay of stored fruit and vegetables.

**Soil**: the top-most layer of the land surface, usually divided into top-soil and sub-soil and the key to all gardening activities. It is important to understand however that whilst containing inert, mineral components of differing sizes and chemical compositions, it is also a dynamic medium, changing as organic matter is added and decomposes, as plants take up nutrients and as the numerous living inhabitants influence it in their own ways, both beneficial and detrimental to plant life.

**Soil sickness and replant diseases**: conditions in which plants decline or fail properly to establish on sites where plants of the same or similar type have been grown previously. Thought to be the result of the build-up of pathogenic fungi in the soil but not fully understood. Rose replant disease and pansy sickness are common examples.

**Solar radiation**: radiation reaching the earth from the sun and divided into numerous components of different wavelength. The most important for gardeners are visible light for photosynthesis, infra-red for warmth and ultra-violet for its degrading action on certain substances such as many plastics.

**Soot**: finely divided carbon deposited from fires during the incomplete combustion of organic matter such as coal. Once used in gardens as a nitrogen source (it contains about 3.6 per cent nitrogen) but also contains toxic materials and should be composted first. Of some value as a slug deterrent.

**Sooty mould**: fungal growth over leaves and other plant parts encouraged by the presence of sugary honeydew secreted by aphids and other sap-sucking pests.

**Spacing**: the spacing of ornamental plants is largely a matter of aesthetics, provided they are not so close they compete adversely for nutrients and moisture. Spacing of vegetables is the key to productivity however and modern research indicates that equidistant spacing (the distance varying with each crop) generally leads to greater productivity than row-cropping.

**Spade**: probably the oldest of all cultivating tools, dating back to the Neolithic period in clearly recognisable form. England is unusual in being one of the few parts of the world where the short handled spade with a cross-piece to the handle is preferred to the long, straight handle.

**Spadix**: type of inflorescence; a club-like spike of unisexual flowers (males above, females below) enclosed in a large spathe. Characteristic of the Araceae.

**Spathe**: large ear-like bract enclosing an inflorescence, usually a spadix as in the family Araceae.

**Species (note that the word has no singular)**: abbreviated to sp., the cornerstone of the classification and naming of organisms but one whose definition is not widely understood. A species is a collection of individual organisms that are readily able to breed among themselves but not generally able to breed with organisms belong to other species.

**Speedwell**: plant of the genus *Veronica* of which many members are common garden weeds and some attractive ornamentals.

The naturalised creeping speedwell *Veronica repens* is the common blue-flowered lawn weed.

**Spent hops**: hop remains produced as waste by the brewing industry. Of some value as an organic soil amendment and contains about 1.1 per cent nitrogen but little phosphorus and potassium.

**Spider**: eight legged Arachnid, of importance in gardens for their role in controlling numbers of pests although they also kill and eat many beneficial insects also.

**Spike**: type of inflorescence, a raceme with the flowers all stalkless.

**Spine**: feature of many xerophytic plants to cut down water loss and provide defence against browsing animals, usually a modified leaf.

**Splitting**: common on many vegetables and fruits as a response to an interrupted water supply. A period of little growth during a dry period is followed by a sudden up-take of water and tissue expansion.

**Spore**: microscopic reproductive structure of many organisms, including fungi, ferns, mosses, liverworts and some bacteria. Quite different in biology and structure from a seed and a general term used for a wide range of bodies that are themselves produced in a wide variety of ways, some by sexual and some asexual reproduction.

**Sprayer**: device for applying pesticide or other chemicals to garden plants. Generally a balance in setting is required between a coarse spray with large droplets that quickly run off plants to a very fine spray (a mist) which is dispersed by the wind before it can adhere.

**Springtail**: wingless terrestrial arthropods, related to insects. Common in soil, especially among leaf litter and other plant debris and a few species cause damage to plant roots, particularly in containers where the compost is very wet.

**Sprinkler**: device attached to a hose-pipe to apply water to gardens. It is important to select a sprinkler that is adjustable and only delivers water where it most needed, not wastefully in all directions.

**Spurge**: general term for many species of *Euphoria*, especially native weed forms such as *Euphorbia helioscopia*, sun spurge.

**Squirrel**: important pests in garden where trees grow nearby. The pest species is the introduced North American grey squirrel which has moved into areas vacated by the native red squirrel. Control is very difficult and netting susceptible plants is the only effective solution.

**Staddle stone**: mushroom shaped stones much used as garden ornaments, but quite inappropriately as their original role was to raise grain stores clear of the ground and so protect them from rats.

**Stake**: important for many herbaceous plants (and should be in place early in the season) and also young trees where short stakes have widely replaced the traditional long form in allowing more natural flexing and strengthening of the plant's stem.

**Stamen**: part of flower that produces pollen grains containing male cells. Divided into a stalk or filament and a terminal swollen anther.

**Standard**: tree or shrub grown on a single stem; a standard rose has the head at a height of about 1m (3ft), a half-standard at 80cm (2ft 7in) and the quarter-standard at 45cm (18in).

**Stem**: part of a plant bearing leaves, buds and flowers, normally green and aerial but may be variously modified. Some stems (rhizomes) for example are subterranean, others much abbreviated (the basal plate of a bulb) or swollen (potato tubers) but all can be recognised and distinguished from roots or other organs by the presence of buds.

**Stem and foot rot**: decay of a plant at or close to soil level, usually caused by soil-inhabiting fungi, often following pest damage.

**Stigma**: the terminal part of a carpel which receives the male pollen.

**Stolon**: horizontally growing stem that roots at the nodes as in a strawberry runner.

**Stoma (pl. stomata)**: pore in plant epidermis through which gas exchange with the air takes place.

**Storage of garden produce**: traditionally, vegetables were largely stored in the ground where they grew, sometimes by wrapping straw or similar material around them. Other popular methods were in a heap covered with soil (a clamp) or in sand in boxes. Tree fruit were stored cool in specially built rooms; soft fruit as jams, preserves or bottled. Today, the freezer has supplanted many of these methods.

**Straw**: useful as an insulation material for stored produce or around the crowns of marginally hardy plants. Also used as a soil amendment and contains about 1 per cent potassium but little nitrogen and phosphorus and best composted before use. Care needed to ensure that it contains no herbicide residues from cereals.

**Style**: the part of a carpel supporting the stigma.

**Sub-species**: abbreviated to ssp., a group of individuals within a species that has developed slight (usually morphological or behavioural) differences, generally brought about by geographical isolation from the main species.

**Sucker**: modified plant root used to achieve adherence in self-clinging climbers; best known examples are species of *Parthenocissus*.

**Suckers (insects)**: small sap-feeding insects, the immature forms of a group called psyllids. Commonest garden example is the bay sucker.

**Sulphur**: chemical element and minor plant nutrient but never deficient in British soils. Sulphur as sulphur chips is sometimes used as a soil amendment to lower pH (increase acidity) for which it is moderately effective. It is also used as a fairly effective fungicide, especially valuable for the control of powdery mildews although some plants are damaged by it; they are said to be 'sulphur shy'.

**Sundial**: attractive device originally for telling the time but now much used simply as a garden ornament. The forms derived from armillary spheres are especially appealing.

**Superphosphate**: the most important phosphorus containing fertiliser with 18 per cent of water-soluble phosphate. It is mainly a combination of monocalcium phosphate and gypsum (calcium sulphate) and is forming by treating natural rock phosphate with sulphuric acid.

**Symbiosis**: association of dissimilar organisms; popularly used to refer to a mutually advantageous association, as in root nodule bacteria on papilionaceous plants.

**Symphylid**: small arthropods related to millepedes and centipedes; live in soil and may cause damage to plant roots, especially in greenhouses.

**Systemic**: generally distributed within an organism. Used to describe the nature of infection by certain diseases or the mode of action of certain pesticides. Some of the most effective pesticides and fungicides are of systemic action but such chemicals take longer to clear from the tissues than contact chemicals so may lengthen the time before edible produce can be used.

**Tar acid and tar oil**: crude chemical mixtures obtained from petroleum or coal and used for the control of over-wintering pests during the dormant period on deciduous trees and shrubs. Damages green tissue but controls algae and lichen.

**Temperature**: all organisms have an optimum growth temperature but because all depend on the same basic biochemical process, almost all grow optimally between about 10°C (50°F) and 20°C (68°F) and little above 25°C (77°F) or below 5°C (41°F).

**Tendril**: stem, leaf or part of a leaf modified as a slender grasping organ for climbing plants.

**Tetramethrin**: synthetic pyrethrum-like insecticide, used in garden pesticides with permethrin.

**Thallus**: a simple, undifferentiated plant body with no obvious division into stem, roots, leaves; as in algae.

**Thiophanate-methyl**: systemic fungicide related to carbendazim, formerly much used in garden products but now limited to a pre-planting dip against clubroot.

**Thrip**: tiny elongated insects, commonly called thunder flies. Larvae and adults of many species feed on plant tissues and can cause mottling damage to surfaces. Some are important virus vectors.

**Tilth**: the condition in which soil is suitable for plant growth.

**Tissue culture**: the artificial growth of plant tissues in a nutrient medium under aseptic laboratory conditions. Now widely used for the rapid multiplication of plants.

**Toad**: common amphibian and to be welcomed in gardens as although they feed mainly on earthworms, they also eat slugs and other pests.

**Tolerant**: able to tolerate attack by a pathogen or pest or action by a chemical. Plants and their cultivars often show degrees of tolerance.

**Tools**: modern garden tools are divided into hand tools, most of which have changed little for many years, if not centuries, and power tools of which new types appear every year. It is important in all cases to handle tools before buying as optimum size, weight and other factors are very personal matters.

**Trace element**: plant nutrient required in very small quantities.

**Training**: another word for the pruning of plants into shapes that render them easier to manage and more productive.

**Translocation**: the movement of chemicals within a plant. Important naturally as the means for the dispersion of nutrients but also taken advantage of by gardeners in the use for instance of translocated weedkillers which reach otherwise inaccessible roots.

**Transplanting**: the transfer of young plants, generally distinguished from pricking out in that the plants are at a more advanced stage of development before being moved.

**Tricalcium phosphate**: a slow release form of phosphorus fertiliser.

**Trickle irrigation**: increasingly popular technique, especially in greenhouses or containers in which water is constantly dripped from narrow bore tubes to maintain continuous watering to plants without the gardener's intervention.

**Triclopyr**: a translocated herbicide, used in gardens for nettle control

**Triforine**: a systemic fungicide, used in gardens in combination with other fungicides or insecticide for the control of rose diseases.

**Triploid**: plant having three sets of chromosomes in its nuclei.

**Tropism**: a response in plants to external stimuli such as light or gravity by growth curvature.

**Tuber**: swollen storage organ which may be a modified root (dahlia) or stem (potato).

**2,4-D**: a translocated selective herbicide for control of broad-leaved weeds among grasses; a common constituent of lawn weedkillers.

**Ultra-violet radiation**: solar radiation with wavelength longer than visible light but shorter than X-rays. Important for its ability to degrade plastic and harmful to skin.

**Umbel**: type of inflorescence with individual pedicels all arising from the top of the main stem, typical of cow parsley and the family Apiaceae.

**Urea-formaldehyde**: artificial slow-release nitrogen fertiliser, much used in potting composts.

**Variety**: often used in the same sense as cultivar but its correct botanical meaning is of a variant that has arisen in a plant species growing in the wild and therefore not subjected to selection through cultivation (for example *Pinus nigra* var. *maritima*). Many plant varieties are cultivated in gardens.

**Vector**: an organism that transports and transmits a pathogen. The most important vectors of plant diseases in gardens are the aphids and eelworms that transmit viruses but some other pests may also be vectors of certain diseases.

**Vegetable**: strictly a plant that is grown for some vegetative part (stem, leaf or root) but popularly used to embrace all kitchen crops that are not sweet tasting and as such embraces many fruit such as tomatoes and cucumbers.

**Vegetative multiplication (reproduction)**: the reproduction of plants by methods that don't entail any sexual process; in gardens, cuttings, layering, grafting, budding and division are all familiar examples.

**Vermiculite**: a mixture of micaceous minerals, especially those containing magnesium, iron and aluminium and used as a substitute for sand when mixed with peat or other growing medium to open up the structure and provide freer drainage and air flow. It can also be used alone to support plant growth or to provide a base for striking cuttings; provided of course that all of the plants' nutrients can be applied in liquid form.

**Vine**: vague term applied to many climbing plants with long flexible stems; most popularly the grapevine.

**Vine weevil**: species of flightless weevil that has become very important in gardens through the root-feeding activities of its larvae and leaf-feeding activities of the adults. A nematode based biological control is effective against larvae.

**Virulent**: (of a pathogen); spreading rapidly and causing serious disease.

**Virus**: structurally simple organisms comprising a nucleic acid and one or more proteins. Absolute parasites in living solely within host cells.

**Viviparous**: giving birth to live young, as in some aphids.

**Vole**: small rodents, distinguished from mice by their blunt faces; can cause serious problems in gardens, especially by their fondness for corms and stored vegetables.

**Wall plant**: general term used to include climbers and those free-standing shrubs that are usually grown, trained in two-dimensional pattern, against a wall.

**Wart**: extremely serious disease of potatoes causing knobbly outgrowths on tubers; now uncommon in Britain but must be reported to the Ministry of Agriculture when discovered.

**Wasp**: often maligned as garden pests although they only cause damage at fruit harvest time and this is counter-balanced by their role in feeding their young on other insects, including many pests.

**Watering**: careful watering is the key to much gardening success but it is important not to water wastefully; a good guideline is only to water plants when the object of their cultivation is maturing.

**Weed**: familiarly, any native plant growing where it interferes with the efficient growing of a garden plant. Weeds are generally very good competitors and their control, ideally by physical rather than chemical means, is vitally important.

**Weed control**: may be loosely divided into physical methods (hoeing, mulching, hand pulling, digging) and chemical methods. Where a choice exists, physical methods are preferable but some perennial species and lawn weeds can only effectively be controlled by chemical means.

**Weedkiller**: see herbicide

**Weevil**: large group (over 50,000 species worldwide) of long-snouted beetles. Include numerous plant pests of which the vine weevil is the most important.

**White blister**: type of disease caused by a small group of Oomycete fungi; sometimes a problem on brassicas and related plants in gardens.

**White rot**: has two meanings: a type of rot disease affecting salad onions, extremely difficult to control and able to persist in soil for up to thirty years; and a type of fungal decay of timber in which the lignin is broken down.

**Whitefly**: small sap-feeding insects related to suckers and psyllids among other garden pests. The glasshouse whitefly and the brassica whitefly are the most important garden pests. They are very difficult to control with chemicals but the glasshouse whitefly can be combated very effectively with biological control using *Encarsia*.

**Wilt**: popularly, any condition in which leaves droop due to water shortage but more specifically, a group of diseases in which fungal attack is the cause of the obstruction of the water conducting tissues. Dutch elm disease is a dramatic example but tomato wilt is common in greenhouses where crops have been grown repeatedly on the same soil

**Wind**: important as both a beneficial force (the carrying of pollen and bringing about the uptake of water through plants by evaporation) and also damaging, (simple physical damage and also the carrying of weed seeds and spores of harmful orgaisms).

**Winter moth**: group of moths whose adults emerge from the pupae between autumn and spring. Includes the important fruit tree pests, the winter moth, March moth and mottled umber.

**Wireworm**: soil-inhabiting larvae of ciick beetles, feeding on grasses but also important root attacking pests in gardens.

**Witches broom**: bird's nest or besom-shaped twiggy proliferation in trees, brought about by fungal or viral attack.

**Woodlice**: terrestrial crustaceans with up to seven pairs of legs. Live in and feed on rotting wood and other plant debris and can cause damage to plants by nibbling soft fleshy parts. Easily controlled with most insecticides.

**Wound treatment on trees**: has changed dramatically in recent years with the discovery that the use of wound paints and the trimming of branches very close to the trunk will inhibit the tree's natural healing.

**Xerophyte**: plant adapted for living in dry climates; commonly characterised by slow growth, swollen storage tissues and spines.

**Xylem**: water conducting tissue in plants that in trees and shrubs, *en masse*, forms wood.

**Zinc**: a chemical element toxic to plants at certain concentrations and can cause problems if galvanised wire netting is placed over them, as in a fruit cage.

**Zone lines**: narrow dark brown or black lines in decayed wood; generally the result of the tree attempting to limit the spread of decay fungus.

# Index

## ACKNOWLEDGEMENTS IN SOURCE ORDER

The publishers wish to thank the following organisations for their kind permission to reproduce the photographs in this book:

**AKG, London**/British Museum, London 29 Top Right **Supplied courtesy of Atco Qualcast Ltd** 51 Bottom Right, 167 Bottom Right, 218 Top **A-Z Botanical Collection** 54, 137 Bottom Right/Dr. Bob Gibbons 137 Bottom Left **BIOFOTOS**/Heather Angel 188 Top, 196, 215 Top, 236 **Pat Brindley** 186 Bottom Centre **Professor Stefan Buczacki** 12 Top Left, 16, 64 Top Left, 71 Bottom Right, 95 Top Left, 96 Top Left, 99 Bottom Right, 99 Top Right, 99 Centre Right, 102 Top Left, 115, 116, 140 Top, 157 Bottom Right, 203 Top, 233 Top, 237 Top **Supplied courtesy of Bulldog Tools, Sheffield, England** 50 Top Left **Cephas Picture Library**/Mark Heasman 11 Top **Eric Crichton** 63 **Ecoscene**/Andy Hibbert 191 Top/Sally Morgan 215 Bottom Right **Elizabeth Whiting Associates** 78 Bottom, 108 Bottom Left, 110 Top Right/Tommy Chandler 94 Top Left/Eric Crichton 36 Bottom Left/Michael Dunne 88 Top Left/Jerry Harpur 127 **Frank Lane Picture Agency**/A Wharton 204 Top **Forest Research Photographic Library** 200 **Garden Picture Library** David Askham 14, 65, 182 Bottom Right, 225 Bottom Right/Philippe Bonduel 79 Bottom Right, 144 Top/Jon Bouchier 53/Lynne Brotchie 112 Bottom Left/Brian Carter 163 Bottom Left, 176 Bottom/Bob Challinor 222 Bottom Left/Dennis Davis 84 Top Left, 228/David England 107/Robert Estall 26/Ron Evans 189 Bottom Right, 241/Vaughan Fleming 17 Top Right, 239/John Glover Spine, Front Cover Bottom Left/ 41 Bottom Right, 66, 80 Bottom Left, 172 Top, 184, /Juliet Greene 25 Top Right /Neil Holmes 149 Bottom Right/Michael Howes 58, 59, 142 Bottom Left, 193, 238/Jacqui Hurst 145/Andrea Jones 90 Bottom Left/Ann Kelley 42 Bottom Left/Lamontagne 24, 77 Top Right, 110 Bottom Left, 140 Bottom Left, 150, 153 Top, 182 Top, 190, 209 Top, 240/Jane Legate 50 Bottom Centre, 75, 109 /Mayer/Le Scanff 12 Bottom Left, 134, 227 Top/Howard Rice 19 Top Right, 199 Bottom/Stephen Robson 77 Bottom Left/Alec Scaresbrook 52/John Ferro Sims 133 Bottom Left/J S Sira 25 Bottom Left, 131 Bottom Right/Friedrich Strauss 117 Top Left/Ron Sutherland 36 Top Left, 49 Top Right/Brigitte Thomas 121 Top Right, 180, 206 Top/Juliette Wade 163 Bottom

Right/Mel Watson 19 Bottom Right, 83 Bottom Right/Didier Willery 235 Top/Steven Wooster 43, 206 Bottom **Garden & Wildlife Matters** 17 Bottom Right, 20 Bottom Left, 42 Top Left, 56 Bottom Centre, 106 Top Left, 135, 189 Top, 203 Bottom Right/John Phipps 89 Bottom Left **Supplied courtesy of Gardening Which?** 48 **Geoscience Features**/Dr. B. Booth 55 **John Glover** 5, 104 Top Left, 117 Bottom Right, 118, 169, 170, 210 Bottom Left, 233 Bottom Right/Hampton Court Flower Show 1997, Designer Julie Toll 23/ Chiff Chaffs, Dorset 32/ High Meadow, Surrey 35 Top Right/ Yorkgate, Yorkshire 38 Bottom Left/ Cutmill, Surrey 39/ Pax Cottage, Surrey 41 Top Right/ Vale End, Surrey 181 Top/ Roger Brook's Cemetary Garden, Bolton Percy, Yorkshire 188 Bottom Left **Haddon Davies** 49 Bottom Left **S. Hamilton Photography** 4, 8-9, 72 Top Left, 78 Top Left, 83 Top Right **Reed Consumer Books Ltd.** Front Cover Top Left, 1 Centre, 101 Top Right, 165 Bottom Left, 166, 195 Bottom/ Michael Boys 22 Bottom Left, 45 Centre Right, 151, 208/ S. Campbell 111 Top Right/Jerry Harpur 173, 178 Bottom Left/Neil Holmes 92, 93, 148 Top, 152 Bottom Left, 155, 158 Bottom Left, 163 Top, 231 Top/Andrew Lawson Front Cover Top Centre, Back Flap, 2 Centre, 3 Top Left, 7, 27 Top Left, 45 Top Right, 211/Peter Myers 13 Top Left, 27 Bottom Left/Peter Myers (Backgrounds - 82, 85, 87, 101, 102, 103, 104, 105, 107, 111)/Howard Rice Front Cover Bottom Right, 60 Bottom Left, 60 Top Left, 61, 62 Bottom Centre, 64 Bottom Left, 67 Top, 67 Bottom Right, 68 Bottom Left, 68 Top Left, 69, 123, 124, 12/Michael Warren 164, 179/Steven Wooster 35 Bottom, 40, 112 Top Left, 114 Top Left, 114 Bottom Left, 195 Top, 197 Bottom Right, 214, 220, 221 Bottom Right, 225 Top/George Wright Front Cover Top Right, 45 Bottom Right, 149 Top, 197 Top, 205, 230 Top **Robert Harding Picture Library**/BBC Gardener's World /R.Harding Syndication 81, 85 Bottom Right, 98 Bottom Left, 199 Top, 223/Michael Brockway 46 Bottom Left/Andreas von Einseidel 31/Tony Latham 34 **Harpur Garden Library**/Designer Edwina von Gal, New York, USA 28/ Designer Phillip Watson, VA, USA 37/Designer Mel Light, CA, USA 183/ 153 Bottom Right, 201/Garden Owner Bob Flowerdew - 84 Bottom Right, 125 Top Centre, 129 Bottom Right, 129 Top Right, 131 Top Right, 160, 161 Bottom Right **Holt Studios International**/Rosemary Mayer 178 Top Houses and

Interiors/Fabbri 198, 216 Bottom Left/Julia Pazowski 172 Bottom Left **Hulton Getty Picture Collection** 30 Top Left **Ken Muir Nursery**/Claire Higgins 121 Bottom Right, 122 Bottom Left, 132 Bottom Left/Michael Warren 126 Bottom Left **Kentish Cobnuts Association**/Meg Game 132 Top Left **Andrew Lawson** 82, 86 Top Left, 213 Bottom Right, 216 Top, 224, 231 Bottom Right, 234, 237 Bottom Right/Bosvigo House Cornwall 29 Bottom Left/Docton Mill, Devon 33/RHS Wisley, Surrey 47/Rofford Manor, Oxfordshire 120/Gothic House, Oxfordshire 202 Top **S & O Mathews** Endpapers, 152 Top, 156 Top, 194, 218 Bottom Right/ North Court, Isle of Wight 10 Bottom Right, 10 Bottom Left/Brook Cottage, Oxon 38 Top Left/Rozelle Close, Hampshire 174//Port Lympne, Kent 175 Top/RHS Wisley, Surrey 175 Bottom/Badgers, Isle of Wight 207 **Reed Consumer Books Limited/Mitchel Beazley** Sue Atkinson Front Cover bottom centre, 187/Stephen Robson 136 Bottom Left, 146 **Clive Nichols Photography** 212/Chelsea Flower Show 1993/National Asthma Campaign Garden, Design Lucy Huntington 161 Top/Picton Gardens, Hereford & Worcester 186 Top/Kew Gardens, London 191 Bottom Right//The Old Vicarage, Norfolk 226 **Photos Horticultural** 15 Bottom Right, 15 Top Right, 18 Top Left, 20 Top Left, 22 Top Left, 30 Bottom Left, 44, 46 Top Left, 51 Top Centre, 56 Top Left, 57 Bottom Left, 62 Top Left, 72 Bottom Left, 74 Bottom Left, 74 Top Left, 76, 79 Top Right, 80 Top Left, 86 Bottom Left, 88 Bottom Left, 90 Top Left, 94 Bottom Left, 95 Bottom Right, 96 Bottom Right, 98 Top Left, 100 Top Left, 100 Bottom Left, 106 Bottom Right, 108 Top Left, 113, 122 Top Left, 125 Bottom Right, 126 Top Left, 130, 133 Top Right, 138, 143 Bottom Right, 143 Top, 147 Top, 148 Bottom Left, 153 Bottom Left, 154, 157 Top, 158 Top, 159, 162, 165 Top, 167 Top, 168 Bottom Right, 168 Top, 171 Top, 176 Top, 177, 181 Bottom Right, 185 Bottom, 185 Top, 192 Top, 192 Bottom Left, 204 Bottom, 209 Bottom Right, 210 Top, 213 Top, 217, 19, 221 Top, 222 Top, 229, 230 Bottom Left, 232, 235 Bottom Right /Capel Manor, Herts 227 Bottom Right **Howard Rice** 156 Bottom Left **Harry Smith Collection** 21, 57 Top Right, 70, 71 Top Right, 73, 85 Top Centre, 91, 97, 102 Centre Left, 136 Top, 139, 141, 142 Top, 144 Bottom Left, 171 Bottom Right, 202 Bottom Left **Supplied courtesy of Suttons Seeds** 147 Bottom Right